PHILOSOPHICAL
PSYCHOLOGY

PHILOSOPHICAL PSYCHOLOGY

SECOND EDITION
REVISED AND ENLARGED

J. F. DONCEEL, S.J.
Fordham University

SHEED AND WARD - NEW YORK

SECOND EDITION
Revised and Enlarged

LIBRARY OF CONGRESS CATALOG CARD NUMBER: 61-7291

NIHIL OBSTAT:

>   REV. FRANCIS ALLAN CONLAN, PH.D.
>   CENSOR LIBRORUM

IMPRIMATUR:

>   ✠ JEROME D. HANNAN
>   BISHOP OF SCRANTON

>   OCTOBER 28, 1960

Third Printing, December, 1963

MANUFACTURED IN THE UNITED STATES OF AMERICA

Preface to the Second Edition

The second edition of this textbook has been considerably revised. New chapters have been added on the origin of life, the origin of species and of the human body (evolution). The chapter on the human soul has been totally reworked and considerably expanded. In the chapters on the intellect and the will more attention has been paid to the objections of the Logical Positivists and of the Psychological Determinists. Valuable new insights, borrowed from Phenomenology and from Existentialism, have been incorporated into the chapters on Sense Knowledge and on the Human Person. Man is treated not only as the highest object in nature but also as an embodied subject, living among other subjects. Many of the improvements brought about in the book should be credited to the challenging questions and objections of my students at Fordham College, to whom I wish to extend my sincere gratitude.

JULY 31, 1960

Preface to the First Edition

Most textbooks of Philosophical Psychology contain at least a few experimental data about such topics as the senses, memory, imagination, etc. In the present book these sections have been expanded, so as to give a fairly complete summary of those chapters of scientific psychology which have the greatest claim to the attention of the philosopher. These sections have been clearly separated from the philosophical parts of the book. Where time is too short they may be omitted, or preferably, assigned for private reading by the students.

The philosophy of man presented in this book is the Aristotelianism of St. Thomas Aquinas, as understood by some of its best modern interpreters. As the spirit of St. Thomas is more important than the letter, quotations from his works have been kept to a minimum, and given only when it was deemed necessary to emphasize some aspects of his doctrine which are frequently overlooked.

To all those who encouraged and helped me in the composition of this book I express my sincere thanks. My gratitude goes especially to the Very Reverend Edward B. Bunn, S.J., President of Georgetown University, Washington, D.C., who sponsored the beginnings of this work, to Father Joseph D. Hassett, S.J., who helped me during the first stages of its preparation, and to Miss Ruth Reidy, who lent me invaluable assistance.

J. F. D.

FORDHAM UNIVERSITY

Contents

PART TWO: PLANT AND ANIMAL LIFE

PART THREE: HUMAN SENSE LIFE

Contents   *xi*

PHILOSOPHICAL
PSYCHOLOGY

GENERAL INTRODUCTION

General Introduction

DEFINITION AND OBJECT OF PSYCHOLOGY

Psychology may be studied at different levels, with different methods. Hence we distinguish four kinds of psychology, which may be called: empirical, experimental, philosophical and metaphysical psychology.[1]

Empirical Psychology may be defined as "the science of the facts and laws of mental life, as acquired by everyday experience." We say "mental life" rather than "conscious life," so as to include the preconscious and unconscious phenomena in man.

Everybody acquires some knowledge of the facts and laws pertaining to mental life through the ordinary process of living. Life would be almost impossible if we did not foresee to a certain extent our own and other people's reactions in given circumstances. Some individuals are better endowed in this respect than others. Some professions require more of this kind of knowledge than others. Labor leaders, salesmen, politicians and teachers must have a solid stock of such psychological knowledge in order to succeed in their professions.

This kind of psychology is to be found, although for the most part in a poorly organized and uncritical form, in proverbs, in the great masterpieces of literature, in the writings of moralists, educators, psychotherapists, ascetical authors, and in popular books about self-improvement. It differs from experimental psychology especially in that its data are not obtained through experimentation and measurement.

An orderly presentation of such facts and laws, which explains

---

[1] This terminology is not accepted by all psychologists. It is presented here only for the sake of clarity.

not only the "how," but also, wherever possible, the "why" of human behavior, is an "organized knowledge through the causes." It fulfills the conditions of a real science, in the wide sense of that word,[2] and can be called the science of Empirical Psychology.

Experimental Psychology, which may be defined as "the Science of behavior," applies strictly scientific methods to the study of animal and human behavior. It originated in the middle of the nineteenth century, and Wilhelm Wundt, who established the first laboratory of experimental psychology in 1879 at the University of Leipzig, is considered its founder.

In its beginnings this science did not differ much from physiology and was mainly concerned with the study of the sense organs. Gradually, more complex functions, such as memory, association and imagination were investigated, and eventually the same methods were extended to the study of the higher functions of thinking and willing.[3]

Philosophical Psychology may be defined as "the science of living bodies which interprets the data of experience in the light of metaphysical principles." It has two sources: (1) the data of experience, supplied mainly by everyday experience and, to some extent, by biology, for the vegetative functions, and by empirical or experimental psychology, for the sentient and rational functions;[4] (2) metaphysical principles, supplied by ontology or by metaphysical psychology.

Philosophical psychology, therefore, is a combination of science and metaphysics as applied to the domain of living bodies, or

---

[2] We mean by science in the strict sense a science which uses measurement and statistics, which presupposes strict determinism in its object, and which is able to predict future events.

By science in the wide sense is meant any organized body of knowledge about a certain topic.

Physics, chemistry, biology, etc., are sciences in the strict sense. History, sociology, theology, etc., are sciences in the wide sense.

In the following pages, the first kind of science will be written with a capital S. We shall use "science" with a lower case *s* to indicate science in the wide sense, or science in general.

[3] Wundt and the early experimental psychologists did not restrict the object of experimental psychology. to behavior; they included within its scope all conscious phenomena.

[4] Hence familiarity with biology and experimental psychology, although useful, is not required for a solid study of philosophical psychology.

organisms. Such a combination of science and metaphysics is sometimes called "natural philosophy," and philosophical psychology
may alternatively be defined as "the natural philosophy of living
bodies."

Because it employs both metaphysics and science, philosophical
psychology is partly deductive and partly inductive. It gives us a
complete picture of living bodies in both their noumenal and
phenomenal aspects. The noumenal aspect of beings refers to these
beings as they are in themselves, independently of our ordinary
way of knowing them. The phenomenal aspect of beings refers to
them as they affect us, as they appear to our senses. The study of
the first aspect belongs to metaphysics; the study of the second
aspect belongs to the various sciences. Natural philosophy combines both aspects.

Metaphysical Psychology is that part of metaphysics which is
concerned with the study of living bodies. Metaphysics, which is
the science of being as such, is divided into general metaphysics,
or ontology, and special metaphysics. Special metaphysics may be
concerned with inorganic beings (metaphysical cosmology), organic
beings (metaphysical psychology), pure spirits (angelology), or the
Infinite Being (natural theology).

Metaphysical psychology is deductive in this sense, that it starts
from a hypothetically necessary fact and discovers, a priori, all the
conditions required to make that fact possible.

For example: We necessarily think by means of judgments. To
deny this involves a contradiction, since the denial itself entails a
judgment. Hence thinking with judgments is of necessity. But such
thinking presupposes certain conditions without which it would be
impossible. These conditions are as necessary as the thinking itself.
Metaphysical psychology investigates these conditions.[5]

Metaphysical psychology is also termed "reflective psychology,"
because it consists essentially in the reflection of the intellect on its
own activity. It differs from other forms of psychology especially
in that "it studies man not as a thing, but as a spiritual and internal

---

[5] Cfr. J. Maréchal, S.J., "Esquisse d'une Psychologie Déductive," in
Mélanges Joseph Maréchal (Brussels, L'Edition Universelle, 1950), Vol. I,
pp. 304-322.

action; not so much under the aspect of an object as under that of a subject."[6]

Psychology is defined etymologically as "the science of the soul." We shall demonstrate that every living body (plant, animal, man) has a vital principle, or soul. Therefore all living bodies, including plants, are studied in philosophical psychology. Since the soul is the innermost reality of every organism, *the soul,* its faculties and activities, is the main object of metaphysical and philosophical psychology.

Modern philosophers, under the influence of Descartes, have restricted the scope of psychology to a study of conscious organisms. Empirical psychology follows this trend, and its object is *consciousness,* or the conscious experience of man. This does not exclude a study of the unconscious, which, however, can be known only through its conscious manifestations.

The psychologists of more recent schools have further restricted the scope of psychology. They are mainly interested in that which can be observed from without, or in that which can be inferred from such observation. The object of experimental psychology is *behavior.*

SOME PRELIMINARY METAPHYSICAL CONCEPTS AND PRINCIPLES

Both philosophical and reflective psychology presuppose a thorough knowledge of metaphysics or ontology. Therefore a brief review of certain metaphysical concepts and principles will be useful.

[6] A. Marc, S.J., *Psychologie Réflexive* (Paris, Desclée de Brouwer, 1949), Vol. I, p. 19. Father Marc takes as his starting point the phenomenon of human language. About his original attempt, read the incisive criticism of S. Strasser, "Le Point de Départ en Psychologie Métaphysique," in *Revue Philosophique de Louvain,* 48 (1950), pp. 220-238. This kind of psychology is sometimes called "psychology in the first person," because it studies man as an "I," not as an "it" or "he." It leans heavily on phenomenology, especially for its starting point. Cfr. the article of Strasser, and also his book *The Soul in Metaphysical and Empirical Psychology.* The reader will notice that although in this book we use the methods of third-person psychology, occasionally, for some essential theses, we shift to the first person, v. g. when demonstrating the immateriality of the intellect from the power of self-reflection.

EXISTENCE AND ESSENCE

Ontology demonstrates that every finite being is composed of two really distinct and strictly complementary principles: existence and essence. Existence is that which makes a being exist, which makes it real. Essence is that which makes a being that which it is.

With regard to every being we can ask two fundamental questions: WHETHER it is, and WHAT it is. The first question concerns the being's existence, the second concerns its essence.

Pure existence is pure perfection, pure act. Of itself it is unlimited. Wherever existence is limited, that limitation must come from another principle, which is called essence. A being which is only existence, which is its own existence, is of necessity infinitely perfect. God is His existence. But it is clear from language alone that we are not existence, not even our own existence. We possess existence, we share it with other beings. In us, and in all finite beings, existence is limited by essence. Essence is to existence as potency is to act.

Under God and above man in the hierarchy of being are the immaterial beings, the pure spirits, whose existence cannot be strictly demonstrated by reason but whose essence can be studied as a possible reality. Pure spirits differ from material beings in that the essence of the pure spirit is simple, whereas the essence of the material being is composed of two complementary principles, substantial form and prime matter. None of these material beings is its essence. My essence, that which makes me a human being, is humanity. I am not humanity, not even my own humanity. I possess humanity, I share it with many others. If my essence were simple, if it did not contain prime matter, I should exhaust it completely. I should possess the whole of humanity, and no other human being would be possible. Every pure spirit exhausts his essence, is his whole species.

Two pure spirits differ from each other, not as two men differ, but rather as a man differs from an animal. Two pure spirits differ from each other through their essences. Two men do not differ from each other through their essences, for the essence is the same in both. What then causes them to differ from each other? The fact that their essence is composed of two principles, that the principle of determination in that essence, substantial form, is received in a principle of indetermination, prime matter.

SUBSTANTIAL FORM AND PRIME MATTER

Substantial form and prime matter cannot be imagined, they must be understood or conceived. Substantial form is not to be identified with the shape of an object; it is not the "form" or "configuration" of the Gestalt psychologists. Prime matter is not the matter studied in physics and chemistry.

To make these difficult concepts intelligible, we might proceed as follows. Suppose that we take some clay and make a ball of it. That ball of clay is a substance, a being which exists in itself. It is round and soft. Roundness and softness are accidents, i.e. realities which exist in something which is other than themselves. Roundness is that which makes the clay round, and softness is that which makes the clay soft. But what makes the clay just clay? We answer: its substantial form. The substantial form is that which makes a being that which it is.[7]

Accidents cannot exist by themselves, they need some substance in which to inhere. Can a substantial form exist by itself? Not in purely material beings. Yet it does not inhere in a substance, since there *can be* no substance before the substantial form is present. The substantial form cannot exist by itself; it does not inhere in something other than itself. It exists-together-with, it co-exists with, matter. In purely material beings these two principles are complementary. They are con-created, they co-exist, they can only be apprehended in their co-existence. That which is directly created, that which exists by itself, that which can be understood by itself, is the material substance, composed of substantial form and prime matter.

Prime matter must be distinguished from the matter studied by the natural sciences. In philosophical language the "matter" of the

---

[7] This is the same definition as the one previously given for essence. The form is the positive element of the essence. In pure spirits, form and essence are the same reality.

natural science is called "second matter." Wood, iron, a rock are second matter. They are substances which are composed of a substantial form and prime matter.

In order that the idea of prime matter may be grasped, it may be useful to consider an example.[8] A cat kills and eats a mouse. The mouse is assimilated by the cat, becomes part of the cat. During this process of assimilation something has disappeared and something has persisted. When digested by the cat, the mouse is no longer a mouse; its "mouseness," its substantial form, has disappeared. But its prime matter persists. The prime matter is neither the cat nor the mouse; it is not the dead mouse or the proteins or other chemicals which analysis may discover in it. It is a principle of being which, when united to the substantial form of a cat, constitutes a cat, and when combined with the substantial form of a mouse, constitutes a mouse. It can never exist in itself, it co-exists with the substantial form.

What happened to the substantial form of the mouse when the mouse was assimilated by the cat? Exactly what happens to the roundness of the clay when you flatten the ball. The roundness disappears exactly *when, and insofar as,* it is replaced by some other shape. In the same way the substantial form of the mouse disappears exactly *when, and insofar as,* it is replaced by the substantial form of the cat. As it is impossible to imagine a piece of clay existing without any shape, so it is impossible to conceive prime matter existing without any substantial form.

It is not the task of the psychologist to demonstrate the reality of substantial form and prime matter. The following considerations are given only to prevent some common misunderstandings.

The reality of substantial form and prime matter cannot be demonstrated by arguments drawn from Science. On the other hand, no objections drawn from Science can invalidate Hylomorphism,[9] which is a metaphysical explanation and not a scientific theory. Hylomorphism is unaffected by any changes in the scientific conceptions regarding the ultimate physical constituents of matter.

A simple argument for the validity of these concepts can be

[8] This example is not intended as a demonstration.
[9] Or the theory which holds that all material beings are composed of substantial form and prime matter.

derived from their usefulness. It seems to be impossible to explain
the relation of body and soul, of organism and vital principle, except on the basis of Hylomorphism. That statement will be demonstrated in the following chapters. If these principles are required to explain living beings, we do not see why they would not
help us also to understand inorganic beings.

The best demonstration of substantial form and prime matter
derives from the fact that we implicitly affirm their existence whenever we know a material being. We shall not present that argument
here, since its exposition supposes an understanding of certain concepts which will be explained further on in the book.[10]

In modern terminology, substantial form might be defined as the
constitutive law of a being. Prime matter would then correspond to
the *undetermined* energy in which this constitutive law is embodied.
That undetermined energy cannot exist or be conceived without
such a constitutive law. It becomes something definite—that is,
something which can exist and can be conceived—only on account
of that constitutive law.[11]

THE DEGREES OF MATERIAL BEINGS

With these ideas it is possible to express in metaphysical terms
the difference between the various degrees of material beings. Every
material being possesses an essence composed of substantial form
and prime matter. The differences between the degrees of material
beings derive from the different proportions in which the two
components are combined.

Form is a principle of perfection; it is restricted by matter, which
is a principle of imperfection. Form is the principle of consciousness, knowledge and spontaneity. Matter is the principle of unconsciousness, passivity and necessity. When form is combined with
matter, the resulting being is deprived of the properties of form to
the extent in which matter has entered the combination. The con-

[10] That argument is briefly presented on page 280.
[11] Cf. the interesting remarks of J. Maréchal, S.J., in 'Le Problème de
Dieu d'après M. Edouard Le Roy," in *Mélanges Joseph Maréchal*, Vol. I,
pp. 237-238.

sciousness and spontaneity of form are, as it were, neutralized by the unconsciousness, passivity and necessity of matter.

The proportions in which form and matter can be combined in material beings vary considerably, and to them correspond the degrees of ontological perfection of these various beings.

In minerals (the "matter" of everyday language and of the Sciences), form and matter are present, so to speak, at equal intensity, so that all the positive qualities of form are counteracted by the negative properties of matter. Form is entirely immersed in matter, it is totally diluted in matter. Minerals possess certain activities, which derive from their form. But because their form is entirely immersed in matter, these activities are necessary, blind and unconscious.

In plants too form is almost entirely immersed in matter. Almost, but not entirely. Here form emerges somewhat from matter, so that its proper effects are not totally neutralized by matter. This explains why some activities of the plant are superior to the activities of minerals, or, more precisely, why the mechanical activities, which the plant shares with the mineral, are all directed to the plant's own welfare, have become *living* activities. The superiority of these activities derives from the slight prevalence of form over matter in the living beings.

In animals the form emerges still more from matter and exerts more of its superior influence. Hence in animals we find conscious activities, sense knowledge and sense appetite.

It would seem that we can go one step farther and apply the same considerations to man. In man, we could say, the form emerges still further and is capable of producing higher activities. But man's substantial form, as we shall demonstrate later, is of a very special kind. The forms which we have considered thus far are material forms; man's substantial form is not material, it is a spirit which acts as the form of a material being. Inasmuch as it is a form united to matter, we can consider it as the next higher step in the hierarchy of forms. But we shall demonstrate that it is more than a material form, that it possesses activities which are never found in material forms. Between the form of the highest animal and the form of man there is not only a difference of degree but a difference in kind. We shall give further consideration to this important aspect of man later on.

METAPHYSICAL PRINCIPLES IN PSYCHOLOGY

Having briefly reviewed these important metaphysical concepts, we must now outline the metaphysical principles used in philosophical psychology.

Besides the principle of identity, or first principle, the principle of causality and the principle of sufficient reason, philosophical psychology uses mainly the following metaphysical principles:

1. "As a being is, so it acts." We know the nature of a being by studying its activities. A chemist discovers that a certain substance is arsenic by finding out how it reacts with other substances. In psychology, we shall be able to discover the nature of our intelligence by studying the operations of that faculty—ideas, judgments, self-reflection. This principle is immediately evident: the nature of a being is the essence of that being, inasmuch as it is the radical principle of its operations. As we can know a cause by examining its effects, so we can know the nature of a being by studying its operations.

2. "An effect cannot possess more perfection than its cause," since the whole reality and perfection of the effect derive from its cause.

3. The principle of proportionality or of analogy: "The ontological perfections are common to all beings, to each according to its degree."[12]

If by ontological perfections we mean the transcendental attributes of being, unity, truth and goodness, this principle is immediately evident. These ontological perfections are but different aspects of being. And since being is common to all beings, these perfections too are common.

But the principle of proportionality has a deeper meaning. It refers not only to the transcendental attributes of being but to all

[12] Pierre Scheuer, S.J., "Notes de Métaphysique," in *Nouvelle Revue Théologique*, 55 (1926), p. 522. English translation in *Cross Currents*, 7 (1957), p. 344. Reprints of this important article are available from *Cross Currents*, 3111 Broadway, New York 27, N.Y.

the pure perfections. All beings derive from God. God is spirit, consciousness, life, intellect, love and liberty. Now every agent produces effects which resemble it—"*Omne agens agit simile sibi.*" Therefore all God's effects, all beings, must be, at their degree, in their own way, spirit, consciousness, life, intellect, love and liberty. These are the ontological perfections implied by the principle of proportionality.

Concerning this principle Fr. Pierre Scheuer, S.J., writes as follows:

According to this principle we are ourselves, in our own being, the first principle of metaphysical explanation. We are, each one of us, the only being which we know from within, in itself. What we discover within us we apply above ourselves by extension and below ourselves by restriction.

The principle of proportionality seems, at first sight, paradoxical and opposed to common sense. Does it not entail panpsychism? Shall we say that a mineral possesses life and intelligence?

We must first remark that words should be given the meaning which they have in everyday usage. We shall not say that a mineral possesses life, because life means the perfection of immanence, at least in that degree which is found from plants upward. Likewise the application of the word "knowledge" begins only with the animal, and of the term "intellect" only with man. We only say that, since all beings are only being, and since being is common to all of them, there is in none of them an ontological perfection which is totally heterogeneous to the other beings. Aside from all terminological discussions, we must affirm that there is in the atom something which is to the intellect what the being of the atom is to the being of a spirit. This formula is above reproach and contains nothing paradoxical. God is only life, spirit, intellect and love; yet He sees in Himself, as a very imperfect participation of Himself, the being of the atom. Would that be possible if the atom were entirely heterogeneous, entirely "alterius rationis" to life, intellect and love? This principle destroys the basis of agnosticism and provides us with the only means of escaping it. It opens the way to that real intelligence of beings which understands the lower ones by means of the higher. The most material determinations are, in their intimate core, nothing but participations of thought and of love. That which is entirely irreducible to the spirit—for instance, local movement or extension as such—is introduced into a being by prime matter.

But this irreducible element can be separated only by abstraction; in reality, it is synthesized with a formal element. The principle of analogy is frequently used by St. Thomas.[13]

Here, for instance, is a text from St. Thomas which implies the principle of proportionality:

It belongs to God's perfection that He bestowed His likeness on created things, except as regards those things with which created being is incompatible: since it belongs to a perfect agent to produce its like as far as possible (*ScG.*, II, 30).

One perfection of God with which created being is incompatible is aseity, or the fact that God depends on no other being, that He is self-existent. But consciousness, intelligence, liberty, et cetera, are not incompatible with finite being, and therefore we expect to find these properties in every creature.

Does not this principle entail the possibility that the ascent from the lowest forms of reality to the highest might be gradual, with the consequence that there is no real discontinuity between the soul of man and that of the animals? By no means, for the principle states explicitly that the ontological perfections are common to all beings, *to each according to its degree*. The degree in which a being possesses the ontological perfections depends on the essence of that being. Whenever there is real discontinuity between two essences, there is discontinuity also in the way in which they partake of the ontological perfections. The principle contains no implication that there is a gradual transition from one essence to the other.[14]

4. The principle of continuity: "The highest point of the lower degree always touches the lowest point of the higher degree."[15]

This principle, which St. Thomas borrowed from Pseudo-Dionysius, is frequently used in his works. It is a heuristic more than a metaphysical principle. It could be metaphysically demonstrated in a philosophy of emanation or of materialistic evolutionism; such philosophies admit a gradual transition from one essence

---

[13] *Ibid.* in *Cross Currents*, p. 344.
[14] Cf. L. Malevez, S.J., "La Méthode du P. Teilhard de Chardin et la Phénoménologie," in *Nouvelle Revue Théologique,* 79 (1957), pp. 594-597.
[15] *De Spiritualibus Creaturis*, a. 2, and passim.

to the next one, hence also a continuity in the whole of reality. In our philosophy, which denies such a gradual transition, the principle has a more restricted bearing. Thus is does not apply to God and his creatures. There is no "lowest point" in God, and even the "highest point" of the most perfect creature remains at an infinite distance from the divine nature.

But within created reality the principle of continuity has a real heuristic value. In every degree of being we can distinguish lower and higher activities. The principle states that "the highest activity of each degree of being resembles the lowest *specific* activity of the degree of being immediately above it." Thus the highest intellectual activity of man, which St. Thomas attributes to the intellect, as opposed to understanding, resembles the intellectual activity of the angels. The highest cognitive activity of animals, their estimative power, resembles the lowest specific activity of man, as found in understanding. We say "specific" activity because it is quite evident that the cognitive activities of animals resemble the lowest cognitive activity of man—that is, his sense knowledge. But sense knowledge is not specifically human. The principle of continuity supposes resemblance between the specific activities of the different degrees of being.

THE CONFUSION IN MODERN PSYCHOLOGY

The distinctions which we have made between the different kinds of psychology are often overlooked by psychologists, with considerable confusion as a consequence. This was especially true during the first decades in the study of experimental psychology. In textbooks of the Sciences—physics, chemistry—there is a certain margin for disagreement with respect to details, but there is agreement with regard to all fundamentals. In psychology for many years the situation was the opposite: agreement with regard to details but utter disagreement on the most essential questions, such as those of intelligence, the will, the soul. Some psychologists tried to explain this wholly on the grounds that psychology was a young Science, engaged in the study of a very complex object. Actually the trouble derives from the very nature of psychology, from the peculiar character of the object which it studies.

We find perfect agreement in the exact, positive or natural Sciences, which use measurement, experimentation and laboratory methods. These Sciences make their greatest gains where determinism is perfect, where the activities under consideration are blind, mechanical, necessary, predictable, where the influence of form is entirely counterbalanced, or neutralized, by that of matter— that is, in the world of minerals. As soon as Science enters a domain where form emerges from matter, difficulties arise. Here we meet activities which show some of the characteristics of form: spontaneity, unpredictability. Spontaneous, unpredictable activities cannot be wholly interpreted within a deterministic frame of reference, and measurement becomes increasingly difficult. Science loses its favorite tools. Form and the influence of form as such can be studied only by philosophy, so that a complete knowledge of these domains in which form exercises its peculiar effects in a perceptible way can be obtained only with the aid of philosophy.

The difficulties start with biology, which is the study of living beings as living. Science can cover most of this domain because all the single activities of the living being are purely material. But the intrinsic finality of these material activities cannot be explained entirely by Science. A study of living beings is incomplete without an explanation of the central phenomenon of life. Science cannot explain life but must recur to philosophy for the consideration of this problem. That is the reason underlying the perennial controversies between mechanists and vitalists in the field of biology.

In animals the influence of form is greater than in plant life. Therefore in the study of animals "as animals," which is undertaken by animal psychology, more problems arise which the scientist feels unable to solve. The nature of animal knowledge and consciousness is no longer a scientific problem but one which must be studied by philosophy.

But it is in the study of human psychology that strictly scientific methods meet the greatest difficulties, since here the influence of the formal element is predominant. Of course, there are Sciences by which man is studied with great success—for example, anatomy. But the Science of anatomy is purely descriptive of man in terms of shape, structure, dimensions; man is studied as if he were a crystal or a mineral. Physiology is concerned with the study of man as if he were a plant, and most of this terrain can be covered in a satisfactory way by means of the scientific method. But when we try to study those functions in man which make him specifically human—his intellect, his free will—we find little help in the Sciences.

The higher we advance in the study of human psychology, the greater is the need for a philosophical method of investigation. The reason for this fact is shown in Figure 1. The two almost

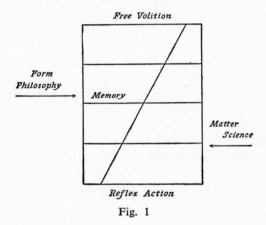

Fig. 1

triangular halves of the rectangle represent respectively the domain of matter, determinism and Science (right half) and the domain of form, spontaneity and philosophy (left half). The various human functions are represented by the horizontal lines. Lower functions, such as reflexes, are represented by the base line, which lies almost entirely in the right half. Hence, for the study of such functions, the methods of Science are quite sufficient. Intermediate functions, such as memory and learning, can be conceived as lying partially in the right and partially in the left half. They have a considerable material component and can to a great extent be investigated scientifically. Yet a complete elucidation of these functions will require the help of philosophy. Thus it is impossible to understand "learning" completely, unless one understands what "knowledge" is. And this requires the help of philosophy.

But in the highest human functions, such as intellection and free volition (represented by the top line), the material element, although still present, is so unimportant as compared with the formal element, that here Science has very little to say, and the explanation must come from philosophy. Science will, and must, try to explain even these highest functions. When we think or freely choose, something happens in the brain; Science must try to investigate this cerebral background of man's spiritual activities. But even when the scientist knows everything about these processes in their physical manifestations, he will not have explained thought and free volition. Only philosophy can, in its own sphere, explain the nature of these functions.

It is easy to understand now why, in most textbooks and courses of general and experimental psychology, the main share of attention goes to the inferior functions, such as reflex movement, sensation, association, perception, learning. The study of the higher functions is necessarily conducted in a superficial way which does not give any real insight into their nature. Consider, for instance, the chapter on intelligence in an ordinary textbook. We hear plenty about the intelligence quotient, the measurement of intelligence and intelligence tests. But we are not told what intelligence really is or how it works.

This is by no means a reproach addressed to the experimental psychologists. The very fact that modern psychologists do not consider these problems shows that they have become aware of the nature and the limitations of their Science. The psychologists of an earlier day treated these problems in their textbooks; they made statements which were not based on scientifically established facts, but which derived from their own, often unconscious, philosophical conception of man. The result of this procedure was a score of conflicting schools holding mutually contradictory positions on essential questions.

Some modern psychologists err in presenting the results of their scientific investigations as a *complete* picture of man. If we consider the study of man as the main purpose of psychology in general, we must state that a strictly scientific psychology is necessarily, and will always remain, an incomplete psychology. It will continually extend the scope of its investigations, but it will never be able to cover the field entirely.

The same limitation applies to metaphysical psychology. Of itself it cannot give us a complete picture of man. Its deductive method does not extend to the material, phenomenal aspects of human nature, without which any picture of man is incomplete.

Therefore in the present study we shall try to combine the scientific and the metaphysical, the inductive and the deductive methods. An attempt will be made to use the data of experience and to interpret them in the light of metaphysics. That is the scope of the natural philosophy of man, of philosophical psychology.

DIVISION OF THE COURSE

Psychology is the science of organisms, or living bodies. There are three main kinds of organisms: plants, animals and men. All three possess vegetative life; animals and men have sentient life; men alone are endowed with rational life.

We are primarily interested in human psychology. But we must also study briefly the life of plants and animals, since these topics belong to psychology as we understand it. Furthermore, man has vegetative life in common with both plants and animals, and sentient life in common with animals. Finally, the study of these lower forms of life will help us to understand more thoroughly, by contrast, the nature of rational life.

Our course will be divided into five parts.

The first part is concerned with the study of life in general.

The second part is concerned with the life of plants and animals.

The third part is given to the study of the sentient life of man. This part will necessarily overlap to a certain extent with the second part, since animals possess sentient life in common with man.

The fourth part is devoted to a study of man's rational life.

The fifth part is devoted to a study of man as a whole, as a person.

READINGS[16]

Allport, "Psychology," in *College Reading and Religion*, pp. 80-114. J. Donceel, S.J., "What Kind of Science Is Psychology?" in *The New Scholasticism*, 19 (1945), pp. 117-135. Maréchal, "Empirical Science and Religious Psychology," in *Studies in the Psychology of the Mystics*, ch. 1. Martin, *The Order and Integration of Knowledge*, pp. 12-28, 256-316. S. Strasser, "Le Point de Départ en Psychologie Metaphysique," in *Revue Philosophique de Louvain*, 48 (1950), pp. 220-238.

[16] Details of publication for the books mentioned in these Readings will be found in the General Bibliography.

PART ONE

LIFE IN GENERAL

1

The Concept of Life

WHAT IS life? Most people are unable to give a satisfactory answer to this question, although the ordinary person can almost always distinguish a living being from one which is not alive. The nature of life is mysterious; its effects or manifestations are familiar to all. It is by a study of these manifestations that we must try to discover the nature of life itself. From the visible effects we must go back to the invisible cause, from the accidents to the nature.

THE POPULAR CONCEPTION OF LIFE

The most usual criterion of life is movement, in particular self-movement. A living cat moves about, a dead cat does not. In some cases, however, such a rough criterion is insufficient. A man may lie quite motionless on the street; we do not at once conclude that he is dead, he may have fainted. We look then for other, less obvious kinds of movement. Is his heart beating? Is he breathing? Here again movement, although of a special kind, is the sign of life. Plants do not move of themselves; yet they are alive if they produce leaves and flowers and fruit, if the sap circulates in their stems and branches, if we discover in them the movement connected with nutrition and growth. In the popular conception, life is the capacity for self-movement.

THE SCIENTIFIC CONCEPTION OF LIFE

Among the features which the scientists consider as characteristic of living beings, we can mention the following:

1. Cellular constitution: living beings are generally built up of cells;

2. Metabolism: a constant exchange of material elements with the environment;

3. Unstable equilibrium: an organism reaches chemical stability only when it is dead;

4. Eventual death, except in the organisms which multiply by fission;

5. Especially organization, which is the "fundamental fact common to every living thing: protoplasm *builds organisms*. It does not grow into indeterminate, formless masses of living stuff. The growth and activity shown by plants and animals are not random processes but are so controlled that they form integrated, coordinated, organized systems."[1]

THE PHILOSOPHICAL CONCEPTION OF LIFE

For the philosopher the great difference between living and non-living beings is that the living beings possess immanent activities, whereas all the activities of the non-living beings are purely transitive.

An immanent activity is one whose effects remain within the subject which acts. When I think, the thinking starts in me and its effects remain within me; thinking is an immanent activity; so are growing, seeing, willing.

A transitive activity is one whose effects pass into another being. When I kick a ball, the kicking starts in me, but its effects pass into the ball. When two cars collide, one smashes the other and is in turn smashed by it; neither car smashes itself.

All living beings manifest a certain number of immanent activities. The number of these activities and the degree of their immanence increase as we ascend in the scale of being. But since we speak here of life in general, of life as possessed by all living beings, even the lowest, we shall consider only those immanent activities shared by all. These are nutrition, growth and reproduction.

---

[1] E. W. Sinnott, *Cell and Psyche: The Biology of Purpose* (University of North Carolina Press, 1950), p. 22.

That nutrition and growth are immanent activities is evident, since the effect of these operations remains within the feeding or growing organism. It is not so clear that reproduction is an immanent activity, since the effect of that activity seems to pass entirely into the new being which is its product. It is true that the final stage of reproduction is transitive; but the first stage is immanent: a living being prepares in itself, as part of itself, certain substances which may eventually give rise to a new being. Only that immanent first stage of reproduction is found in all living beings; the final, transitive stage may never be reached.

That nutrition, growth and reproduction are found in all living beings is evident. That these activities are never found in non-living beings is a fact of common experience. Hence a living being is one which is capable of immanent activities, and life is that which makes a being *capable of immanent activities*.

It could be objected that every machine is capable of immanent activities: it is argued that the machine moves itself, the effect of its movement remains within itself. In fact, machines have no immanent activities, because they possess no natural unity. Their unity is extrinsic, artificial, produced from without. Therefore we cannot say that they move themselves, but only that one part moves another. Only where there is intrinsic, natural unity can we speak of real immanent activities. A living being is *naturally* capable of immanent activity, and we can complete our definition of life by saying that it is that which makes a being *naturally capable of immanent activities*.

A more serious objection derives from a consideration of the intra-atomic movement of inorganic matter. According to modern physics, matter is constituted not of solid particles but of an immense number of infinitesimal systems in which electrons move around a central nucleus. Here is an activity which is natural and whose effects remain within the atom. Why should we not call this an immanent activity?

In a certain sense we could say that it is, or at least that it is some approximation to it, something analogous to it.[2] The difference between this activitiy and the immanent activities of living

[2] ". . . every natural movement in respect to natural things has a certain likeness to the operations of life" (*S. Theol.*, I, 18, 1, ad 1).

beings is that intra-atomic movement only maintains the energy of the atom, whereas the immanent activities of a living being not only maintain but also develop and increase the energy of the organism. They are not only immanent but are *perfective* of the acting subject. That nutrition and growth are perfective of the organism is evident, whereas reproduction is at least perfective of the species.

We can now add this last qualification to our definition, and say that life is that which makes a being *naturally capable of self-perfective immanent activity*.

THE METAPHYSICAL CONCEPTION OF LIFE

In order to penetrate more deeply into the meaning of life, we must use metaphysics, in particular the principle of proportionality.

"Using ourselves as the first principle of metaphysical explanation and applying that which we discover in ourselves above ourselves by extension and below ourselves by restriction,"[3] we can proceed as follows:

We find in ourselves some very perfect types of immanent action. I know that I know, I am aware of being aware, I decide to decide. In all these actions I am both subject and object. The subject of the action coincides with its object. The subject is luminous to himself, is present to himself, identifies himself actively with himself. That kind of immanent action is more perfect than any immanent actions we discover in plants or animals; yet it is far from the supreme perfection which immanent activity reaches in God.

Between our highest immanent actions and the immanent activity of God there are three main differences:

1. We do not always consciously know and love ourselves, our self-identification is not continuous. God, on the other hand, knows Himself and consciously loves Himself continually.

2. Even when we reflect upon ourselves, we are not conscious of our whole selves, but only of the operation of our mind in the act of self-reflection. There remain perpetually in us vast areas of unconsciousness. After many centuries of scientific investigation,

---

[3] Scheuer, "Notes de Métaphysique."

man remains a mystery to himself. God, on the other hand, knows Himself perfectly, and nothing in Him is outside the grasp of His consciousness. He is nothing but consciousness, intellect and will.

3. We become conscious of ourselves after having first become conscious of an exterior object. The movement of our consciousness is first outwards, then, through reflection, inwards. A human being who was unable to know any exterior object would never know himself, would not be aware of his own existence.

That is why St. Thomas speaks of a "return to our essence," which supposes that we have first gone out of it. That is why we speak of an "active identification with ourselves," an operation of becoming identical with ourselves, which presupposes a stage at which we were not identical with ourselves.

God, on the other hand, need not first know any exterior object before He knows Himself. To declare that He is subject to this necessity is the fundamental error of idealistic pantheism. He knows Himself first, continually, eternally. In Him there is not self-identification but active self-identity. He is essentially such an active Self-Identity.

No creature possesses such perfect self-identity. Angels know themselves continually and without the need of exterior objects, but they depend on God for their self-knowledge. Man knows himself partially, intermittently, and with dependence not only on God but also on exterior objects. Animals do not know themselves, but they are aware of external objects. Plants do not even know external objects. Their immanent activity is restricted to the operations by which they feed, grow and reproduce themselves. Yet these simple operations of nutrition, growth and reproduction are that in the plant, which, at its degree, corresponds to the perfect Self-Identity of the First Cause, or to our human self-consciousness. In other words, life is the first step of matter towards a greater similarity with God.

The principle of proportionality can therefore be stated concretely as follows:

$$\frac{\text{Perfect Self-Identity}}{\text{God}} = \frac{\text{Self-consciousness}}{\text{Man}} = \frac{\text{Consciousness of objects}}{\text{Animal}} = \frac{\text{Immanent action, Life}}{\text{Plant}}$$

We can go further. Even in the mineral there is something which, at its lowly degree, corresponds to the perfect Self-Identity which is God. In other words, although there is no really immanent activity in the mineral, there must be something akin to it, foreshadowing it, according to the principle of proportionality and the principle of continuity.

In fact, we find in crystals phenomena resembling growth; we find in many material bodies a spontaneous restoration of equilibrium which resembles the phenomena of regeneration in organisms. Intra-atomic movement is an activity whose effects remain within the atom, and which resembles the immanent activity of living bodies. When W. Köhler[4] saw a similarity between the "Gestalten," or configurations, which occur in the world of physics and those which occur in the organic and psychic world, he was not wholly wrong. His mistake was to emphasize only the similarity, not the differences. The principle of proportionality draws our attention to both.

[4] *Die physischen Gestalten in Ruhe und im stationären Zustand* (1920).

2

The Nature of Life

WHAT MAKES living beings so different from non-living beings? What gives them the power of performing self-perfective, immanent operations?

The answer is: life. But how do we explain that mysterious life? Is it some kind of material energy, like electricity or magnetism or radio-activity, or a special combination of such material energies? Or is it something superior to purely material energy?

The first hypothesis is defended by mechanism, the second by vitalism.

THE MECHANISTIC INTERPRETATION OF LIFE

Mechanism holds that life is some kind of material energy, or a resultant of a combination of material energies; that it can be explained, or will eventually be explained, by the laws of physics and chemistry; that a living being is only a complicated machine. The difference between living and non-living machines is that the latter are products of human ingenuity, whereas the former are products of nature, of evolution, of the blind powers of matter. Mechanists readily admit that living machines are vastly more complicated than the most complicated man-made machines. But sooner or later, they maintain, the human mind will be able to construct the machinery of life.

Philosophically considered, mechanism is a doctrine which rules out all final causes and explains living beings by means of mechanical causes. A mechanical cause is an efficient cause which acts without purpose, blindly and necessarily.

31

We shall briefly indicate two ways in which mechanism, as a doctrine, can be refuted:

1. Mechanism cannot explain the origin of living beings. A complete mechanist must hold that they are the products of chance. What he does not hold for a watch, an airplane or a bridge, he holds for the much more complicated structures which we call living beings. While the paleontologist considers the presence in a cave of a few rudimentary tools sufficient proof of the passage of man, the mechanist ascribes the origin of fantastically complicated organisms to the action of chance. The impossibility of such an explanation is immediately evident for a philosopher, and quite a number of scientists admit this impossibility.

2. Some mechanists admit the impossibility of explaining the origin of the first living beings by the forces of matter alone. They accept some extra-mundane cause as the first origin of life, or they claim that life has always existed in some part of the universe. Either position means the abandonment of the mechanistic explanation of the origin of life; yet they hold that, once life is given, it can be explained entirely in terms of the forces of matter.

The best refutation of this claim is still to be found in the famous experiments of Hans Driesch. This German biologist and philosopher performed some remarkable experiments on the embryos of sea-urchins. When the embryo contained only two or four cells, he separated these cells from each other and saw each one of them develop into a complete, although smaller, animal. When the embryo was composed of eight cells, he modified the position of these cells, he "shuffled" them. In spite of this he obtained a normal animal. When the embryo contained about a thousand cells, he took away an indefinite number of cells, at any place in the embryo; if not too many cells had been removed, the embryo developed into a normal animal of smaller size.

The same experiments have been performed upon the embryos of other animals, with identical results. It appears that only technical difficulties making the experiment impracticable prevent the scientist from obtaining the same results with the embryos of every animal.

Such phenomena do not occur in machines, and their presence

in living beings is considered by Driesch to be a sufficient refutation of the mechanistic conception of life.

Later research in experimental embryology has shown that these remarkable phenomena of regeneration can be explained by the influence of "organizers," of specialized parts of the embryo which direct the regenerative activity. If an embryo is dissected into two parts, one of which contains such an organizer while the other lacks it, only the first part will regenerate.

Embryologists have further demonstrated that these organizers operate by means of certain chemical substances. It might seem, therefore, that there is really nothing mysterious in these phenomena, since they can be analyzed in terms of physics and chemistry. In reality, however, the mystery of life has not been solved, but only further removed. As Professor E. W. Sinnott points out,[1] the organizing chemicals produce their results only if they are distributed in a definite way, if they appear at a definite time, if they are present in a definite quantity. The biologists do not know the factors responsible for this "prospective adaptation." Moreover, these chemicals presuppose living cells susceptible of being influenced by them. The mystery of the element in these cells which makes them react in a certain way to the influence of the organizers has not been solved.

Undoubtedly new discoveries will shed more light on the mechanical causes at work in every organism. Science will indefinitely continue to find answers to the problems which it meets in the investigation of life. But every answer will raise new problems. A final answer, which would explain how all the mechanical factors co-operate harmoniously towards their immanent goal, the perfection of the organism as a whole, lies beyond the reach of Science and must come from philosophy.

Hence some outstanding theoretical biologists have given up the mechanical explanation of living activities. For them, as Sinnott puts it, "biological organization and psychical activity are fundamentally the same thing."[2] We shall not go as far as they do. But we accept their statements as a proof that life cannot be explained entirely by the forces of matter alone.

[1] *Cell and Psyche*, p. 37.
[2] *Ibid.*, p. 48.

THE VITALISTIC INTERPRETATION OF LIFE

If life cannot be explained mechanically, we must admit some other kind of causality. The mechanical causes, which are undoubtedly at work in every living being, seem to be under the direction of some "guiding idea" which steers their activity toward the realization of the specific type of this plant or that animal. We call this guiding idea the vital principle. Such is the position of vitalism.

Most biologists have a deep-seated aversion for vitalism. Even those whose explanations seem to coincide with the vitalistic position do not want to be known as vitalists. This strange attitude can be said to arise from two sources: (1) a misunderstanding of the real nature of vitalism; (2) the erroneous idea that vitalism is presented as a *scientific* theory.

THE REAL NATURE OF VITALISM

When a modern biologist hears about vitalism, he immediately thinks that what is meant is the theory which we call "exaggerated vitalism." According to this, a living being is constituted of a complete material being plus a vital principle which directs the activities of that material being and explains its life. A living being is like a car with a driver: the car exists without the driver, but it needs a driver to turn the ignition key and direct its movement; the living being exists and acts without the vital principle, but it needs this principle to direct its countless activities towards its own immanent perfection.

That is not our interpretation. For us the vital principle not only directs the activities of the plant, it explains the very existence and nature of the plant. Without the vital principle, not only would the plant not be alive, there would be no plant at all.

All material beings, including inorganic substances, are composed of prime matter and substantial form. Hence, according to exponents of exaggerated vitalism, there would be first a complete material being, constituted of matter and form, and above and beyond that a vital principle, which would be a second and higher kind of form.

But moderate vitalism states that the vital principle IS precisely the substantial form of a plant, or other living being. There is no need for a guiding principle in addition to the substantial form. The difference between a rock and a plant is not that the plant has a special guiding principle, but only that in the plant the form is more perfect than in the rock; this higher perfection explains why the plant is alive, while the rock is not. Such a substantial form is called a "soul," and we can speak of the soul of a plant.

Our position lies between the two extremes of mechanism and exaggerated vitalism. For mechanism, a living being is only a complicated machine. For exaggerated vitalism a living being is a complete material system provided in addition with a guiding principle which directs its activities. We claim that a living being is a material being constituted, like all other material beings, of prime matter and substantial form. But in living beings this substantial form is more perfect than in non-living beings, and it is therefore called a vital principle, or a soul.

VITALISM NOT A SCIENTIFIC THEORY

Even after these explanations there remains in the mind of the biologist a lurking suspicion that, if he embraces vitalism, he must give up any further attempts at scientific explanation of the facts of life. Everything is now explained by this mysterious entity, the vital principle.

Nothing could be further from the truth. Vitalism is not a scientific explanation of the nature of life. It does not supersede the scientific theories of biology. A vitalist admits that each single operation of the living organism, taken separately, can and should be explained by the forces of matter alone. Each single step of cell-division, for instance, can or will be explained physico-chemically; each one could be artificially reproduced in the laboratory, without the intervention of any vital principle.

The scientist can and should, therefore, explain every single step in the vital activities of an organism by means of the laws of physics and chemistry. There are no mysterious new energies at work in an organism which cannot be interpreted in terms of these laws.[3] A scientist as such should never explain any operation in a living being by referring it to the vital principle. When he does that, he gives up Science and passes into philosophy. As a scientist he is engaged in the study of the single operations of the organism, which he must explain mechanically.

What cannot be explained mechanically is the fact that all these single operations co-operate in the same immanent purpose, the good of the organism. The intrinsic finality of a living being cannot be explained by physics and chemistry.

A biologist may balk at this statement, since it may seem to put certain biological problems beyond his competence. He will not only try to explain each single activity, he will also attempt to discover the mechanisms which are responsible for the co-ordination and the succession of these single activities. He will, in fact, discover a steadily increasing number of these mechanisms. And since he has thus succeeded, or will eventually succeed, in explaining every single operation in the organism, and the connection between two successive operations, without appealing to any but mechanical factors, he will conclude that, as the whole is but the sum of its parts, he has explained the total activity of the organism. But that is precisely our point: in a living being the whole is more than the sum of the parts, each part is what it is and acts as it does only because of some influence deriving from the whole.

It is at this point that biologists who have thus far worked harmoniously together will go their separate ways and adhere to conflicting schools of thought. Some deny the difficulty and claim that absolutely all problems of biology can be entirely solved by the ordinary methods of Science. This is not a scientific but a philosophical statement; it is a profession of mechanism not only as a method but as a philosophy.

For those who reject both mechanism and vitalism, two avenues remain open. They may use explanations which, although not mechanistic, are still considered strictly scientific. The fact is that these explanations are generally nothing but scientific transpositions

[3] In philosophical language: the vital principle is a formal, not an efficient cause.

of philosophical explanations and more complicated or inaccurate ways of advocating vitalism. Thus the many biologists who insist upon organization, configuration, holism or Gestalt in order to explain the problem of life advocate in their various ways the influence of a formal cause (without ever using that term) which we have called the vital principle.

Others have adopted explanations which are patently philosophical, whether or not they are aware of it. This applies especially to the proponents of life as a psychic reality. Strictly speaking, this explanation is untenable, but if we look at it in the light of the principle of proportionality it can be interpreted in an acceptable way. The vital principle is to a living organism what the psyche is to a sentient organism.

Summarizing, we can say that adopting *mechanism as a method* is the only possible attitude for the scientist. It is only when we try to find the final explanation of the co-ordination of all the single (mechanical) operations and their intrinsic finality that mechanism is no longer sufficient. But such a final explanation is not a scientific but a philosophical problem. And therefore *mechanism as a philosophy,* that is the doctrine which denies the existence of all but mechanical factors in organisms, is false.[4]

Every material being is constituted of substantial form and prime matter. In the lowest degree of beings—the minerals—form is entirely commensurate to matter, it is entirely immersed in matter, so that all activities of these minerals, although they derive ultimately from their form, are necessary and blind and can be explained totally by the laws of physics and chemistry.

As we come one step higher, in the plants, each single operation is still entirely explainable by the same laws. Something, however, can no longer be explained in that way: the fact that the effects of these operations remain within the being—their immanence, their intrinsic finality. To explain this intrinsic finality we do not require

[4] There are other instances in which a superior influence uses factors of a lower nature and, without any apparent interference in their regular order, directs them towards a higher purpose. Such are freedom and divine grace in our human activity, and divine Providence in the events of daily life. In all these cases, each single action or event can be explained by ordinary physiological, psychological or social causes. Yet from within they are somehow directed by a superior influence towards a higher end.

a new directing principle in the plant. We say that the plant's substantial form is more perfect than the mineral's, that it is able to exert some of its peculiar effects, to direct the material activities of the plant towards the good of the plant.

READINGS

Bertalanffy, *Modern Theories of Development and Problems of Life: An Evaluation of Modern Biological Thought.* Carles, *Unité et Vie: Esquisse d'une Biophilosophie.* Lillie, *General Biology and Philosophy of Organism.* Mason (ed.), *The Great Design,* a collection of contributions by famous biologists; cfr. especially Driesch, "The Breakdown of Materialism," pp. 283-303. Ruyer, *Eléments de Psycho-Biologie.* Schrödinger, *What Is Life?* Sinnott, *Cell and Psyche: The Biology of Purpose.* Windle, *Vitalism and Scholasticism.*

3

The Origin of Life

SCIENTISTS AGREE that life did not always exist on our earth. They estimate that it began about a billion years ago. In this view, the earth itself would have originated about four billion years ago. For billions of years there was no life on earth. How, then, did it start? What do we know about the origin of life?[1]

Concerning this problem the philosophers are divided into two main groups, those who claim that life originated from matter alone and those who claim that life originated from God and matter.

LIFE DID NOT ORIGINATE FROM MATTER ALONE

This statement should be fully understood. We do not claim that matter—that is, mineral substances—had no share in the first production of life. It will be pointed out that some causality of matter in this first production is most probable. But we deny, and shall try to refute the claim, that the first living beings were produced by matter and chance alone, by the mere instrumentality of the physico-chemical factors at work in the inorganic world. The theory which we reject is known as the theory of absolute emergence, and it is defended by all materialists.

The ancients believed with Aristotle that a certain number of living beings originated spontaneously from inorganic matter—that maggots, for instance, issued from carrion and mice from rubbish. The Schoolmen, including St. Thomas, clung to this strange opinion. There was no materialism involved, however, as they attributed

[1] The origin of *human* life is not under discussion here but will be treated in a later chapter.

such spontaneous generation to the influence of the sun, viewed by them as a higher kind of animated being. As late as the eighteenth century the famous scientist Van Helmont described the methods to be used for the spontaneous generation of mice and of scorpions.[2]

The nineteenth century gave up the notion of the spontaneous generation of mice, maggots, scorpions and similar creatures, but clung tenaciously to the idea that the infusoria—the microscopic, one-celled animals found in liquids—had such an origin. It took Pasteur's genius to explode this theory and to establish once and for all that in the present state of our earth every living being derives from a living being.

Occasionally a scientist puts forth the claim that he has produced life from inanimate matter. Typical of such claims is the famous case of Stephane Leduc, professor at the Ecole de Médecine of Nantes, France (1906). Having put some sugar and copper sulphate in an artificial plasma composed of water, potassium ferrocyanide and salt, he set in motion a chemical reaction which looked, to all intents and purposes, like the budding of a seed and the growing of a cactus-like plant. However, what looked at first like a real production of life turned out to be nothing but an interesting example of osmosis in semipermeable membranes.

In other instances where life had supposedly been produced in a laboratory, closer examination established either that there was no real life, and the phenomena in question were merely physico-chemical in nature, or that some living substance had been employed for the production of life.

Nowadays scientists who are looking for a point of transition between living and non-living substances turn increasingly to the study of viruses. These mysterious creatures act at some times like minerals, as when they are isolated in crystalline form; at other times like real organisms, as when they reproduce their kind. Scientists do not agree as to whether or not they are alive. One seemingly widespread opinion is that they might be living beings

---

[2] The "recipe" for mice is very simple. "Fill a vase with wheat, seal it with a soiled shirt, preferably that of a woman. Some ferment emanating from the shirt, being transformed by the wheat, changes it into mice. Time: about three weeks." J. Carles, *Les Origines de la Vie,* p. 11.

which have degenerated through parasitism, genes which have lost their connection with chromosomes and cells. It is difficult to see how, in that case, they could be the steppingstones from inorganic to living matter, since, parasitic by nature, they *presuppose* a living being as their host.

We may conclude that scientists have demonstrated that at the present stage of our planet's existence the spontaneous generation of complete organisms does not occur. From this, however, we cannot validly conclude that spontaneous generation has never occurred or that it is altogether impossible.

Science, in the strict sense of that word, is not able to demonstrate that some event is impossible. It can only show that this event is so utterly improbable that it is practically, statistically impossible.[3]

Where Science cannot strictly demonstrate that something is impossible, philosophy can. An effect can never be superior in perfection to its total cause. But if inorganic matter should, by its own forces, produce life, the effect would be superior in perfection to the cause. The superiority of the living beings over inorganic matter has already been demonstrated and is obvious enough. Therefore, by itself alone, inorganic matter cannot produce any living being, and spontaneous generation, in the sense of absolute emergence, is impossible.

LIFE ORIGINATED FROM GOD AND MATTER

This statement is demonstrated in Natural Theology, where it is shown that every contingent being derives directly or indirectly from the First Cause. The question which interests us here is whether the first living beings were directly created by God or were made by Him out of pre-existing inorganic materials.

God could have created the first living beings. He could have made them out of nothing. But when we consider that according to Science inorganic matter had existed for millions of centuries

---

[3] Lecomte du Noüy tries to demonstrate the statistical impossibility of a chance production of life out of matter in his book *Human Destiny* (New York, Longmans, 1947), pp. 33 ff.

before the first organism appeared on earth, and that God generally uses secondary causes whenever possible, we are led to think it more probable that He made the first living beings out of pre-existent inorganic matter.

Having admitted this, we would also like to examine the question of how He made the first organisms. Since their material cause (the minerals) was already in existence, the only problem concerns the origin of their formal cause, the vital principle. Aristotelian Thomism holds that the vital principle is "educed from the potency of matter,"[4] which is to say that as soon as the specific organization is effected by the agent in the matter, the form is present. This specific organization of the matter IS, in a certain sense, the substantial form. In other words, as soon as a collection of atoms has been given the mode of organization which it actually has in a living being, that collection of atoms is alive.

Hence the vital principle of the first organisms must have derived from the cause which organized the atoms in such a living pattern. What is this cause? A scientist would say: matter itself and the energies of matter. And we shall say: matter indeed, but under the influence of God. Both answers are right, and there is no conflict between them. The scientist as such is interested only in the secondary causes, and these causes were at work in the production of the first organisms. If God used mineral substances in making the first living beings, He used them as mineral substances, that is, as endowed with material energies, as exerting some activities. Radiation, pressure, temperature, moisture, magnetic and electrical attraction must have co-operated in the formation of life, and a scientist as such can only study such factors.

We must repeat here what we have said in our discussion of vitalism. In the long sequence of microscopic events which must have slowly led up to the first organisms, every single step and every connection between two successive steps may be exhaustively explained by the laws of physics and chemistry. Yet the transformation considered as a whole is more than the sum of its parts and supposes some higher causality which, under the circumstances, could only have been the influence of God. In the case of a living being this higher causality comes from the vital principle; in the

[4] *Spir. Creat.*, Q. 2, Art. 8; *Comment. in Met.*, VII, lect. 7, 1417-1423.

first origin of life it comes from God. The vital principle acts as a formal cause; God's causality is at once an efficient and an exemplary causality.

The foregoing considerations will make us very prudent when the question is raised whether scientists will ever be able to synthesize life in their laboratories. The answer is that if they become capable of putting into matter the ultimate disposition for life, such matter will become alive. And it is difficult to see why scientists should not eventually succeed in producing this ultimate disposition. Such a synthetic production of life would not, of course, be a case of spontaneous generation. Here the effect would not be more perfect than the total cause, since the cause would comprise not only the energies of matter but also man's intelligence. If God has endowed inorganic matter with the virtuality of life, to become actual if and when a certain set of circumstances are realized, we do not see why such circumstances, which must have existed on earth about a billion years ago, could not be artificially duplicated by the human mind in the laboratory.

READINGS

Sr. Adrian Marie, O.P., "Viruses: Are They Alive?" in *The New Scholasticism*, 31 (1957), pp. 297-316. A. Bauchau, S.J., "Vers la Synthèse Artificielle de la Vie," in *Nouvelle Revue Théologique*, 80 (1958), pp. 395-409. Bawden, "Evolution and Viruses," in *Symposium on Evolution*, pp. 9-26. M. Calvin, "Chemical Evolution and the Origin of Life," in *American Scientist*, 44 (1956), pp. 247-263. Carles, *Vers la Conquête de la Vie*. M. Ducasse, "Life, Telism and Mechanism," in *Philosophy and Phenomenological Research*, 20 (1959), pp. 18-24. Editors of *The Scientific American, The Physics and Chemistry of Life*. Facultés Catholiques de Lyon, *L'Origine de la Vie sur Terre*.

PART TWO

PLANT AND ANIMAL LIFE

Introduction

OUR PHILOSOPHICAL conception of plants and animals follows from the general principles outlined above. Both plants and animals are material beings, composed of prime matter and substantial form. In this respect they differ neither from minerals nor from men. The difference lies in the degree of perfection of the substantial form, of its emergence from matter.

In minerals (the "matter" of ordinary language) the substantial form is so entirely immersed in matter that it can give the mineral only its material existence and its material activities. In man form emerges so far from matter that it can produce operations which are intrinsically independent of matter. We shall demonstrate later that man's soul is more than a substantial form, that it is a spirit which functions as a substantial form. This explains why man's soul can exist apart from matter.

Plants and animals lie between these two extremes; in both the form cannot exist without matter, in both it emerges enough from matter to produce some effects which are never found in minerals.

This emergence is slighter in plants, in which the substantial form (soul, or vital principle) can produce no activities which cannot individually be explained by the laws of physics and chemistry and artificially reproduced in the laboratory. This applies equally to the vegetative functions or the physiological activities of animals and men. There is nevertheless in the plant some degree of emergence of form from matter, which explains why all these material activities are directed towards the greater perfection of the whole, why the plant possesses intrinsic finality or life.

In animals the emergence of form from matter is more consider-

able, producing a higher kind of immanent operations. Though
strictly in the material domain, these activities must be ascribed
mainly to the influence of form. Such are the conscious activities
of the animal, its knowledge, feelings and drives. They involve a
higher degree of immanence than the activities associated with
nutrition, growth and reproduction; they are more highly perfective
of the organism. Their effects remain not only within the acting
subject, but within the acting power of the subject. Matter continues to be a partial cause in these operations, but the influence
of form is predominant.

THE PLANT SOUL

Psychology has little to say about plants. We have already demonstrated that the occurrence of immanent, self-perfective operations in the plant induces us to affirm the presence of a vital
principle, or soul. We must briefly consider the nature of the plant
soul.

The plant soul is material. A thing is material either (1) when
it can be seen, touched, weighed, measured, when it is perceptible
to the senses; or (2) when in all its operations, and for its very
existence, it is intrinsically dependent on matter.

The plant soul is not material in the first sense. It is material in
the second sense; it is intrinsically dependent on matter.

A being is intrinsically dependent on matter when matter is a
co-cause of its operations and its existence.

Matter is a co-cause of its operations: when such a being acts,
the action is not produced entirely by the being itself but involves
the causal influx of matter. Every action of that being is the effect
of a dual causality: the being in question and prime matter.

Furthermore prime matter is a real co-cause of the very existence
of the plant soul. Neither the plant soul nor the prime matter can
exist independently, but only the whole substance, the plant. Soul
and matter alike are substantial principles, constituting together
one substance which exists. Therefore the plant soul cannot exist
in itself; it depends on prime matter for its very existence, in this

sense, that only in combination with prime matter can it constitute a substance capable of existing.

Contrast this with realities which are only extrinsically dependent on matter—that is, for whose operations matter is only a necessary condition,[1] not a real co-cause. Such a reality is our intelligence. No thought or judgment is possible in man without the co-operation of the body, especially the brain. However, the brain is not a cause of thinking or judging, but only a necessary condition. This important statement will be demonstrated later.

The plant soul is material; both environmental matter and the mineral components[2] of the plant itself are really co-causes of nutrition, growth and reproduction in a plant. This is so evident that there is no need to labor the point. The vital principle alone cannot feed, or grow or reproduce; matter is really involved as a co-cause of these activities.

Therefore in its characteristic and highest operations the plant soul is intrinsically dependent on matter. But as a being is, so it acts. Therefore the plant soul is intrinsically dependent on matter, not only in its operations, but also in its existence.

It follows that the plant soul is material. It cannot exist without matter, any more than roundness can exist except in something round. When the plant dies, the soul disappears, as roundness disappears when a ball is flattened. The plant soul is replaced by a mineral form, as the roundness is replaced by some other shape.

---

[1] A necessary condition is that which enables a cause to produce its effect without actually contributing toward the production itself. A cause is that which contributes in some positive manner toward the production of another thing.

[2] Prime matter is an essential constituent of these mineral components and is therefore a real co-cause of the plant's operations.

4

The Origin of Plant and Animal Species

IN THE previous chapter we briefly examined the problem of the origin of life. Our next problem is the origin of the various forms of living beings. How did the great variety of living beings originate on this earth? Among these living beings we shall not include man; his origin we shall consider in a later chapter. This chapter is therefore exclusively concerned with the origin of the plant and animal species.

Two main answers have been given to our question: (1) The theory of *fixism* holds that the various species of living beings were directly created, or made, by God as we know them today. (2) The theory of *evolution* claims that the various forms of life which we know today originated gradually, by natural descent, from one or a few original living beings.

The first theory is, of course, perfectly tenable. God could have made every individual species, either simultaneously when life began on earth or each one at its appointed time. All scientists, however, prefer the second theory, which we shall briefly consider in the following pages.

The problem of the evolution of the various species of plants and animals may be considered from the scientific, from the philosophical and from the theological point of view. In this chapter we shall examine only the first two of these aspects, leaving the theological problems which arise in connection with evolution to an Appendix.

BIOLOGICAL EVOLUTION CONSIDERED FROM
THE SCIENTIFIC POINT OF VIEW

This very complex problem can be treated here only in a most elementary way. We might summarize its present status as follows: (1) That evolution has occurred is admitted by all scientists today; (2) but there is uncertainty about the extent of evolution and about its explanation.

THAT EVOLUTION HAS OCCURRED IS
ADMITTED BY ALL SCIENTISTS TODAY

The bases for this conviction are traditionally grouped under five headings:

Comparative Anatomy

1. The difficulty of systematic classification of plant and animal species. Every attempt at such a classification raises great problems. A considerable number of organisms seem to belong to no clear-cut category; they fall between the groups which have been set up, constituting transitional forms. This is easy to explain if they are held to descend from common ancestors.

2. The presence of homologous organs. These are organs found in different animals, having the same anatomical structure yet performing different functions. Thus, in the words of Darwin, "the hand of man formed for grasping, that of a mole for digging, the leg of the horse, the paddle of the porpoise, and the wing of the bat are all constructed on the same pattern, and . . . include similar bones, in the same relative positions."[1]

3. The presence of vestigial organs. These rudiments, found in quite a number of animals, are of no possible use. Such are the vestigial eyes of many cave animals, the vestigial wings of certain species of birds, the rudiments of hind limbs in some snakes and in the whalebone whale.

[1] *The Origin of Species* (New York, Modern Library, 1936), p. 334.

Paleontology

1. In the oldest geological strata of the earth, which go back to the Archeozoic and Proterozoic eras, we find fossils only of invertebrates; the exploration of more recent strata yields, in succession, fossils of fishes, amphibians, reptiles, mammals and men. This implies that the various forms of life did not appear on our earth all at once, but that they succeeded each other in the order given above.

2. As the paleontologists go back into the past, they notice that the differences between the species, genera, families and classes of animals become vaguer. Forms have been unearthed which are considered by some scientists as intermediary between fishes and amphibians, amphibians and reptiles, reptiles and mammals.

3. We possess evidence of series of animals following each other in time and showing a gradual modification or evolution (orthogenetic series). The most famous is that of the horse.

Biogeography

How can we explain the origin of the animal species on the oceanic islands? The best explanation is that in the distant past the forebears of these animals reached these islands from the continent, either by their own powers (swimming, flying) or swept along by wind or water currents or borne on the branches or uprooted trunks of trees. The absence on these islands of any animal form which could not have travelled in any such way confirms this explanation.

But these animals differ considerably from the species which live on the nearest continents. The dissimilarities increase in proportion to the distance of each island from the continent, and they may go all the way to a difference not only in species but in genus or in family.

The best available explanation of this fact is that the species which landed on these islands long ago, having evolved in isolation from their continental counterparts, have developed their own characteristics during the course of their separate evolution.

Embryology

Haeckels's famous Law of Biogeny states that "Ontogeny is a short recapitulation of Phylogeny." This means that each animal, in its development, passes quickly through certain stages traversed very slowly by its forebears during the course of their evolution. Thus during its embryonic development an ape would show in succession some typical features of an invertebrate, a fish, an amphibian and a reptile before developing its own mammalian features. This law is very difficult to apply in practice, because it is so hard to distinguish in the embryonic forms what is a genuine recapitulation of phylogeny and what is simply an adaptation to the embryo's very special kind of life.

Yet there seems to be no doubt that some aspects of embryonic development confirm this law. Thus certain species of birds, for instance the parrot and the ostrich, show during a stage of their development rudimentary teeth which later on disappear. The same phenomenon occurs in other toothless animals, such as the whale and the platypus. It seems rather difficult to explain these "false starts" if one does not admit evolution.

Genetics

Geneticists can, to a certain extent, see evolution occurring under their very eyes in the laboratory. A careful study of hundreds of generations of short-lived animals, such as the fruit-fly, discovers slight changes in their inherited characteristics, resulting in many new races. Some of these races may eventually differ enough from each other to be viewed as new species.

These changes may happen spontaneously. In other cases, they may be induced by the geneticist himself. Thus it has been possible to double the number of chromosomes of certain plants, a fact which permits the expectation that eventually even more striking changes may be produced in the nature of some organisms.

**BUT THERE IS UNCERTAINTY ABOUT THE
EXTENT OF EVOLUTION AND ABOUT ITS EXPLANATION**

All scientists admit that there has been some evolution at least within the confines of a definite species, resulting in the production of new races and varieties. This is a fact of observation. The most extreme fundamentalists admit that all present human races are descended from one original couple, and this supposes a certain amount of evolution.

But there are fewer facts and more hypotheses as we pass from species to genus, to family, to order, to class and to phylum. A considerable number of observations point towards an evolution of very wide extent; many facts can be easily explained on the basis of that hypothesis which are difficult to interpret "scientifically" in any other way. Yet universal evolution (from ameba to ape) cannot be considered to be an established fact and will most probably always remain a hypothesis, although the great majority of scientists favor that view.

As for the way of explaining the evolutionary process, there has been, until rather recently, considerable disagreement between the proponents of evolution.

The three most important explanations are: (1) Lamarck's explanation through adaptation and the inherited transmission of acquired characteristics; (2) Darwin's explanation through natural selection; (3) De Vries' explanation through mutations.[2]

LAMARCK (1744-1829), a French naturalist, posited the two following laws: (a) In every animal which has not passed the limit of its development, the frequent use of any organ gradually strengthens and develops that organ, while constant disuse gradually weakens it until it disappears; (b) when such modifications have been acquired by both sexes in a species, they are transmitted to their offspring.

The first law may be valid, but it is difficult to see how it could explain the formation of entirely new organs. The difficulties revolve especially around the second law. The idea of hereditary transmission of acquired characteristics finds little favor among scientists. Only that which affects the germ plasm or the genes seems to be transmitted through biological heredity, and the immense majority of acquired characteristics do not affect the genes. Time and again some scientists have come up with the claim that they have demonstrated the second law of Lamarck, but their evidence has regularly been rejected as inconclusive.

DARWIN (1809-1882), the great British naturalist, postulated

---

[2] Nowadays most scientists seem to favor a combination of these explanations known as the Synthetic Theory of Evolution. See following note.

three factors to explain evolution: (a) The accidental variations occurring continually in nature. In every litter some of the off-spring are stronger, faster, etc., than the others; (b) The struggle for life. The food supply is limited, and each animal has to fight to get its share of it; (c) Natural selection. In this struggle the stronger and faster individuals will survive, while the weaker and slower are eliminated. The fittest survive, and since they tend to mate with the fittest, the generations of offspring gradually improve.

That these factors are really at work in evolution cannot be doubted, and the Neo-Darwinians rightly attach great importance to them. But no convincing reply has ever been made to the following objection: natural selection cannot explain the origin and development of new organs. For such organs, e.g. eyes or wings, would develop very gradually, they would be of no possible help to their owners until they were in working condition; there is no reason, therefore, why the organisms which started by accident to develop such rudiments of new organs should have survived in the struggle for life.

DE VRIES (1848-1925), a Dutch botanist, discovered the phe-nomenon called "mutation," which consists in a sudden change in one or several of the genes of a newborn individual, producing more or less considerable changes in the animal's specific features. Such mutations have been studied extensively and even produced arti-ficially in laboratory-bred organisms, especially in the fruit-fly. They also occur spontaneously in nature, where they are known as "sports."

It is generally admitted that mutations must have had a consider-able influence in the process of evolution. But it seems difficult to explain the whole of evolution through the random occurrence of mutations. First, most mutations are lethal, or at least deleterious. Either the individuals in which they occur die, or they are rendered weaker or less fertile, so that they would be eliminated in the struggle for life. (It is not without reason that scientists are afraid of the effects of atomic fall-out upon the next human generations.) Secondly, why should the thousands of mutations required during the course of evolution have consistently proceeded in the same direction? Why should not subsequent random mutations have undone the progress made by the former ones? Thirdly, none of the mutations which have been reported has ever produced a new organ.

Our conclusion is that neither the adaptations emphasized by Lamarck, nor the natural selection of Darwin, nor the mutations of De Vries can *of themselves alone* explain evolution. These factors were most certainly at work in evolution, and a scientist as such should look only for them and try to explain everything by means of them.[3] Yet, the over-all progress of evolution cannot be explained by the blind influence of these mechanical factors. Some kind of finality seems to be required if we want to present a complete explanation of evolution.

Finalism holds that evolution does not result from the blind interaction of the forces of nature but is informed by a purpose; it strives towards an end, it embodies an idea, a design, it supposes a directing mind. Not all forms of finalism claim that therefore every new form of life, every step in evolution, is the result of purpose or of design. Many of the individual steps in the long march of evolution could be explained by chance. But the main steady upward trend requires some deeper explanation. We are now becoming familiar with this important idea. As every single operation of a living being, as every step in biogenesis, can be explained entirely by the laws of physics and chemistry, so every single step in evolution can be adequately explained by the laws of biology. A scientist as such should look only for that kind of explanation; his efforts in that direction will be steadily rewarded by new discoveries. To explain single steps in evolution by an appeal to purpose or design is to give up the scientific ideal. Thus we can understand why the immense majority of evolutionists avoid any mention of finality in their explanation of evolution. They present purely mechanistic theories, which, in a certain sense, are quite acceptable. The point at which we part from these authors is where they stop speaking as scientists and assume the function of philosophers, adopting mechanism not only as a method (in which they are

[3] This is done by the Synthetic Theory of Evolution, which is prevalent in the field today. According to this hypothesis, mutations occur at random in animal populations; natural selection maintains the favorable adaptive mutations. Owing to its emphasis on natural selection, the theory is also called Neo-Darwinian.

right) but also as a doctrine (in which they are wrong). A total
explanation of evolution by means of mechanical factors is an
inaccessible "limit" which will never be reached, although steady
progress will always be made in its direction. To explain the total
meaning of evolution is no longer a scientific problem, it is the
task of the philosopher. He claims that in evolution as in life a
formal factor is at work which directs the efficient causes (the
only ones which the scientist as scientist can reach) towards their
common goal.

A Christian historian knows that history is directed by Divine
Providence. As a historian, however, he must look only for
ordinary psychological, economic, social and political antecedents
to explain every single event in history. *Mutatis mutandis,* the same
rule holds for the student of evolution.

BIOLOGICAL EVOLUTION CONSIDERED FROM THE PHILOSOPHICAL POINT OF VIEW

Philosophically speaking, there are two main interpretations
of evolution; they are known as the theory of absolute emergence
and the theory of restricted emergence.

According to the theory of absolute emergence, all the higher
forms of life derived genetically from one form, or from a few
simpler forms, of life, or even from inorganic matter, under the
sole influence of the laws of matter and of chance. This theory
does not restrict itself to a consideration of the mechanical factors,
as a scientist limiting himself to the proper sphere of Science is
perfectly entitled to do; it explicitly denies the influence of any
other factors within the whole process of evolution.

Philosophically speaking, the impossibility of such an explanation is at once evident. The perfection found in the effect cannot
be greater than that which is present in the cause. If the perfection
of the effect were greater than that of the cause, this effect would
not be intelligible, it would be deprived of sufficient reason.

But it is evident that the instincts, the consciousness and the
"intelligence" of higher animals are superior to anything which
is found in inorganic matter or in the lower organisms.

The theory of restricted emergence likewise admits that the higher forms of life developed from the lower forms, in which they are present potentially. But it holds that these virtualities, from which the higher forms emerge, come from the Creator.

In other words: the sequence of events we see in ontogeny also occurred in phylogeny. Ontogeny is the development of each individual from a single cell to full animal maturity; a tiny speck of protoplasm slowly develops into a complicated organism. We attribute that development to the efficient causality of the material energies and the formal causality of the vital principle, inherited from the parents and ultimately derived from the Creator. In the same way, an ameba might have been the origin of all higher animals, if it had received from God the power of evolving. We would attribute such an evolution to the instrumental efficient causality of the energies of matter and to the principal efficient causality and the exemplary causality of God, who willed life to evolve, setting the stage for man.

Some Scholastic authors oppose this theory on the ground that it contradicts the principle of the immutability of the species, according to which an animal of a certain species can generate only individuals belonging to that same species. Natural generation is univocal.

This objection seems to be based on the confusion of ontological with phenomenal species, of species understood in the philosophical sense with species understood in the scientific sense.

It is not easy to decide what a species is, either scientifically or philosophically. Scientists find it increasingly difficult either to define the concept of natural species or to distinguish the boundaries of each particular plant and animal species. Their conception of species tends to become statistical: they consider the specific type to be the average type realized by a living group,[4] with many small, and a few important, deviations from that average. Although the specific average types are easy to distinguish and to describe, some of the deviations of neighboring types tend to overlap.

Nor is it any easier to define an ontological species. One extreme position, which has the advantage of being clear and unequivocal, holds that there are only four ontological species in the

[4] Or by a collection of sub-groups, often called "populations."

material universe: minerals, plants, animals and men. According to this view, only those species whose quiddity can be defined in terms of an "intelligible" genus and specific difference—that is, in terms which do not imply a direct reference to sense qualities—would be really ontological. Terms such as living and non-living substance, conscious and not-conscious substance, rational and not-rational substance are "intelligible" in that use of the word. On the other hand, it is impossible to define a dog or a wolf without referring to such sense qualities as color, size, figure, texture, and so on.

The adherents of this position further hold that the ontological species are indeed immutable, that there is no transition between one species and the next higher one. However, they deny that the same thing holds true for the phenomenal species. Thus, in terms of this hypothesis, no objection against biological evolution can be drawn from the principle of the immutability of the species, since all animals would belong to the same ontological species.

If one raises the objection that animals as different from each other as, say, a bee and an elephant cannot possibly belong to the same ontological species, one is faced with the necessity of deciding where to draw the boundaries between ontological species in the animal realm. That this is not easy is shown by the plight of one open-minded author who, having first decided that such a boundary was to be found on the level of the genera of the systematic classification, has been slowly retreating before the accumulating evidence of paleontology, and has now arrived at the orders (carnivora, herbivora, et cetera) as the real ontological species. Meanwhile paleontology, continuing to unearth new evidence, has come up with fossils which are clearly common ancestors of the different present orders.[5] It seems preferable to take one's stand at once in a position from which there is no danger of being dislodged.

Another opinion holds that there are real ontological species within the animal realm and that a gradual transition from one such species to the next higher is possible. According to this hypothesis, the divine causality which is required to explain evolution will not only actualize the virtualities latent in the lower species but will also make the species capable of producing effects not contained

[5] See E. C. Messenger, "A Roman Theologian on Evolution," in *Theology and Evolution*, pp. 155-171.

in these virtualities. As an instrument is capable of producing effects which go beyond its own limited power, so the lower species, operating as instrumental causes under the motion of the Creator, would be capable of producing descendants which stood higher in the scale of being than their progenitors.[6]

If we wanted to discover the deeper philosophical roots of evolution, we might proceed as follows:

Every organism is composed of existence and essence, the essence being further composed of substantial form and prime matter. Existence, of itself, is unlimited; it is restricted to a certain degree by the essence. Form also, of itself, is unlimited in its line; it is restricted to a certain individual being by matter.

This restriction of existence by essence and of form by matter should be conceived not statically but dynamically. Existence is restricted by essence, and form is restricted by matter, not as a property is restricted by the wall built around it, but rather as steam is restricted by the boiler which contains it. This kind of restriction produces an inner tension, a driving force, a dynamism.

Form tends to overcome the restriction imposed by matter, and it succeeds to a certain extent by means of generation and the multiplication of the individuals within the species. The form of a dog is better realized in the millions of past, present and future dogs, with their countless variations, than it would be if only one single dog existed. Univocal generation is explained by the dynamism of form.

Existence tends to overcome the restriction imposed by essence, and it succeeds to a certain extent by striving towards greater unity, greater spontaneity, greater consciousness, greater ontological perfection. This tendency manifests itself in the slow acquisition, over successive generations, of accidental variations which, in their main direction and not excluding many deviations, tend toward the realization of higher forms of organisms. The differences which we notice between two successive generations are very slight; we shall never meet, in nature, the transformation of one phenomenal

---

[6] We might even consider the environment itself as an instrumental cause, working in behalf of the Supreme Cause. See J. De Finance, S.J., *Existence et Liberté*, p. 262. Also J. Maritain, *The Range of Reason*, pp. 35-38.

species into another. But if we take a long-range view in time, if we compare organism A with organism B, the direct descendant of A through millions of generations, the differences are considerable, leading not only to new phenomenal species but to new families or new phyla.[7]

St. Thomas, following Aristotle, rejected the possibility of a passage from one phenomenal species to another. No scientific data had been discovered which might have challenged that traditional opinion. His philosophy of nature is hopelessly static. But his metaphysical conception of nature is dynamic and sees the whole of creation carried along in an irresistible upward movement towards God. These fundamental conceptions might have given him the basis of a philosophical theory of evolution. Here is the most famous of these passages:

Since, as we have said, everything which is moved or which changes, tends thereby to the divine similitude, that it may be perfect in itself, and since everything is perfect in so far as it is actualized, it follows that *the intention of anything existing in potency is that it shall tend through motion to actuality.* Hence the later and the more perfect an actuality is, so much the more is the appetite of matter directed towards it. Hence the appetite of matter, whereby it desires a form, tends to the furthest and most perfect act which it can possess, as to the ultimate end of generation.

Now, in the actualizations of forms, there is a certain gradation. For prime matter is first in potency to the form of an element, and when it exists under the form of an element, it is in potency to the form of a compound; considered under the form of a compound, it is in potency to a vegetative life-principle, for the soul is the act of such a body. Again, *the vegetative soul is in potency to a sensitive, and the sensitive soul to an intellectual soul.* . . . Hence the ultimate stage of the whole process of generation is the human soul, and to this matter tends as to its ultimate form.[8]

The two passages which we have italicized in this text might

[7] For a philosophical theory of evolution along similar lines, see E. Brisbois, S.J., "Transformism and Philosophy," in E. C. Messenger, *op. cit.,* pp. 109-123.

[8] *ScG.,* III, 22. Translation of the English Dominicans (Burns and Oates, 1928), p. 461.

be put together as the major and the minor premises of a syllogism whose conclusion would affirm the existence of evolution.[9]

This justifies the following interesting remarks of Fr. Maréchal:

In the presence of ascending, progressive causality, going from *less* to *more,* our revised and filtrated scholasticism shows a timidity which the medieval Masters did not know to the same extent. Let us admit it: the most Aristotelian among them showed less fear than we do of borrowing something from Platonic "wisdom," which pays such steady attention to the ascending movement of all beings. We naturally think of the two opposed phases of the proodos and the exodos among the neo-Platonists: how are they treated in most of our scholastic textbooks? The first phase—creative emanation and descending causality—is treated as thoroughly as by the neo-Platonists; on the other hand, the exodos, the phase of the active return of the creatures towards their Principle, may seem to be cut short and to begin really only at the level of intellectual spontaneity; as if the levels below the spirit were not permeated with any ascending effort and offered to our spiritual activity nothing but a lifeless collection of passive materials. Between the spirit and things the dynamic continuity has been broken. . . .[10]

St. Thomas, who used to insist that "every truth, by whomever it may be proposed, comes from the Holy Spirit" would have welcomed the modern findings about evolution and integrated them without difficulty in his system.[11]

[9] It might be objected that if these considerations are true, evolution should be going on in our time. We answer: there is no difficulty against this conclusion, as far as evolution within the plant and animal realm is concerned, but we cannot witness it in nature because the process is so very slow. We shall demonstrate later that if there has been evolution of the human body, this evolution, unlike biological evolution, requires a special divine intervention.

[10] J. Maréchal, S.J., Preface to A. Hayen, S.J., *L'Intentionnel selon Saint Thomas* (Brussels, Desclée de Brouwer, 1954), 2d ed., pp. 10-11.

[11] For the theological problems involved in evolution the Catholic reader is referred to the Appendix, pp. 459ff.

READINGS

Scientific Aspects of Biological Evolution:
Dodson, *A Textbook of Evolution*. J. F. Ewing, S.J., "Précis on Evolution," in *Thought*, 25 (1950), pp. 53-78. A. Wolsky, "A Hundred Years of Darwinism in Biology," in *Thought*, 34 (1959), pp. 165-184. (See p. 174 of that article for further references.)

Philosophical Aspects of Biological Evolution:
Books or articles mentioned in the footnotes; also: Otis, *La Doctrine de l'Evolution*. N. Luyten, O.P., "Implications of Evolution," in *The New Scholasticism*, 25 (1951), pp. 290-312; "Darwin Symposium," in *The New Scholasticism*, 33 (1959), pp. 411-513. van Melsen, "Philosophical Aspects of Evolution," in *Symposium on Evolution*, pp. 57-80.

5

Animals Possess Consciousness,
or Sentient Life

WE SHALL explain later exactly what we mean by sentient life, or consciousness. For the present discussion the everyday notion will suffice. It is generally admitted that animals, at least most animals, know some objects, are affected by them in some way (feelings, emotions) and tend consciously towards them or away from them.

Descartes was led by his philosophical premises to deny the existence of consciousness in animals and to assimilate them to machines or robots. Recently some psychologists have revived this doctrine on the basis of scientific claims and have tried to explain all animal activities in terms of tropisms or reflexes.

We must first point out the difficulties involved in such an interpretation; next we shall mention some characteristic features of animal behavior which can best be explained by attributing consciousness to animals.

TROPISMS ALONE CANNOT EXPLAIN THE
ACTIVITIES OF ANIMALS

In general a tropism is the movement of an organism towards or away from a simple stimulus, such as light, heat, gravity or water. It is called positive when the organism is attracted, negative when it is repelled by the stimulus. Examples are the positive geotropism of plant roots and the negative geotropism of the plant stem (towards or away from the source of gravity); the positive or negative phototropism of many plants and animals (towards or away from light).

Plant tropisms can be explained mechanically. The positive phototropism of polyps of Hydrozoa is "probably caused simply by an unequal growth at the illuminated and the non-illuminated side of the polyp, and there would seem to be no reason to admit that any psychical element is involved in it."[1]

Even in animal tropisms, such as the positive phototropism of the common moth or the negative phototropism of the cockroach, it is difficult to demonstrate the presence of psychic elements, or consciousness. Consciousness may be present, but it is not required to explain these movements.[2]

However, it has been shown that these tropisms can become modified by experience, and in such cases we have a good proof of the presence of psychic factors. Thus Bless succeeded in training positively phototropic Daphnias to swim away from the light in order to get out of a glass tube.[3] Tropisms may explain certain activities of lower animals in such a way as to exclude any intervention of consciousness. But even these animals are able, when circumstances require, to engage in a higher kind of activity from which consciousness is not absent.

REFLEX MOVEMENTS ALONE CANNOT EXPLAIN THE ACTIVITIES OF ANIMALS

A reflex movement is a muscular or glandular reaction to a stimulus, not directed by any consciousness either of the stimulus or of the movement. Most familiar is the knee-jerk reflex, produced by sharply tapping the tendon below the knee-cap, and consisting in a quick, involuntary upward thrust of the leg. Such stimulation is conducted to the spinal column and is there, without passing through the brain, directly translated into muscular movement.

Some reflexes are linked in what is called a "chain-reflex." In such cases, the situation in which the organism finds itself as a result of the first reflex movement becomes the stimulus for the next

[1] J. A. Bierens de Haan, *Animal Psychology* (London, Hutchinson's University Library), p. 76.

[2] A description of artificial animals with inbuilt tropisms will be found in *The Scientific American*, May 1950 and August 1951.

[3] Bierens de Haan, *op. cit.*, p. 81.

reflex, the situation produced by the second becomes the stimulus for the third reflex, and so on.

Thus the stimulation of the flank of a dog may produce a "scratching reflex," by which the hind leg moves rhythmically to and fro. A dog in which the connection between brain and spinal column has been severed (a spinal dog) continues to execute walking movements when the soles of the feet are stimulated.

Some mechanists have tried to explain all movements of animals, and even of man, in accordance with a chain-reflex pattern. Instinctive actions especially have lent themselves to this kind of explanation. Thus the nesting instinct is explained as follows: when a bird is in a suitable physiological condition in the spring, the sight of a feather or some other material useful for a nest acts as a stimulus. Stimulus "feather" produces reflex action "flying to feather," from which results the situation of "being near feather." That situation is in turn the stimulus for the next reflex, "picking up feather," which produces the situation "feather in bill." This is followed by the reflex action "flying to nest." No consciousness is required, every movement is explained mechanically, as in a complicated machine.

The difficulty in the acceptance of such an explanation is the perfect adaptation of every movement of the animal. Here are the arguments given by William McDougall against this mechanistic explanation of animal behavior. McDougall describes the usual characteristics of real "behavior" in animals and shows that such behavior is really different from reflex action.[4]

1. Animal behavior shows a certain spontaneity of movement. The movement begins in the animal, is not produced by outside forces pushing or pulling it. A running dog "behaves," a dog which is thrown out of a window is only put in motion, it does not behave. Reflex actions are not spontaneous, they are specific reactions to specific stimulations.

2. Animal behavior may persist even after the effects of the stimulus have ceased. A rabbit starts running when it hears a sound, and it may continue to run even when the sound is no longer heard. Reflex action lasts only for the duration of the stimulus and then ceases until the stimulus is repeated.

[4] *Outline of Psychology* (New York, Scribners, 1923), pp. 43ff.

3. Behavior consists of movements which are perfectly adapted to the environment. An animal following a prey will avoid obstacles, leap across ditches. Reflex movements are stereotyped and show hardly any adaptation to the environment.

4. Behavior comes to an end when it has brought about a particular change in the situation of the animal. A squirrel running away from a dog stops moving as soon as it is safe on a tree. The stimulus (the barking dog) is still active, but it no longer elicits the response of movement from the squirrel. A reflex action persists unchanged as long as the same stimulus is applied.

5. Behavior frequently indicates readiness in the animal for some anticipated movement. The cat crouches and is ready to spring on the mouse. The dog which hears steps outside the house prepares to attack the approaching intruder. Reflex action does not show this readiness for anticipated activity.

6. Behavior generally shows improvement with repeated performance. The animal learns from experience. There is no improvement with repetition in reflex activity.

7. Behavior implies a total reaction of the organism. When an animal behaves, all its limbs and energies are intent on its purpose. Reflex action is the response of a specific part of the organism to an appropriate stimulus.

All these characteristics of behavior point to its most fundamental feature: behavior is *purposive*. It is exercised for the sake of a certain end which must be more or less clearly anticipated. Such purposive action supposes in the animal some knowledge of the goal and some conscious striving towards it. The animal must be aware of it, must be attracted or repelled by it. Therefore we say that in their most characteristic actions animals manifest some degree of consciousness. That consciousness may be very faint and vague, but it is to some extent an essential factor in every case of real "behavior."

This does not imply that there are no reflexes or chain-reflexes in animals or in men. The presence of such elementary ways of reacting has been clearly demonstrated. They may be sufficient in simple, routine situations. In more complicated situations they are used as means, and they stand in the service of consciousness.

6

Animals Do Not Possess Rational Intelligence

BY RATIONAL intelligence we mean intelligence as it is found in man, as it is described in philosophy. This kind of intelligence (which we shall in general call "intellect," to avoid confusion) can be defined as the faculty which knows universals as universals, which is aware of its own activity, as the faculty of perfect self-reflection.

Many modern psychologists use the word intelligence with quite a different meaning. For them it is defined as "adaptability to new circumstances," or "the power of learning from experience," or "the faculty of improving upon inborn instinctive actions in the light of past experience."[1] Intelligence thus defined is found in many animals. It differs essentially from rational intelligence, or reason, or the intellect, whose existence in animals we deny.

Some activities of animals, especially of insects and higher vertebrates, may produce in the observer the impression that they involve reason. These are the instinctive activities and the activities which suppose learning. They will be examined in the following two sections.

INSTINCT IN ANIMALS

Instinct has been defined by William James as the faculty of acting in such a way as to produce certain ends, without foresight

[1]Bierens de Haan, *Animal Psychology*, p. 96.

of the ends and without previous education in the performance.

The highest development of such instincts is found, not in the higher animals, but in the insects, especially in the hymenoptera—the bees, wasps, and ants. In vertebrates, especially in mammals, such as dogs, horses, monkeys and apes, there is a foundation of instinctive activity which is considerably modified and enriched by experience and learning.

Countless descriptions have been offered of the marvelous performances of instinct in the hymenoptera. We present only one, the example of the Yucca-moth.

The Yucca-moth is a small moth, the *imagines* of which come out of the pupa at the same time as the flowers of the Yucca-plant . . . open for a few nights. Males and females of the moth find each other and copulate; then the female flies to an open flower of the Yucca, takes some pollen from the stamina of it, and kneads it into a ball with the help of her great sickle-shaped maxillary tentacles. She then carries the collected pollen to another Yucca-flower. There with the aid of her sharp ovipositor, she opens the ovary of the flower and deposits her eggs between the ovules of the plant; then she climbs upwards along the style to the stigma and presses the pollen she brought with her into the opening of it. Herewith she achieves the fertilization of the plant, an event which probably would not have occurred without her help, as this moth is one of the few insects, or the only one, which pollinates Yuccas. Through this complicated behavior, however, the moth achieves the propagation of her own species as well as that of the plant, since her growing larvae feed only on the developing ovules of the Yucca and would therefore perish if these ovules were not brought to development.[2]

Typical instinctive activities have the following characteristics:

1. They are inborn—not acquired through experience, anterior to any learning. The Yucca-moth, for example, has never seen another moth perform the operation described above. The inborn character of instincts is evident in the many insects which never know their parents: the latter die during the winter and the new generation is born in the following spring.

[2] *Ibid.*, pp. 84-85.

2. They are uniform—the same in all individuals of the same species. All Yucca-moths go through their instinctive activities in the same way. All bees of a single species make the same kind of hive.

3. They are immediately perfect. While the skills of man develop slowly by trial and error, instinctive activities are perfect at once and are executed without mistake if the insect can perform them in its normal environment. Some insects, such as the Yucca-moth, perform a complex instinctive activity only once during their lifetime. The survival of their species depends on its being perfect from the start.

4. They are constant, remaining the same throughout the life of the animal. Spiders do not improve the technique of weaving their webs, and swallows do not make a more comfortable nest the second or the third time.

5. They are specialized. Each animal is a specialist, there are no universal instincts. A bird or a bee does not have a general building instinct, not even a general instinct for building nests or hives, but only a specialized instinct for building this particular kind of nest or hive.

Finally, instinct shows two more features on which we must insist, because they make it possible to present an interpretation of instinctive activities. Instinctive activities are adapted to the environment when that environment happens to be the normal one for the animal. But instinct does not involve awareness of the final purpose for which it operates.

6. Instinctive activities are adapted to the normal environment of the animal. Although a spider always builds the same kind of web, only the general design is constant. Some adaptation is required to fit it to the ever changing environment. The spider will use two parallel twigs, or the crotch of a tree, or any other circumstances suitable for its activity. *Osmia papaveris,* a bee,

. . . builds its nest in holes in wood or in the spaces between stones; by preference, however, in the empty shells of snails. Then the form of the nest is adapted to the available space: in long stalks, the cells are placed in one long row; in openings between stones, in an irregular heap; in snail-shells, cells are built in a simpler row in the narrower convolutions of the shell, while nearer to the opening of the shell, the cells are laid side by side.[3]

Furthermore if, accidentally or through human intervention, part of the structure is damaged *while the insect is at work,* it may repair the damage.

This power of adaptation to varying local circumstances—and especially the power of repairing damage to the work—shows clearly that instinctive activity is not blind or automatic, that it cannot be explained in terms of a mere chain of tropisms or reflexes but supposes some guiding consciousness in the animal.

7. Instinctive activities are not directed by the consciousness of their ultimate goal. This is demonstrated by the many cases of what has been called the "folly of instinct." Here are two examples:

A striking example is reported by Hingston. *Messor barbarus* is an ant which collects seeds of grass and carries them into the nest, where they are peeled and stored, after which the husks are carried out of the nest to a special refuse heap at about eight inches distance from the nest. Hingston once found a nest that, by way of exception, was built on the vertical surface of a wall. Now the ants did not take advantage of the convenient position of the nest opening to throw the husks out, but continued to carry them eight inches from the nest and lay them carefully against the wall as if to make a heap there. Naturally the husks always fell down directly; yet for months the ants continued this useless work.[4]

The other example, taken from Fabre, is the famous case of the Pine Processionary. These caterpillars have the habit of crawling in single file, the head of each touching the rear of the preceding one. As each one advances it continuously secretes a silken thread which the succeeding caterpillar carefully follows, while contributing its own thread to the resulting ribbon. Thus only the leader of the procession is free to go where it fancies, all others follow blindly, adhering to the guiding thread. Fabre succeeded in bringing the head of the leading caterpillar in contact with the rear of the last in line. They now formed a closed circle without any independent leader,

[3] *Ibid.,* p. 61.
[4] *Ibid.,* p. 51.

each blindly following the one ahead of it. For seven days the caterpillars turned round and round in this mad circle, taking time out
only to rest at night. Fabre computed that they had crawled for
84 hours, covered a distance of more than a quarter of a mile, and
described the circle 335 times before it finally broke up.

These two examples, which could be multiplied many times over,
show clearly that animals do not know the why of their instinctive
activities. Performed in their usual habitat, under normal circumstances, these activities happen to be useful. But if some accident or
human interference modifies these circumstances, the animals,
guided only by their instinct, are unable to introduce the necessary
changes, and their action becomes purposeless.

Therefore we conclude that instinct is neither a purely mechanical
activity nor an activity directed by intelligence. It supposes some
knowledge, it does not involve rational knowledge. We say that it
involves the sense knowledge of the animal.

Instinctive activities become less mysterious when, with Bergson,[5]
we consider them as the continuation of the physiological processes
of the organism. When in embryology we study the slow but steady
transformation of a chicken egg into a chick we are amazed at the
"wisdom" of this budding organism which, if circumstances are
normal, unfailingly guides the countless steps of its development in
the right direction. At the end of this embryonic development within
the egg, the chick breaks the shell with its bill. This, its first *instinctive reaction,* looks very much like a continuation of the long
series of physiological transformations. One new element has been
added: consciousness, awareness in the organism of what is happening. That consciousness may be, and most probably is, very dim and
vague at first. It seems to increase gradually, as the animal is required to adapt its activities to the ever-changing environment. Thus
the chick will be pushed by its instinct to pick up and swallow small,
hard things lying within its reach. But this activity implies consciousness: the animal sees the grains of wheat, and we have good
reasons for admitting that, in some vague way, it "wants" them.

The vital principle which had been at work *unconsciously* in the
physiological development of the organism, "inspiring" its countless

[5] H. Bergson, *Creative Evolution* (New York, Modern Library, 1911), p. 139.

physico-chemical reactions and guiding them to their goal, continues its work on two levels: the physiological level, on which all operations continue to occur without any awareness in the organism either of the ultimate goal or of the many activities leading up to it; and the psychological level, on which, although the animal is still unaware of the ultimate goal, it is conscious of every single action which it feels impelled to perform in order to reach that goal.

If the animal were aware of the long-range purpose for which it acts, and were capable of ordering its activities accordingly, we should have to credit it with reason or intellect. The aberrations of instinct when acting in unusual circumstances exclude this possibility. An animal acting by instinct knows what it is doing but does not know the remote end for which it is acting.[6]

But if the animal is not aware of the end for which it acts, why does it act at all? Because it derives pleasure from the actions which lead it unconsciously towards this end.

When we are thirsty we drink, not because we have reflected that water will quench our thirst but because we feel like drinking. When hens suffer from a lack of calcium in their diet, with the result that their organism cannot produce shells for their eggs, they eat all the calcium they can find, not because they know that calcium is useful but because when they are in this condition calcium has a special appeal for them. In the same way we can explain that an insect goes through its specific round of instinctive activities because it feels like performing them, because these activities happen to be pleasurable.

These explanations do not really solve the mystery of instinct. How did these simple beings acquire such marvelous powers? The ultimate answer is, of course, that they received them from God. But did they receive them ready-made, or did they slowly acquire them in the course of evolution? Either answer is possible. Scientifically speaking, the second answer is more acceptable. But it raises a host of difficulties which will probably never be solved, questions for which only hypothetical answers are available.

We reproduce in the following passage one such hypothetical ex-

[6] In other words: the animal knows the immediate end of its actions (for the squirrel: to bury this nut), but not the remote end of it (to have food in wintertime). Aquinas calls this an imperfect knowledge of the end. (See *S. Theol.,* I*ª*, II*ªᵉ*, 6, 2.)

planation, as presented in the general framework of the theory of evolution. Speaking of the Mesozoic era, Lecomte du Noüy writes:

The climate was mild; there were no seasons, except in the regions near the poles. Everywhere else the temperature was almost uniform, as in the South Sea Islands nowadays. This was probably the age during which the insects developed their prodigious instincts. Our modern trees were beginning to push back the ancient conifers in certain places. Poplars, willows, birches, beeches, oaks appeared, and with them the flowers. The progressive change in vegetation affected the number of insects. With practically non-existent seasons their lives were not shortened by the rigors of winter. They could live long enough to acquire experience and to take care of their young. As their activity was limited to a small number of gestures, always the same and inspired by the same circumstances, these gestures ended by becoming automatic, like habits, and resulted in an organization of the brain which was transmitted hereditarily. These habits became conditioned reflexes, spontaneously accomplished at determined epochs. At any rate, it is plausible to imagine, as do certain great zoologists, that things occurred in this way. When winters started—around the middle of the Tertiary period . . . —they separated successive generations but did not abolish the organizations acquired in the course of millions of years. The insects have continued to act as in the past, and seem to know at birth the things they are too short-lived to learn.[7]

We give this theory for what it is worth. Dr. du Noüy himself admits that it is highly hypothetical. It supposes among other things the hereditary transmission of acquired characteristics, which is rejected by most scientists. It raises more questions than it answers. Yet if we want a scientific explanation of the origin of instinct, it seems that we must look in that direction.

LEARNING IN ANIMALS

Few animals depend on their instincts alone for survival. The vertebrates especially can profit from experience, can adapt themselves to new circumstances, can learn. Animals which manifest these powers are said, in modern parlance, to show "intelligence."

[7] *Human Destiny*, pp. 78-79.

As we have explained above, this is not the intelligence which philosophers have been studying for centuries. There is a qualitative difference between human intelligence, or the intellect, and this animal intelligence.

Not all psychologists admit this difference. Some claim that between man and the animals there is only a difference of degree, not one in kind. We must therefore briefly examine the facts in order to establish that there is really a difference in kind. These facts are not to be collected from the many anecdotes about animal cleverness. Such reports are usually unreliable because they are presented by untrained, often by biased, observers and cannot be checked. Animal psychology has become a genuine science with well-established data. These data are well worth the attention of the philosopher, because they have made it clear that the animal mind, although separated by a real hiatus from its human counterpart, is nevertheless capable of remarkable performances.

There has been a tendency among the later Scholastics to underestimate the psychic powers of the "brutes." St. Thomas, on the other hand, applying the principle of proportionality and remembering that the highest point of the lower touches the lowest point of the higher, speaks of the "particular reason" and of the "prudence" of animals.

Thirdly, this is proved from a property of man and of other animals. For we see in the latter a certain participation of prudence by means of a natural judgment, in regard to certain particular acts (*S. Theol.*, I, 96, 1, c).

All animals have by natural judgment a certain participation in prudence and reason, which accounts for the fact that cranes follow their leader, and bees obey their queen (*Ibid.*, ad 4).

There has also been a tendency to define too loosely that which distinguishes the animal mind from the human intellect. It has been said, for instance, that abstraction, generalization, the perception of universals or of relations and the use of tools are specifically human accomplishments. In a certain sense this is true, but the terms we use must be carefully defined. Actually animals give evidence of some power of abstraction, generalization, perception of universals or of relations, use of tools. Nevertheless there remains in every respect a considerable divergence between animal and human be-havior, which points to a difference between animal and human knowledge. It is the purpose of the following pages to show these divergences.

In the study of the animal mind the introspection so useful in the study of human psychology will not serve. We must derive our data from the observation of the achievements of animals, and from these exterior manifestations infer the powers from which they issue. In general, the explanation proposed must always be the simplest pos-sible. An action which can be explained in terms of an inferior power must not be attributed to a higher faculty. Psychologists accept what is known as Lloyd Morgan's canon, according to which, "in no case may we interpret an action as the outcome of the exercise of a higher psychical faculty, if it can be interpreted as the outcome of the exercise of one which stands lower in the psychological scale."[8] This is an application of Ockham's razor: "Beings should not be multiplied without need."

All animal learning is based on instinctive reactions. An animal learns new things because it is impelled to make a variety of move-ments in order to satisfy its hunger, thirst, sexual need or curiosity. All animal learning derives from its striving towards pleasure and its avoidance of pain.

Sometimes the pleasure- or pain-giving object is signalized by an indifferent element to which the animal would not normally react, but which evokes a positive or negative reaction after it has fre-quently been associated in the animal's experience with something of biological importance. Countless such associations can be estab-lished between the animal's needs and elements in the environment. Learning consists precisely in the formation of such new associa-tions.

Sometimes these associations are established with scarcely any active intervention on the part of the animal. It is repeatedly sub-jected to a sequence in which an important stimulus is signalized by an indifferent object, until a connection between the two is estab-lished in its mind. This is called "conditioning."

At other times the animal is active; under the impulse of some

[8] C. L. Morgan, *An Introduction to Comparative Psychology* (Scribner, 1894), p. 53.

drive it makes a number of movements which, at first unconnected and haphazard, gradually become organized. When this organized set of movements has become firmly connected with the goal, the animal has learned by "trial and error."

In both these cases the animal reacts to certain relations in its environment, but without explicitly noticing these relations. In some instances, the animal explicitly grasps the relations (although not as relations). It cannot solve the problem presented to it unless it meaningfully connects part of the situation with the goal. Some higher vertebrates are capable of solving problems in that way. They learn by "insight."

CONDITIONING

We have already mentioned simple *reflexes*. They are reactions of a part of the organism to an elementary stimulus. If you put some meat powder upon a dog's tongue, the dog salivates abundantly. That is a simple reflex. If every time the dog receives meat powder a light is flashed, a connection is gradually built up in the dog's mind between the food and the light, so that, after a certain number of repetitions, the animal will salivate on the presentation of the light alone. The light, to which the animal was at first indifferent, has become a "conditioned stimulus." The animal reacts to it by a "conditioned reflex." This important phenomenon has been studied extensively by the Russian physiologist Pavlov.

If the light is flashed a few times on the same day without being accompanied by food, the conditioned reflex gradually diminishes in intensity, and finally disappears. It is "extinguished." If, on the next day, the light is flashed again, the conditioned reflex reappears. Therefore the "extinguished" reflex had not been eliminated but had only been temporarily inhibited.

Conditioned reflexes have made it possible for psychologists to study many aspects of the animal mind. Thus the power of discrimination has been studied in animals by means of such reflexes. Suppose that an animal has learned to salivate at the flashing of red light. If a green light is presented, the animal will salivate, for it has learned to react to "light." If, however, the red light is always accompanied by food and the green light never, an animal which can distinguish between them—which is not color-blind—will, after a certain number of trials, stop salivating for a green light and continue to do so on the presentation of a red light. In this way it has been possible to find out whether animals can distinguish between colors, between certain shades of the same color, between sounds.

Most animal training is based on the establishment of conditioned reflexes. If you whistle while feeding sparrows, they will, after a while, come to you as soon as you start whistling. Infinite patience in the trainer, who tries to elicit certain reactions in his trainee which he constantly associates with a reward, may produce remarkable results, as a visit to the circus will demonstrate. These results are sometimes so remarkable as to induce some people—especially the confirmed admirers of the animal mind—to speak of animal intelligence as if it were no different from the specifically human form of intelligence.

No better example could be given of such high achievement, and of the great prudence required in interpretation, than the famous case of "Clever Hans." Hans was a horse trained by Herr von Osten, who firmly believed in the great intellectual powers of horses in general and of his Hans in particular. He set out to demonstrate his conviction and for a time seemed to have succeeded. After long months of patient training, the animal was able to add, subtract, multiply and divide, extract square roots and tell the time. The problem was written on a piece of cardboard and shown to the animal, which started at once to tap out the result with its hoofs. There seemed to be no deception involved. Anybody was allowed to ask the questions, even when the trainer was not present. This remarkable case baffled psychologists for some time.

The solution of this puzzle was finally discovered by Pfungst. He demonstrated that the horse did not count at all but carefully observed cues which the questioner gave without being aware of it. Suppose Hans were asked to multiply 4 by 6. The experimenter had to know the result himself, in order to check the correctness of the horse's answer. He counted the number of times Hans tapped his hoofs, and when the result was reached, he told himself "That's it," making at the same time, unconsciously, an almost imperceptible movement which translated his thought. The watchful animal observed the cue at once and stopped tapping. None of the experimenters, least of all Herr von Osten himself, had been aware of the cue given unconsciously to their pupil. How did Pfungst demonstrate his explanation? He showed the horse a piece of cardboard bearing a problem. He himself did not know the data of the problem or the answer, and consequently he did not make any tell-tale movements. In this setup the horse watched the experimenter and continued to tap endlessly, as if waiting for a cue which did not come. Clever Hans showed remarkable powers of sense observation, but not the slightest sign of real intelligence.[9]

We have described this case in some detail in order to show how skeptical one should be when one hears of some extraordinary feat performed by an animal. Even when such accomplishments have been accurately reported and the accounts can be checked, the explanation will often be simpler than some supporters of animal intelligence would have us believe.[10]

TRIAL AND ERROR

In the conditioning process the animal is more or less passive. In "trial and error" learning, it is more active, it discovers the solution by its own efforts. For example, it is hungry, it sees or smells food but cannot reach the food directly. It makes all kinds of movements, not quite at random, for they all tend in the general direction of the food. It tries, makes mistakes, tries again, makes more mistakes, until, sooner or later, one of its efforts succeeds and it arrives at its goal. When, after this experience, the same problem recurs, the animal goes through very much the same procedure until its repeated efforts meet with success. Gradually, however, after the problem has been encountered and solved a number of times, the mistakes decrease, the goal is reached more rapidly, until eventually the animal reaches it without making a single mistake.

This is, of course, a real instance of learning, but no one claims

[9] Cfr. D. Katz, *Animals and Men* (New York, Longmans, 1937), pp. 2-7; O. Pfungst, *Clever Hans, The Horse of Mr. von Osten.*
[10] The works of C. L. Hull and other modern psychologists have considerably changed Pavlov's conception of conditioning. These new theories are too complicated to be explained here.

that it involves real, rational intelligence. The most familiar example of this kind of learning is that of mice or rats learning to run a maze. Animals can learn many other things in this way.

Some performances learned by conditioning or trial and error seem to indicate that animals can count. Thus a bitch from whose litter 3 puppies have been removed keeps looking for them. She notices the difference, say, between 6 and 3 puppies; she appears to have counted. It is true that the animal notices the difference in the number of her offspring, but it does not follow that she can count. When only 1 puppy out of 6 is taken away, the animal notices nothing. The reason is that there is a difference between the global impression made by 6 and that made by 3. There is no need for counting, the difference is obvious at a glance. But there is no such global difference between 6 and 5. The perception of a difference between 6 and 5 requires an analytic approach, entails real counting, and the animal is incapable of that.

Experiments have demonstrated that animals, even among those which stand rather low in intelligence, observe global distinctions between numbers of objects. Thus Revesz taught a rooster to choose between numbers of grains, so that it would eat only from the bigger of two heaps. It succeeded in noticing the difference between 3 and 2, 4 and 3, 5 and 4, 6 and 5, 8 and 6, 10 and 7 grains. It was unable to differentiate between 8 and 7, 10 and 9, 10 and 8.[11]

In other trial and error experiments animals are taught to react positively to a triangle and to avoid other geometrical figures such as squares, circles, diamonds. When this problem has been mastered, the features of the original triangle are changed; it is presented in a different size, in a different color; different kinds of triangles are introduced. In Gellerman's experiments with chimpanzees[12] these modifications did not appreciably affect the reactions of the apes. Does this not imply that the animals have some notion of a triangle as such, have an abstract and universal idea of the triangle?

Here again the true explanation is simpler. Some features of the phenomenal domain—such as brightness, color, size, shape—re-

[11] Quoted by G. de Montpellier, *Conduites Intelligentes et Psychisme chez l'Animal et chez l'Homme,* 2d ed. (Louvain, Institut Supérieur de Philosophie, 1949), p. 145.

[12] L. Gellerman, "Form Discrimination in Chimpanzees and Two-Year-Old Children," *J. Genet. Psychol.,* 42 (1933), pp. 3-27.

main constant in the sphere of perception, even when the stimuli deriving from the physical objects are considerably modified. For example, two sheets of white paper, one exposed to sunlight, the other lying in a dark corner, both seem white, although actually the white paper lying in the dark corner reflects less light to the eye than would a sheet of black paper lying in sunlight. A wheel of which we get a side view looks round to us, although the outline it produces on the retina of the eye is elliptical. A dog recognizes its master despite the great variations in the physical stimuli emanating from him. Perception is global, and unconsciously it takes into account the differences deriving from a different illumination, a different angle of observation. No one claims that this adjustment involves intellectual elements. Likewise there is no reason for admitting intellectual elements in the explanation of the constant reaction of apes to a triangle.

Furthermore, the Gestalt psychologists have shown that figures such as triangles, circles or squares have a pronounced global character. They are spontaneously perceived without analysis. The animals do not observe, say, three blue lines of equal length, but a whole triangle. On the following occasion they do not notice another figure, with three blue lines of unequal length, but again just a triangle. To analytic observation these two triangles are different: one is equilateral, the other is scalene. For spontaneous global perception they are both triangles, and the animal does not have to abstract their common features in order to discover their triangularity.

Therefore the fact that animals react to a common feature in many different situations does not mean that there is real generalization or abstraction. We have already noted that a dog which has been conditioned to a green light will react positively to any light.[13] Instinct, too, shows some kind of generalization or abstraction. A

[13] Lashley and Wade have explained this apparent case of generalization in a different way. They contend that it is due only to a failure to discriminate. "When a single stimulus is presented, reaction is associated only with the most conspicuous character that differentiates it from the otherwise uniform environment (the stimulus is some *thing* that varies on a constant background)" (p. 81). It is not surprising, then, that other somewhat similar stimuli provoke the same reaction. No process of generalization must be postulated. Cfr. K. S. Lashley and M. Wade, "The Pavlovian Theory of Generalization," in *Psychol. Rev.*, 53 (1946), pp. 72-87.

cow wants grass, not just this or that grass but any grass, anywhere, at any time. When young chicks emerge from their shells, they start picking at any small object, not only at grains of corn but also at small pebbles, bits of paper, their own toes. No one claims that this is real generalization involving intellectual elements. Generalization is real only when the general feature is known explicitly as general, when it can be abstracted from the concrete context, compared with other features, given a name. There is no evidence of such activities in animals.

LEARNING BY INSIGHT

In the experiments described above the animals learned to react to certain relations. But they discovered these relations in a haphazard way, by essaying all kinds of movements in the general direction of the goal. The general organization of the field is not noticed or examined by the animal.

In the following cases the animal observes and examines that organization; it discovers relations existing between itself and elements of the environment. The learning is no longer haphazard, gradual, proceeding by the slow elimination of mistakes. The animal sees the goal, observes that it cannot be reached directly, looks around for ways and means of reaching it and, if the problem is not too complicated, discovers them. Usually it employs the trial-and-error method first. If that does not succeed, it pauses, examines the whole field, looks puzzled; suddenly its face lights up[14] and without further hesitation it uses the right method.

Psychologists have studied this learning by insight, especially with monkeys and apes, by offering the animals a series of problems of gradually increasing complexity. This complexity, of course, is only relative; problems which present little or no difficulty to human beings are quite beyond the powers of the highest apes. Here are a few examples taken from the famous experiments of W. Köhler.[15]

Outside the cage in which a chimpanzee is confined lies a banana.

[14] German psychologists have called this the "Aha-Erlebnis," the experience of "I've got it."

[15] W. Köhler, *The Mentality of Apes,* trans. by E. Winter (New York, Harcourt, 1926).

The animal tries first to reach it with his arms, but it is out of range. Then he sees a stick lying close by, picks it up and with it nudges the banana until it is within his reach.

The banana is out of reach. A stick has been placed in the cage, but it is too short to reach the banana. Outside the cage lies a longer stick which can be reached by using the shorter one. Some animals manage to get hold of the longer stick first and thus reach the banana.

The banana is hung from the ceiling of the cage. The apes jump for it, but it is beyond their reach. There is a box in a corner of the cage. Some animals drag the box to some point under the fruit, then jump from the top of the box to reach the banana. This problem is difficult for the apes, and only a few succeed in solving it without aid from the experimenter.

The fruit is out of reach outside the cage. A stick is suspended from the ceiling of the cage, too high to be reached by jumping. A box is available. Some animals learn to drag the box to the point where the stick is suspended, jump from the box to get the stick, then use the stick to reach the fruit.

In all these cases the "tool" was available, and the problem for the subject was to perceive it as a tool and use it accordingly. The following examples show the animals actually "making tools."

The fruit is out of reach and there is no stick available. But there is a tree inside the cage. Some apes break off a branch and use it as a stick.

Others use a bundle of straw and even fold it in two in order to make it more substantial.

A piece of wire is straightened out and used as a stick.

One box is not enough to reach the banana. Several boxes are available in the cage. Some apes succeed in piling them on top of each other (generally in a very clumsy way) and in using this tottering structure as a base for jumping.

Two sticks are available, but neither is long enough to reach the fruit outside the cage. The sticks can be fitted together like the parts of a fishing rod. The brightest animal solved this problem only by trial and error.

In the interpretation of these experiments, wherein animals discover relations and make use of tools, or invent tools, the following points must be kept in mind:

1. The performance, although not explainable in terms of instinct alone, is often based upon instinctive activities. Not only is the motivation always derived from some instinct or drive (generally the hunger drive), but the way of solving the problem is frequently a modification of actions which the animal would instinctively perform. Monkeys and apes have learned, during their arboreal life, that by pulling a branch towards them they can bring the fruit borne by this branch within their reach.

2. The solution of these problems does not call for any abstract reasoning. All the data of the problem are actually present to the senses, and the solution can be worked out on the level of perception. It seems to arise from a shifting or regrouping of elements in the total field of perception present to the animal. Let us explain this by means of a simple example. Look for a while at the cube on page 128. You will notice a sudden shift in your perception, which makes the drawing look quite different. What was first the reverse side of the cube is now seen as the front side. No intellectual effort is entailed; this reorganization occurs spontaneously. In the same way we may assume that at first the animal sees the banana and the stick as two unconnected elements of the total picture. After a while the stick is no longer seen as an indifferent object but as "something-to-get-the-fruit-with." The solution is *seen,* it is not thought out.[16]

This interpretation is strongly suggested by the fact that the animal is able to solve the problem only when the data can be seen together in the same field of perception. A chimpanzee which sees a banana hanging from the ceiling but cannot see at the same time, in the same perceptual field, the box which might help it reach the fruit, will not find the solution. It must see end and means simultaneously. Furthermore, even when the box and the banana can be seen simultaneously, if another animal happens to be sitting on the box no solution is possible. In this instance the box is seen as "something-to-sit-on" and cannot be perceived as "something-to-reach-the-banana-with."[17] Once the animal has discovered the solution to a specific problem, a simultaneous perception of means

---

[16] Cp. Max Scheler, *Die Stellung des Menschen im Kosmos* (München, 1949), pp. 35-37.

[17] Cfr. Köhler, *Mentality of Apes,* pp. 35, 37, 53, 108, 110, 125.

and goal is no longer required. But then the performance must not be attributed to insight or learning but to memory.

Hence learning by insight does not force us to admit the presence of abstract intelligence, of real reason, in animals.

USE OF SYMBOLS AND LANGUAGE

We have seen above that animals can learn to connect a sign with the object signalized. Can they learn to connect a symbol with that which it symbolizes? There is a considerable difference between these two forms of association. Between the sign and that which is signalized a simple association in time and space is sufficient, and animals make such associations frequently in their daily experience. The symbol, on the other hand, signifies, represents, *means* that which is symbolized. To grasp a symbol as such the animal must be able to grasp a *meaning*. A moving shadow signalizes an approaching object, it does not symbolize it. A coin symbolizes buying power, it does not signalize it.

Some psychologists claim that animals can react to symbols and really grasp meanings. They point towards certain experiments, two of which we shall briefly discuss.

1. The temporal maze

In the temporal maze as first used by Hunter, the animal is made to run twice through the same alley; when it arrives at the end of the alley on the first run it must make a right turn to find the exit; on the second run, a left turn.[18] Since, except for the situation of the free or blind terminal, the alley remains the same and presents no differential elements in the course of this twice-repeated run, the cue for the turn must originate in the animal itself, and it seems to be based on some counting, which is an activity involving the use of symbols.

Some psychologists, however, present a simpler explanation of this performance. They admit that there are no spatial cues to tell the animal which way it must turn. But are there no kinesthetic

[18] While the animal runs the maze, the experimenter modifies the position of the blind alleys, so that the same part of the maze may call for a right turn when the rat reaches it for the first time and for a left turn when it gets there the second time.

cues—that is, cues deriving from the motor activity of the subject? A second run down the same alley has a different "feel" from the first run. It is possible that the animal has associated the left turn with this different "feel." As long as a simpler solution of this kind is not excluded by further experiments, it is not permissible to claim that the animal's activity in solving the problem of the temporal maze involves a grasp of symbols.

2. The use of money

Wolfe and Cowles at Yale University have taught chimpanzees to use poker chips to obtain food or other rewards. The animals have learned to put the chips into a food-vending machine. They learn not only to work the machine but also to evaluate the "coins." Some of these are worthless, and the chimpanzees soon learn to neglect them; others produce an extra amount of food, have thus a greater value, and the animals show special eagerness and make particularly intense efforts to obtain them. The animals also learn to distinguish between the chips—those which produce food, drink, or some other kind of reward. The chips acquire a certain value in themselves, since the animals make efforts to obtain them even when they cannot be used right away, when a certain number (from 10 to 30) must be accumulated before they can be used.[19]

Are these tokens real symbols? Do they represent, or mean, the food, or the possibility of getting it? Here again a simpler explanation has been offered. The chips are simply tools by means of which the animal can obtain what he desires. A chimpanzee which sees a banana outside its cage makes efforts to reach a stick which will help it reach the fruit. The stick is not a symbol of the fruit but a means or tool to reach it. In the same way the chips may be regarded as tools by means of which the food can be reached. This simpler interpretation should first be eliminated before we can speak of real processes involving a grasp of symbolism in the chimpanzees.

3. Language in animals

Do animals use language? The answer to that question de-

---

[19] J. B. Wolfe, "Effectiveness of Token-Rewards for Chimpanzees," *Comp. Psychol. Monogr.,* 12 (1936), p. 72. See also J. T. Cowles, "Food-Tokens as Incentives for Learning by Chimpanzees," *Comp. Psychol. Monogr.,* 14 (1937), p. 96.

pends on our definition of language. Not every kind of communication is language, but only the intentional communication of one's feelings, desires and ideas to another being.

Animals do communicate with each other. The mother hen clucks when she finds food for her chicks. When one dog barks in anger the dogs of the neighborhood start barking with it. The anger is communicated to all of them. When one sheep becomes panicky, the fear is quickly spread to all the others. Even among insects, such as bees and ants, we observe some communication of that kind.[20] However, in all these cases, what is communicated is a present emotion, feeling or desire. And this communication is conducted, not by means of symbolic substitutes—by words or gestures, used and intended as such, as between human beings—but by some kind of emotional contagion. It is the kind of communication which we ourselves may experience when we hear a piercing cry of fright. In such a case we may become frightened too, although we have no idea of the reason for this fear which has been communicated to us. Our fright has an instinctive basis and involves no intellectual elements.

But animals are quite unable to communicate ideas—anything referring to the past or the future or to abstract contents. The reason they cannot communicate ideas is not the lack of means of communication. Some animals, such as the parrot, can use human words, but they use them without knowing them as words, without reference to meaning. Other animals, such as apes, have vocal cords which they could use for speech if they felt the need for it. Even animals which possess no vocal cords, or only such as would be inadequate instruments for producing the variety of sounds contained in human language, could use simpler ways of communication. If dogs wanted to communicate with each other, why could they not emit combinations of long and short barks after the manner of a simple Morse code? Most animals would be physically able to use a gesture language if they experienced a need for language. The reason why animals do not communicate with each other concerning the past or the future or any abstract contents is to be sought, not in the lack of appropriate organs, but in the lack of any conception of past or future and any abstract ideas.

It is obvious that if real language existed among animals, we

[20] Cp. the interesting book of Karl von Frisch, *The Dancing Bees*.

should look for it in those animals in which the nervous system and brain is most highly developed—in monkeys, and especially in apes. Efforts have been made to induce apes to talk, but these efforts have led to very poor results. Instructive in this regard is the book of C. Hayes, *The Ape in Our House*. Mr. and Mrs. Hayes, both psychologists, decided to bring up a young chimpanzee in their home, treating her as much as possible as a human baby. They were anxious to find out to what extent she could be educated. Everything went rather smoothly in the prelingual stages, and the animal infant developed a remarkable number of skills. But when the time of vocalization was at hand, the progress was most disappointing. In spite of long, patient efforts the ape's vocabulary did not even reach that of an average parrot. Years previously another such couple reached the same dead end in a similar experiment.[21]

It is true that the ape had learned to react differentially to a considerable number of phrases spoken by her trainers. There is, however, no reason for admitting that the animal understood the "meaning" of these phrases, any more than a horse understands the meaning of "Whoa." The horse's and the ape's reactions can be explained as a mere conditioning to different combinations of sounds, usually accompanied by appropriate gestures.

Therefore the communication of animals is restricted to present experiences and excludes anything of the past or future. Furthermore, it excludes any abstract contents and refers only to drives, feelings or emotions. Finally, it seems evident that such communication as there is between animals is unintentional, merely instinctive. The animal does not intend to share its joy or anger but instinctively makes certain sounds or gestures whose effect is to transmit the creature's feelings to others of its kind.

GENERAL CONCLUSION ABOUT ANIMAL INTELLIGENCE

The purpose of this chapter was to demonstrate that animals have consciousness but no rational intelligence. There can be no doubt about the first part of the statement. The second part is more

[21] W. N. Kellogg and L. A. Kellogg, *The Ape and the Child*, 1933.

difficult to demonstrate, because it is a negative statement. It is easier to show that something is than to demonstrate that something is not. However, if we note the following points, we arrive at a practical certitude that common sense is right in denying the existence of reason in animals.

Rational intelligence, or reason, or intellect is that power which can reflect perfectly upon itself, which is aware of its own activities. Through it man knows that he knows, he is conscious of being conscious, he can say "I am myself." We cannot directly observe the absence of such a power in animals. But we do observe the absence of certain activities which should follow upon the possession of such a power.

A being in possession of perfect self-reflection knows universals as universals, relations as relations. Do animals have any such knowledge? We cannot directly demonstrate that they do not possess it, but we can show that not one of their activities supposes this kind of knowledge.

Where such knowledge of universals as universals and relations as relations exists, there is also the power of becoming aware of them as objects, distinct from one's self as subject; the capacity of objectifying them, of naming them, of comparing them with other contents, of communicating them to other beings. Therefore the presence of reason entails the power of speech. But speech under its many forms (gestures, talking, writing) is the basic essential of culture and civilization. Hence the best way of showing that animals do not possess reason, and of demonstrating the wide hiatus between the minds of animals and men, is to point to the absence of speech, and consequently of culture, in animals.

We have discussed the problem of speech in animals in the preceding pages. Culture has been defined as "social heredity"; it comprises knowledge, skills and attitudes which an individual acquires as a member of society. An animal acquires almost nothing as a member of its society; it learns almost exclusively through its own experience. What it learns by watching its parents or other members of its species amounts to very little, for animals can transmit their own experience to other animals, even their offspring, only in a concrete, never in an abstract way; only accidentally, never intentionally.

A mother fox, for example, may have learned from sad experience to keep away from traps. If she meets one of these devices while roaming afield with her young, she may show signs of fear and carefully avoid it. This fear may spread to the young foxes, with the effect that they will, in the future, keep clear of traps. But if the vixen never meets any traps while accompanied by her young, she cannot impart this caution to them. Thus an animal cannot learn from the experience of its race; there is only biological, no social heredity.

Man, on the other hand, learns much from education, through which he is enabled to share the experience of the whole human race. Thus progress, culture and civilization are made possible. Every generation can carry on from where the previous one left off.

The lack of real language, and consequently of culture, is the clearest demonstration of the absence of reason in animals. It also shows conclusively that between man and the animals there is not merely a difference of degree but a difference in kind. We shall show later that this radical distinction derives from the presence in man of a spiritual component, which is totally lacking in animals. The absence of a spiritual component in animals also explains why we do not discover in them the slightest manifestation of religious feeling, morality or art.

NOTE ON THE ANIMAL SOUL

The characteristic operations of animal life are sense knowledge and sense appetite. We shall demonstrate later that matter is a real co-cause of these operations. Hence they are intrinsically dependent on matter, they are material. Since a being acts in accordance with what it is, the animal soul, from which these material operations derive, is also intrinsically dependent on matter, is material. Therefore the animal soul cannot exist without a body, and when bodily life ceases, that soul disappears, as roundness disappears in a flattened ball.

READINGS

Bierens de Haan, *Animal Psychology*. Katz, *Animals and Men*.
Köhler, *The Mentality of Apes*. de Montpellier, *Conduites Intelligentes
et Psychisme chez l'Animal et chez l'Homme*. Muckermann, *Humanizing the Brute*. Stone (ed.), *Comparative Psychology*. Teale, *The
Insect World of J. Henri Fabre*. Tinbergen, *The Study of Instinct*.
Werner, *Comparative Psychology*.

PART THREE

HUMAN SENSE LIFE

Introduction

BEFORE WE begin the study of human psychology we must discuss a few questions in which philosophical psychology and modern experimental psychology are at variance with each other. These questions are: (1) the use of introspection, (2) the concept of faculty, (3) the division of psychic functions.

THE USE OF INTROSPECTION

Introspection is the examination of the data of our own consciousness. By means of introspection we know and can report what takes place in ourselves—what we see, hear, feel, think. For example, try to imagine Rockefeller Plaza and tell me what you see in your imagination, how vividly you perceive it. Or, you are suffering from a bad toothache; describe how that pain feels to you. Introspection is the natural method for obtaining data about man's mental life. Nevertheless modern psychologists raise serious objections against it. They say:

1. Introspection can be used only by the subject on himself. The exactness of the reports cannot be checked by any other person. But science requires facts which can be checked by many independent observers.

2. Some important psychological facts cannot be studied by introspection since intense concentration of the mind is impossible if you try at the same time to attend to what is happening in you. For example, strong emotions and introspection do not go together; either the emotion makes introspection impossible or introspection eliminates the emotion.

Some authors answer this objection by pointing out that when we cannot introspect, we can at least retrospect—that is, analyze afterwards how we felt while we were experiencing, say, a strong emotion. They replace introspection by retrospection, the observation of a present fact by the memory of a past event.

3. Even in ourselves some psychological facts escape introspection altogether, namely the unconscious activities. During hypnosis, a subject may be given a suggestion which he is to carry out when he awakens from hypnotic sleep. He may act on it without knowing why. There is a tendency in him of which he is totally unaware and which escapes all introspection.

4. The introspective method cannot be used with animals or young children, with feeble-minded or psychotic individuals.

These real limitations of the method of introspection have induced many modern psychologists to reject it altogether as incomplete and unreliable and to advocate instead the objective method— that is, the observation and description of what an individual does, how he behaves in a certain situation. For instance, we see that a dog can distinguish between a square and a circle by the fact that, after some training, he will take food when it is presented on a square platter but will never touch it when it is given to him on a round platter.

This objective method presents many advantages from the scientific point of view. The conditions under which a certain act is performed can be standardized in detail, so that anyone can duplicate the experiment and verify its findings. Apparatus can be used to measure the activities. First used with animals, this method was defended as the only possible method for the whole field of psychology by the Behaviorists, some of whom went so far as to deny the very existence of consciousness. The majority of psychologists do not go to that extreme; but without denying consciousness and the possibility of introspection they rightly maintain that the scientific purposes of psychology are better served by the objective method.

We should note, however (most psychologists are aware of this), that the objective method can be misleading, especially with regard to human beings. The same kind of behavior may be inspired by any of a number of different motives, and it is difficult or impossible to obtain information on this point, except through introspection and report. Furthermore, some problems cannot be studied at all by this method. How could we study our dreams or the nature of our after-images by purely objective observation? What progress would have been made in the interpretation of so many clinical tools and projective techniques?

Our conclusion, showing again the strange position of psychology among the sciences, will be:

If you want a strictly scientific psychology, you must use the method of description of behavior. But you will necessarily have to omit some of the most important problems of psychology.

If you want a complete psychology, covering the whole field of mental phenomena in man, you will have to use introspection. But your method, if exclusively introspective, will not fulfill the strict requirements of scientific observation.

It is very instructive to compare, from that point of view, the Continental and the Anglo-Saxon approach to Experimental Psychology.[1] The American textbooks are undoubtedly more scientific than their Continental counterparts. Their authors can back up most of their assertions with pertinent research data. But they carefully avoid any discussion of some of the most important problems of human psychology—or if they touch these topics at all, they do so in a perfunctory and shallow way. They avoid in particular anything which may smack of a philosophy of human nature. But it is impossible to study man even scientifically without a philosophy of man, whether explicit or implicit. The philosophy of the American textbook is generally of the implicit and unconscious kind, and consequently too often it is rudimentary, or positively naive.

The authors of the European textbooks are not afraid of philosophy, and they try to cover all aspects of human nature. Where no experimental data are available, they use introspection, intuition, phenomenology, and so on. As a result they probe the very depths of human nature, but many of their assertions have to be taken on authority, without any facts or experiments to back them up.

[1] Or, more concretely, to compare the average American textbook of Experimental Psychology with two of the leading Continental textbooks: the French *Traité de Psychologie Générale* of Maurice Pradines and the German *Aufbau der Person* of Philipp Lersch.

Their psychology covers a lot of ground, but it is no longer a Science.

The ideal would be to reserve the philosophical problems of human nature to Philosophical Psychology and to study in Experimental Psychology only those topics which can be tackled with the methods of the natural sciences. In other words, the future of Experimental Psychology seems to lie in the direction of the American approach. This is confirmed by the fact that some of the more progressive Continental schools of Experimental Psychology are heading definitely in that direction. But these schools are also clearly aware[2] of the importance of the Philosophy of Man, as a distinct discipline, never to be superseded entirely by Experimental Psychology.[3]

THE CONCEPT OF FACULTY

We use this concept frequently in everyday speech: "I have a poor memory: I want to develop my intelligence." Memory and intelligence are examples of faculties.

Modern psychologists have many objections to the use of this concept. They claim, for instance, that to explain psychological activities by attributing them to some faculty is no scientific explanation. To explain that we can remember past events because we possess a memory, or that a bird builds a nest because it has the instinct for building nests, is as unscientific as to explain the explosion of some chemical substance by means of its "exploding power."

Scientifically speaking, this objection holds. To account for any activity merely by ascribing it to a faculty is not a scientific explanation. The scientist will have to look for some other explanation. Modern psychologists are so convinced of this that they avoid —or rather, try to avoid—the concept of faculty altogether. Yet they speak of "functions" or "powers" or "abilities," which only amounts to using other terms for expressing the same or a similar idea. Ordinary language needs certain philosophical terms, among

[2] As are the psychology departments of Catholic universities and colleges in this country.

[3] Cfr. the penetrating remarks of G. W. Allport in *College Reading and Religion* (Yale University Press, 1948), pp. 80-114.

which faculty is included. The concept of faculty corresponds in the psychic domain to that of an organ in physiology. A physiologist does not claim that he has explained the process of digestion by ascribing it to the stomach. Yet he does not reject the idea of the stomach or of an organ. The same can be said of the use in psychology of the concept of a faculty.

A faculty is defined as the proximate or immediate principle of mental operations. We say "proximate" to distinguish it from the "radical" or "remote" principle of all mental operations (and of all other operations as well), which is the "nature" of the being.

I perform many operations—such as breathing, digesting, thinking, seeing. The *principle which* performs these operations is the Ego, "I." The *remote principle by which* I perform these operations is my nature. The *proximate principle by which* I perform physiological operations is an organ. The *proximate principle by which* I perform mental operations is a faculty.

Hence from the scientific point of view we do not insist on retaining the concept of faculty, since it does not explain anything. Nevertheless even scientists need some idea corresponding to it and express such an idea frequently, because all human language has a philosophical foundation.

From the philosophical point of view the concept of faculty is absolutely necessary. We have clearly defined it, and we shall use it in the sense in which it has been defined.

We must be careful, however, not to consider these faculties as complete and separate beings, which act on their own and independently of each other. A faculty does not act, it is something by means of which I act. It is not the eye which sees or the mind which thinks, but I see through my eyes and I think with my intelligence. Many false problems will be avoided by remembering this important observation.

CLASSIFICATION OF HUMAN FACULTIES

Man has many faculties. What order, if any, exists among them? Here again there is disagreement between Scholastic philosophers and some modern psychologists.

The Scholastic philosophers (and, for that matter, all philosophers

who admit an essential difference between man and the animals)
distinguish between faculties which man has in common with animals, the sentient or organic faculties, and others which man shares
with the pure spirits, the rational or spiritual faculties. This distinction is of the utmost importance, and we shall solidly establish it
later on. All materialists reject it, because for them there is no real
difference between animals and men.

Sentient and rational faculties are further subdivided into cognitive and appetitive faculties. The cognitive faculties give us knowledge of exterior or interior reality. The appetitive faculties are those
by which we strive towards, or away from, the objects we know.
The scholastic classification of human faculties is set down in the
following table:

	COGNITIVE	APPETITIVE
RATIONAL	INTELLECT	WILL
ORGANIC	SENSES	SENSE APPETITE

Experimental psychologists avoid the concept of faculty. Many
of them do not try to classify the functions of the human mind,
but those who do attempt such a classification add to the cognitive
and appetitive categories mentioned above the category of the affective phenomena, comprising the feelings, emotions and sentiments. This yields the following table:

	COGNITIVE	AFFECTIVE	APPETITIVE
RATIONAL	INTELLIGENCE	SENTIMENTS	WILL
ORGANIC	SENSES	FEELINGS	DRIVES
		EMOTIONS	INSTINCTS

The content of this table is not homogeneous, since it includes
faculties (intelligence, will), functions (drives, instincts) and psychic phenomena (sentiments, emotions). Despite this defect we

shall use the classification for convenience in organizing the empirical and experimental data concerning man's mental life.

The Scholastics had no separate category for the affective phenomena because they considered them to be mere modifications of the cognitive and appetitive activities. For example, we observe some danger (cognition), we try to avoid it (appetite), and while we are thus knowing and striving, we are affected by fear (affection).

A deeper reason for the dichotomous classification of the Scholastics seems to lie in the fact that the outlook of St. Thomas is universal and embraces the totality of being. But in the superior beings, the pure spirits and God, we find only cognition and appetite, no emotions, feelings or sentiments. Emotions and feelings occur only in material organisms. Even the sentiments,[4] such as the sentiment of duty or the esthetic sentiment, although implying an intellectual element, are sentiments only owing to the repercussion of this higher element upon a human, material, bodily sensibility.

The third part of our course is divided into two main sections, an experimental and a philosophical section. In the experimental section we shall use the threefold classification into cognitive, affective and appetitive functions. In the philosophical section we shall classify the faculties into cognitive and appetitive faculties.

[4] Some psychologists use the term "sentiment" in a different sense and consider sentiments as appetitive phenomena.

Experimental Study of Man's Sense Life

Introduction

TWO METHODS can be used in the experimental study of man's psychic life. We may start with a picture of man's complex behavior and try to analyze it, to discover the different elements which contribute their share to it. Or we may start with the elements, and by putting them together, try to reconstruct the total picture.

Both methods have advantages and disadvantages. The first method is more lifelike: it follows the natural process of our perception, which is to seize the totality first, and only as a second step proceed to analyze it. But this advantage is offset by a lack of clarity. The second method is generally clearer, since it passes gradually from the simple to the more complex. But it has the disadvantage of studying as independent entities elements which are never given in isolation; it involves the danger of taking abstractions for realities.

We must emphasize that at every moment man's psychic life is a complex totality of all kinds of phenomena. They are intimately connected with each other, they fade gradually into each other, they influence, weaken or strengthen one another. Man's consciousness is under most circumstances a blend of perceptions, feelings, images, judgments, concepts, decisions, emotions, sentiments. Only exceptionally does one of these phenomena become so predominant as to occupy the whole field of consciousness.

Unfortunately, the living reality of man's psychic life is too complicated to be studied as a whole. Therefore we shall distinguish in it, by means of abstraction, some elementary phenomena which have long been distinguished by traditional philosophy and which many experimental psychologists continue to study separately.

105

7

Sense Knowledge

THE CENTER of man's knowledge is judgment, by which he affirms or denies something of something. When man knows an object, he does so in a judgment. We discover that in a judgment there are concepts, that is, intellectual, universal representations of some reality. If we abstract the intellectual element contained in these concepts, we are left with either a perception or an image. Even a perception is a complicated unity which we can further subdivide until we reach elementary sensations. The first part of this chapter will be devoted to the study of sensation.

SENSATION IN GENERAL

A sensation cannot really be defined. It can be described as the most elementary cognitive reaction of an organism to a simple stimulus. We never experience a pure sensation. If we could ever have a pure experience, say, of "red," not connected with any object, not localized in space or time, we should then experience a sensation.

A sensation presupposes the interaction of some stimulus with a specialized part of an organism. This specialized part is called a sense organ, to which corresponds a sense, or elementary cognitive function.

Not all organisms have the same number of senses. Unicellular living beings possess only the sense of touch, while the higher mammals and man are endowed with a great variety of senses. Traditionally they have been enumerated as the five senses of sight, hearing, smell, taste and touch. Modern psychology has subdivided the sense of touch into several more senses, each of which possesses its own specialized nerve endings and conveys its own specific kind of sensations. Therefore we have the following table of senses and sensations.

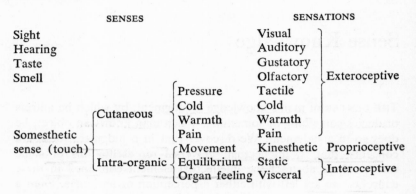

SENSES				SENSATIONS	
Sight				Visual	
Hearing				Auditory	
Taste				Gustatory	
Smell				Olfactory	Exteroceptive
		Cutaneous	Pressure	Tactile	
			Cold	Cold	
			Warmth	Warmth	
Somesthetic			Pain	Pain	
sense (touch)		Intra-organic	Movement	Kinesthetic	Proprioceptive
			Equilibrium	Static	Interoceptive
			Organ feeling	Visceral	

The last column of this table contains terms which are frequently used in modern psychology to designate wider categories of sensations. Exteroceptive sensations give us knowledge of something outside our own body; interoceptive sensations inform us about objects or states in the interior of our body; proprioceptive sensations inform us about parts of our body. Thus undigested food in our stomach may be sensed by an interoceptive sensation. The movements of our limbs, which are not within our body but are parts of our body, are known by proprioceptive sensations. The distinction between these two categories is not very sharp.

Sensations have certain characteristics: quality, intensity and duration. Quality is that which distinguishes one category of sensations from all others. Thus the difference between visual and auditory sensations is one of quality.

What makes sensations differ in quality? What makes a visual sensation differ from an auditory sensation? The answer seems obvious: it must be the nature of the stimulus. The sensations are different because the stimuli are different. When light radiation strikes our eyes, we experience a visual sensation; when sound waves strike our ear, we have an auditory sensation. What would happen if a sound wave affected our eyes? The question would seem to be purely academic, since in fact sound waves do not affect our eyes. However, it is not wholly idle, as some stimuli may affect sense organs different from those designed to receive them, or may affect more than one organ. Thus a mechanical blow, which is a tactile stimulus, may affect our eyes, and from experience we know that we then "see stars," we have a visual sensation. Likewise electric stimulation may affect several sense organs, and we know that each organ reacts in its own specific way. When the optic nerve is electrically stimulated, we see light; when the acoustic nerve is thus stimulated, we hear a sound; electric stimulation of the gustatory nerve produces a taste sensation. In the famous paradoxical cold sensation, a warm stimulus reaching a nerve ending specialized in conducting cold sensations produces a sensation of cold.

These facts have given rise to the famous law of the "specific nerve energies," first formulated by Johannes Müller, according to which, whatever be the stimulus, a sensory nerve always reacts with its own specific sensation. It follows from this law that if sound waves should affect the eyes, they would be experienced as light, not as sound. It follows also that if, by a clever operation, the optic nerve could be connected with the acoustic brain-center, and the acoustic nerves with the optic brain-center, we should hear light and see sound.

Does this not imply that knowledge obtained through the senses is necessarily subjective and that any objective knowledge of the world of reality is consequently impossible? Our sensations would tell us what nerves in our body are affected but not the nature of the stimuli which affect them. Because of this consequence some try to minimize the law of Müller.

There seems to be no real foundation for these misgivings. We shall often have occasion to point out that our basic certitudes come from our intellect, not from our senses. The senses give us pragmatic certitude, and that certitude is not endangered by the law of specific nerve energies. For it is a fact that the different senses are adapted to their respective stimuli and that only occasionally, and under artificial circumstances, will a sense organ react to the stimulus of another sense. Our intelligence warns us of these special circumstances and keeps us from error.

VISUAL SENSATIONS

The sense of sight and that of hearing together constitute the most important part of our human sense equipment. We rely primarily upon these two senses for the acquisition of our intellectual knowledge. People who are deprived of one of these senses, and especially of both, have to overcome great handicaps in their education.

The human retina has two kinds of specialized sensory cells, which, because of their shapes, are called the rods and the cones. The rods are extremely sensitive to light, but they do not register differences in color. The cones are less sensitive to light, but they react to color differences. Rods and cones are not evenly distributed over the retina: there are no rods on the fovea (the part of the eye we use when we focus on an object), but they occur in increasing concentration towards the periphery. The cones are numerous on the fovea and in the central part of the retina, and their numbers decrease towards the periphery. This explains why the fovea possesses excellent color-discrimination and is almost useless in very dim light, why the peripheral area is color-blind. The rods adapt themselves to dim light by building up "visual purple," a chemical extremely sensitive to light. It takes about thirty minutes for the rods to build up their maximum amount of visual purple in total darkness; afterward the eye may be a million times more sensitive to dim light than at the start of this process. A short exposure to intense light destroys the visual purple at once, producing a dazzling or blinding impression.

Man therefore has a double system of vision: a twilight system, very sensitive to brightness, insensitive to color, and a daylight system, much less sensitive to brightness but able to distinguish the various colors. This is the gist of the "duplicity theory," first formulated by the German physiologist von Kries.

Visual sensations, or colors, can be divided into two main groups: achromatic colors (black, white and gray) and chromatic (all other hues). The achromatic colors can be represented by a straight line, going from black to white through all the shades of gray. The chromatic colors can be represented by a circle, described by the following series of colors: red, orange, yellow, green, blue, indigo, violet, purple, and again red. Some of these colors are intermediate hues, obtained by blending the two neighboring colors. If we keep only the colors which cannot be obtained by blending others, we find the following four fundamental colors: red, yellow, green and blue. All other colors can be obtained by mixing some of these fundamental colors.

Therefore the chromatic colors are better represented by a square, each corner of which is occupied by one of the fundamental colors. And the totality of all colors is often represented by a double pyramid, whose main axis is the line of the achromatic colors, and whose basis is the color square.

Every color has three characteristics: hue, brightness and saturation. Hue is that which makes one color of the spectrum different from another. Brightness is the similarity of a color to white. Saturation refers to the richness, the fullness of the color. Thus blood-red is saturated red, whereas pink is unsaturated red.[1]

Colors are mixed psychologically when two different hues are projected simultaneously, or almost simultaneously, onto some part of the retina. When mixed in that way, some chromatic colors produce an achromatic result. Thus when blue and yellow are mixed psychologically they produce white or gray. The same thing occurs when green and red are mixed. Colors which, when mixed psychologically, produce either white or gray are called complementary colors.[2]

Complementary colors have the further characteristic of tending to induce each other in their immediate neighborhood. This phenomenon can be observed in a room where red and white lights are used simultaneously: all the shadows in the room are green. We expect them to be gray, but because they are surrounded by large red fields which tend to induce their complementary color, they

[1] The Gestalt psychologists have emphasized the fact that the colors studied in the early stages of experimental psychology are all surface colors. Nature offers other kinds of colors, such as the color of liquids, fog, smoke, glass, glowing embers, etc.

[2] Impressionistic painters mix their colors psychologically, in the eyes of the observer, while their predecessors mixed them physically on their palette. That explains the luminosity of the impressionistic masterpieces: the more colors you mix psychologically, the brighter the end product; the more colors you mix physically, the darker your end product.

take on a greenish cast. This is the phenomenon of simultaneous contrast.

Successive contrast occurs when, having looked for about half a minute at an object of a certain hue, we rest our gaze on a gray surface and see a spot of the complementary color. This is called a negative after-image.

Complementary colors are further combined in the phenomenon of color-blindness. The normal eye is color-blind at its periphery, where only black, white and gray are perceived. The central part of the eye perceives all hues. Between the central zone and the periphery there is an intermediate zone in which, of the chromatic colors, only blue and yellow are perceived.

In some individuals color-blindness extends over the whole retina. The hues they do not see are generally red and green. About four per cent of all men suffer from this defect, which is much rarer among women. In some cases there is yellow-blue color-blindness. Very rare is total color-blindness, wherein only the achromatic colors are perceived.

AUDITORY SENSATIONS

Auditory sensations are divided into two main categories: noises and tones. Noises are irregular, rough, arising from complex physical stimuli. Tones are regular and smooth, produced by a simple stimulus. Although most sounds affecting our ears are noises, the psychologists have especially studied the tones.

Tones have three main properties: loudness, pitch and timbre. In loudness, tones range from slight to loud. Loudness depends on the physical intensity of the stimulus, more specifically on the amplitude of the sound vibrations. In pitch, tones range from low to high. The pitch of a tone increases with the frequency of the vibrations. The timbre of a tone, or its quality, allows us to distinguish a tone of the same loudness and of the same pitch, when played on different instruments. Timbre depends on the complexity of the sound waves.

The human ear can perceive tones ranging in frequency from about 20 to 20,000 vibrations per second. The high limit usually comes down as people advance in age. Music uses tones ranging in frequency from about 16 to 4,000 vibrations per second. Pitch discrimination is best within that range.

Tones cannot be classified in groups like the colors. However, proceeding from lower to higher, we observe that certain tones can be blended more smoothly than can other combinations. These tones have frequencies which stand in a simple mathematical relation to each other. Thus two tones whose respective frequencies stand to each other as 1 to 2 blend so harmoniously that an untrained ear cannot distinguish them. They differ by an octave. Tones having a relation of 2 to 3, 3 to 4, et cetera, are also harmonious in combination; they correspond to the different notes of the octave.

The sounds which are most useful for man's intellectual life are the sounds of human language. They are classified either as consonants or as vowels. Consonants are noises, and they are complex in their physical structure. Vowels are tones, and their physical structure is relatively simple.

SMELL AND TASTE SENSATIONS

The sensations of taste and smell have little importance for man's intellectual life; on the other hand, they are of great biological importance and generally possess a strong affective character; usually an odor or a taste is agreeable or disagreeable, rarely is it a matter of indifference.

These two senses work in intimate association. In particular, many so-called tastes have a strong olfactory component. There are only four basic taste qualities: sweet, salt, sour and bitter. The great variety in the taste of foods and drinks must be explained mainly by differences in aroma, in smell. Furthermore, the basic taste sensations are often blended with sensations of temperature, of touch (crispness), even of pain (horse radish).

There is immense variety in the smell sensations, and psychologists have met with great difficulties in their attempts to classify them. The classification which is most generally accepted at present is that of Henning, who distinguishes six main odors. These odors, with an example of each, are: flowery (violets), fruity (peaches), spicy (cloves), resinous (turpentine), burnt (coffee), foul (carrion).

The phenomenon of contrast occurs in the domain of taste: lemonade tastes sweeter after pretzels. The sense of smell shows a marked capacity for adaptation: an odor which is very noticeable at first is no longer consciously perceived after a while, e.g. in a hospital.

CUTANEOUS SENSATIONS

The cutaneous sensations, whose nerve endings are localized in the skin, correspond to the former fifth sense, the sense of touch. They are the most essential for biological survival; many animals possess only these senses, and no animal is without them.

Modern psychologists distinguish four categories of cutaneous sensations: pressure, cold, warmth and pain. This classification is based on the theory (on which some doubt has lately been cast) that each category has its own specialized nerve endings in the skin. If the skin of the forearm is gently pricked with a hair, certain spots yield a definite sensation of pressure, of touch, while other spots do not react. Pressure spots are unevenly distributed over the skin; some parts of the body possess many of them, e.g. the tips of the fingers and of the tongue; others have very few, e.g. the abdomen and the thickened skin on the soles of the feet. Pressure sensations show great adaptability, which explains why we are not aware of the pressure of clothes on the skin.

If the skin is touched with a blunt, cold object, certain spots give a clear sensation of cold. It is even possible to stimulate some of these spots by means of a warm object; the cold spot then reacts with its specific response and yields an impression of cold (paradoxical cold sensation). Other parts of the skin react with a sensation of warmth if stimulated with an object whose temperature is higher than that of the skin.

The sense of cold and that of warmth give us relative, not absolute knowledge[3] of the temperature, as can be demonstrated by

[3] We shall show later that all sense knowledge is relative.

the following simple experiment. Plunge your left hand into warm water and your right hand into cold water. Then put both together into lukewarm water. This water will feel cold to your left hand and warm to your right hand. Objects which have the same temperature as the skin do not produce any temperature sensation. Skin temperature is called the "physiological zero"; any object whose temperature is above the physiological zero is felt as warm, any object whose temperature is below it is felt as cold. The physiological zero can be moved slightly up or down through adaptation, as shown in the above experiment.

Pain sensations are obtained at definite spots in the skin when these are lightly stimulated by some sharply pointed instrument. Where there are no pain nerve endings, this slight stimulation is not felt, or is felt only as pressure. Of the four kinds of cutaneous nerve endings the pain spots are the most numerous. They react more slowly than any of the others and show little adaptation.

Certain portions of the skin yield a special reaction called tickle —particularly little-used parts, such as the skin of the armpits and under the instep. These sensations are a peculiar mixture of pleasure and pain and have a marked affective character. Certain authors claim that they belong to an older "protopathic" kind of sensibility. This sensibility does not produce much information about the outside world, but only affective reactions; it has been overgrown by the "epicritical" sensibility in most parts of the body.

INTRA-ORGANIC SENSATIONS

The cutaneous sensations have their nerve endings in the skin and inform us with regard to conditions affecting our body from without. The intra-organic sensations have their nerve endings within the body and inform us about the position, the movement or the state of parts of the body or the body as a whole.

There are three groups of intra-organic sensations: the static, the kinesthetic and the visceral.

The static sensations inform us first about the position of our body with relation to space or to the force of gravity. We usually know whether we are standing upright, or leaning at a certain angle, or lying in a horizontal position; we gather this information from visual or touch sensations. However, it has been demonstrated that, even when these visual and tactile sensations have been eliminated or neutralized, we still have a certain idea of our position in space. This information is supplied by the static sense. Very often we do not experience our static sensations directly, but only through the reflex actions which they elicit. Thus when we are riding a bicycle, we must continually make slight movements whose purpose is to maintain our equilibrium. These movements are automatic, and they are guided by the static sense.

The static sense informs us also about the movement of our body as a whole through space. This does not apply to steady movement in a constant direction. But every acceleration or deceleration, any change of direction in our movement, is felt by the static sense. Generally we rely so much upon visual and tactile sensations that we do not notice these data of the static sense. When the movement of our body is very irregular—e.g. in a tossing boat—the static sense may produce reflex reactions of a highly disagreeable nature, such as dizziness, nausea, sea-sickness.

The organs of the static sense are situated in the inner ear.

Kinesthetic sensations inform us about the position of our limbs and about the strains and pulls which they undergo. If you move your arm slowly with your eyes closed, you will be aware of its successive positions. And you can evaluate with fair accuracy the weight of an object which you hold in your hand without seeing it.

Kinesthetic sensations are very important in the management of our own body. When a baby begins to move his limbs he is in somewhat the position of a man who has to learn without an instructor how to operate a complicated machine with many levers and switches. The child will spend years building up thousands of connections between his visual or auditory sensations and his kinesthetic sensations. The easy skill of a great athlete is based on such connections. All our own skills and movements depend on them. Take the function of speech. How do we know the exact position of the mouth, the lips, the tongue, the exact amount of contraction of the vocal cords required for the many words of our language? We learn by experimenting until the emitted sound seems to be right.

Connections are established between our auditory sensations, which tell us when we are right, and our kinesthetic sensations, which direct the various positions and contractions of our speech organs.

The great importance of our kinesthetic sensations is tragically demonstrated in cases of ataxia, which consists in an impairment of the kinesthetic function. Patients suffering from this disease can no longer control their muscular reactions. When they reach for an object, they reach too far or not far enough, and only with great difficulty can they bring their hands to the right place.

The organs of the kinesthetic sense are embedded in the muscles and tendons.

Visceral or organic sensations inform us about the conditions of the various parts of our body, especially about disturbed conditions of the organs. To this group belong the sensations of fatigue, exhaustion, inner pain, freshness, "pep."

Other visceral sensations derive from the digestive organs. Such are hunger, which is accompanied by contractions of the stomach; thirst, which is connected with a dehydrated condition of the membranes of the mouth; sensations of indigestion and nausea. Other sensations originate in the circulatory and respiratory tracts. Finally we must mention a general bodily feeling, a blend of many visceral sensations, which gives us an all-over impression of the state of our body and may produce a sense of general well-being or of vague discomfort. This general impression is sometimes called *coenesthesis*. It has a strong affective tonality and provides the basis for our general mood.

Visceral sensations explain how we are aware of the passing of time; how, without a watch or any other outside help, some individuals have a fair idea of how much time has elapsed. Some people, wakening in the night, may be able to tell the time with remarkable accuracy. This feeling of time is connected with sensations deriving from the visceral organs.

PERCEPTION OF SPACE

In the preceding paragraphs we have considered our most elementary cognitive reactions, the sensations. Next we must examine more complex cognitive operations, by means of which can be known, not some abstracted aspect of a total situation, but real objects and the space in which they are situated. These mental operations are called perceptions.

We shall first consider the perception of space. Four problems will be examined: (1) the relation between space perception and the retinal image; (2) the monocular perception of space; (3) the binocular perception of space; (4) whether the perception of the third dimension is inborn or acquired by experience.

1. We mention the problem of the relation between space perception and the retinal image because it shows how flexible our perception is and what a complex background of experience even the simplest perceptions presuppose.

The problem is this: why do we not see objects upside down, since their image on our retina is upside down? This question assumes that there is a strict point-to-point correspondence between every spot on the retina and a definite point in space. That there is no such exact correspondence has been clearly demonstrated in the famous experiment of Stratton.[4]

Stratton built a system of lenses which, when held before the eye, inverted the retinal image, so that objects appeared on the retina right side up. He wore these lenses over one eye for a whole week, taking them off only in the dark. (He kept his other eye out of service during the experiment.) At first all objects were seen upside down. He had great trouble getting around in the most familiar places, and the trouble was aggravated by the fact that objects were "felt" in their right locations, although they were not seen there. The sound of someone approaching came from the right, and that person entered the visual field from the left. All his visual-kinesthetic and visual-auditory connections were disturbed. His past visual experience had helped him build up a picture of reality which was not conformable to the present situation.

After he had stumbled about for a few days, parts of the visual field came into order again. Objects appeared in their right position. At the end of the week, the visual field looked quite normal; only

---

[4] J. M. Stratton, "Vision without Inversion of the Retinal Image," *Psychol. Rev.*, 4 (1897), pp. 341-360 and 463-481.

some of the connections with the other sensory spheres were still resisting the necessary adjustments.

From this experiment we conclude that the position of the retinal images does not matter. What matters is the associations established between these images and the other sensory fields and the movements of the body. Early in the experiment, when an object affected the upper portion of Stratton's retina, he would reach for it in the lower part of his visual field, and the object would be seen there. At the end of his experiment he reached for that object in the upper part of the visual field, where the object was now seen. It is a question of associations and past experience. Our simplest visual perceptions are not passively received pictures of reality but have been actively constructed with the aid of experience.[5]

2. How do we perceive the third dimension with one eye?

The retina is a two-dimensional field. There is no difficulty in understanding how it can record the width and the height of objects. But how can it represent their depth? How can it grasp the third dimension?

This problem is analogous to the problem of the third dimension in drawing and painting. Students of the history of art know how long it took painters to master this problem. Leonardo da Vinci, the great Italian painter of the Renaissance, was the first to set down the rules of perspective. He mentioned the following monocular cues for the third dimension. The same cues are at work in our monocular perception of depth.

a. Linear perspective. The farther an object is from us, the smaller it looks. We have all seen how railroad tracks, a road and telephone wires seem to converge in the distance at what is called a "vanishing point."

b. Aerial perspective. Remote objects lose all their details; their colors become duller and grayer. Nearby objects show many details and their colors are clear-cut.

c. Shadows. Shadows are of two kinds: those which appear on an object because of the angle at which light strikes it or the

---

[5] The far-reaching implications of this experiment are profoundly discussed by M. Merleau-Ponty in his *Phénoménologie de la Perception*, pp. 282 ff. See also A. De Waelhens, *Une Philosophie de l'Ambiguité*, pp. 186 ff.

irregularity of its surface, and those which the object itself casts on neighboring objects. Both kinds make the objects stand out in strong relief and give a vivid impression of depth. Compare two photographs of the same face, one without and one with shadows.

d. Overlapping or covering. If an object covers part of another object in the visual field, we know that the former is nearer to us.

Furthermore there is a kinesthetic monocular cue of the third dimension which is called accommodation. A camera must be focussed if we want a clear picture. This is done by modifying the distance between the objective and the film. It is, of course, impossible for the human eye to modify the distance between the eyeball and the retina. The focussing of the eye is accomplished through a modification of the curvature of the lens. The kinesthetic sensations which accompany this curving of the lens have been frequently associated in our experience with the varying distances of objects. Hence the sensations, of which we are vaguely aware, can become cues to distance. However, experimental research has established that such a cue is only approximate and is of little use in most cases.

3. How do we perceive the third dimension with both eyes?

The best cue of depth perception within a range of twenty yards derives from the fact that we have two eyes and the picture we get of the same object is slightly different for each eye (binocular disparity). Look at the inside of a box first with the left eye, then with the right eye alone. With the left eye you will see more of the right inside wall, with the right eye more of the left inside wall.

If we imagine the two retinas put one over the other, we can say that the points which cover each other are corresponding points; points which do not cover each other are called disparate. An object striking corresponding points upon both retinas is seen as single. If it strikes disparate points, it is seen as double. However, if it strikes points which are only slightly disparate, which are almost corresponding, the object is seen in relief, in three dimensions. This is the principle of the stereoscope; two slightly different views of the same object are presented, one of which is seen by each eye;

the pictures are somehow fused in the brain, and the effect is a striking impression of depth, or relief.

A kinesthetic binocular depth cue sometimes mentioned is that deriving from convergence. When we look at a far-away object, the eyes look in parallel directions. When we look at an object which is very close, the eyes converge on it. The nearer the object, the greater the convergence of the eyes. The kinesthetic sensations produced by this movement of convergence, having been frequently associated in our experience with the distances of objects, eventually serve to indicate such distances. It has been shown experimentally that this cue is not very important.

4. A much-debated question is that of nativism versus empiricism. Is space perception inborn or is it acquired by experience?

As long as Associationism prevailed in psychology, it was held that space perception was entirely, or almost entirely, a product of experience. The first and simplest perception is that of a point. Experience, it was said, taught us to combine points to produce lines, lines to produce planes and planes to produce volumes.

The Gestalt psychologists, or Configurationists, whose theory is essentially anti-associationistic, claim that perception of the third dimension is spontaneous and inborn. They do not deny that experience exerts an influence on the perception of depth; experience renders that perception more precise, better articulated. But they have presented strong evidence in support of the inborn character of our perception of space.

The Associationists pointed out that, since our retina is a two-dimensional field, our original space perception could not be three-dimensional. This is denied by the Configurationists. "The retina is the boundary surface of the tri-dimensional optical sector of the brain, and the forces set up in this boundary surface determine a process extended over the whole tri-dimensional sector."[6]

The Associationists considered the simplest visual stimulation to be that produced by a single point in space affecting a single spot on the retina. The Gestalt psychologists deny this, pointing to the phenomenon of auto-kinetic movement. If in total darkness a

---

[6] K. Koffka, *Principles of Gestalt Psychology* (New York, Harcourt, 1935), p. 115.

subject is shown a single luminous spot, he will see that spot—
which is objectively motionless—travelling extensively over his
visual field. The perception of a single point is a complex phenomenon. For the Gestalt psychologists the simplest stimulation is that
produced by a perfectly uniform field affecting the whole retina.
Under these conditions the observer will "feel himself swimming
in a mist of light which becomes more condensed at an indefinite
distance."[7] Such a uniform field could be constituted by an actual
fog. But it can also be a white wall, every point of which sends the
same amount of light into the eyes of the observer.

Metzger performed an experiment using such a wall as stimulus.
The observer sat in front of it, at a distance of slightly more than a
yard. The visual field of the observer was restricted by means of
side-screens, so that he could see only the wall. As long as the
illumination was low, the subject saw only a three-dimensional mist.

If, however, the illumination was increased, something new happened.
The fog became condensed into a regularly curved surface which surrounded the observer on all sides; its appearance was filmy like the
sky, not surfacy, and similar to the sky it was lightly flat in the centre.
. . . If the illumination is still further increased, the surface straightens
out into a plane whose apparent distance may increase very definitely
beyond the real one.[8]

Why was the selfsame stimulus which first appeared as a regularly curved surface seen later as a flat surface? Because with the
influx of stronger illumination the field was no longer homogeneous.
The wall surface was not perfectly flat, it had grain, and the small
irregularities showed up with the greater illumination and better
accommodation of the eyes.

Hence for the Gestalt psychologists the original perception is
tri-dimensional and becomes two-dimensional only when the field
is no longer homogeneous. Experience may improve the perception
of depth, but it does not create it. The terms of the problem have
been reversed, and the psychologist's main task is now to explain
how the perception of two-dimensional and one-dimensional stimuli
is possible.

[7] W. Metzger, quoted by Koffka, *op. cit.*, p. 111.
[8] *Ibid.*, p. 114.

PERCEPTION ACCORDING TO THE
GESTALT PSYCHOLOGISTS

The Gestalt school of psychology originated in Germany at the beginning of this century as a reaction against Associationism.[9] The Associationists tried to explain all complex psychic phenomena as aggregations of elementary states; against this the Gestalt psychologists assert that in reality and in our experience the complex phenomena come first, and that the elements are perceived later, if at all, and only through abstraction. They have supported their claim very successfully in the domain of perception, and this is a good place to examine their system.

According to what has been called the "mosaic" or the "bundle" theory of Associationism, what come first in our experience are the elementary sensations, corresponding to so many elementary stimuli. We put these elementary sensations together and obtain the more complex perceptions. Or rather, these elements combine spontaneously under the influence of the laws of association. The human mind is passive in this process. The perceived "wholes" are simply copies of the wholes existing in reality. When I see a wall, every part of that wall sends light impressions to some part of my retina. These simultaneous stimulations unite in my mind under the influence of the laws of association, and their sum-total yields the perception of the wall. This associationistic conception emphasizes the primacy of the parts over the whole and the passivity of human perception.

The Gestalt psychologists reject these views and emphasize the primacy of the whole over the parts and the spontaneity, the activity, manifested in our perception. The first thing we perceive is the totality, the whole, the configuration, the Gestalt. At first no details

[9] The works of the founders of Gestalt psychology abound in statements of a philosophical nature. Many of these statements have a mechanistic or materialistic flavor. The Configurationists seem to deny any real difference between the configurations which occur in the physical world and the configurations which are found in the mind. When they speak of the mind they seem to mean the brain, and only the brain. They forget that the brain is an animated organ which, like the body, is informed by the soul. Therefore the mental configurations are not produced by the brain alone but by the brain working under the formal causality of the soul.

are noticed, or only such details as are very striking and unusual. For example, when we see a crowd, we do not first perceive a great number of individuals which we put together in our mind and thus see the crowd. We first see a crowd and only afterwards we distinguish individuals.

Furthermore, these wholes which we perceive, of which we are aware, are not passively reproduced copies of the wholes as they exist in reality. They are actively constructed by our own mind, more or less after the model of the objective data. Consider the physiological difficulties which would be involved in a purely passive perception of the objective configurations. We might admit that the retinal image is a passive reproduction of the outside data, but this retinal image is translated into nerve impulses and further into the mysterious activity of the brain cells. How could a point-to-point reproduction of the objective scene be maintained in the course of this cerebral activity?

The problem can be stated in different terms. What meets our eyes is a mosaic of irregular patches of color. Why do we not see these patches of color, but instead trees, houses, a river, a road, a house? The Associationists admitted that at first we saw only these irregular blots of color. Slowly, through repeated experience, we come to associate them with definite objects. After a while these associations become so strong that the objects are perceived at once.

It cannot be denied that experience has a share in our perception of objects. The reason why the language spoken by foreigners, even a language we have studied, sounds to us like an uninterrupted series of sounds, in which we do not recognize the words we have learned from the dictionary, is precisely that we have not sufficient experience of these words. We do not have any such difficulty where our own language is concerned, even when we hear it spoken very rapidly.

But experience alone is not enough, since it presupposes some knowledge. The question remains: how did we recognize these objects, these words, as units the first few times we met them in our experience? Recognition of units presupposes an original cognition of these units.

For the Configurationists our very first perception, previous to any experience, is not of an irregular assortment of disconnected patches of color. It is from the beginning organized, structured; it contains figures and a background; some parts are grouped together to form units, or wholes. We do not know at once that these wholes are houses or trees; that knowledge presupposes some experience. But before we know what these configurations are, they exist clearly in our perceptual field. In other words, there is within the mind itself a factor which organizes the data of our perception the very first time we perceive them. Our perception is not a passive receiving of impressions but entails active reconstruction and organization.

The Gestalt psychologists offer many experimental data to establish their claims. We shall now mention some of these data.

1. We may perceive an object or a whole before finding out what it is. Thus we see "something," "some object" in the distance or in a fog. We do not know what it is, we do not recognize it, but we perceive it immediately as a distinct unit.

2. The Configurationists have studied the factors which make for such spontaneous groupings in our perception. They mention especially the following:

a. Nearness, or proximity. Stimuli which are near each other are perceived as groups. Thus the nine lines in Fig. 2 are not perceived spontaneously as nine lines but as three groups of three lines.

$$/// \quad /// \quad ///$$

Fig. 2

The law of nearness explains why men have at all times seen some constellations in the sky. Stars which are perceived near each other are seen as groups, or constellations.

b. Similarity or resemblance. In Fig. 3 we spontaneously see vertical lines of crosses and circles, not horizontal lines made up of alternating crosses and circles.

c. Common fate. Planes travelling in the same direction and at the same speed are naturally seen as groups, as perceptual wholes. Nearness and similarity of movement combine here.

d. Good continuation, good curve, good figure. These factors

are easier to explain by means of examples than in words.
When two lines can be seen as continuing each other smoothly,
they will be seen as one. Max Wertheimer, one of the founders
of Gestalt psychology, used to camouflage his initials in the

```
+ o + o + o
+ o + o + o
+ o + o + o
+ o + o + o
+ o + o + o
```

Fig. 3

following figure, 4,[10] in which the M and the W are difficult to
see. Good continuation makes us see the two outside lines as
units, and the central diamond as a whole.

Fig. 4

A figure which is harmonious, balanced, well-proportioned, is
seen as a whole. Circles, triangles, squares are good figures, and
they show great internal cohesion in perception. This may explain why some animals can be trained to react uniformly to
certain of these figures even when they are presented in different
contexts and with many variations. The abstraction and uni-
versalization which seem to occur in such cases are activities
which take place on the perceptual level.

We have much more experience of the word "little" than of
the upper part of Fig. 5:

Fig. 5

[10] Figure 4 is reproduced from Koffka's *Principles of Gestalt Psychology*
through the courtesy of the publishers, Harcourt, Brace and Company.

Nevertheless we see that figure, and not the word "little" to which a few lines have been added. If the extra lines do not contribute to the formation of a good figure, they do not interfere with our perception of LITTLE.

3. Perception, especially visual perception, organizes itself spontaneously in "figure" and "background." We see trees and houses (figures) against the background of the sky; furniture and paintings against the background of the wall; words and pictures against the background of the white page. Figures have contour, consistency and unity, and our attention goes spontaneously towards them; the background is unlimited, it seems to continue behind the figures, it is vague and we do not pay much attention to it.

This organization of our perception occurs spontaneously, without previous experience. It is very striking in some cases where figure and background are unstable and shifting, as in Fig. 6. The odd shapes disappear, become background, as soon as you see the word HAT.

Fig. 6

The same phenomenon of sudden, spontaneous reorganization of a perception is also evidenced in some "ambiguous" figures. Look for a while at the cube in Fig. 7 and you will suddenly notice a radical change in its appearance. What seemed to be the reversed side of the cube has now become the front side. This change of organization is almost continuous in Fig. 8.

These examples deserve a word of comment. In the very act of observing these figures, our perception is organized in a certain way. We become clearly aware of this when suddenly, without apparent reason, without any effort on our part, this organization changes, with a corresponding change in the perception. It is evident that this is not an intellectual or voluntary process. It happens entirely on the level of perception, in the sense domain.

This may help us to explain some cases of insight in higher animals. When a chimpanzee suddenly discovers the possibility that a stick or a box will help him reach the desired banana, a similar shift may have just occurred in his perceptual field. At first the stick or the box was in the background, the only figure was the fruit.

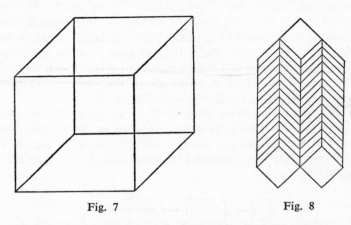

Fig. 7   Fig. 8

Under the influence of an intense desire to reach the goal, perception undergoes a sudden reorganization and the stick or the box assumes the features of a figure. This explanation is suggested by the fact that the animal must see tool and goal together, in the same visual field, if he is to discover the solution of the problem.

4. In some diseases of perception the patient loses the power of perceiving forms. Their visual acuity is unimpaired, they recognize ordinary objects through color, size, et cetera; but they do not recognize any form or configuration. In particular a drawing, in which an object is outlined by its general shape, has no more meaning for them unless they follow the outline with a finger, or at least with a movement of the head. They manage to read in the same way, and if they are asked to read an ordinary word through which a few cross lines have been drawn, they have the greatest difficulties. In the perception of a normal person these cross lines do not interfere, because they are seen as background against which the word, as figure, is clearly observable. But the perception of these patients marks no distinction between figure and background. Wherever one

of the lines crosses a letter of the word, the patients hesitate, unable to decide in what direction they should continue their reading movement. Where the normal reader easily distinguishes a letter crossed by a line, the patients might as well perceive some meaningless outline.

From these and many other facts the Gestalt psychologists derived their new theory of perception. At first they claimed that a perception is more than the sum of its elements, that it is constituted of the totality of these elements plus a *Gestaltqualität,* or "form quality," which holds the elements together. Later they went further and denied the very existence of the elements. Our perception is a whole, a totality, it is that landscape before our eyes. If I analyze it, I discover not elements but smaller wholes: trees, houses. Under scrutiny these may, in their turn, yield still smaller wholes. Elements represent the ultimate limit of an analysis pushed to the extreme. Our perception, say the Gestalt psychologists, is "structured," that is, it can be analyzed into smaller components, each of which is itself a totality that derives its meaning from its relation to all the other parts of the global field.

What has been said about visual perception applies also, *mutatis mutandis,* to perception in the other sensory domains. Thus we can easily distinguish figure and background in an auditory perception: a conversation to which we attend against a background of sundry noises, a soloist playing against the background of an orchestra. Thus again, in the auditory domain, the global units come first: a child learning his mother tongue does not start with letters and syllables (as was done in the older, artificial method of learning to write) but with short sentences. He will discover words and syllables and letters later through analysis. And each of these components constitutes itself a smaller totality.

The Gestalt theory also gives us the best explanation for the optico-geometrical illusions, most famous among which is the Müller-Lyer illusion (Fig. 9).

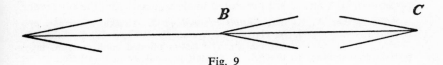

Fig. 9

The two objectively equal lines AB and BC seem unequal in length. The reason is that we do not really see these lines in themselves, but as parts of the two whole designs in which they are submerged and which are objectively of unequal length. The illusion points to the primacy of wholes in our perception.[11]

PERCEPTION OF MOVEMENT

The movements of our own body are perceived by means of our visual, kinesthetic and static sensations. We are interested here in the perception of the movement of objects distinct from us.

For the perception of movements in the third dimension we use the same cues as for the perception of the dimension itself. When an object appears to become smaller as we look at it, vaguer in outline and dimmer in color, and we are conscious of accommodation and divergence in our vision, we know from past experience that it is moving away from us.

For the perception of movements across the visual field, when some object moves from our left to our right, or vice versa, we use several cues. We can compare the position of the object with that of stationary objects. We can turn our eyes and our head to follow the movement of the object. From experience we know that such movements in our own body mean movement of the object. If we do not turn our eyes, the moving object will affect different parts of the retina.

In the latter case our perception of the movement seems to be purely passive. The impressions are passively received and constitute the perception of the movement. However, the Gestalt psychologists claim that even here we are active, we reconstruct the movement in our own perception. In order to demonstrate this assertion, they point to instances where no real movement is given, although a movement is really perceived (the phi-phenomenon). On a screen before the observer two luminous spots, A and B, are presented. If A and B are presented in slow succession, the observer

[11] See further W. Köhler, *Gestalt Psychology*, K. Koffka, *Principles of Gestalt Psychology*, G. W. Hartmann, *Gestalt Psychology*, W. D. Ellis, *A Source Book of Gestalt Psychology*. The last-mentioned book contains important contributions to the field of Gestalt psychology in translation.

sees first A, then B, then A again, and so forth. If A and B are presented in quick succession, they are seen simultaneously; the eyes are too slow to notice the interruption of the stimulus. If A and B succeed each other at a moderate speed, the observer sees only one luminous spot which seems to move, which seems to jump from point A to point B. Although this luminous spot never occupies any of the intermediate positions between A and B, the observer has the impression that it passes through them. This perception of apparent movement explains our ability to perceive motion pictures.

The Configurationists conclude that when a certain number of conditions in the stimulus are fulfilled, we perceive movement, whether the exterior object is really moving or not. Movement is a Gestalt, a configuration, which is evoked when certain well-defined conditions are fulfilled. This happens generally when real movement is given in the stimulus field. But even then we do not passively receive it but actively reconstruct it after the data coming from outside.

Professor Michotte of Louvain University has recently demonstrated something similar in the perception of causality. Many philosophers have claimed that the exercise of efficient causality cannot be perceived by the senses but only conceived by the intellect. If we are to accept their claim, it means that whereas we see the active movement of the cause and the passive movement of the effect, we do not see the cause producing—actually causing—the effect. We see, for example, the knife entering the loaf and the slice taking shape, but we do not really see the knife cutting the bread. Michotte has devised clever experiments which demonstrate that causality can be perceived. This perception takes place when a certain number of conditions are fulfilled, even if no causal influence is actually at work. The Louvain psychologist has carefully investigated the conditions required for us to perceive one object exercising a causal influence upon another; he has demonstrated that empirical causality, just like movement, is a Gestalt, perceived by us whenever a certain number of conditions are fulfilled.[12]

---

[12] A. Michotte, *La Perception de la Causalité*. See also J. Paulus, "La Perception de la Causalité selon M. Michotte van den Berck," in *Revue Philos. de Louvain*, 44 (1946), pp. 530 ff.

Experiments like those of Professor Michotte are looked upon with little favor by a great number of experimental psychologists, because they rely rather heavily on the introspective reports of the subjects and because they bring up philosophical problems.

The same remark applies to Gestalt psychology in general. It has certainly meant a great step forward in our understanding of perception, as compared with Associationism. The latter theory involved the attempt to interpret mental phenomena as if they were physical events. The former comes much nearer to a real comprehension of their specific nature.

Yet even Gestalt psychology seems to have been too objectivistic in its approach to mental life, and a more thorough effort is being made by some phenomenologists to understand sensation and perception from within, as they are really experienced by the subject, rather than to study them from without as objects.

There is not much hope that the experimental psychologists will look favorably upon this new approach. If they had objections against Gestalt psychology because of its many subjective interpretations, its proneness to philosophizing, they will have many more against phenomenological psychology on this score. This illustrates once more the ambivalent nature of experimental psychology; the experimental psychologist is trying to produce a Science, but he cannot succeed without giving up the possibility of a thorough exploration of the most essential psychological phenomena. It seems premature to attempt to summarize here the very complex data of phenomenological psychology. The interested student is referred to the writings of its originators.[13]

EXTRA-SENSORY PERCEPTION

Can we perceive objects or other people's thoughts without any help from the sense organs? Some people claim that we can, and they offer as evidence the phenomena of telepathy and clair-

---

[13] M. Merleau-Ponty, *La Structure du Comportement* and *La Phénoménologie de la Perception*. A good study of these difficult works in A. De Waelhens, *Une Philosophie de l'Ambiguité: L'Existentialisme de Maurice Merleau-Ponty*. Cf. also Erwin W. Strauss, "Aesthesiology and Hallucinations," in Rollo May et al., *Existence*, pp. 139-169.

voyance. In telepathy a mental content is supposed to pass from the mind of one person into that of another without any intervention of the senses. In clairvoyance a person is supposed to become aware of some material object without intervention of the senses.

Most cases of so-called telepathy or clairvoyance must be treated with great caution, because they are reported by untrained observers and cannot be checked. Furthermore, the element of coincidence cannot be excluded, since the positive cases alone are reported and the negative cases are completely ignored. Suppose that you are a boarder, and that one morning you wake up depressed and unusually worried about the health of your mother. You have a feeling that something has happened to her. And indeed, at ten o'clock a telegram arrives telling you that Mother died that very morning. An evident case of telepathy, which will be duly reported to all comers. Suppose, on the other hand, that nothing had happened to Mother. That would be a negative case, about which nobody would hear. If for 1000 negative cases there is 1 positive case, would this allow us to exclude the obvious explanation of a chance coincidence?

All this is not intended as a demonstration that telepathy and clairvoyance do not occur, but as a warning that it is not easy to demonstrate the genuineness of the cases that are reported.

However, Professor J. B. Rhine, a psychologist at Duke University (North Carolina) who has spent many years in a scientific study of such phenomena, has reported results which deserve attention. He uses a deck of twenty-five cards. The deck contains five cards with a star, five with a circle, five with the plus sign, five with a square and five with wavy lines. The subject of the experiment is supposed to identify each card without seeing it. In telepathy experiments the experimenter sees the card and the subject is supposed to "read his mind"; in clairvoyance experiments, the subject is supposed to tell the order in which the cards occur in the deck. By chance alone the subject should be right once out of five times, therefore five times for each deck. A subject who was consistently right for all cards (provided, of course, that there was no cheating) would show either real telepathic powers or clairvoyance. Rhine reports no such achievement. But he does report many cases of subjects making scores which cannot be explained by mere chance.

Elaborate precautions are taken against irregularities in the conduct of the experiment, and the use of statistics excludes the possibility of explaining these results by chance.

Nevertheless most psychologists maintain a reserved attitude towards extra-sensory perception. Some admit it as a possibility, most of them are withholding their decision until more evidence is available.[14]

SYNESTHESIA

Synesthesia consists in the action of one stimulus on more than one sense. A rather common example of this phenomenon is called "colored hearing"—i.e., some individuals experience the impression that certain sounds have a definite color. Thus a sound may be heard as high C and produce the impression of whiteness.

The existence of this phenomenon was long ago recognized, but until recently it was considered unusual, occurring only in subjects abundantly endowed with imagination, especially artists. The Configurationists, however, have shown that in certain circumstances synesthesia is a normal occurrence. In line with their general theory, they insist upon the unity of the senses and the relations existing between them, and the consequent possibility of one sense influencing another. According to the theory of evolution, all the senses are developments and specializations of one fundamental sense. Since they have a common root, it is not surprising that they maintain intercommunication.

In the study of language we see that there are intersensory adjectives—for example, in English, *dull,* which can be applied to a color, a sound, an odor, a pain; and *bright,* which can likewise be used for several sense modalities. The French verb *sentir* is used indiscriminately with reference to sensations of pain, pleasure, taste, or touch. Such words seem to be numerous in primitive languages.

Synesthesia can be produced experimentally, especially with labile, subjective psychic phenomena. Thus an after-image can easily be influenced by a sound simultaneously perceived. Subjects

[14] See further J. B. Rhine and J. G. Pratt, *Parapsychology,* 1957.

who were asked to correlate certain shades of gray with definite sounds showed an agreement which could not be explained by chance.

ORDINARY IMAGES

With this paragraph we begin the study of what the Scholastics call the internal senses. The first which comes up for consideration is the imagination, and its products, the ordinary images. We call them ordinary images in order to distinguish them from special images, such as eidetic images, dream images and projected images.

An image can be defined as a sensorial mental content which represents an object in the absence of any stimuli deriving from the object. When I look at the Statue of Liberty, I have a perception of it; when I picture it to myself in my mind, I have an image of it.

Images exist in all sense domains; there are visual, auditory, olfactory, gustatory, tactile, kinesthetic images. The liveliness of imagery varies considerably from individual to individual. Intellectual development generally decreases the vividness of a person's images, unless the development occurs in the artistic domain.

For a long time it was held that there were definite imagery types among individuals—i.e., that some people belonged to the visual type and had predominantly visual images, others to the auditory, and still others to the motor type. Educators especially were interested in finding out to which type individual students belonged, with a view to adapting methods of presentation and study to each type. Later research has disclosed, however, that there are very few individuals in whose mental life one type of image is clearly predominant. Most people have visual, auditory and kinesthetic images. The other kinds of images are usually less distinct, and in fact are hardly noticed. The variation between individuals consists rather in the degree of vividness of whatever images they experience. In rare individual cases images are almost as vivid as actual perceptions; at the other extreme we find individuals in whom images are very vague, schematic, reduced to the greatest possible simplicity.

In man we must distinguish between two functions of imagination, the reproductive and the productive. The first reproduces pictures of objects previously perceived. Although deriving from the past, they are not recognized as belonging to the past. Recognizing former perceptions is a function of memory.

Productive, or creative, imagination recombines previously perceived images to form a fresh synthesis. Walt Disney's many creations are the products of this kind of imagination. It is not creative in the sense that it produces something absolutely new; only the arrangement of the elements is original. This function is closely associated with intelligence and indispensable for the easy and quick solution of problems—that is, for intelligence in the sense of brightness.[15]

Since images can be extremely vivid and perceptions very indistinct, instances inevitably occur in which the distinction between image and perception is difficult to make. When an image is mistaken for a perception we speak of an illusion, or a hallucination. Generally speaking, however, we have no difficulty in making the distinction. We use the following criteria:

1. The indistinctness of images, as opposed to the vividness of perceptions.

2. The lack of detail in the images, as opposed to the abundance of detail we can distinguish in our perceptions.

3. The subjective character of our images, as opposed to the objective character of a perception. We can change our images, produce and dismiss them at will; but a perception is not influenced by our desires.

4. In general, an image lacks many of the features which we know, from past experience, that the perception should possess. Imagined fire does not burn.

All these criteria depend on former experience. Hence the question arises how, before any experience, an image can be distinguished from a perception. Previous to any experience the distinction is not made at all. The human mind spontaneously objectifies all its contents. For a very young child there is no

15 See p. 210.

difference between what he imagines and what he perceives. Experience teaches him that some of these contents are not real.[16]

Images which have occurred simultaneously in our experience become associated. They form clusters which are reproduced as such later on. Images also form associations with perceptions. This process is called "association of images," or "association of ideas."

The principal laws of Association, already noted by Aristotle, are:

1. The law of contiguity. Mental contents which have been experienced at the same place or at the same time have a tendency to evoke each other. If we have witnessed an automobile accident at a certain street corner, we may think of it again when we pass that corner.

2. The law of similarity. Mental contents which resemble each other have a tendency to evoke each other. A suspension bridge met in our travels may evoke in our mind the memory of a similar bridge in our home town.

3. The law of contrast. Mental contents which contrast with each other tend to evoke each other. Black evokes white, day evokes night.

The British school of psychologists known as the Associationists tried to explain all the phenomena of mental life in terms of these simple laws. Their effort did not succeed, for although it is true that these laws are constantly at work in our minds, they are inadequate to explain any of the higher intellectual functions of man. For a while it was held that they were sufficient to explain such functions as perception and memory, but the Gestalt psychologists have demonstrated that even on this level association cannot explain everything.

All the perceptions of an adult are accompanied by images which enrich the present perception with data from similar perceptions of the past. When we stand looking at a house, we have the impression that we are seeing a house. The fact is that very often we are seeing only one side of the house, a wall with a door and windows. If we had never seen a house before, we should see only that wall. But

---

[16] Cfr. J. Maréchal, S. J., *Studies in the Psychology of the Mystics,* trans. by Algar Thorold (New York, Benziger, 1927), ch. 2.

our present perception is completed by images derived from past
perceptions in which we have seen houses from many angles. This
amplification of a present perception by remnants of former perceptions has been called "apperception," a term which is used with
a quite different meaning by many modern philosophers.

PECULIAR IMAGES

We shall now briefly consider illusions and hallucinations, projected images and eidetic images.

Illusions and hallucinations are both images which present a false
interpretation of reality. They are mistaken for real perceptions.
An illusion is an erroneous perception with a basis in reality. When
on a dark night we take a tree stump for a crouching man, we have
an illusion. Something is there, the perception has a basis in reality;
but our apperception is wrong, and we misinterpret the stimulus,
thinking it is something which it is not. This usually happens when
the subject is under the influence of some emotion, such as fear,
hope or anger.

A hallucination is an erroneous perception with no basis in
reality. It may be caused by some irritation of the sense organ concerned or some disorder in the corresponding brain center. When
a delirious patient sees a nonexistent robber entering his room
through the window, he is suffering from a hallucination. These
phenomena, too, are generally experienced under the influence of
affective factors.

In both illusions and hallucinations there is a projection of subjective images into objective reality under the influence of some
emotion or drive. We can therefore learn much about the affective
and instinctive life of a person by studying his projected images.
That is why psychologists have devised methods to induce the
projection of images.

The subject is shown a stimulus which is vague and ambiguous,
and is invited to interpret it. This projective method of testing was
first used by Rorschach. He offered his subjects a certain number
of irregularly shaped ink-blots in black or in various colors and
asked them to tell him what these blots represented. Most people

have no difficulty in seeing something definite in these queer shapes. Rorschach studied abnormals and neurotics and discovered, after testing hundreds of patients, that there was a relation between what the patient saw in the ink-blots and the trouble from which he was suffering. This test, whose value has been demonstrated for the examination of mentally disturbed individuals, is being used more and more in the examination of normal subjects.

Other projective tests have been devised. We shall mention only the Thematic Apperception Test of Murray. An untitled picture showing a simple scene is presented to the subject without comment, and he is invited to explain what is taking place in that scene. From the manner in which the subject interprets the picture, an expert psychologist can gather useful information about his feelings, drives and attitudes.

Eidetic images occur especially among children, although a few cases have been reported in adults.[17] The child is shown a picture containing much detail. He is allowed to look at it for only a few seconds. Then he is invited to "see" that picture again on a screen— that is, to project it. If the subject is eidetically endowed, he will be able to do so, to re-examine the picture he has projected on the screen and discover details he did not notice before. Erich Jaensch, who discovered this phenomenon, claims that it is quite common among his German subjects. Other psychologists, examining children in other countries with the same methods, have found very few cases. Did Jaensch unconsciously use suggestion on the children? Or are there regional differences in the frequency of eidetic subjects? Both hypotheses have been advanced to explain the discrepancies between the results of different investigators. Most psychologists now admit that eidetic images exist but think that they occur less frequently than Jaensch claimed.[18]

MEMORY

Memory is the function which retains, reproduces and recognizes the representations of objects formerly perceived. The main differ-

[17] See Dorothy Wayman, *Bite the Bullet*, p. 12.
[18] E. R. Jaensch, *Eidetic Imagery* (New York, Harcourt, 1930).

ence between imagination and memory consists in the factor of
recognition. Memory not only retains and reproduces, as does the
imagination, it also recognizes, it is aware (vaguely or clearly,
consciously or unconsciously) that a certain mental content has
been met in the past.

Memory has been a favorite object of study for experimental
psychology. Many of the results of these investigations are presented
in the chapters on learning, which are among the most important in
every textbook of psychology. This material is too extensive and
too specialized to be presented here, even in summary. We shall
mention only a few points which are of particular interest to the
philosopher.

Different kinds of memory must be distinguished. The first distinctions will be between what can be termed motor memory, mental
memory and pure memory.

Motor memory is the memory of the living body in motion.
When certain movements have been repeated often enough in a
fixed sequence, they become automatic, they are executed without
volition and with a minimum of attention. Motor memory ac-
cumulates and conserves the many skills which every man or animal
needs for everyday life. Walking, talking, writing, reading, using
tools are different manifestations of motor memory. Many forms of
animal training and learning by animals come under this heading.

Mental memory stores its acquisitions in the form of knowledge,
consisting in memory images, ideas, judgments or conclusions. This
kind of memory frequently operates in conjunction with motor
memory. Thus when we have memorized a poem or a song, the
vocal movements may have become automatic (motor memory)
and we remember the ideational content (mental memory). When,
on the other hand, we simply remember the content of a poem or
of a lecture, only mental memory is involved.

Pure memory is the result of the spontaneous inscription in our
mind of some event we have experienced. This kind of memory just
"remembers," whereas motor memory "learns how to" and mental
memory "memorizes." Suppose you learn a poem by heart. You
read it several times, and after a few repetitions you are able to
recite the strophes. This entails the function of motor memory for
the vocal movements and mental memory for the ideas of the poem.

But your pure memory has been at work too. Through it you remember that you started studying that poem after hearing it on the radio, that you read it a couple of times while you were sitting at your table, that the two last readings were done while you walked in the garden. No effort has been required to remember these details. They were at once inscribed in your memory as experience, they have become a part of your private past. Compared with the two other kinds of memory, this one has a personal, concrete, living character, because it concerns events in your own history, because it conserves the stuff of which your own concrete duration is made.

Owing to this kind of memory, everything we do or feel or decide or experience becomes in a certain sense part of our own past, of our empirical personality. To a certain extent we are what we have done: there is a cumulative pressure of the past around the core of our personality. We are, and we shall always remain, the one who has done this, omitted that, suffered this or that pain and enjoyed this or that pleasure.

This kind of memory, which has been neglected by experimental psychology, is strongly emphasized by clinical psychology in the techniques of the case history and anamnesis. It is very important in the development of personality, and we shall mention it again when we treat that topic.

Do animals possess such a thing as pure memory? They do, because the animal also is, to a certain extent, the product of its own past. A dog which was treated kindly as a puppy will be different from another dog which was treated harshly at that stage. However, animals cannot remember these facts of their own past distinctly and explicitly. Human beings can; they are able to relive their own history in their memory.

Another important distinction is that between sense memory and logical memory. Sense memory recalls concrete events and individual objects; it does not recognize the past explicitly as past. Logical memory recalls abstract contents and recognizes the past as past.

Sense memory does not recognize the past as past. An animal has no explicit idea of the past. How, then, does an animal recognize something? How, for instance, does a dog recognize his master? Owing to the fact that the master produces in him a feeling of familiarity which consists, according to Bergson, in "the animal's consciousness of a certain special attitude adopted by his body, an attitude which has been gradually built up by his familiar relations with his master, and which the mere perception of his master now calls forth in him mechanically."[19]

This kind of sense memory is also part of man's equipment, but it usually operates in conjunction with intellectual memory, i.e. an explicit recognition of the past as past. Because intellectual memory is more distinct, we do not pay much attention to sense memory. Nevertheless, we can experience the operation of sense memory as such on occasion—e.g., when we recognize one tool among several others just by its "feel," or proceed along a complicated but familiar route without adverting to the directions we are taking.

The word "reminiscence" is used with differing meanings by the Scholastics and modern psychologists. For modern psychologists it refers to the fact that, during a short period after learning, memory traces may increase in strength instead of weakening. Thus a subject who has learned 100 Russian words may be able to recall 80 of them in an immediate test. Next morning, without any further study, he tries again to reproduce the words and is able to recall 85 of them. Overnight the memory traces, instead of diminishing, have grown in strength. This is reminiscence in the modern sense of the word.

For the Schoolmen reminiscence consists in the voluntary recall of past memories. Only man is able to reminisce in that sense. He has a general idea, a "dynamic scheme," of what he is looking for, and he probes his memory for it. He may find it right away or he may be unable to discover it during his search. But later on it may arise spontaneously, as if the efforts made to find it had prepared it for discovery.

In this connection we must say a few words about the important question of the "transfer of training," which has been investigated especially in the sphere of memory. The problem can be stated as follows: when we train a function such as memory in a certain

[19] H. Bergson, *Matter and Memory* (New York, Macmillan, 1911), p. 93.

field—e.g., by memorizing poetry—are the effects of that training transferred to other memory domains—e.g., the memorizing of dates or names—or are the effects strictly confined to the specific sphere in which the training occurred? The importance of this issue becomes immediately apparent if we apply it to human intelligence and ask, for example: Does the study of classical languages produce an over-all development of the intelligence, or does it only make the mind fitter for the study of classical language? Does the study of mathematics develop a general aptitude for exact reasoning in all fields or are its effects restricted to the field of mathematics?

Until the advent of experimental psychology the prevailing opinion was that such transfer of training took place, and this view was one of the arguments in favor of Liberal Arts education.[20]

Experimental psychologists have devoted much effort to the investigation of this important problem. The first results gave no support to the theory of the transfer of training. The experiments showed that exercising a function in a specific task strengthened the function only for that task and did not affect it so far as other fields of endeavor were concerned. Only when identical elements were involved in two tasks would there be any transfer. Thus training in addition would improve aptitude for multiplication, because every multiplication contains an addition; multiplication and addition possess identical elements.

This extreme position, denying all real transfer of training, is no longer held by many psychologists. They admit that there is no purely formal development of a function, that a faculty cannot be developed like a muscle. But they add that certain general attitudes and attainments acquired through mental work—application, methods, procedures, motivation, ideals—can be and are transferred from one domain to another. Concretely this means that whereas merely studying Latin will not produce a general development of the mind, if this study helps a student to acquire habits of accuracy, careful analysis, comprehension, and synthesis, these attitudes or procedures may be transferred to other domains.

[20] We say: *one* of the arguments, because other arguments can be adduced in favor of that kind of education which are in no way affected by the present discussion.

In conclusion two practical suggestions can be made with regard to memory work. Generally speaking, spaced memorizing is better than massed memorizing, and global memorizing is superior to part memorizing.

Memorizing is spaced when the memory effort is made in short periods, interspersed with periods of rest. Massed memorizing means that the work is continued without interruption until the whole "lesson" is learned. When we set ourselves to learn 100 words of a foreign language, or 100 verses, progress will be faster and retention more certain if the effect is distributed over four half-hour periods than if two solid hours are spent in study. The same principle applies to the acquisition of new skills, such as playing the piano or typing.

Global memorizing is the method of taking the thing that must be memorized as a whole, instead of dividing it into parts to be memorized separately. It is generally better to study a poem of 100 verses, or a speech, as a whole than to master one strophe or one paragraph at a time. This is especially true of meaningful materials and with adult learners, who are not discouraged if no notable progress is made quickly.[21]

[21] Readings: cf. p. 161.

8

Affective Functions

ON THE SENSE level we may distinguish two kinds of affective phenomena: feelings and emotions.

FEELINGS

Feelings are elementary affective states which cannot be further analyzed. Psychologists are generally agreed that the elementary feelings can be reduced to only two: pleasantness and unpleasantness, or pleasure and pain (although the word pain is often restricted to a specific kind of unpleasant sensation).

Experience seems to indicate that there are more than two elementary feelings. Thus we speak of feelings of sadness, tiredness or depression. Strictly speaking, however, sadness is an emotion, tiredness is a visceral or organic sensation, depression may be either an emotion or a visceral sensation. The distinction between these phenomena is often difficult to make.

Our affective life is said to have dimensions, since the affective states vary between two extremes. Pleasantness has all the gradations between mild and intense, and so has unpleasantness. We pass along this scale from the extreme of one to that of the other. Therefore there must be some neutral point at which we experience neither feeling, although this is of rare occurrence in our psychic life.

Feelings scarcely ever occur in isolation. They are generally elements in a complex whole. We have already emphasized the affective character of many of our sensations (taste, smell, pain, visceral sensations). Ideas, drives, decisions can be felt as pleasant or un-

145

pleasant. It is only by abstraction and for greater clearness that we distinguish feelings as a group of mental states.

Some authors claim that an affective state must always be preceded by an act of knowledge: i.e., *something* must be felt pleasant or unpleasant. Generally speaking, it is indeed true that feelings develop in us because we have become aware of something that pleases or displeases us. Yet the same feelings may be produced by physiological causes of which we are not aware and which can hardly be identified with any cognitive process. We may have a pleasant or unpleasant feeling without knowing why. There are, of course, causes for these feelings, but they are either merely physiological or unconscious.

It frequently happens that in such cases we project our feeling on to external circumstances or people in our environment, as if we were looking for some reasonable justification for feeling the way we do. For instance, we may have an unpleasant feeling deriving from purely physiological causes, but we explain it by remarking that some person or persons are very disagreeable today. We believe that we feel out of sorts because people are disagreeable, whereas the fact is that people seem disagreeable only because we aren't feeling well.

EMOTIONS

Affective states of greater intensity and shorter duration are called emotions. The main emotions are: anger, fear, joy and sadness.

Emotions are always accompanied by typical physiological reactions. This has been known from antiquity. The ancients placed the seat of the emotions in the heart or in the viscera. We know now that the physiological modifications which accompany the emotions are under the direct control of the autonomic nervous system and the indirect control of the midbrain, especially of the thalamus. Under the influence of these agencies the activities of the stomach slow down, the beating of the heart accelerates, glucose is poured into the blood. The organism is keyed up and ready for an emergency.

In the ordinary theory of the emotions the sequence of development is described as follows. We become aware of some stimulus (frightening, saddening, provoking), and this produces in us the typical psychological state known as an emotion (fear, sadness, anger). As a result of this emotion the physiological modifications described above exert their effects throughout the body.

This classic theory of the emotions has been sharply challenged by two psychologists, James and Lange. They claimed that the physiological modifications precede the conscious emotion, that they are directly produced by the stimulus and the emotion is nothing but the awareness of these modifications. We see a bear coming towards us, we begin to tremble, and because we tremble we feel afraid. Such is the gist of the James-Lange theory of the emotions.

This theory is generally rejected by psychologists, and weighty experimental evidence against it has been presented. Nevertheless it contains its grain of truth. The classic theory overemphasized the distinction between the psychic state of emotion and the physiological modifications. We might perhaps say that these modifications neither follow the emotion, as claimed by the traditional theory, nor precede it, as claimed by James and Lange. Emotion and modification occur simultaneously and are but different aspects of the same reality.

What is the purpose of the emotions? Are they useful or are they mildly pathological phenomena? The question may justly be raised. The useful reaction to danger is the movement of escape, not the trembling and blanching which result from fear. Anger is a disturbing factor in a fight; the angry man will strike powerful but ill-directed blows, and his own defenses will often be down. It is better to fight coldly, without anger.

Several theories concerning the finality of the emotions have been presented. Some authors assert that the emotions are actually psychic disorders, offering in evidence of this claim the disturbances in the motor apparatus (trembling, shaking, clumsiness), in the sensory functions (decrease of acuity), and in the intellectual functions (obnubilation) which accompany strong emotions. Other psychologists, without going to this extreme, admit that an emotion is an abortive form of an instinctive reaction, having somewhat the effect of a short circuit in electricity. When danger threatens one should immediately try to take appropriate action—either mental or physical—to avoid it. If this effort is not made or does not succeed, the purposeful reaction will be displaced by the emotion of fear.

On the other hand, Cannon claims that the emotions themselves are purposeful reactions. He emphasizes the fact that the emotion puts the organism into a state of readiness for emergency. Functions which are not essential to the present exigency—such as digestion—are slowed down or suspended; the acceleration of the heart-beat sends more blood to the muscles; quickened breathing increases the intake of oxygen, and glucose is poured into the bloodstream to provide fresh fuel for energetic movements.

The French psychologist Wallon has presented a hypothesis which reconciles these contradictory theories. In his view an emotion is both useful and harmful; it is useful as long as it is kept under control, harmful when out of control. When an emergency arises, we normally experience emotion. This emotion produces a mobilization of all our powers which enables us to act with extraordinary vigor and dispatch. If we act at once, the emotion abates; it has performed its useful function and may now disappear. If no action occurs, the emotion takes control of our whole system. It floods the body, producing all kinds of disturbing effects. A man who sees a bull bearing down on him feels fear; that fear is said to "give him wings." He should use these "wings" right away to get out of danger. During his flight little or no fear is experienced, he is totally intent on running. But if fear is so strong as to paralyze action, or if some exterior obstacle makes flight impossible, the emotion will take over; the man begins to tremble; he may "lose his head" and be helpless in face of the danger.

Therefore an emotion is useful if it is kept under control and replaced as soon as possible by a reaction, whether instinctive or deliberate, adapted to the circumstances. It is harmful if it is allowed to exert its full influence. Emotional reactions are controlled by the midbrain; in an emergency control should pass from the midbrain to the lower brain centra which control instinctive reactions or to the higher centra which direct conscious adapted behavior.

But if emotional extremes are harmful, why do they occur so

frequently in man? Wallon explains their presence in us as a psychic vestige of the evolutionary process. These emotional seizures served a useful purpose earlier in the development of the race and the individual. In gregarious animals they may still be useful, since they are a powerful means of unifying the herd and making it capable of concerted action, common flight or fight. A strong emotion spreads automatically, by some kind of psychic contagion, from one individual of the herd to another. Where language is lacking, it is the best means of unifying a group. In much the same way a mob of human beings which has lost all intellectual control of its actions is united in rage or panic.

Strong emotions may also be useful in the development of the individual. Before the child's higher functions are active, he cannot adapt his behavior to his needs. A baby who is in pain or is hungry cannot help himself by any purposeful activity. But he manifests a strong emotion of fear, grief or anger which will powerfully influence his mother and thus produce the needed relief.

In other words, strong emotions are useful in man before the higher brain centra are developed. They are no longer useful in the adult because he has better methods of adapting himself to his environment. Their occurrence in adults is a vestige of an earlier stage of development.[1]

EXPRESSION OF THE EMOTIONS

We have already described certain physiological modifications which accompany the emotions. Some of the modifications are visible and serve as external expression of the emotions—for example, trembling, blushing, blanching, sobbing, smiling, laughing, et cetera. Others can be observed only with the aid of special apparatus—e.g., the increase of blood pressure and the psychogalvanic reflex.

Because of their special interest for the philosopher we shall briefly consider two of these expressive movements, the psychogalvanic reflex and laughter.

[1] H. Wallon, *Les Origines du Caractère chez l'Enfant* (Paris, Boivin, 1934).

1. The psychogalvanic reflex (P.G.R.) consists in a lowering of skin resistance to an electric current under the influence of an emotion. It is measured by the pathometer, better known as a "lie-detector."

When a light electric current is sent through a human body by means of two electrodes placed in the subject's hands, great resistance is opposed to it by the organism. But if the subject is suddenly frightened or affected by some other emotion, his resistance decreases and the current passes through more easily. It has been demonstrated that the resistance comes from the skin and that its diminution with the onset of emotion is brought about by the secretion of microscopic drops of sweat on the palms of the hands. The glands which secrete these sweat drops are controlled by the sympathetic division of the autonomic nervous system, which also commands all the other physiological modifications accompanying an emotion. It is a remarkable fact that even when the subject is able to control all other external expressions of his emotion, and even when he does not "feel" any emotion at all, this phenomenon occurs and can be measured. We have here a very sensitive indicator of the slightest activity of the sympathetic nervous system.

Is this activity always accompanied by an emotion? Only if the word "emotion" is taken in a very wide sense. Experimental research has established that the P.G.R. always accompanies an "emergency," be it ever so slight, even if it consists only in an embarrassing or unexpected question. A new event of some kind has taken place to which the subject must make an appropriate response. Therefore, when an innocent suspect is questioned with a lie-detector, his skin resistance will go down. If the questions are repeated several times, they lose their newness, and the P.G.R. wanes and disappears. With the guilty suspect, who lies consistently when answering compromising questions, the emergency persists and so does the P.G.R. Even in such a case, however, a competent psychologist will not affirm that the subject lies, but only that he shows continued signs of emotion, of embarrassment, when a certain question is repeated.[2]

---

[2] Not all pathometers or lie-detectors use the P.G.R. to detect emergency feelings of the organism. Others use changes in blood pressure or in breathing.

The psychogalvanic reflex is interesting for the philosopher because it demonstrates so clearly the intimate interaction between the psychic and the physiological components of the organism.[3]

2. Laughter interests us as philosophers because it is so characteristic of man that Aristotle and the Scholastics called it a "proper accident" of human nature, something which occurs in all men and only in men, and which can therefore be considered to be a distinguishing feature of the human being.

First, a few words about the related phenomenon of smiling. Many muscles of the face are involved in smiling, not only the muscles of the mouth, but also those of the cheeks, the nose, the eyelids, the forehead—all the facial muscles except those of the chin.

Smiling is generally the manifestation of a feeling of joy, well-being, or euphoria. Such a feeling produces a slight stimulation which is expressed by the most mobile muscles of the organism. The muscles involved will be those which contract easily, which have no heavy parts to move and which are synergic—that is, which work naturally together. In man these muscles are the muscles of the face. In animals they may be located elsewhere. Thus a dog shows the slight stimulation produced by joy or euphoria by contracting the most mobile muscles of his body, which happen to be located in his tail. A dog smiles with his tail.

In man smiling may arise from physiological or psychological causes. The physiological causes consist in organic euphoria, such as may be produced by a good meal or a feeling of health or energy. That kind of smile appears very early in the baby. The psychological causes usually involve some mild amusement or some agreeable sentiment, such as approval or benevolence. The resulting smile is typically human and supposes a certain development of the higher functions.

Physiologically, laughter is more complex than smiling. The contraction of the facial muscles is more intense. There is contraction of the internal intercostal muscles resulting in the convulsive expiration interrupted by inspiration which is so characteristic in laughter. Furthermore the sides of the glottis contract, causing the vocal

---

[3] Cf. W. Summers, S. J., "Science Can Get the Confession," *Fordham Law Review*, 8 (1939), pp. 334-354.

phenomena in laughter. In violent laughter, many more muscles of the body may be involved.

Laughter, like smiling, may be produced by physiological and psychological causes. The mechanism of these two kinds of laughter is the same but their meaning is quite different. The first is the result of a feeling of bodily well-being; the second is generally caused by the perception of something funny.

Why does the perception of something funny contract the muscles of the face, the ribs and the glottis? Why is it that it can, in some cases, shake the whole human body? This fact is best explained by the theory which attributes laughter to a sudden release of tension. As we await the outcome of a funny situation or listen to the telling of an amusing story, a certain amount of suspense or tension is usually built up, which is then suddenly released. The body gets rid of that tension by the muscular contractions which laughter provokes. However, this theory does not explain all instances of laughter.

9

Appetitive Functions

IN THIS chapter we shall consider first the inborn sensory tendencies of man, then his acquired sensory tendencies, or habits. This distinction between innate and acquired tendencies is clear enough on paper but very difficult to maintain in practice, since man has in fact no tendencies which are totally inborn, yet every one of his acquired tendencies is based upon innate elements. A further difficulty derives from the fact that in the sphere of the tendencies, as in man's whole mental life, there is an intimate connection between the sensory and intellectual levels. Finally, in this same sphere, the existing terminology is so abundant and so ill-defined that there is danger of considerable confusion among the various synonyms used in everyday language to designate human tendencies.

What is the relation between terms such as tendency, striving, appetite, inclination, drive, impulse, need, passion and instinct—to mention only a few? Very roughly, we may suggest the following distinctions. Appetite will be used as a technical term of the widest meaning to designate all mental processes through which we strive towards some good or pleasure or try to avoid some evil or pain. The words "tendency" and "striving" may be considered everyday equivalents of "appetite." An "inclination" is a relatively weak, a "drive" is a strong, form of tendency. An "impulse" is a tendency to act. A "need" is a tendency produced by the conscious lack of something. A "passion" is a powerful and lasting tendency deeply rooted in the mind and associated with strong feelings or sentiments. Finally, an "instinct" is a tendency which is inborn and present in all the individuals of a species.

INBORN SENSORY DRIVES OF MAN

In ordinary speech inborn sensory drives are called instincts. But does man actually have any instincts? This question has been

153

vigorously debated for the last half-century. Before the study of experimental psychology began, the use of the term instinct was ordinarily reserved for animals, and man was considered to have no instincts, although an exception was usually made with respect to the sex instinct. William James, in reaction against this position, claimed that man possessed several real instincts. He was followed by William McDougall, whose very popular *Introduction to Social Psychology* was based in great part on the concept of human instincts. With the advent of Behaviorism another reaction set in which went all the way to the opposite extreme, at least among experimental psychologists. Many of them asserted that there were absolutely no instincts in man and some tried to eliminate the concept of instinct even from the study of animals. The Behaviorists claimed that all tendencies were learned, derived from experience and molded by environment. However, one important school of psychologists resisted this anti-instinctivist trend; in the psychoanalytic school and the systems derived from it, the concept of instinct has never been relinquished. The sex instinct and—of later date—the aggressive instinct are essential features of the Freudian system.

At present a new trend is taking shape in psychology which reconciles the divergences between the older and more recent psychologists and correlates the theories of experimental and clinical psychology. Experimental psychologists have come to admit more of an inborn element in human drives, and clinical psychologists are paying greater attention to the influences of learning and environment.

The present theory may be summarized as follows. Man possesses a certain number of inborn tendencies. However, these tendencies are considerably modified by experience and learning. Real instincts, ready to enter into action from the moment of the individual's birth, are found only in lower animals. In the higher animals and especially in man the instinctive tendencies are molded to a great extent by influences from the environment.

With these restrictions many of the ideas of McDougall may be adopted, and they have, in fact, been taken up again by some modern psychologists.[1] McDougall distinguished three aspects in

[1] Cfr. R. B. Cattell, *Personality* (New York, McGraw, 1950), ch. 7.

every instinct: a cognitive aspect, which explains why the individual pays attention to certain objects in the environment; an affective aspect, which produces in him a certain feeling in the presence of such an object; an appetitive or active aspect, which causes him to perform certain movements aimed at that object.

In the study of animal instinct, only the first and last aspects are emphasized, the intuitive knowledge of the animal and its complex activities in certain specialized domains. We have no means of knowing how the animal feels while under the influence of its instinct, but when there is question of human drives,[2] the affective aspect may be observed by means of introspection. McDougall claims that this affective component is the most reliable clue to the presence of a drive. The other two components may be considerably modified by experience. Consider, for instance, the aggressive drive and the corresponding emotion of anger. The cognitive aspect of that drive may be modified by learning: a baby becomes angry if you pin his arms against his body; an adult becomes angry when he hears that taxes are going up. The active aspect of the same drive has been modified too: the baby sets up a powerful howling; the adult votes against the party in power. Both the baby and the adult feel angry; the affective aspect of the drive has remained unchanged.

McDougall distinguished the following human drives with their corresponding emotion:

Drive	Emotion
Escape	Fear
Combat	Anger
Repulsion	Disgust
Parental	Tenderness
Mating	Lust
Curiosity	Wonder
Submission	Subjection
Assertion	Elation

McDougall recognized more than these eight unlearned drives in man. The other drives are not listed in this table either because

[2] Where McDougall speaks of instincts we shall speak of drives, in order to emphasize more than he did the acquired features of our tendencies.

there are no emotions corresponding to them or because the corresponding emotions are too undefined to be designated by specific names.

Instead of mentioning the other drives enumerated by McDougall, we shall here transcribe the more complete table given by R. B. Cattell and derived from the work of McDougall and other psychologists who have studied this complex field. Cattell warns us that his list is preliminary, or tentative:

I. Organic Needs:
   To seek air; to avoid physical pain, heat, cold; to seek water; to urinate and defecate.
II. Propensities which are organic, viscerogenic. . . .
   1. (a) To seek stimulation, exercise, activity, when well rested.
      (b) To play.
   2. To avoid stimulation, lie down, sleep, and rest when tired.
   3. To seek food. This may be functionally connected with storing food, with restless wandering (as in the herbivorous animals) or with hunting readiness (as in carnivorous).
   4. To court and mate (sex drive).
   5. To feed, protect, and shelter the young.
   6. To reject and avoid noxious substances.
III. Propensities showing no clear organic rhythm. . . .
   7. To escape from violent impressions by
      (a) flight.
      (b) "freezing" to the spot.
   8. To defer, obey, abase oneself in the presence of superiority and dominance behavior in others.
   9. To appeal, cry aloud and seek help when utterly baffled.
   10. To acquire, collect, possess, and defend whatever is found useful or attractive.
   11. To explore strange places and things or manipulate and pull to pieces strange objects.
   12. To remain in or seek the company of one's fellows.
      With this go the functionally related tendencies

> (a) to assume, by primitive sympathy, the feelings of the group;
>
> (b) to evoke emotional responses from others; and
>
> (c) to imitate.
>
> 13. To assert oneself, achieve, domineer, lead, display oneself.
> 14. To resent resistance to the expression of any propensity; to attack and destroy such resistance.
> 15. To laugh and destroy tension in certain tension-provoking situations.
> 16. (Questionable) To construct shelter and implements.[3]

The question may be raised: How are we certain that these are real inborn drives, and not just tendencies acquired under the influences of education and environment? To make sure that his instincts were really inborn, McDougall used mainly two criteria: (1) they must be found in animals as well as in man—at least, in the higher animals; (2) they must sometimes assume pathological forms. McDougall had no difficulty in demonstrating, for instance, that the instinct of escape operates in all animals and that in man it sometimes assumes the pathological form of one of the various phobias.

That these various drives, although primarily inborn, need environmental influences to complete their development is demonstrated by the fact that a few of them may be entirely lacking in some individuals, and even (if we are to believe the reports of ethnologists) in entire tribes. Thus we have all encountered people who seem to lack the parental or the acquisitive drive, and some ethnologists have reported the discovery of primitive tribes among whom the fighting drive seems to be nonexistent. There is no question of the absence in these individuals or tribes of the innate core of such drives. Environmental factors have prevented the development of these propensities. A different environment would have evoked the same fundamental drives as are seen in the average human person.

[3] Cattell, *Personality*, pp. 180-181.

HABITS IN MAN

A habit can be defined as a disposition to act in a uniform and easy way in certain circumstances. Before we study human habits, it is imperative to make a few distinctions. Much confusion obscures this topic because the necessary distinctions are not made and properties are attributed to all habits which belong only to certain kinds of habits.

We can distinguish at least four kinds of habits: physiological, motor, psychological and moral. In this chapter we shall not consider the last-mentioned. Moral habits are habits of a free will and will be considered when we study that faculty.

A physiological habit is a habit developed by the body. It would be more precise to call it a "habituation," since it occurs when the body becomes accustomed, or habituated to, say, a certain climate or a certain altitude, or to smoking. Such habits produce a facility in the body for performing the action corresponding to them and also a real need for the repetition of that action. The first cigarettes are usually disagreeable and may make the smoker sick. He smokes them for extrinsic reasons—in order to act like a grown-up or because everybody else smokes. Gradually, however, the body gets used to this mild drug and develops a need for it.

Motor habits are skills. They consist in a complex organization of movements which, through practice, have become easy, smooth and well-adapted. Thus we have all acquired the habits of walking, talking, writing and reading. We may acquire the habits of typing, playing the piano or the violin, driving a car, playing tennis or golf. Such habits make the corresponding actions easier to perform, but they do not of themselves induce any need for the repetition of those actions. A professional typist feels no need for typing, a taxi-driver develops no addiction to driving his cab.

Motor habits *in the making* are usually enjoyed for their own sake; they produce a need for repeating the corresponding action. A child learning how to walk enjoys walking for walking's sake. A new driver loves to drive. Some motor habits are never entirely mastered and may be exercised with pleasure for a very long time, e.g. playing tennis or golf. As long as we meet opponents who are not too easy to beat, these skills will be enjoyed for their own sake, but to play tennis or golf with an inferior opponent is not pleasurable, since we have sufficiently mastered the habit to defeat him with great ease. On the other hand, a well-mastered skill may be pleasurable as a means to an end. The "cabbie" who hates to drive through the streets of New York may enjoy a drive in the country with his family.

Under the label "psychological habits" we have put the vast collection of habits which are neither physiological nor motor nor moral. To this group belong such habits as rising early, brushing one's teeth, taking a nap, reading the paper, avoiding drafts, watching television; workmanship, thrift and orderliness.

The characteristic feature of the perfected motor habit is the ease and smoothness with which rather complicated actions or movements are performed. There is nothing of this nature in the psychological habit; it takes no great skill, requires no long practice, to get out of bed, to watch television or to save money. Skills may be involved in these habits (e.g., in reading the paper), but they are only tools used by the habit, they do not constitute the habit itself. The typical feature of this group of habits consists in a certain need for repetition which they bring with them. I feel unhappy or restless if I did not rise early, or if I cannot read the paper right after breakfast, or if everything is not orderly in my room. Psychological habits may therefore be considered *acquired* needs, as opposed to the inborn needs mentioned in the previous chapter.

All these psychological habits do not originate in the same way, and they are not kept alive by the same forces.

In some cases, the need is predominantly inborn but the way of satisfying it has been learned. Curiosity is an inborn need, and therefore every normal person likes to hear news. One way of satisfying that need is to read the paper. But why do we insist on reading the paper at a certain time, in a certain place? Why do we feel that something is wrong with our day if we did not have the paper right after breakfast? This habit requires another explanation. Man is a spirit in matter. Because of his material component he is unable to be unintermittently spontaneous and creative in his actions; the continuous effort of attention required would tax his mental energies. He will wisely reserve his attention for special situations in which it is needed. As for unimportant daily actions, he will allow himself to glide slowly into a certain routine which frees him of the duty of continual reflection and deliberation. This routine is felt as satisfactory, it runs very smoothly, a growing need arises to leave it undisturbed. Reading the paper right after breakfast is part of that routine, it is a daily rite. We naturally look forward to it, and it is not surprising that a certain amount of displeasure is felt if circumstances make that daily rite impossible.

Then there are habits in which the need itself, not just the manner of satisfying it, has been acquired. A certain course of action has been frequently repeated under the influence of social pressure or some other extrinsic factor. That action produces useful results which are increasingly appreciated by the individual. Let the social pressure or the other extrinsic factor then disappear, and the individual will continue with the same action because of the advantages he derives from it. In this event, what was first a means to reach a certain end, e.g. parental or social approval, has become the means of reaching some other personal end. Thus a boy may have learned to rise very early each morning because his parents wanted him to. Rising early was a means of obtaining parental approval. Slowly he came to recognize the many advantages of this course of action. His parents are no longer with him, but he rises before the sun. He has acquired the habit of rising early.

Of like kind are habits in which a certain action, having long been used as a means to an end, has become an end in itself. Take, for example, the habit of thrift. We presume that it is not exercised for moral reasons but is merely a psychological habit, that the thrifty person is unable to explain why he parts so reluctantly with even small amounts of money. To explain such a habit, G. W. Allport introduced the notion of "functional autonomy."[4] Thrift may have been useful or necessary to such an individual during his first years of earning his living. Now he has become a very wealthy man, yet he remains so thrifty that some people call him a miser. The habit was acquired as a conscious means to an end. It has now become an end in itself, it is autonomous.

[4] *Personality* (New York. Holt. 1937). ch. 7.

A final remark to close this chapter. Although we have distinguished various ways in which a habit may originate and be kept alive, few habits can be confined entirely to any single category. Several influences are usually at work in a habit. Thus, to return to our example of the early riser: his habit has been explained as a psychological habit; yet it is undeniable that a physiological habit is also involved—the body has become accustomed to a certain rhythm of retiring and rising, to the extent that the young man may spontaneously awaken around his usual time of rising and find it rather difficult to go to sleep again. This physiological component is a powerful adjuvant of the psychological habit.

READINGS

Bugelski, *A First Course in Experimental Psychology*. Gannon, *Psychology: The Unity of Human Behavior*. Harmon, *Principles of Psychology*. Hilgard, *Introduction to Psychology*. Krech and Crutchfield, *Elements of Psychology*. Morgan, *Introduction to Psychology*. Munn, *Psychology*. Ruch, *Psychology and Life*. Schneiders, *Introductory Psychology*. Walters and O'Hara, *Persons and Personality*. Wickens and Meyer, *Psychology*.

SECTION II

Philosophical Study of Man's Sense Life

10

Cognitive Faculties

BEFORE WE study the cognitive faculties in detail, we must know something about knowledge in general.

KNOWLEDGE IN GENERAL

Knowledge is one of the greatest mysteries confronting the human mind in the natural order. The phenomenon of knowledge is so common, so continually with us, that we do not realize how mysterious it really is. It is the task of the philosopher to wonder at those elementary mysteries which habit makes inconspicuous.

Take a simple act of knowledge, I see a tree before me, and I affirm: This is a tree. A simple act of knowledge. Yet how difficult to understand and to explain! From the physical tree are reflected light waves which affect my retina, produce in it chemical transformations which provoke physiological modifications in the optical nerve and the optical brain center. And then, suddenly, the mysterious thing happens: I *know* that tree, I *become aware* of that tree. How the passage from the ultimate physiological modifications in my brain to the act of awareness and of knowledge occurs, nobody has ever been able to explain. Between these material modifications and the immaterial act of knowledge there is an abyss, and our act of knowledge somehow bridges that abyss. This is one aspect of the great problem of the relation between matter and mind, between body and soul. We know that there is a relation between them, but how it operates we cannot understand. We stand before a real mystery: How is knowledge possible?

Yet if we look at reality from another point of view, the problem changes entirely; the question becomes: How is it possible that some beings do not know, are not conscious? This way of putting the question may bring us nearer to an understanding of knowledge.

If we try to understand what being really is, we shall realize that it consists fundamentally in consciousness, in an "active identification with oneself." To be is to be conscious, to identify oneself with oneself. Where do I come into contact with being in the most perfect way? In my own being. If I reflect on my own being, on that fundamental, inescapable truth "I am," I notice that it means "I am myself, I am conscious of myself, I will myself." Each of these expressions points towards a duality—I, myself—and an identification of this duality: I know myself, I will myself, I am conscious of myself.[1]

In God this identification is infinitely more perfect. It is not only an active identification, but an active identity. One way of conceiving God is for us to think of Him as an Infinite Intelligence which knows Itself in an infinitely perfect way, or as an Infinite Will loving Itself in an infinitely perfect manner. In God too there is active Self-Identification (God knows Himself, God wills Himself)—or rather, God is Active Self-Identity. For an identification supposes a previous stage at which the two elements were not identical, and this never occurs in God. In fact, between the elements which are identified there is in God no distinction.

We have already indicated some of the differences between God's Infinite Self-Knowledge and our own finite, imperfect self-knowl-

[1] "Consciousness understood in its widest possible meaning is a possession of oneself in oneself, an immanence of all that which we are in all that which we are, a perfect identity of being with itself, a manner of being which makes us exist in ourselves and for ourselves, so that we are not for ourselves as if we were not, in a word a manner of fully existing.

"The notion of consciousness coincides with the notion of being. Being is knowable and known insofar as it is in act. Hence to be conscious is to be. But it is to be so thoroughly that one is oneself for oneself, that one possesses one's own being by and in oneself merely by being. Non-conscious beings do not know themselves, and they remain shut off from themselves and strangers to themselves." E. Mersch, S. J., *La Théologie du Corps Mystique* (Brussels, L'Edition Universelle, 1946), Vol. I, p. 94. (Our translation.)

Father Karl Rahner, S. J., also emphatically insists on this point, which is one of the main themes of his remarkable study *Geist in Welt*. "Knowledge is the self-presence of being (*Erkennen ist Beisichsein des Seins*), and this self-presence is the *being* of that which is" (2d ed., München, Kösel, 1957, p. 82).

edge. We know ourselves explicitly only at times, God knows Himself continually. We know ourselves only imperfectly; God knows Himself perfectly. We know ourselves only after having first known something else; God knows Himself at once, eternally, without any need of an object distinct from Himself. He does not become Self-Knowing (that is the error of pantheism), He is Self-Knowledge.

Therefore we can say that to be is to be present to oneself, to be conscious of oneself, to know and to will oneself, to identify oneself actively with oneself, to return to one's own essence.[2] This is just a more psychological way of repeating the truths established in Ontology, that being is one, is true and good.

But since every being is one, true and good inasmuch as it is being, it would seem that every being should be conscious of itself, should know and will itself. The principle of proportionality or of analogy affirms that there is indeed, even in the lowest beings, in minerals and plants, something which is to their essence what consciousness, knowledge and love are to the essence of spiritual beings. We do not claim, however, that there is real knowledge or consciousness in minerals and plants.[3]

Why is there no knowledge or consciousness in minerals and plants? Because they are too material. Consciousness and being vary together. Hence the more being is extenuated, the weaker consciousness becomes. But matter is precisely that which limits or extenuates being. It follows that the perfection of a being's knowledge is measured by the degree of that being's immateriality.

God is entirely immaterial and contains no potency whatsoever: therefore His knowledge is infinitely perfect. A mineral is entirely material, its form is immersed in matter; therefore there is no knowledge in a mineral. In a plant the form emerges somewhat from matter, but the plant's immateriality is too slight to allow of any real knowledge. Yet there is in the plant something which foreshadows knowledge, a beginning of active self-identification—the plant's immanent, self-perfective activities, its intrinsic finality.

[2] "To return to its own essence means only that a being subsists in itself." *S. Theol.*, I, 14, 2, ad 1.

[3] Notice, however, that our philosophy, which denies the presence of knowledge in plants and minerals, maintains that plants and minerals possess a "natural appetite."

However, it is only with reference to the animal that we begin to speak of real knowledge. Here the form emerges still further from matter, and some knowledge is possible. But this knowledge is imperfect, because the animal's degree of immateriality is still insufficient. An animal knows objects, but it does not know itself. Its being is too material to make possible self-possession, self-consciousness or self-knowledge. Only in man does the form emerge sufficiently from matter to make that self-knowledge possible. But that self-knowledge is still imperfect because of the element of materiality in man.

Knowledge is something very mysterious when we look at it from the scientific point of view. When we look at it from the central point of view of metaphysics it is not mysterious. Knowledge goes with being and the real mystery is: How is it possible that some beings do not know?

We must immediately add another fundamental principle. Each being is "knowable," or "cognoscible," insofar as it is immaterial. The degree of a being's immateriality determines not only its degree of knowledge, but also its degree of knowability. The most knowable being is God, the least knowable being is the mineral—or rather, prime matter, which is not knowable at all in itself, but only "co-knowable." Many people do not admit this. For them it is much easier to know minerals than to know God; they claim that the more material a being is, the better we can know it.

That is partially—or accidentally—true. But it derives from the imperfection of our intelligence, not from any lack of cognoscibility in God. If our intelligence were perfect, no being would approach God in cognoscibility. The more luminous an object is, the better our eye can see it. Yet the sun, the most luminous of objects, is not a fitting object for our eyes, not because it is not visible but because it is too visible, because our eyes are too weak to look at it. God is in the world of intelligible reality what the sun is in the world of visible reality. No being is more intelligible than God because no being is further removed from matter than God. As for our vaunted knowledge of the material world, metaphysically speaking that knowledge is very inadequate. We know a lot "about matter," but we "know matter" hardly at all.

Continuing our study of knowledge in general, we discover another fundamental principle: "The more perfect knowledge is, the more it comes from within," and vice versa, "The more knowledge comes from within, the more perfect it is."

At first sight this statement seems to be false. We have the impression that real knowledge comes from without, from a close examination of its object. Subjective knowledge is considered unreliable. So far as our imperfect human knowledge is concerned, that is very often true. But even with respect to human knowledge it is not always true. Nobody knows a bridge or a ship better than its designer. He does not have to look at it, or to read about it: he knows it in himself, where he first conceived it in his mind.

But our principle applies especially to God's infinitely perfect knowledge. God knows everything perfectly without ever having to "look outside Himself." He knows all reality *in* Himself. God does not look at me in order to know what I am and what I do. He knows all this in Himself, without experiencing any influence from outside. Yet, although His knowledge is entirely from within, it is absolutely perfect, sure and infallible. We should even say that because His knowledge is from within it is perfect and absolutely certain. All knowledge which really comes from within a faculty shares in this certitude.

If we go down one step in the scale of beings, we see that in angels also all knowledge comes from within.[4] Angels are not passive in relation to exterior reality, they know it by means of ideas which they have received directly from God. A pure spirit knows the universe not because he sees it or has studied it, but because he finds, in his own intelligence, a perfect picture of it. You may know the whole structure of a great mansion without ever having been near it, if its architect gives you a blueprint of it. God, the architect of the universe, has imprinted in the mind of the angels a blueprint of reality. This knowledge is absolutely certain and reliable, because it comes from the Creator of reality.

Quite naturally, then, the question arises: Is there anything similar in us? Are there in human knowledge any elements coming from within? It would be most surprising if there were no such ele-

[4] Philosophy can strictly demonstrate that *if* there are pure spirits, all their knowledge must come from within, must be a priori.

ments. In God, the Infinite Spirit, all knowledge is from within. In the angels, finite spirits, all knowledge is from within, although it derives ultimately from God. That in man, finite spirit in matter, all knowledge should come from without seems entirely impossible. In that case man would not be a spirit. There must be in us some element whereby our knowledge resembles, although in a humbler degree, the knowledge of the pure spirits. Knowledge which was derived entirely from without would not in any respect resemble angelic knowledge. And in such an event it would no longer be true that "the highest aspects of a lower being resemble the lowest aspects of a higher being."

On the other hand, experience tells us and traditional philosophy teaches that "there is nothing in the intellect which has not first been in the senses." All our knowledge passes through the senses, comes from without.

Thus we arrive at two seemingly contradictory conclusions. On one hand, there must be in our intellectual knowledge some elements coming from within. On the other hand, we maintain that our knowledge comes entirely through the senses, from without.

Both statements are true, and they can be reconciled. In every act of intellectual knowledge there are some elements which come from within and others which come from without. We never have any intellectual knowledge without some contribution from the senses and some contribution from the intellect.

The contribution of the intellect consists in the first principles. These principles are "habitually" present to our intellect. We have a "habitual knowledge" of them (*habitus primorum principiorum*). The certain knowledge which we have of them is inborn to our intellect, comes directly from God, although explicit knowledge concerning them requires some co-operation of the senses. That habitual knowledge of the first principles makes our intellect resemble the angelic intellect. While the angel receives all his knowledge directly from God, we receive directly from Him the virtual or habitual knowledge of the first principles.

Because this essential aspect of St. Thomas's thought is often overlooked, we must mention a few texts which emphasize it.

"For the intellect knows principles naturally, and from such knowledge in man comes the knowledge of conclusions, which are known by him not naturally, but by discovery or by teaching" (*S. Theol.*, I, 60, 2, c).

"Although the knowledge of the human soul is properly by way of reason, yet there is in it some sharing of that simple knowledge which is found in the higher substances" (*Ver.*, 15, 1, c).

"For in every man there is a certain principle of knowledge, namely the light of the agent intellect, through which certain universal principles of all the sciences are naturally understood as soon as proposed to the intellect" (*S. Theol.*, I, 117, 1 c).

"As from the truth of the divine intellect proceed in the angelic intellect the inborn forms of things, according to which the angel knows everything; so from the truth of the divine intellect proceeds in an exemplary way into our intellect the truth of the first principles according to which we judge of everything" (*Ver.*, I, 4, ad 5).

Yet in other passages St. Thomas seems to say just the opposite. Thus, for instance, "Some people have believed that the agent intellect is nothing but the habitual knowledge of the first indemonstrable principles in us. But that is impossible, since we know the first indemonstrable principles themselves through abstraction from the singular" (*De Anima*, 5, c).

Actually there is no contradiction between these statements. St. Thomas means that, even in order to know the first principles, we must first have obtained knowledge of their terms from the senses through abstraction. Thus the principle "Whatever happens has a cause" cannot be understood by us unless from experience, by means of sense knowledge and abstraction, we know what is meant by "happen" and "cause." But as soon as we understand these terms, the principle is evident, and this evidence does not derive from sense experience. We have passed "from experience to the first principles which are known as soon as their terms are understood."

Although we possess these principles naturally, we cannot discover them in our intelligence before, or independently of, any sense experience. But as soon as some object from without enters our intelligence, that faculty impresses upon the object the seal of these principles. Therefore it is in the objects themselves, as known by our intelligence, that we discover them. They seem to come from without although we do really possess them within ourselves.

In this context St. Thomas adopts a remarkable expression first
used by Aristotle. Speaking of the "first principle" he says, "Ad-
venit quasi habenti ipsum"—"It comes from outside to somebody
who, as it were, possesses it already."[5] That is exactly the formula
of a virtual a priori.

A comparison may help us to understand this. When you drive
at night on a highway, the road signs stand out in clear light. That
light seems to come from the signs, although actually it comes
from your own headlights. You may not see the light of your car,
except as reflected on the signs, yet it is the light of your own car.
Thus our intellect sees objects in its own light, the light of the
first principles.[6] That light seems to come from the objects; in reality
it comes from our intellect, and what we see in the object is its
reflection.

These principles are possessed naturally although virtually by the
intellect. But we cannot know them or see them directly in the
intellect itself: the intellect imprints them upon every object entering it, and it is in these objects only that they can be directly studied.
They are the fundamental principles of metaphysics, or Ontology.
This explains the supreme dignity and importance of the science of
metaphysics.

Take the most fundamental of these principles, "Whatever is, is,"
or, in its negative form, "It is impossible for a being to be and not to
be at the same time." We know that principle with absolute certitude.[7] Do we know it from experience? Must we first study a certain
number of objects before we are certain of it? Would it apply likewise in a different universe, with other kinds of possible beings? We
know with absolute certitude that this principle applies always and
everywhere—in the past, in the present, in the future, in this universe or in any possible universe. Such certitude cannot be based on
sense experience.

[5] In *IV Metaph.*, lect. 6.

[6] "Whatever is known intellectually is known as illuminated by the light
of the agent intellect and received into the possible intellect. Therefore,
as in every color we see the material light, so in every intelligible object
we see the light of the agent intellect, not however by way of an object,
but by way of that by which we know the object." In *I Sent.*, d. 3, q. 4,
a. 5. Cf. the commentary of K. Rahner, S. J., in *Geist in Welt*, 2d ed., pp.
226 ff.

[7] In the sense that its denial involves a contradiction.

It should be well understood that we do not claim to possess any inborn *ideas* or *concepts,* not even *virtually* inborn ideas. Every idea supposes an actual co-operation of the senses, comes therefore from without. But we affirm the existence in us of virtually inborn *principles,* of habitual *affirmations,* which we apply spontaneously to the ideas which enter our minds through the senses. Thus I can never get the idea of a tree unless I have some previous sense knowledge of trees. Once, however, I have such an idea, I implicitly affirm of the tree which I know, all the following judgments and many more: This tree is a tree, it cannot not be a tree, it has a sufficient reason and a cause, it is composed of act and potency, it is one and true and good, and so on. These fundamental affirmations are an explicitation of the "habitual knowledge of the first principles."

In this way we have reconciled the two statements: that there are in our intellectual knowledge some a priori elements; that all our knowledge comes from the senses, a posteriori. It is only when the two kinds meet that we have real intellectual knowledge. And we correct the fundamental realistic principle thus: "There is nothing in our intellect which was not first in the senses, except the intellect itself" (Leibniz).

Another question naturally arises. Do we find anything similar in sense knowledge? Does the faculty here too contribute something to knowledge, or does sense knowledge come entirely from without? An entirely passive faculty is inconceivable; knowing is an activity, and only prime matter can receive in a purely passive way. If the faculty is not entirely passive, it contributes its share to the object of knowledge. That share from within will, of course, be less important in sense knowledge than in intellectual knowledge, because the senses are more material, and hence more passive, than the intellect. That share from within consists in the forms of space and time.

This does not mean that we agree with Kant's dictum that space and time are nothing but the a priori forms of our senses. Space and time exist in reality, independently of our mind. But space and time as we imagine them are not exactly like space and time as they exist in objective reality. Our senses invest all objects with a space and a time which correspond rather closely with their objective counterparts, but the correspondence is not necessarily perfect. If we were pure spirits, we should not know space and time as we know them now. It is most probable that animals do not experience space and time in the same way we do.

Hence we must distinguish an imaginary space, which is the a priori form of our external senses, and an objective space, which exists in reality. This explains a certain number of facts.

Metaphysics gives us absolute certitude in the domain of being, and from this we have concluded that metaphysical knowledge is not entirely a posteriori. Geometry gives us hypothetically absolute certitude.[8] We must therefore conclude that it is partly a priori. If we accept Euclid's postulates (and we naturally do), we are absolutely sure that in all triangles the three angles add up to two right angles. This certitude can be explained only if we admit that in geometry we study the necessary laws of our own way of imagining space. Yet we know now that although triangles in reality seem to obey these laws rather well, they do not obey them perfectly. This goes to show that our imaginary space corresponds closely, but not perfectly, with real space.

Imaginary space is neither finite nor infinite. If it existed in reality, it would have to be one or the other. However, it is not an objectively existing reality but the form of a movement. As such it is indefinite, you can go on indefinitely imagining more space. Objective space is finite, but without boundaries.[9] You can imagine that nothing whatsoever exists in space, but you cannot imagine that there is no space, because you cannot use your imagination without projecting your imaginary space. Similar remarks could be made concerning time.

We have seen in the study of Gestalt psychology that it can be shown even experimentally that the perceiving functions contribute something of their own to our perceptions, e.g., the movement in a

---

[8] Hypothetically absolute, because the certitude is based upon our acceptance of the postulates of Euclid. Once we accept these postulates, the whole of geometry follows with absolute necessity.

[9] If this seems difficult to understand, you might try to imagine how baffled creatures which knew only two dimensions would be on hearing that in their two-dimensional space the surface of a sphere is finite, yet without boundaries.

moving picture. It would be surprising if we did not find something similar in our philosophical study of sense knowledge.

From the preceding we see that our system occupies a middle position between the two extremes of empiricism and the theory of innate ideas. The theory of innate ideas maintains that some ideas are actually inborn in the mind and that we can become aware of them independently of any data of the senses. We deny the existence of such inborn ideas. Before sense knowledge there are no ready-made ideas in the mind. All our ideas come from the senses.

Nevertheless our knowledge does not come entirely from the senses. The intellect contributes a share to its formation. Therefore we reject empiricism, which claims that our knowledge comes entirely from sense experience. For the empiricists our intellect is merely passive in knowledge, it is like a wax tablet on which nothing has been written (tabula rasa). Such a system leads logically to scepticism and materialism. Sometimes the Thomistic system is so presented that it is difficult to see wherein it differs from empiricism. This version of Thomism avoids the destructive consequences of empiricism only by evading the conclusions which would logically follow from its own premises.[10] Empiricism is right when it denies the existence of innate ideas; it is wrong when it asserts that our knowledge comes entirely from sense experience.

But does not our own conception lead to subjectivism, does it not give rise to serious doubts about the validity of our ideas? This is a problem of Epistemology which cannot be treated here. It will be enough to remark that anything which is contributed to our knowledge *by the very nature* of a faculty comes directly from the Maker of that faculty, from Truth Itself.

GENERAL THEORY OF THE INTENTIONAL FORM OR IMPRESSION

Knowledge is an immanent action, more perfectly immanent than nutrition, growth and reproduction. It begins and ends within us. It is more perfect than the immanent operations of the plant

[10] See the author's article "A Thomistic Misapprehension?" in *Thought*, 32 (1957), pp. 189-198.

because its effects remain not only within the acting subject, but within the acting faculty of the subject.

Knowledge is immanent, it occurs entirely within the acting faculty. But the object we know is generally exterior to the faculty. How can the act of knowledge take place entirely within the faculty if the object of that knowledge is outside? The object itself must in some measure be present in the faculty. Since it cannot be there in its natural, physical reality, it must be there by means of some representative, some substitute. That is why every act of knowledge requires what we call an "intentional form" or "impression"[11] to make cognition possible.

To understand this better, we may compare a camera taking a picture of a tree with the visual faculty seeing that tree. In both cases the first stages of the process are much alike. Light waves coming from the tree impinge upon the plate of the camera and the retina of the eye respectively. In the operation of our visual faculty, the physical impression proceeds from the retina, through the optical nerve, to the optical brain center. Hence we have in the camera a chemical modification corresponding to the tree, in the visual faculty a physiological modification corresponding to the tree. But there the resemblance ends. The camera does not know the tree, whereas my visual faculty does. Therefore further processes are required in my visual faculty. To the concrete physiological modification in my brain must correspond an invisible mental modification which affects the faculty as such. This is called the "intentional form" or "impression." It is not material in the everyday meaning of that word, it cannot be seen or in any way experienced by the senses. It is a purely mental modification, corresponding to the physiological modification in the brain. It replaces the object in the act of knowledge.

This helps us understand the profound analysis which St. Thomas makes of knowledge in general. For him beings which know are superior to beings which do not know, inasmuch as the knowing being not only possesses its own form, but also the forms of all the objects which it knows.[12]

Every being has a form—or, rather, many forms, one substantial

[11] We prefer this English word to the Latin *species impressa*.
[12] Cfr. *S. Theol.*, I, 14, 1.

form and many accidental forms. These forms have two modes of existence: a natural and an intentional mode of existence. The natural mode of existence refers to the way in which the form exists in the physical object. The intentional mode of existence refers to the way in which the form exists in the faculty which knows the object.

When we know an object, we possess the form of the object, not the natural form but the intentional form. Possessing the form of that object, we become that object, not naturally but intentionally. To know an object is, in a certain sense, to become that object. We become intentionally all that which we know. Knowledge allows us to become everything.

DIFFERENT KINDS OF KNOWLEDGE

The main cognitive operation by which man knows reality is the judgment. Judgment is an act of the intellect by which we affirm or deny something of something. That river is wide. Paul is not big. If we want a more psychological definition we may say that the judgment is the act by which we guarantee the objective value of a subjective state. Every judgment is a complicated act in which many elements can be distinguished. We must first distinguish:

1. The matter of the judgment, which consists in the terms of the judgment considered in themselves as simple concepts. River, wide, are the two terms of our first example; they constitute the matter of that judgment.

2. The form of the judgment, which unites these two concepts and guarantees that they really do belong together.

We shall consider here only the matter of our judgments, the concepts. A concept is materially the same as an idea, a simple apprehension, a notion. It can be defined as the act by which the mind grasps or becomes aware of an object, without affirming or denying anything of it.

In fact, our intellect cannot grasp an object without affirming something of it—at least that it is, or that it is possible. Therefore the judgment is the first act of our intellect, and a new concept is reached only in and through a judgment.[13] Notice how you acquire new concepts. "That is a finch"—"A mastodon is a species of prehistoric elephant." These new concepts come to you in judgments. The judgment is the central act of man's intellectual life from which all others derive.

In every concept we may distinguish intellectual and sense elements. It follows that animals have no concepts, since they have no intellect. When we take away by abstraction the intellectual elements of a concept, that which remains is either a perception or an image.

It is a perception if the object is actually present to one or more of our senses. If the object is not actually present to the senses, we have either a memory image or a pure image: a memory image if we remember having seen or otherwise known the object before; a pure image if we do not remember anything of that kind.

When a dog sees a cat, it has a perception of that cat. A perception is the sensuous cognition of an object in space.

Human beings never have a perception without an idea, at least some vague idea. In us the intellect and the senses always work together. A perception is not the same as a sensation. Generally a perception contains several sensations; furthermore, it is projected into space and completed by a certain number of images supplied by past experience.

If man never has pure perceptions, a fortiori he never has pure sensations. Our sensations are always enveloped in a complex structure. Our senses are never mistaken about their proper object, sensations as such cannot be false. But we may err in our perceptions because memory may supply elements which do not really pertain to the present object.[14]

---

[13] Logically, concepts are prior to judgments; chronologically, both are given together; ontologically, the judgment comes first.

[14] Readings: see pp. 194-195.

THE PHILOSOPHY OF SENSE KNOWLEDGE

THE DIFFERENT STAGES OF SENSATION

In every sensation[15] four stages may be distinguished: the physical, the physiological, the passive psychological and the active psychological stage.

1. The physical stage consists in the action of external forces or stimuli on some sense organ—light waves impinging on the retina, sound waves striking the eardrum, etc. This stage is studied in Physics.

2. The physiological stage consists in the physiological or neurological reaction produced by the physical stimulus in the sense organs, in the nerves running from them to the brain and in the brain itself. When light strikes my eyes, all kinds of physiological reactions occur in my retina, in my optical nerve and in my optical brain center. This stage is studied in Physiology.

3. The passive psychological stage. The previous, physiological stage does not occur merely in the body, as opposed to the soul. The body is an animated body. Inasmuch as the animated *body* is affected, we have physiological phenomena; inasmuch as the *animated* body is affected, we have mental or psychic phenomena. We shall call them, collectively, the passive psychological stage.

This stage consists in some intentional modification of the sense power, corresponding to the physiological modifications occurring in the brain center. The form of the object is impressed upon the senses; not its substantial form, which can only be known by the intellect, but some accidental form, such as color or sound. This form is not physically impressed upon the senses, for that would make them colored or sonorous. But it is intentionally impressed, enabling the faculty to become conscious of these accidental forms of the object.

Can we compare the intentional form to a photograph of the object? Preferably not. The only way the intentional form resembles

[15] Although we shall use the traditional term of sensation throughout this section, much of what we shall say applies also to perception. Sensation is taken here in a wider sense, for every form of external sense knowledge, for sense perception.

a photograph is in that both are effects of the object and make us know it. But a photograph is a permanent effect; once it is printed the object is no longer required. Whereas the intentional form lasts only as long as the object is acting on the sense power. It is the actual impact of the outside object upon my animated body. There is another important difference: when I look at a photograph, I do not see the object itself but its reproduction. Whereas I do not know the intentional form itself (except indirectly, in philosophical reflection), by means of it I perceive, I see, I hear, I feel the object. Therefore the only picture the intentional form can be compared with is the retinal image of an object in my eye. That image too lasts only as long as the object is impinging upon the retina, and the image itself is never seen directly, but by means of it the object is seen. Technically speaking, such pictures are called *formal signs*. The intentional form (the *"species impressa"* or "impression") is a formal sign; it is not that which is perceived but *that by means of which* (*id quo*) we perceive.

4. The active psychological stage. Until this stage we are still without knowledge, or consciousness of the object. If the process of sensation were to stop at the third stage, we should not know anything. We should be ready to know, everything would be in readiness for a perception, but there would be no actual knowledge.[16] When, at the third stage, the "impression" of the object is present within the faculty, the only further requirement for knowledge is light, consciousness. At this fourth, the active psychological stage, there is, as it were, a flash of light, a surge of consciousness, an active turning of the faculty towards the object as it is actively influencing me, and through this I become aware of the object in its impact upon my sense power, I see or hear or touch it.

Therefore this is really the central stage of sensation, for which the other three stages were only a preparation. Every act of knowledge is an immanent operation, an operation which begins and ends within the faculty. Only this fourth stage possesses this immanence. The object of our knowledge must be in us, must in a certain sense have become us, before we can know it.

Chronologically, however, the third and fourth stages are simultaneous. They are the interlocking of a double activity and passiv-

[16] This would be an "unconscious" sensation.

ity. From a certain point of view, emphasized in the third stage, the object is active and the faculty passive. From another point of view, emphasized in the fourth stage, the faculty is active and the object is passive.

WHAT WE KNOW THROUGH OUR SENSATIONS

The Thomistic theory of sense knowledge is profound and difficult. One of the reasons for this difficulty is that we never meet pure sensations in our experience. In man sensation is always accompanied by concepts and judgments. Pure sensations, or rather, pure perceptions, occur in animals, but we do not know how they are experienced by them. Even if we did know we should not be helped much in our investigation, because animal perceptions are quite different from human perceptions.

As the human soul is present in the body, making the body exist and animating it throughout, so the human intellect is present in the senses, making them exist[17] and animating them throughout. A human body without a soul is not a human body; human senses without the intellect are not human senses. Yet we must somehow try to understand the nature and the activities of these senses in themselves, abstracting from all intellectual influence.

In order to understand what we know through our sensations, we shall exclude a few false conceptions which are rather widespread:

1. *Naive realism* holds that the objects enter our senses in somewhat the way that sunlight enters a room when the shades are up. No problem here. Sense knowledge seizes the objects and introduces them to the mind, where they are known as they are in themselves, in their noumenal reality.

The Thomistic position is one of realism, but not realism of this naive sort. The Thomist insists that knowing is an immanent action, which occurs entirely within the subject; that it does not reach out and grasp objects in exterior reality. Knowledge must be preceded by preconscious activities which bring the objects into the subject, making the latter thus capable of knowing them.

Furthermore, our senses do not know objects as objects. To know

[17] *S. Theol.*, I, 77, 7, c.

an object as object, you must know yourself as subject. But the senses are incapable of self-reflection; or, more correctly, man insofar as he possesses sense knowledge does not know himself as subject. Moreover, to know an object as object implies the knowledge of the substantial form of that object; but the senses know only the accidental forms of objects. All this amounts to saying that the senses give us no noumenal knowledge of reality. They do not know objects or their qualities as they are in themselves.

2. *Representative realism* holds that we do not know the objects, but only the impression they make upon us, the representations we have of them. We are aware only of the way in which we are affected by the object. The tree reflects light waves, which produce physiological and psychological modifications in me. Of these modifications, and of them alone, am I aware.

But how then, according to this theory, do we know the things around us? We do not, for example, see trees, or hear the piano, or taste the steak, or touch the kitten; we see pictures of trees, we perceive acoustic images of the piano, gustatory images of the steak and tactile images of the kitten. The upholders of representative realism are willing to admit this. But they immediately add, by way of explanation, that these pictures and images which we perceive resemble the outside objects and that thus we have a real, although indirect, knowledge of them. They are, however, rather embarrassed when asked how they can demonstrate that these pictures and images resemble outside reality. In order to be sure of this resemblance, we should have at least once perceived the originals to compare them with their representations. And that is utterly impossible in this theory: the similarity between originals and images must be dogmatically asserted.

Some proponents of representative realism acknowledge this. They say that we do not know how things external to us look, how they sound and taste, but that we do know there are external objects corresponding to the pictures and impressions we receive. We unconsciously apply the principle of causality, and from the pictures and images we experience, which we ourselves do not produce in our minds, we infer the existence of outside objects which do produce them.

Suppose that we admit as legitimate the use of the principle of causality in this connection. The only thing we know is that some cause is producing these effects in us; we have no idea of the nature of that cause. This theory leads naturally to Berkeley's form of idealism.

One fundamental error in the preceding theories is that they conceive of perception as a kind of telephone message. The objects send off messages which are picked up by the receiving systems of our senses and transmitted over the wires of our nerves to the brain, whence they pass into the mind, there to be read and interpreted.

The difficulty against this explanation is that there are no receiving systems or wires. The sense organs, the nerves, are part of the subject; they are, to some extent, the subject himself; there is no receiving subject distinct from them.[18]

But are there no light vibrations, no sound waves, etc.? And can they not be considered as transmitting a message? That is the way science sees it, and from the scientific point of view these statements are true. But if we want to find out how science knows about these light vibrations and sound waves, we shall ultimately be referred to ordinary sensations. And, for our purposes, we are not advanced by explaining our sensations by means of scientific constructs which must themselves ultimately be explained by sensations! In philosophy we must stay with our ordinary experience.

Therefore, taking for granted in our metaphysical context of moderate realism that objects exist outside us, we accept the everyday conviction that we do really see trees, really hear the piano, taste the steak and touch the kitten. We are not just aware of pictures of them, of messages emanating from them or of effects ascribed to their influence.

However, when, through a difficult abstraction, we consider only our sense knowledge, without any intellectual elements, what we thus perceive are not the objects as they are in themselves but the objects as they affect us. We might also say that we perceive ourselves as affected by these objects. We are animated bodies. Our body is part of us and also part of the world. There is no great problem in finding out how we can ever step outside ourselves in order to know the objective world. In a certain sense we are con-

[18] Gabriel Marcel, *Journal Métaphysique*, passim; R. Troisfontaines, S. J., *De l'Existence à l'Etre*, Vol. I, pp. 165-173.

tinually outside ourselves because of our body, a bit of the world which is also a part of us.[19] Because we are bodies we can be influenced by all the other bodies in the world. We are bodies animated by a soul which is not totally exhausted by this task of animation but "emerges" considerably from the matter it animates; therefore, whenever a body exterior to us acts on our body, the point of contact becomes luminous, conscious; we perceive an object as it acts upon us and we react upon it. Hence that which we perceive is the boundary common to the outside world and our own animated corporeity. Sensation, therefore, is neither strictly objective nor strictly subjective, it is relative.

If sensation is relative, it follows that if our senses were altered, reality would look different to us. Reality looks slightly different to color-blind people because their visual sense differs slightly from that of the majority. As Dr. Carrel puts it, "should the retina record infra-red rays of great wave-length, nature would take on a different visage. The color of water, rocks and trees would vary with the seasons because of the changes in temperature."[20] What would happen if, by a clever operation, the optic nerve were linked up with the brain center for hearing, and the acoustic nerve with the brain center for vision? Some psychologists hold that in this eventuality we should hear colors and see sounds. Or rather, we should hear where we now see, and see where we now hear.

Does this not lead to utter scepticism? Absolutely not. Our senses, however altered, would be as reliable as they are now; they would know objects as they affect us, which is the only function they are supposed to serve, taken in isolation. Our fundamental certitudes do not come from the senses alone but from the senses in conjunction with the intellect.

[19] "Ultimately the sense object does not penetrate into the sense power, but the sense power is, as '*actus materiae,*' already present at all times in the outside world. As '*actus contra materiam*' it possesses such an intensity of being that whatever penetrates into its medium reflects upon itself, becomes conscious and is nothing but a formal delimitation of that world-possession which through its very being the sense power is at all times" (Rahner, *Geist in Welt,* p. 107). The same author goes on to show that this explains the absence of an "agent sense" corresponding to the "agent intellect" and the presence of the "sensible *in act*" as opposed to the "intelligible *in potency*" in the outside world.

[20] A. Carrel, *Man, the Unknown* (New York, Harper, 1935), p. 66.

Since scientific knowledge is always based on the data of the senses and uses the sense element as an essential constituent, the natural Sciences give us only phenomenal knowledge of reality; they tell us how the world affects us, not what it is in itself.

We have claimed that sense knowledge perceives the objects as they affect us. How then do we know that these objects are distinct from us? The fact is that through sense knowledge alone we do not know that the objects are *entitatively* distinct from us, as one being is distinct from another. That kind of distinction is known only by the intellect. Animals do not know that they are entitatively distinct from the objects they perceive. But they perceive a *spatial* distinction between themselves and the things around them. Space, as we have seen, is the a priori form of the external senses. Whatever is perceived is perceived in space. But space differentiates, extraposes, exteriorizes; what is perceived in space is known as spatially distinct from the knower.

. . . every actual sense representation "extraposes" virtually on both sides of itself a space and a time, in which all other possible representations will have to arrange themselves. . . . If the sensing subject acquires a spatial representation of itself, that representation will necessarily possess the property of exteriority in relation to all other spatial representations; no spatial confusion is possible between the image of the subject and the image of the objects. . . .
Hence sensation is objective: slightly objective, to be sure, since its proper objectivity is nothing but spatial exteriority. But sensation is subjective too, revealing the sensing subject to itself; slightly subjective, however, just as it is slightly objective; or, more exactly and in one word, as it is slightly immanent.[21]

THE MATERIALITY OF SENSATION

Sensation is a material process. Material, as we have seen, can have two meanings: first, something which can be seen, touched, or

[21] J. Maréchal, S. J., *Le Point de Départ de la Métaphysique* (abbreviated henceforward: *PDM*), Cahier V, 2d ed. (Paris, Desclée de Brouwer), pp. 175-177.

in another way examined by the senses; secondly, something which is intrinsically dependent on matter.

Sensation is material in the second, not in the first sense. Sensation cannot be seen or touched, but it is intrinsically dependent on the brain, the nerves and the sense organs. These parts of the body are not only a condition but a real cause of our sensations.

Our sensations have certain properties, such as quality, intensity, extension. These properties are determined by the sense organ, the nerves and the brain center. Therefore these parts of the body are a real cause of our sensations.

Thus the quality of our sensation, the fact that it is visual or auditory or olfactory, is determined at least in part by the nerves and the brain center affected, as is demonstrated by the law of specific nerve energies.

That the intensity of our sensations is proportionate, at least roughly, to the physical intensity of the stimulus affecting the organ is a fact of experience.

In the sensations which possess extension this property is proportionate to the area which receives the stimulus. Thus we get a more extensive sensation of warmth when we plunge our whole arm into warm water than if we put only our finger into it.

Hence the parts of the body are a real cause (together with the vital principle, or soul) of our sensations. Our sensations are intrinsically dependent on matter, they are material.

We shall demonstrate later that our ideas are not material, that the brain or the body is not a real cause of them.

We may then, in conclusion, make a brief comparison of our ideas with our sensations. Our senses know only material things, and they know them in a material way—that is, as singular, concrete, individual objects. Our intelligence can know both material and immaterial objects, and it knows both in an immaterial way, without intrinsic dependence on matter. Therefore our ideas apply to all individuals of a species. The mountain I see is a singular, concrete, individual mountain. The idea I have of a mountain is universal and applies to all mountains.

Furthermore, our senses know their objects only insofar as they affect us, not as they are in themselves. Our intelligence knows them, at least to some extent, noumenally, as they are in themselves independent of our knowledge of them.

In ordinary mental activity the senses and the intelligence are always used together. The intellect gives us universal and abstract knowledge which we apply to individual objects by means of our senses.[22]

THE INTERNAL SENSES

Internal senses are senses which are not directly in contact with external reality but refer to it indirectly, through the agency of the external senses. Thomistic philosophy distinguishes four internal senses: the central sense, imagination, memory and the estimative power. Whether these senses are really distinct, or only four aspects of one power, is undecided. We prefer the second hypothesis.

CENTRAL SENSE

The central sense is the center where all the data of the external senses are collected and integrated. Three main functions are generally ascribed to the central sense:

1. The central sense makes the animal (and man on the sense level) aware of the activity and the objects of its external senses. Without that sense the animal would see and hear but would not be aware that it saw and heard. When a dog sees a cat, it is aware that it sees that cat. It is not the eye that is aware of this fact, for the eye does not see that it sees; a sense cannot reflect upon itself. There is, moreover, in the animal no intelligence which can make it aware of its sensations and their objects. Therefore there must be in the animal a higher sense which performs that function. We call it the central sense.

Through the central sense the animal possesses sense consciousness. That sense consciousness in the animal corresponds at its degree to the self-consciousness of man (law of proportionality). Man's consciousness is capable of reflecting perfectly upon itself;

[22] Readings: see pp. 194-195.

man is conscious of being conscious, he is aware that he is aware. The animal is not conscious of being conscious, but it is conscious of its acts and of their objects. The exterior senses are not conscious of their own activity; the central sense is not conscious of its own activity, but it is conscious of the activity and of the objects of the external senses. Therefore we call the reflection of the central sense an "imperfect reflection." In perfect reflection subject and object coincide: I am aware of being aware. In imperfect reflection one aspect of the subject coincides with some other aspects: I am aware of seeing a boat.

2. The central sense enables me to distinguish between the different sensations deriving from the various senses. The eye can distinguish black from white, the taste organ differentiates between bitter and sweet. But I can also distinguish black from sweet. Neither my eye nor my taste organ enables me to do that, since these senses know only their own qualities. Therefore there must be a superior sense which receives the impressions of all external senses and can compare them with each other.

3. Finally the central sense integrates the data of the external senses and refers them to their common object. It is the same pie whose color and shape I see, whose odor I smell and whose savor I taste. I refer all these sensations to the same object. My individual senses cannot do this, it is the function of my central sense.

MEMORY AND IMAGINATION

The greatest part of our information about these two internal senses derives from empirical and experimental psychology and has been reviewed in the preceding section. A short philosophical note will complete this information.

All knowledge requires an intentional form or "impression." This applies also to memory and imagination. But memory and imagination need in addition another kind of form, which is called the "expressed intentional form" or "expression."

If we recall the four stages which we distinguished in external sensation, we shall understand at once that in the case of memory and imagination there is no physical stage, because their object is not present to, and cannot actually affect, these senses. There is, however, a physiological stage, which consists in the reactivation of some neural trace of past perceptions. Next follows the passive psychological stage, with the "impression." Finally comes the active psychological stage. At this stage, the external senses actively turn towards the object which is influencing them. But memory and imagination cannot turn actively towards an object which is not present. They bring forth a conscious substitute, a representation of the object, which we call the "expression," in which these senses know their object. This is the "image," either the pure image of imagination or the recognized image of memory.

The differences between "impression" and "expression" can be summarized as follows:

IMPRESSION	EXPRESSION
Presupposed by knowledge	Its production is the act of knowledge
Unconscious	Conscious
That by means of which I know	That in which I know

THE ESTIMATIVE POWER

This is the traditional Scholastic name for the fourth, internal sense. It corresponds to the cognitive aspect of instinct. The concept of instinct is wider than that of estimative power, since it includes the motor aspect, which makes the animal capable of performing complex activities.

We are forced to admit the existence of such a power on the sense level, to explain the fact that animals, which have no reason, can perceive what is useful or harmful to themselves and to their species. Usefulness and harmfulness are not sensory qualities which might be perceived by the external senses or by the internal senses mentioned previously. The squirrel avoids the dog not because it is disagreeable to look at, or because its odor is repellent, but because it is dangerous to squirrels. Therefore the squirrel must have some cognitive power enabling it to perceive qualities which are beyond the reach of the other senses.

That power involves some kind of judgment, but a judgment which uses no ideas, which is singular, concrete and pragmatic. Squirrels do not know that dogs in general are dangerous to squirrels in general, but when they see a representative of the canine species, they know at once that this creature is dangerous to them.

Using the principle of proportionality, we can say that the estimative power is analogous on the sense level to reason on the intellectual level. It observes relations (useful to, harmful to), but it observes them in a concrete way.

Man also possesses an estimative power. In man this power is called the cogitative power. Its scope is wider than that of the estimative power in animals.

The cogitative power in man is the bridge between the intellect and the senses. It is, so to speak, the extension of man's spiritual powers into the field of sense knowledge. The phantasm, man's highest form of sense knowledge, is formed in the cogitative power under the unconscious guidance of the agent intellect.[23] By means of that power man applies his abstract concepts and universal judgments to the concrete objects and individual situations of experience.

CO-OPERATION BETWEEN EXTERNAL AND
INTERNAL SENSES

We must consider more carefully why the co-operation of the internal senses is required in all sense knowledge.

Every act of knowledge supposes the unification of its raw data. What kind of unification must the subject impose upon the form which is passively received in the sense faculty? . . . First, of course, a unification of its spatial dispersion. For the extension of the form, which is materially received in the organ, is nothing more, in this first stage, than a point-to-point and, as it were, disjunctive correspondence between the extension of the subject and the extension of the environment. But the . . . only kind of unity which space or extension can

[23] Cp. pp. 264ff.

receive, in order to become the "specifying form of a strictly immanent operation," seems to be the formal unity of an interior movement which would take up in succession the juxtaposed parts of that extension or space, in order to fuse or totalize them in a definite temporal continuity. The unification of space is performed by means of time.[24]

An example will make this clearer. From the top of a hill you are admiring a wide sweep of landscape. You see it as *one* beautiful spectacle, although your eyes can never take it in at one glance. When you look to your left, you do not see the river at the right, and when you look right, the farm houses are out of your visual field. But your eyes keep moving right and left, up and down, and this movement of your eyes brings together all the elements of the picture. What you cannot take in at one single moment of time, you know in succession, through the movements of your eyes. Your visual field is unified by this movement which occurs in time. You have unified space by means of time.

The impression of the observer is that the landscape itself is a unity, and that the unifying element is space. Reflection shows, however, that space does not unify but disperses. In space every point is outside every other point, there is merely a juxtaposition of countless details.[25] This multiplicity is unified only in and by your knowledge, which seizes all the elements in temporal succession.

Nevertheless, such temporal succession likewise lacks real unity. Every moment of time is outside every other moment. Time itself needs unification. Time will be unified only if each passing moment is not entirely lost but persists somehow in you. This is the function of memory, which retains something of every moment of the past. The movements of your eyes would not help you to get a complete picture of the landscape if, as soon as you stopped looking at one part of it, you should completely forget what you had seen. Time, which unified space, is itself unified by memory.

The unifying function of memory is likewise very clear in the field of auditory sensations. We should be unable to understand a simple sentence if a word were entirely forgotten as soon as it was

[24] Maréchal, *PDM*, V, pp. 170-171.
[25] The objects in space are, of course, unified. Not by space, however, but by their own substantial form, which the senses do not know.

heard. What we should hear in such a hypothetical case would be a succession of unconnected words, not a sentence. The same remark applies to the hearing of a melody.

Therefore every sensation or perception supposes the co-operation of memory. The external senses suppose the continual co-operation of the internal senses.

It might be objected that such a unification of space by time is required only when the field of perception is wide. When the field is narrow, its whole content can be taken in at one glance and no unifying movement is necessary. When I see my watch on the table, my gaze does not travel all over it, the whole watch is seen at once.

We must remember, however, that actually the watch is represented by a retinal image composed of many points, each one of which is outside every other; that these points must be unified by some movement in time. In this instance we are not aware of the unifying movement, but it must occur, since we cannot otherwise explain how the spatial diversity is unified. Without such a unification there can be no knowledge.[26]

Does this not contradict the Gestalt theory, which insists that the whole is perceived before any of its parts? In our "scanning" hypothesis the parts seem to be known before the whole. This would indeed contradict the Gestalt theory if the scanning process were conscious. But generally it is unconscious; the parts are not "known" before the whole, although they may be "taken in" before it. Knowledge will never be understood correctly unless we are well aware that its conscious aspects are preceded by a considerable amount of unconscious activity.

Therefore we say that the external senses invest their data with the form of space, and the internal senses invest their data with the form of time. The space in which the landscape is unified is not objective space, exterior to my mind, but my own space, supplied by my senses, what we can call my "imaginary space." And the time which unifies that space is not the mathematical time of

[26] Some psychologists claim that there can be no perception in the visual or tactile domains without some movement in the sense organ: "A motionless eye is a blind eye."—M. Pradines, *Traité de Psychologie Générale* (Paris, Presses Universitaires de France, 1948), Vol. I, p. 46. See also L. A. Riggs and F. Ratcliff, "Visual Acuity and the Normal Tremor of the Eye," *Science,* 114 (1951), pp. 17-18.

our clocks but my own time, the duration which I personally experience.

Hence in a certain sense Kant was right when he claimed that space is the priori form of the external senses and time the a priori form of the internal senses. Kant's error consisted in denying the existence of real objective space and time, both independent of my knowledge. As Fr. P. Scheuer, S.J., puts it, "Every faculty has its form, its way of knowing things, according to the principle, 'That which is known is in the knower after the manner of the knower.' As universality is the form of our intelligence, so spatiality is the form of our sensibility. To say that space is the form of our sensibility means that the senses necessarily perceive everything spatially, as intelligence necessarily conceives everything universally."[27]

Every single sense has its own formal object; thus the formal object of the visual sense is color, the formal object of the auditory sense is sound. But these formal objects have a common element, which is space. Our eyes see color in space, our ears hear sound in space. And thus the doctrine of the a priori character of imaginary space meets an ancient doctrine of Aristotle and the Scholastics, the doctrine of the "common sensibles."

Size, shape, and the like, which are called *common sensibles,* are midway between *accidental sensibles* and *proper sensibles,* which are the object of the senses. For the proper sensibles first and of their very nature, affect the senses, since they are qualities that cause alteration. But the common sensibles are all reducible to quantity. . . . Now quantity is the proximate subject of the qualities that cause alteration, as surface is of color. Therefore the common sensibles do not move the senses first and of their own nature, but by reason of sensible quality, as the surface by reason of color.[28]

Fr. Maréchal comments on this text as follows:

Everything which, in sense perception, can be reduced to quantity (size, figure, concrete number, motion or rest) is therefore, from that

[27] Unpublished Notes.
[28] *S. Theol.,* I, 70, 3, ad 2. Quoted from A. C. Pegis' translation in *Introduction to St. Thomas Aquinas* (New York, Modern Library, 1948).

point of view, a "common sensible," that is, a formal object which is common to the specialized objects of the various senses. But for the Scholastics the formal object reveals directly a formal aspect of the active faculty itself. . . . Therefore, according to the Scholastics, there must exist, in the sense faculty, a general disposition—an a priori condition—corresponding to the common quantitative determinations of the sense data. Kant says nothing more when he speaks of the a priori form of space or (mutatis mutandis) of time.[29]

Therefore, although St. Thomas never spoke of space and time as a priori forms of our sensibility, he held a doctrine which can be interpreted as analogous if not identical. But he held, and we affirm with him, that space and time correspond to something in objective reality. Denying this was Kant's mistake.

READINGS

Knowledge in General:
St. Thomas Aquinas, *Summa Theologica*, I, Q. 14, 1, 2, 3, 5; Q. 84, 3, 6. (All readings from St. Thomas Aquinas can be found in Pegis, *Introduction to St. Thomas Aquinas*.) Gilson, *The Philosophy of St. Thomas Aquinas*, pp. 260-283. Marc, *Psychologie Réflexive*, Vol. I, pp. 61-86. Maréchal, *Le Point de Départ de la Métaphysique*, Cahier V, pp. 105-130. Maritain, *The Degrees of Knowledge*, pp. 134-143. Rahner, *Geist in Welt*, pp. 71-90. Rousselot, *The Intellectualism of St. Thomas*, pp. 17-60. Sertillanges, *Foundations of Thomistic Philosophy*, pp. 10-44.

The Philosophy of Sense Knowledge:
St. Thomas Aquinas, *Summa Theologica*, I, Q. 78, a. 3. Marc, *Psychologie Réflexive*, Vol. I, pp. 87-102, 133-163. Maréchal, *Le Point de Départ de la Métaphysique*, Cahier V, pp. 131-146. Rahner, *Geist in Welt*, pp. 91-109. Wild, *Introduction to Realistic Philosophy*, pp. 413-426.

The Internal Senses:
St. Thomas Aquinas, *Summa Theologica*, I, Q. 78, a. 4. Gaffney,

[29] *PDM*, V, pp. 179-180.

The Psychology of the Internal Sense. Klubertanz, "The Discursive Power," in *The Modern Schoolman* (1952). Marc, *Psychologie Réflexive,* Vol. I, pp. 103-110. Maréchal, *Le Point de Départ de la Métaphysique,* Cahier V, pp. 146-184. Rahner, *Geist in Welt,* pp. 110-128, 302-311. Wild, *Introduction to Realistic Philosophy,* pp. 426-436.

11

Appetitive Faculties

BEFORE STUDYING sense appetite, we must know something about appetite in general.

APPETITE IN GENERAL

Our general conception of appetite follows from our fundamental conception of being as an "active identification with oneself."[1] An identification supposes two terms which are to be identified and which we can call subject and object. Since there is identification, subject and object are in reality one and the same being, but conceived under two different aspects. This active identification can occur in two directions and in two directions only. Either the subject draws the object into itself, and then we have knowledge; or the object draws the subject towards itself, and then we have striving, or appetite.

In both cases the action is immanent. Fundamentally each being knows itself, wills itself. But when it knows itself, the subject represents itself to itself; being as object becomes present to itself as subject through some activity of the subject. In appetite the same being unites itself to itself, but here it is not the object which comes to the subject and which is, as it were, passively received by it, but it is the subject which is drawn by the object, which goes out towards it and unites itself with it under an influence proceeding from the object. Under the first aspect being is called true, under the second aspect it is called good.

[1] What follows is taken from the unpublished lecture notes of Fr. P. Scheuer, S. J.

197

In knowledge the subject remains within itself, it interiorizes the object which was first exterior. In appetite, the subject ceases to be interior and becomes exterior to itself, steps outside itself.

The intelligence operates like a progressive enlargement and enrichment of the subject, while the will as it progresses, assumes more and more the aspect of renunciation, a giving up of self. The subject loses itself, in order to find itself in the object. However, in this life, intelligence, although it means a progressive enrichment, is the less effective way of coming into contact with being. Intelligence assimilates objects to itself, it brings them down to its own level, so that any reality which is greater than the knowing subject is stripped of all that by which it exceeds the capacity of this subject. The will, on the other hand, is attracted by the object as it really is in itself. The object of the will is being as it is in itself; whereas the object of intelligence is being as it is known, as it is possessed intentionally.

Therefore, in this life, real contact with the Supreme Reality is established through the will; it is through the will that we enter into contact with the Absolute. The will reaches further than the intellect; but since its union with the good does not entail a representation of that good, it brings no light to the intellect.

DEGREES IN APPETITE

The degrees of appetite correspond to the degrees of being (principle of proportionality).

The first object of appetite is the reality of the subject. Any other reality can become the object of appetite only insofar as it becomes one with the primary good, which is the subject's own being.

Divine Being is infinite. Therefore in God there is perfect identity, the Divine Will is perfectly in act. Its good is fully realized. God wills, by one and the same act, all other realities, because they all depend on Him. God does not love creatures for their own sake, as if they had any goodness independent of His goodness. Yet He loves the intrinsic goodness of all creatures as participations of His own goodness.

In a creature the primary object, the creature's own being, is not fully in act, it is not identical with absolute goodness. Therefore the will cannot rest in it. A created being loves itself, but it is also attracted by the Infinite Being; it can really love itself only inasmuch as it is a participation of that Infinite Being. As every human intellect strives unconsciously towards the knowledge of the Infinite Being, so every human will strives unconsciously towards the possession of the Infinite Being. And as we can, on the natural level, know God only by way of negation and supereminence, so the will must give up finite goods, transcend them, and strive towards the Infinite Good.

It follows that, in the human will, there is always a mixture of enjoyment and desire: enjoyment of the good which is present, desire for more and ever more. This mixture corresponds to the ontological composition of act and potency.

Man loves his spiritual nature in the same way in which he understands it. As our intellectual activity is intimately connected with our sense knowledge, so our volitional activity is connected with our sense appetite. The possible deviations are the same in both faculties. Our intellect confuses sensible being with being as such, and from this derives error. The will confuses the sensible good, that which is good for our material nature, with that which is absolutely good. Therefore, like our intelligence, our will needs education. The great difference between intellect and will is that error in the intellect is due to the union of the intellect with the senses, not to the intellect as such; whereas that which is in the will is willed by it—the confusion between the two kinds of good is voluntary, it is a sin. In the intellect a disorder happens; in the will, it is willed.

SENSE APPETITE

Appetite in general implies striving towards some good or away from some evil. Appetite is divided into natural appetite and elicited appetite. Natural appetite is possessed by all beings; it is a striving which is not directed by any knowledge. Thus the roots of a plant strive towards moisture; chemical substances strive towards other substances for which they have an affinity.

Elicited appetite is a special faculty by which conscious beings strive towards a good or away from an evil which has been previously perceived by a cognitive faculty. It is striving preceded by knowledge. It follows that there will be as many kinds of elicited appetite as there are different kinds of knowledge. In man there are two different kinds of knowledge, sense knowledge and intellectual knowledge; hence also two kinds of appetite, sense appetite and intellectual appetite, which is called the will.

Since sense knowledge knows only material, single, concrete objects in a material way, sense appetite will strive only towards or away from material, single, concrete objects in a material way, that is, with intrinsic dependence on matter.

Because sense appetite is material, it is not free; it strives necessarily towards pleasure or away from pain. In an animal a drive can be inhibited only by another drive which happens to be stronger at a given moment. Thus a hungry dog, on meeting food, must necessarily eat it, unless his hunger drive is inhibited by a stronger fear drive. In man, too, sense appetite may be inhibited in the same way, as when a man refrains from stealing because he is afraid of the police. However, in man the lower appetites may also be inhibited by the higher appetite which we call the will.

Our sense appetite is constituted by our drives and instincts. Although we have them in common with animals, and they are thus "lower," they are not evil. Because they are not free, their activity involves neither responsibility nor sin. As long as their striving is in accordance with the order imposed by reason, it is perfectly legitimate. Even when they strive towards something which is forbidden by reason and opposed by the will, this is not, in itself, wrong or sinful. Sin occurs only when the will yields to such a striving and identifies itself with it. Then the rational appetite acts like sense appetite; man descends to the level of the unfree animal; there is moral disorder and sin.

St. Thomas distinguishes two main aspects in sense appetite, the concupiscible and the irascible appetite. The concupiscible appetite strives towards pleasure and away from pain, the irascible appetite deals with obstacles which impede the functioning of the concupiscible appetite. The various motions of both appetites are called the passions. St. Thomas distinguishes eleven of them, six in the concupiscible appetite and five in the irascible appetite.

Of the six passions of the concupiscible appetite, three refer to that which is good and three to that which is evil. Directed towards the good in general, there is love; towards an absent good, there is desire; towards a present good, there is joy. Towards evil in general, there is hatred; with regard to an absent evil, there is aversion; with regard to a present evil, there is sorrow.

Of the five passions of the irascible appetite, two deal with some good which is difficult to reach, three deal with some evil which is difficult to overcome. When the difficult good is within range of possibility, there is hope; when it is not, there is despair. When the evil can be overcome, there is courage or anger; when it cannot be overcome, there is fear.

St. Thomas' Treatise on the Passions (*S. Theol.,* Ia IIae, QQ. 22-48) contains what we might call his "Empirical Psychology." Using the accumulated psychological knowledge of Aristotle, the Stoics and the Fathers of the Church and completing it with the results of his own observations, he has left us in these pages a wealth of practical psychological knowledge. As Sertillanges remarks, one of the best ways of becoming acquainted with the highest abstractions of Thomistic philosophy is to study these Questions. Although the framework in which these data are presented may seem antiquated and although the opposition between the concupiscible and the irascible appetite is given up by some Thomists,[2] modern Phenomenology insists that it corresponds to a fundamental opposition between two categories of human drives.[3]

[2] A. D. Sertillanges, O. P., *La Philosophie de St. Thomas d'Aquin,* rev. ed., Vol. II, p. 185.

[3] Cfr. P. Ricoeur, *Philosophie de la Volonté,* pp. 111 ff.; S. Strasser, *Das Gemüt,* pp. 133-153.

READINGS

St. Thomas Aquinas, *Summa Theologica*, I, Q. 19, a. 1, 2; Q. 80, a. 1, 2; Q. 81, a. 1, 2, 3; Ia IIae, Q. 6, 1, 2. Gilson, *The Spirit of Mediaeval Philosophy*, pp. 269-303, and *The Philosophy of St. Thomas Aquinas*, pp. 284-303. Marc, *Psychologie Réflexive*, Vol. II, pp. 9-61. Wild, *Introduction to Realistic Philosophy*, pp. 469-475.

PART FOUR

HUMAN RATIONAL LIFE

SECTION I

Empirical Study of Man's Rational Life

12

Human Intelligence

Human intelligence differs considerably from the intelligence of animals. Taken in its everyday meaning, it is not quite the same function as the "intellect." Our intellect does not grow, it cannot be measured, it does not differ measurably from individual to individual. We know, on the other hand, that experimental psychology studies the growth of human intelligence, measures the degree of its development, and can determine how intelligence is distributed in a certain population.

What, then, is the relation between these three terms: animal intelligence, human intelligence and the human intellect? We might express it as follows.

Man is both an animal and a spirit. As an animal he possesses a cognitive function similar to that of the higher animals, which makes him able to adapt himself to new circumstances and to learn from experience. As a spirit he is endowed with a cognitive function akin to the angelic intellect, which makes him capable of reflecting on his own intellectual activity and of being conscious of himself as a subject. Human intelligence is neither of these two functions but may be considered a combination of both.

The relation between intelligence as the power of learning and the intellect as the faculty of self-reflection is analogous to the relation between matter and form. In human intelligence the material element is represented by the power of learning from experience, whereas the formal element consists in the purely spiritual function of self-reflection. Because of its material element our intelligence gives evidence of growth, can be measured, is unequally distributed among men. Because of its formal element, human intelligence is totally different from its animal counterpart. From a certain point of view, considered materially, human intelligence is comparable to animal intelligence. From another point of view, considered formally, it is entirely different from the animal mind.

If, in spite of material similarities, there is an essential difference between human and animal intelligence, that difference must manifest itself in the ordinary activities of man's intelligence. In fact we discover such differences. Man engages in abstract thought, the animal does not. Man is capable of formally knowing universals and relations, while the animal discovers them only materially if at all. From these deficiencies of animal intelligence derive the two most visible differences between animal and human development: the total lack in all animals of real language and real culture.

How can we explain the quantitative development, the quantitative differences in human intelligence? The intellect as such is intrinsically independent of matter, as will be demonstrated in the next section. Therefore all quantitative differences must derive from the material element of intelligence. Since this material element itself depends on the senses and their organs, it seems that the degrees of intelligence are ultimately based on the body, the sense organs, and especially the brain. The kind of intelligence an individual possesses, whether brilliant or dull, quick or slow, depends mainly on the kind of brain he has inherited from his parents. The specific feature or quality of the brain which makes for high intellectual endowment has not yet been discovered. The new science of Cybernetics, which studies the structure and functioning of electronic computing machines and artificial brains, will probably shed some light on this important problem.

Will computing machines ever be able to think exactly like a man? The answer is a definite No. We have distinguished in human thinking a material and a formal aspect. Electronic brains are capable of performing, with more speed and accuracy even than man, some of the material, purely mechanical operations of thinking, as they occur for instance in mathematical computations. But these machines will never know that they are performing these operations. The formal aspect of thinking, which consists essentially in self-awareness or perfect self-reflection, is forever beyond their reach.

Thinking is the typical activity of human intelligence. The senses perceive, memory recalls, imagination pictures objects before the mind; intelligence alone thinks. What thinking is in itself can be explained only by philosophy. Yet empirical psychology can tell us something about the thinking process in man.

Empirical studies of human thinking can be found in the works of philosophers such as John Dewey and psychologists such as G. Heymans and E. Claparède. Our exposition in the following paragraphs will be substantially that of Heymans. In its broad outlines it agrees with the conclusions of the other authors in the field.

1. That which sets the thinking process in motion is always some problem. We are arrested in our daily routine by some question which invites or demands an answer. It may be a practical problem: how to play a hand at bridge, where to find a drink of water? Or it may be a theoretical problem: is the universe finite or infinite, are sponges animals or plants?

2. Supposing that the necessary data are available, the first requisite for solving such a problem is concentration. We must be able to focus our mind upon the problem at hand and to keep it focussed until a solution is reached. If we do not or cannot concentrate, distractions arise, our mind loses track of the problem and no solution will be found.

Concentration supposes attention. There are two kinds of attention, spontaneous and voluntary. Spontaneous attention is that with which we advert to objects that interest us, whether this interest arises from inborn factors and is related to biological needs (e.g., we naturally pay attention to strong noises), or is acquired (a philatelist pays spontaneous attention to new stamps). Voluntary attention is the attention which we direct consciously and voluntarily towards some object. In spontaneous attention the object and the immediate motive of attention coincide, while in voluntary attention object and motive are distinct. We fix our attention on a difficult book not because the book itself interests us, but because our study will help us to acquire knowledge which we desire for an ulterior motive.

The concentration required for solving problems is generally based on voluntary attention, so that successful thinking requires a highly developed power of voluntary attention. However, a genuine interest in the problem at hand makes concentration easy and natural, and therefore one of the best ways of alleviating the difficulty of thinking is to acquire and develop a wide range of interests.

3. It sometimes happens that as soon as a problem arises before the mind, the solution takes shape without any effort on our part. Generally, however, some effort is required. Several possible solutions or "hypotheses" present themselves, and each must be examined for its applicability.

Suppose that I am writing a poem and looking for a word which rhymes with "sweet." If my mind is working efficiently, several such words are evoked at once, allowing me to make a choice and select a word which fits into the context of my poem.

Efficient thinking demands that the possible solutions shall arise in the mind quickly and in great numbers. Such efficiency depends on a good memory, which recalls solutions used in similar situations, and especially on a highly developed creative imagination, able to rearrange many data from the past in new, original ways, well adapted to the present situation.

4. The next step in the solution of our problem consists in a rapid review of the proposed hypotheses and the selection of the best among them. Although this step is distinct from the previous one, in practice the two are continually overlapping.

A good solution must fulfill a certain number of conditions. Therefore our mind must be able to examine each suggested hypothesis and its consequences in relation to every one of these conditions. This process would be complicated enough if all the conditions were simultaneously and clearly present before the mind. But that is impossible, because the mind can grasp only one fact at any given moment. To compare each hypothesis explicitly with every condition would be a long and tedious process. If the "censoring" of each hypothesis is to proceed quickly, it will have to take place unconsciously. The mind must be endowed with some power through which the possible objections to each solution can be sifted without emerging into the full light of consciousness.

Consider the following situation. You meet the mother of a

very good friend unexpectedly and learn that he has just been killed in an automobile accident. You must say a few words to the grieving mother. Your words will not be appropriate unless you take into account what you know about your friend, about his mother, about their relationship. Some expressions come to mind which you immediately reject because they are too trite, or would not sound sincere, or would recall things that would increase the mother's distress. You have no time to consider all these factors explicitly, and yet somehow you must take them into account. An efficient mind performs this task very quickly; in some mysterious way it produces a formula which satisfies all the vaguely recognized requirements of the concrete situation.

We possess a great mass of information concerning the problem at hand, acquired from past experience or from reflection. All this information must actually be used. It is not enough to have it present somewhere in our memory; its influence must be brought to bear on the present situation while we are quickly weighing each possible solution. This entails what some psychologists have called a strong "secondary function." The secondary function of a mental content is the influence which such a content exerts on our conduct even when we are not at that moment aware of it. In people with a weak secondary function the past is not only lost from consciousness, it is even forgotten to the extent that it has no bearing on their present conduct. Those who have a well-developed secondary function can, without recalling past experiences, take them into account when making a decision. They are able to check quickly and accurately any hypothesis arising in their minds for its fitness and adaptation to the present circumstances, without even becoming aware of the reasons why they reject one solution and prefer some other. They "feel" which solution is best, and that feeling is usually reliable.

Summarizing, we may say that the following factors are required for efficient thinking: concentration, which allows the subject to bring all his mental powers to bear on the problem; a lively creative imagination, which provides him at once with a great variety of possible solutions; a strong secondary function, which makes it possible for him to test and weigh each solution as soon as it occurs to him.

When these three abilities are highly developed in an individual, we have a very intelligent person. Very intelligent people constitute a minority in a population. This can be attributed not only to the fact that each of these abilities seems to be the result of the chance combination of a great number of independent factors, but also to the further circumstance that these abilities have a tendency to exclude each other, at least if any one of them is overdeveloped. Thus an excessive power of concentration adversely affects the power of creative imagination. A too lively imagination impedes the secondary function. Only an optimum development of the three factors makes for a superior mind.

If only two of these three abilities are well developed, we have a mind in which some factor necessary for superior intellectual achievement is lacking. A lively imagination and a strong secondary function combined with weak powers of concentration produces the intelligent dilettante who is acquainted with many fields of knowledge but has a solid grasp of none. Excellent powers of concentration and a strong secondary function combined with an insufficiently developed imagination are found in scholars and savants who know everything in their own specialized fields but seem incapable of creative innovations, who possess plenty of erudition but little or no originality. Finally, when we have great powers of concentration and a lively imagination combined with a deficient secondary function, much will depend on the nature of the deficiency. Where the secondary function is uniformly undeveloped, there may be brilliant flashes of insight, making possible occasional bits of solid intellectual work, but the mental process will lack the logical coherence required for outstanding achievement. If, on the other hand, the secondary function is one-sidedly developed, we may find a "one-track" mind, clever in presenting and defending its own point of view but unable to see anything beyond it.

QUANTITATIVE STUDY OF INTELLIGENCE

Intelligence as generally understood is present in various degrees in different individuals. Some people are "more" or "less" intelligent than others. They show it by the way in which they solve the various problems, theoretical or practical, which confront them in everyday life. In the field of education especially, an evaluation of the pupil's intelligence by the teachers has been a customary practice. Education aims to develop the intelligence of the students. Therefore, if we are to gauge the value of educational systems and methods, it seems imperative to measure the degree of intellectual development obtained by means of these methods.

Teachers measure the intellectual development of their students by asking them questions or by having them solve problems and observing how they perform these tasks.

The intelligence tests used by psychology for the measurement of intelligence employ fundamentally the same methods. Questions are asked and problems are submitted, and the subject's reactions are recorded and evaluated. But the test method introduces great improvements into the traditional ways of evaluating intelligence.

1. In a test all the questions are asked and all the problems presented within a short time (usually not more than two hours), whereas in the ordinary method the process is extended over months and years.

2. In a test a great variey of questions and problems are included, so that every kind of intelligence is given a chance. Too often teachers rely on a small variety of tasks when they are evaluating intelligence in the ordinary way.

3. The questions in a test have been carefully devised, they are generally clear and unambiguous—and this cannot always be said for the questions used by a teacher.

4. In a test the questions are generally so worded as to allow of only one solution. This solution is known to the person applying the test, which makes the scoring of the answers quick and objective. In the traditional methods many good solutions are possible, and the subjective element is very important in the evaluation of the answers.

5. The norm used in evaluating test results is clearly defined. In the ordinary methods of evaluating intelligence a norm is always used, but it is vague and usually very subjective. A teacher finds the answers of his pupil outstanding or weak to the extent that they stand above or below what he expects from the average student in

the group. But he would be unable to define precisely the standard that he expects from an average student.

Suppose that 1,000 individuals of a more or less homogeneous group (e.g., college freshmen chosen at random) have taken a test comprising 200 questions. One member of the group, John, has 172 answers right. This figure alone does not tell us how well he did. But if we are told that among the 1,000 freshmen who took the test, 500 had more than 172 right answers and 500 had less than 172 right answers, we conclude at once that John's score is average.

The results of a test are often given in "percentiles." Among the 1,000 subjects who have answered the test questions we take the 1% whose answers are best. Let us say that they have 195 or more right answers. If John has 196 right answers, he is said to fall within the 99th percentile, and we know that among 100 college freshmen taken at random only one will equal or exceed his mark. If, on the other hand, we are told that Paul falls into the 15th percentile, we know that 85% of an unselected group will do as well as or better than he. In this way the use of tests makes it possible to avoid such vague terms as "excellent," "good" or "poor" in the evaluation of a subject's responses and allows us to state with great precision where he stands in comparison with others of his group.

Much painstaking work goes into the preparation of a good test, and great care is taken to make sure of the test's validity and reliability.

A test is valid when it really measures what it purports to measure. Thus an "intelligence test" which in fact measured almost exclusively the testee's memory or imagination would not be a valid test. The validity of a test is ascertained by comparing its results with those obtained by other methods of measuring the same function, where these methods have been demonstrated to secure reliable measurements. Although one teacher who has known a pupil for only a short time may be wrong in evaluating this pupil's intelligence, it is generally admitted that a sound estimate of the pupil's intelligence can be given by a good teacher who has observed his performance over a long period, or by a number of teachers, even though the period during which they have observed the pupil's work is shorter. If, therefore, the results of a test agree with such reliable estimates, this test will be considered valid.

A test is reliable when it yields fairly constant results in repeated applications. A yardstick which shrank or expanded to any real extent with changing temperatures would not be reliable. An intelligence test which, when used several times on the same subject, yields results which are considerably at variance, is not reliable. Checking the reliability of a test is a rather complicated procedure which we cannot explain in this book. One of the main difficulties involved is that the subject may remember the questions of a test and the answers he gave to them, so that a repetition of the test would measure his memory more than his intelligence.

A valid and reliable intelligence test given by a competent psychologist is a useful means of finding out how intelligent a given individual is. However, even in the best circumstances, too much reliance should not be placed on the results of such a test, especially when these results are negative.

One reason for this is that certain kinds of intelligent answers or reactions are difficult to put into words or write down. A man may do poorly in an intelligence test, yet be able to run his business in an efficient and intelligent way. The average intelligence test measures what has been called "Academic Intelligence," the intelligence required for success in academic pursuits, and although this kind of intelligence is not entirely different from the kind that makes for success in everyday life, these two forms of intelligence are not equally well-developed in every individual.

Experimental psychologists are well aware of this difficulty. They have devised tests of practical intelligence, also called "performance tests" since questions and answers are not presented in words but certain practical problems are submitted to the testee and his performance is watched and measured. However, these practical problems are necessarily simple as compared with some problems of real life, and therefore an outstanding performance on such tests of practical intelligence does not always demonstrate that the subject will be highly successful in real-life situations.

Another reason why test results may give a wrong idea of a subject's intelligence is that most tests put a premium on speed, which is not an essential component of real intelligence. A subject who is quick in his mental operations will often get better results in such a test than a slower person who is actually more intelligent.

Finally, since the score in an intelligence test is based on the work done in a set period of time, it may happen that a subject who, for some accidental reason (headache, worry), is unable to muster all his intellectual resources will be considerably underestimated.

For these reasons high results on tests are more reliable than low results, in this sense, that high results (supposing that there has been no cheating) can be explained only by the presence of a high degree of at least "academic" intelligence, whereas low results may occasionally be explained by causes other than an undeveloped intelligence. This applies especially when only one test has been administered.

The most famous of all tests is the Binet-Simon test. It was the first as to date and is still used extensively. Early in this century, the French psychologist Alfred Binet devised a certain number of questions or problems and tried them out on a fairly large number of children taken at random from the schools. He wanted to establish the standard of accomplishment which could be expected at each age level, and his object was to find a small number of problems of such a nature that the majority of children at a certain age could solve them, whereas the majority of children who had not yet reached that age could not. Take a group of simple problems which can be solved by most 8-year-old children but are too difficult for most 7-year-old children; then the mental development required for solving these problems is the 8-year level, and a child who can solve them has a Mental Age of 8 years. Now if the subject is able to answer not only the questions devised for age 8 but also all the questions for age 9 and even a few of the questions for age 10, he will be credited with a Mental Age of 9 years and a few months. Another child of the same age who is able to answer only the questions of age 6 will be considered as having a Mental Age of 6 years.

The Intelligence Quotient (I.Q.), which is generally used as a measure of intellectual development, is obtained by dividing the

Mental Age by the Chronological Age and multiplying this quotient by 100. Hence I.Q. $= \dfrac{\text{M.A.}}{\text{C.A.}} \times 100$. An average child of 8 will have an Intelligence Quotient of 100; a child who at the age of 8 has an M.A. of 10 possesses an I.Q. of 125; a child who at the age of 8 has a M.A. of 6 has an I.Q. of 75.

Binet prepared three editions of his famous test and published it in its last form a short time before his death in 1911. Ignored in France, his work was accepted eagerly in other countries. Several revisions and adaptations have been published, the most intensive and complete of which is the revision made by Professor Terman of Stanford University, widely known as the Stanford Revision of the Binet Test, or the Stanford-Binet Test.

The Binet test is an oral individual test. The questions are asked and the answers given orally. Only one individual can be tested at a time. Other tests have been devised which can be administered in writing and to a group. They are known as the paper-and-pencil group tests.

The aim of all these tests is to measure the native intelligence of the subject; hence they are called Intelligence Tests. Other tests are used to measure abilities which seem to be, to a certain extent, independent of intelligence—for instance, mechanical ability, musical ability. Such tests are known as Aptitude Tests.

Another group of tests are designed to measure the progress made by children in the different branches of the curriculum—spelling, arithmetic, biology. These are the Achievement Tests, and they are in fact nothing but standardized examinations.

DATA DERIVED FROM INTELLIGENCE TESTING

From the great number of investigations carried out by means of tests, it is possible to reach certain conclusions with regard to the distribution of intelligence among individuals, how it grows, its relation to other functions, and so on.

How is intelligence distributed in a normal population? All investigations point to the conclusion that this distribution is normal, in the statistical meaning of that word. Whenever an Intelligence

Test is administered to a great number of subjects chosen at random from a large population, we discover that the results can be graphically represented by the probability-curve of Gauss. This means that the I.Q.'s of the subjects will tend to occur in the greatest density around the average I.Q. of 100; in proportion as the extremes on either side, the very high and very low I.Q.'s, are approached, the number of subjects decreases regularly. In other words, there will be very few I.Q.'s which are either very high or very low; most quotients are average; they gravitate around 100, as many below that figure as there are above it. In the scale of intelligence ranging from the genius to the idiot, with the average individual at the center, there is no gap but a gradual transition.[1]

It has been demonstrated that whenever a phenomenon is distributed according to the curve of Gauss, the different degrees in which this phenomenon occurs can be explained by the operation of many factors acting independently of each other. If you throw a dozen dice and record the number of points you obtain at each throw, your scores will agree with the probability-curve, especially if you keep at it for quite a while. From this psychologists have deduced that the development of human intelligence depends on a great number of independent factors. Some of these factors are organic, either hereditary or acquired—for example, the quality and number of the brain cells, the blood supply which reaches them. Other factors are social or environmental, such as the intellectual development of the parents, the training they give their children.

Suppose that a highly developed intelligence should depend on only one hereditary factor, on the presence of only one gene. Then all those who possessed that gene would be very intelligent, those who did not possess it would be dull. If high intelligence depended on the presence of two genes, A and B, there would be four possibilities. Some individuals would possess A and B, others only A, others only B; finally, some neither A nor B. Under that hypothesis, one individual out of four would be very intelligent, one would be dull, and two would be average. Continuing in this line, and supposing that the development of intelligence required the presence of three genes, A, B and C, we discover that there are now eight

---

[1] It has been objected, not without reason, that the tests are generally made up in such a way that they yield a normal distribution. However, this does not seem to have been the case with the first Intelligence Tests.

possible combinations: ABC, AB, BC, AC, A, B, C, and, finally, the case in which none of the three is found. Here again there would be one very intelligent and one very dull individual. Three would be above average and three under average in intelligence.

There are, of course, many more than three hereditary factors influencing the development of intelligence, and to them must be added a host of environmental factors. As the number of factors increases, the ensuing distribution of intelligence assumes more and more the outline of the curve of Gauss (Fig. 10).

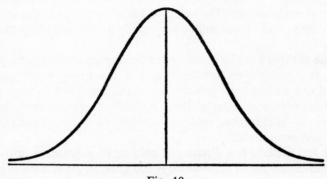

Fig. 10

The following table,[2] based on a great number of cases, shows how the various I.Q.'s are distributed in a large unselected group of people:

I.Q.		% IN POPULATION
above 140	Genius	1
130-139 ⎫	Very superior	2
120-129 ⎭		8
110-119	Superior	16
100-109 ⎫	Average	23
90-99 ⎭		23
80-89	Dull average	16
70-79	Borderline	8
60-69	Mentally deficient	2
below 60		1

[2] This table is reproduced from R. S. Woodworth and D. G. Marquis, *Psychology*, 5th ed. (New York, Holt, 1947), p. 54.

The mentally deficient are further subdivided into idiots, imbeciles and morons. An idiot is absolutely unable to take care of himself; he cannot wash or dress himself or avoid ordinary dangers. His speech is restricted to a few unconnected sounds. The I.Q. of this group varies between 0 and 25. Imbeciles have an I.Q. which varies between 26 and 50. They can take care of their own biological needs, they are able to speak, but they cannot learn how to read. Only the most intelligent among them are able to perform some simple work, under continual supervision. The I.Q. of morons ranges from 51 to 70. Morons can hold a very simple, routine job in a rural environment. The complex life of big cities is too confusing for them, and in that milieu they easily drift into delinquency or crime.

Some authors have attributed most incidences of delinquency and crime to undeveloped intelligence, but the many investigations carried out with delinquents and criminals have not substantiated this view. Although some of these individuals are decidedly below average in intelligence, quite a number of them possess well-developed mental ability.

The test method has discovered only small differences in the intellectual development between boys and girls. In general intelligence the two sexes show no reliable differences. A slight superiority on the part of boys has been demonstrated in mathematics and mechanics, for girls in verbal ability. It is impossible to say whether these differences should be explained by hereditary or environmental factors. Many psychologists prefer the second hypothesis. It has also been demonstrated that around the time of puberty girls develop more quickly than boys.

Children coming from wealthy families and attending private schools often have higher results in intelligence tests than children from less privileged milieus. This difference must be explained mainly in terms of factors in the environment, especially the greater intellectual stimulation to which the child is exposed in a more prosperous environment.

It is very difficult, and often impossible, to compare the intelligence of widely different races by means of ordinary intelligence tests. The background, say, of an African Bushman is so utterly different from that of a white American that, even if there were no language barrier or if performance tests were used, no common measure is available. Where psychologists have been able to measure racial differences, as in the United States, a considerable superiority on the part of the white race has generally been indicated. From this it does not follow that the average white individual is congenitally more intelligent than the average colored individual. Most test results point to the difference in educational opportunities as the main, if not the only, explanation of such differences. This is suggested, for instance, by the fact that the I.Q.'s of Negro children who have moved from Southern rural districts into New York City increase regularly, the increase being proportional to the length of their residence in the city, and also by the fact that, although the average white recruit had a higher I.Q. than the average colored recruit in the Armed Forces Testing Program of the First World War, Negroes from Ohio, Illinois, New York and Pennsylvania did better, on the average, than Whites from Mississippi, Kentucky, Arkansas and Georgia. These findings can be explained by the fact that, in general, the educational opportunities for the Whites were superior to those available to the Negroes, although the colored schools of some Northern states were better than the white schools of a few southern states.[3]

Intelligence tests have been used to good effect in studying the growth of intelligence. These studies show that growth proceeds rather quickly during childhood and early adolescence, after which it slows down and finally stops. However, some psychologists do not admit this conclusion, because they claim that the test items used at different age levels are not equidistant in difficulty.

When does intelligence stop growing? No definite answer can be given to that question. The limit is placed by various authors between the ages of 14 and 20. This does not imply that no new mental acquisitions are possible after the age of 20. It only means that such acquisitions are no longer the effect of spontaneous growth but are the result of personal reflection or intentional learning.

Does the I.Q. remain constant throughout life? This question has more than a theoretical importance; it may have great practical consequences. If we can measure the intelligence of a six-year-old

[3] Cf. O. Klineberg, *Race Differences* (New York, Harper, 1935); A. Anastasi, "Psychological Research and Educational Desegregation," in *Thought*, 35 (1960), pp. 421-449.

child, and if furthermore we know that his I.Q. will remain the same during the ensuing years, we can decide very early whether that child is fit to undertake advanced studies.

Most psychologists agree that if the environment remains constant, the I.Q. of an individual living in that environment will also remain fairly constant. A radical change in the environment may result in a corresponding change in the subject's I.Q. This explains why intelligence tests administered to pre-school children are generally not a sufficient basis for long-range prediction of their future achievements, because the passage from the home to the school may mean for many children a considerable change in environment.

Intellectual endowment and scholastic achievement are not necessarily parallel. Achievement generally supposes effort and hard work, and these factors depend on the subject's motivation, not on his I.Q. A hard-working student with an I.Q. of 115 may get better results in his studies than a lazy student with an I.Q. of 130. Hence the knowledge of an individual's I.Q. usually allows us to predict his capabilities but not necessarily his future achievements.

The famous British psychologist Spearman noticed that the best intelligence tests, those whose results agreed most closely with the estimate of experienced teachers, always examined a great number of mental capacities, such as sound judgment, discrimination, reasoning, imagination, even sense acuity and motor co-ordination. Yet the ultimate result is given as a measurement of "intelligence." Therefore intelligence is a factor which determines at least in part the degree in which these abilities are present in an individual.

Spearman tried to demonstrate this conclusion mathematically, by means of statistical computations which are too complicated to explain here. He claimed that all these functions are determined by two factors: a general factor designated by the letter g, which remains constant in each individual and influences the level of all his performances, and as many specific factors (factor s) as there are distinct abilities.

Furthermore, the respective influence of either factor varies greatly from one ability to another. Some abilities seem to be due almost entirely to factor g, whereas in others the specific factor is more important. Thus in learning Latin and Greek the importance of the general factor would be about fifteen times that of the specific factor. On the other hand, the specific factor is about four times more important than the general factor in musical ability. It follows that an individual in whom factor *g* is well developed has great aptitudes for classical studies and may show little progress in music.

Further research has established the existence of group factors, not as general as factor *g,* but less specialized than factor *s.* Thus such tasks as finding synonyms and antonyms, sentence completion, etc., require, besides general ability and a specific ability for each function, a verbal ability common to all of these functions. The presence of such verbal ability helps the subject to get good results in all tasks connected with words. Other abilities which have been discovered experimentally are: numerical ability, which is required for success in handling numbers; spatial ability, which facilitates the grasping of spatial relationships; musical ability; mechanical ability.

The fact that each mental performance requires the presence of three factors: general, group and specific, explains the great variety of correlations discovered in psychology.

A correlation exists between two functions when these functions vary together although not at the same rate. Physics discovers relations between phenomena. Thus there is a relation between the expansion of mercury and the rise of temperature; to each increase in temperature corresponds a proportional expansion of the mercury. Psychology discovers no such strict relations between mental functions. Intelligence, memory, imagination do not vary at exactly the same rate. Yet they have a tendency to vary together. An increase in intelligence is generally accompanied by an increase in the other two functions, although the rate of increase is not identical in the three of them.

When two variables increase or decrease at exactly the same rate, we have a relation, or a perfect correlation, indicated by $+1$. When one function increases at exactly the same rate at which another function decreases, the correlation between them is -1. Such perfect correlations are never found in psychology. When there is no connection whatsoever between the variations of two functions, the correlation is 0. A correlation of 0.40 is considered low,

a correlation of between 0.40 and 0.70 is medium, correlations
superior to 0.70 are high.

Psychology never discovers a correlation of $+1$ between two
mental functions, even when the functions in question are almost
identical, as, for instance, memorizing dates and memorizing names,
finding synonyms and finding antonyms, canceling a's and canceling
e's. This fact can be explained by the presence of a specific factor
for each function. On the other hand, all mental functions in a subject show positive correlations. This can be accounted for by the
presence of the general factor. Finally we discover in every subject,
functions between which the correlations are high, whereas these
same functions show low correlations with other groups of functions. The simplest way of explaining that fact is to admit that each
of these groups is influenced not only by the subject's factor g, but
also by such group factors as verbal, numerical, mechanical ability.

The factor analysis of intelligence, begun by the British psychologists, especially Spearman, has been developed and improved
by American psychologists, especially L. L. Thurstone. These investigations have assumed a highly technical character and cannot
be explained in this book.

READINGS

Data about the quantitative study of intelligence will be found in
the textbooks of Experimental Psychology listed on p. 161.

Dewey, *How We Think*. Dimnet, *The Art of Thinking*. Heymans,
Einführung in die Spezielle Psychologie, pp. 53-71. Moore, *Cognitive
Psychology*. Spearman, *The Abilities of Man* and *The Nature of
"Intelligence" and the Principles of Cognition*. Stoddard, *The Mean-
ing of Intelligence.*

13

The Human Will

In the preceding chapter we have explained the difference between intellect and intelligence. Although these two human functions are intimately related, they do not coincide. There are no degrees in the spiritual intellect, and that faculty does not grow. Intelligence grows and individuals differ in intelligence.

A similar observation can be made with regard to the will. As a spiritual faculty the will does not grow, and it is the same in all human beings. Yet we speak of the education of the will; we say that some people have a strong will, whereas in others the will remains weak throughout life. Unfortunately we do not have two different words to distinguish these two aspects of our higher appetitive power. It is possible to speak of the will considered empirically and the will considered as a spiritual faculty, but to avoid these cumbersome expressions we shall make the necessary distinction by speaking, more simply, of "will-power" and the "will."

The relation between will-power and the will is the same as that which exists between intelligence and the intellect.

Like intelligence, will-power involves sense elements; it is directly connected with the organic drives and indirectly with the body. This explains the possibility of real growth in will-power, the presence of quantitative degrees in that function which allows us to declare that some people have more will-power than others.

However, unlike the term "intelligence," the terms referring to our higher appetitive power, "will" and "will-power," are never used of animals. Even in our present day and age only man is credited with will.

225

Success in life depends more on the will than on intelligence. Great achievements are not possible without a strong will. Hence it is important to know what is meant by a strong will and what means can be used in the development of will-power.

WHAT IS A STRONG WILL?

A strong will is a will which strives constantly towards a self-chosen goal under the influence of self-supplied motivation.

This definition of a strong will involves three elements: constancy, a self-chosen goal and self-supplied motivation.

It is obvious that constancy and perseverance are indispensable ingredients of real will-power. The true test of will-power is not found in the decisions the individual takes or in the eagerness with which he sets to work, but in the way he behaves when obstacles and other difficulties present themselves in his path. These impediments may come from without—people or the circumstances of life —or from within—weariness, discouragement, the very monotony of the task. It takes a strong will to overcome all difficulties and keep up one's efforts in spite of them.

Furthermore, real will-power supposes a self-chosen goal, a goal freely accepted by the person. A drug addict may show great constancy and perseverance in the pursuit of his goal, the enjoyment of his morbid pleasure. He is ready to sacrifice his health and wealth, his reputation, the honor and well-being of his family in order to indulge his craving. All the obstacles which society multiplies around him are thrust aside whenever his demon possesses him.

Yet this is not real will-power, because the individual has not freely chosen his goal; he has submitted to the tyranny of an unruly drive, he is the prisoner of a blind passion. In his better moments he is aware of this degrading servitude and deplores it. He would like to shake it off, but it is stronger than he.

It does not follow that passion and will-power are always in conflict. Passion, which we can describe as a powerful drive deeply rooted in a person's mind and polarizing all his energies, is a powerful adjuvant of a strong will if that passion has been wholeheartedly accepted by the person, if it is harmoniously integrated with the rest of his personality. Typical of this is an ambitious man who has freely decided to live only for the acquisition of power, or a Saint whose passionate love of God directs all his energies towards the service of the Divine Majesty. But wherever passion is not harmonized with the personality, wherever it grows like a cancer at the expense of the sound elements of that personality, it is incompatible with real strength of will.

The other element of our definition, "under the influence of self-supplied motivation," is also essential. Quite a number of people who do not possess a strong will nevertheless strive constantly towards a self-chosen goal. They persevere in their efforts only because motivation is continually supplied to them from without, by their environment. Take any student who is "getting an education." From the age of six to the age of twenty he may persist in this purpose. He has freely chosen it, he really wants an education. He meets obstacles of all kinds, especially in himself: weariness, monotony, desire for a more interesting or more immediately rewarding occupation. Despite all these obstacles he keeps striving towards his goal. But the motivation which keeps him in his course is supplied mostly from outside, by his parents, the school, the whole environment. Quizzes, examinations, praise and rebuke, sanctions for absence or for failure keep him steadily at his work. Would he continue to strive towards his distant goal if all this social pressure were withdrawn? In most cases the answer would be no. A student who would not slacken his efforts in the absence of such outside motivation can be credited with real will-power, because he strives constantly towards a self-chosen goal under the influence of self-supplied motivation.

METHODS FOR DEVELOPING WILL-POWER

Some authors claim that the will, like any other faculty, is developed by practice and training. The child is supposed to perform tasks which are disagreeable or difficult, and it is presumed that after prolonged practice of this kind he will have developed a strong will.

Many difficulties can be raised against this theory. The will is not a muscle which can be strengthened by repeated use. Experimental psychology has demonstrated that training a power or function in one definite task does not automatically result in an over-all development of that function. The many experiments performed on "transfer of training" have clearly shown that there is transfer only when methods, attitudes, motives, or principles acquired in one field can be applied in the other field. Furthermore, where will the child find the will-power required for the repeated performance of these difficult tasks? How will he keep up such a training program unless he already possesses the will-power which this program is supposed to develop?

There can be no doubt that practice and exercise help to develop the will, but only in connection with strong motives, only when and inasmuch as they make these motives more personal and cause them to become more deeply rooted in the mind. Practice without simultaneous development of motive is useless.

Another method which is often recommended for the development of will-power is the acquisition of habits. This theory claims that every habit makes the corresponding action easier to perform and produces a need for repetition of that action. We have already shown that this is true for physiological and psychological habits, but that it applies to motor habits, to the skills, only when these habits have not yet been perfectly mastered. Perfectly mastered motor habits make the corresponding action easier to perform, but do not impel the subject to repeat that action.

Moral, or voluntary habits may make the action easier to perform, but of themselves they do not impel us to repeat that action. I may by frequent acts of patience have acquired the virtue or the habit of patience, but I shall not look for opportunities of repeating acts of patience the way a smoker looks for opportunities to smoke or a golf-player looks forward to his next game.

We may even wonder whether a moral habit as such, considered apart from its motivation, makes the action easier to perform. In other words, we doubt whether real moral habits can be acquired without strong motivation. Everyday experience confirms our doubts. For example, newly married people generally start their life with excellent dispositions, and they repeat, time and again, acts of kindness, patience, self-forgetting charity for each other.

Repetition should engrave these habits in their nature, so that such actions should become easier as the years go by. We know that this is not always the case. Let the first flush of love (that is, the motivation) wane, and what came easily and as a matter of course a few months ago becomes more and more difficult. The habit, which should have developed from frequent repetition, seems to have grown weaker instead of stronger, because the motivation has been allowed to decrease.

When we speak of moral habits, we too easily forget the important observation of St. Thomas,[1] that only intense actions will strengthen a habit, not the mere repetition of any kind of action. It is not repetition as such, but only the repetition of intense actions, which produces a moral habit. And what makes these actions intense? Not, of course, the habit itself, but only the motives which inspire the actions. Hence habit formation is useful for the development of the will only when it is backed by strong motives.

Everyday experience and philosophical reflection therefore agree on this basic truth: the will is a striving faculty and, like any other striving faculty, it is set in motion only by some apprehended good. A motive is precisely such an apprehended good. Any good, any value presented to the will through the senses and intelligence, may set that faculty in motion, will at least attract it. Hence in order to influence and to educate the will, we must learn how to use the most powerful motives.

There is a scale of motives as there is a scale of values. Not all motives are equally useful for the formation of the will. We can distinguish, in ascending order, the following groups of values or motives:[2]

1. The sensory values, which satisfy any of our segmental drives or the body as a whole. Such are food, drink, rest, comfort, sex.

2. The vital values, which derive from the harmonious development of the body: health, strength, forceful and harmonious activity, physical beauty, playing. These values have their greatest appeal during later childhood and adolescence.

---

[1] *S. Theol.*, Ia IIae, q. 52, a. 3, c.

[2] To every group of positive values corresponds a group of negative values, which repel the will and which the person tries to avoid. Thus negative sensory values are lack of food, pain, etc.

3. The social values, which satisfy the individual as the member of a group: love of the parents, heterosexual attraction, friendship, human society, reputation, power.

4. The spiritual values, which appeal to the spiritual faculties of man, to his intellect and will; they can be further subdivided into intellectual values (knowledge, discovery, truth), aesthetic values (artistic beauty in its many forms), moral values (goodness, honesty, justice, generosity).

5. The religious values, which refer to God and to our life after death. Some of these presuppose the supernatural virtues of faith, hope and charity. Others are accessible to unaided human reason. The former include the fear of hell, the desire of heaven, the love of God.

It is with these values, or rather with a combination of some of them, that the educator must operate when he wants to strengthen the will of his charges.

WHAT IS REQUIRED FOR EFFICIENT MOTIVES?

The values or motives mentioned above will be efficient if they fulfill the four following conditions:

1. The motives must be adapted. A value may be very noble and high, but if it does not appeal to the mind it will remain fruitless. In general we may say that the higher the motive, the less it will appeal to the undeveloped mind of the child. Promise him some candy or a visit to the movies, and you will get immediate results. But appeal to his sense of social responsibility, point out to him that the progress of the human race demands that he should study his lessons, and the results will be disappointing. The conclusion seems to follow that in the education of young children, we must use only the lower values, the sensory values and, to a certain extent, the vital and the social values. The higher values are useless in early education.

2. The values must be lasting, enduring, permanent. This requirement seems to be incompatible with the former one. Lower values are not lasting. They produce immediate results, but they drive no permanent roots into the mind. They have to be presented ever anew from outside. On the other hand, the higher values are

permanent and lasting, deeply rooted in man's intelligence and will. Anyone who can develop a real enthusiasm for intellectual, aesthetic or moral values will find in them a source of permanent motivation, of durable will-power. This leads us to the following rather discouraging conclusion: the adapted motives are not permanent and the permanent motives are not adapted.

The same difficulty can be presented under another form, which may lead us to a solution. The lower values derive their power from the fact that they are backed by drives and instincts, whereas the higher values appeal only to the will. Because they are backed by drives, the lower motives push; the higher motives draw, and they draw only those who have taken hold of them intellectually.

Therefore, just as it is impossible to educate the intelligence of the child except through the medium of his senses, it is impossible to develop his will without using his drives and instincts. Real educators have always realized this truth. They have generally presented the higher values in such a way as to make them appeal, at first, not directly to the will, but to the drives. We can demonstrate this best in relation to the highest of all values, the religious values, which are also the most easily adaptable. These values, as presented to the child, should not take the form of considerations about the Mystical Body of Christ, but the simpler form of heaven with the Celestial Banquet (sensory motive), or of the eternal Crown which rewards virtue (social motive). Virtue is presented not as the most reasonable form of conduct but as the real test of strength or the essential requisite of beauty (vital motive). As his mind develops, the child should, of course, be gradually introduced into a deeper understanding of the inexhaustible meaning of these values.

3. Motives must be comprehensive in order to be useful in the formation of the will; that means that their influence must extend to all the actions of life, not just to one category of actions. An athlete who has his heart set on winning a race or a game, or on breaking a record, will find in this motive a source of strength for all that lies in the line of his goal. It will carry him through strenuous training, help him to be temperate—to abstain from smoking, drinking and all forms of dissipation. But it will not help him in the least to be honest, truthful and charitable, because these virtues do not come within the scope of his motive.

The higher the motives are, the more comprehensive they become. Secular education in general uses social-moral values or a social-moral ideal,[3] such as "becoming a good citizen, or a useful member of the community, or a real gentleman." Such an ideal is indeed very comprehensive, and it covers most natural and social virtues. But it is inadequate in relation to some of the most intimate struggles of the individual, the struggle for purity, the struggle with apparently meaningless pain. One can be an excellent citizen and member of the community, and have all the makings of a gentleman, and yet have an unclean mind or an inability to accept pain and humiliation. A person confined to bed for long years by a crippling disease does not derive much inspiration from such motives.

It seems that only the religious motives cover absolutely all the activities of life, as is immediately evident to anyone who understands their scope and meaning. This does not mean that they should be used exclusively of the others. The best motivation seems to derive from a combination of social, moral and intellectual values, supported and animated by strong religious motives. Any young man who is inspired by an intense desire of becoming an outstanding Catholic doctor, lawyer or scientist or an accomplished Christian gentleman is well on his way to perfect voluntary control.

4. Motives must be conscious, they must constantly be kept before the mind. We do not derive any strength from motives to which we do not advert. This requirement is most difficult to realize. If we try to probe this aspect of efficient motivation, we shall sooner or later come up against the essential mystery of the will. There are some superficial and artificial methods which may be used to keep the motives in the focus of consciousness, or at least to bring them there on frequent occasions. Such are slogans, written resolutions. There is the better method of meditative reflection by which the motives are, at stated times, renewed before the mind and woven into the very fabric of our life.[4]

---

[3] An ideal is an integrated group of motives, often personified in a real or possible model.

[4] In his famous book *The Education of the Will* Jules Payot recommends meditative reflection as the best method for developing will-power. A good retreat, with plenty of meditation, can have a powerful influence upon a person's will because it makes him clearly aware of the great religious motives.

The great differences existing between individuals in regard to will-power seem to derive mainly from the availability, the degree of consciousness, of their motives. Most people want to succeed, to forge ahead in their careers, to accumulate wealth, power or knowledge, to have a happy family life, to improve their personalities, etc. But only those who want these things badly enough are going to get anywhere, because they will make the necessary efforts to achieve them. "To want things badly enough," to want them intensely, seems to be the essential condition of success. This is precisely the point where great differences exist between individuals. Some people are haunted by the desire to succeed, to make money, to help others, and so on. They are, in the good sense of that word, "ambitious." Whenever they are inclined to slacken their efforts, a powerful motivation, the idea of whatever they want to achieve, rises before their mind and gives them no rest until they are again hard at work. These are the strong-willed individuals. Others want the same things too, but in a theoretical, detached way, which allows them to forget their purpose for long stretches of time, during which no endeavor is made to reach it. Such people are unable to want something badly enough. They may be very intelligent, but they are definitely *minus habentes* in the domain of the will.

The real way, therefore, of developing a strong will is to "want it badly enough," to will it. This seems to lead to a vicious circle. In fact it leads to an awareness of the peculiar nature of the will, which, like the intellect, is capable of reflecting upon itself, in this sense: that as the intellect knows that it knows, the will may will to will.

READINGS

Aveling, *Personality and Will*. Barrett, *Strength of Will*. Eymieu, *Le Gouvernement de Soi-même*. Lindworsky, *Training of the Will* and *Psychology of Asceticism*. Moore, *The Driving Forces of Human Nature*, pp. 321-387. Payot, *The Education of the Will*.

14

The Higher Tendencies

HIGHER TENDENCIES AND DEPTH-PSYCHOLOGY

The will is essentially a rational love of that which is good, or seems to be good. But many things are or seem to be good for man, and therefore his will manifests itself in many different ways. The main directions which the striving of the human will may take can be called the higher tendencies of man, as opposed to the lower or sensory drives which we have studied in a previous chapter.

Experimental and clinical psychology have not been very successful in the study of these higher tendencies. True, the Würzburg school of systematic introspection has devoted a certain number of investigations to the study of the human will.[1] But the results of these studies have not been satisfactory because introspection applied to the elusive higher phenomena in man seems to discover nothing but the conscious or unconscious philosophical preconceptions of the scientist who introspects. As a consequence, where a spiritually-minded psychologist discovered, through introspection, a real consciousness of free choice, his materialistically-minded colleague discovered only images accompanied by muscular tensions in his chest.

Depth-psychology, that is, the psychology of Freud and all the systems directly deriving from it, has emphasized the study of human drives and tendencies. But because it started with a strong materialistic bias and studied exclusively the abnormal aspects of mental life, its findings are woefully incomplete and give a distorted picture of the normal personality.

[1] They have been summarized and critically evaluated in Fr. J. Lindworsky's *Der Wille,* 3d ed. (Leipzig, Barth, 1923).

Depth-psychology claims that the sex drive and the drive for power are the main tendencies in man, and that all higher tendencies somehow derive from these two fundamental drives.

It is evident that these two drives are very important in human life and that many psychological disturbances have their roots in them. But this does not derive from the fact that they are the only, or even the main human drives, but from the fact that they are the most liable to clash with the norms imposed by society and with man's higher tendencies.

1. The sex and the power drives are the ones most liable to clash with the norms imposed by society. This has always been true, but the observation is especially applicable to our time, to modern society torn between Christian and pagan influences. Most of our contemporaries pay lip-service to the Christian ideal of morality, which emphasizes the control of the sex drive and of aggressiveness. In practice, however, the sex drive is often given free rein, and ruthless competition is the rule rather than the exception. Is it surprising, then, to find that so many psychic troubles can be traced to this ambivalent attitude produced by the cleavage between theory and practice, between early education and the realities of adult life? And should we not expect that the two drives upon which these problems generally center have assumed an importance out of all proportion to their real place in the human mind?[2]

2. The sex and the power drives are not only in conflict with social norms, they are also frequently in conflict with other drives in man. Man is both an animal and a spirit—or rather he is, in a certain sense, a combination of both. As an animal he possesses drives whose satisfaction is not always compatible with his spiritual drives. Unlike the animal, therefore, man is bound to meet psychic conflicts within himself. When he freely indulges his animal drives, his spiritual tendencies continue to exert their pull in other directions. If he tries to satisfy these spiritual inclinations, the animal drives will often rebel and produce mental turmoil. Complete harmony is possible only if his animal drives are subordinated to his higher tendencies. This is not too difficult to achieve with such drives as hunger and thirst, but it is much more difficult where the

[2] Cp. J. Nuttin, *Psychoanalysis and Personality* (Sheed & Ward, 1953), pp. 166-167.

sex drive and the power drive are concerned, and this explains why these drives may take on such ominous dimensions in his mental life.

MAN'S HIGHER TENDENCIES

The human will is a universal appetite for the good as possessed by an individual being.

Inasmuch as it is a universal appetite for the good, it strives necessarily, albeit unconsciously, towards the perfect good, which is God. Therefore man's deepest *unconscious* tendency goes out towards God.

Inasmuch as it is an appetite possessed by an individual being, the will strives necessarily and consciously towards the possession of what this individual considers to be his supreme good, towards happiness. Man's deepest *conscious* tendency is the tendency towards happiness.

Here lies the root of a fundamental conflict in human life. Man's conscious willing should coincide with his deeper, unconscious striving. It should, but it does not necessarily coincide, for the will is free. Man may freely decide that his happiness does not lie in the knowledge and the loving possession of God, but in some created good, such as duty, social progress, wealth, power, pleasure.

Happiness is the realization of all man's desires, and implies perfect self-realization. Therefore we may also state that man's deepest conscious tendency is the tendency towards self-realization. If man considers himself as what he really and basically is, a creature, his craving towards self-realization will ultimately be a craving for God. If he overlooks or ignores the fact that he is a creature, his fundamental conscious tendency towards self-realization will assume the form of a drive towards the possession of some created good.

In both cases man wants to realize himself as a being endowed with an intellect and a will, as a being who knows and loves. As a *being who knows,* man wants knowledge and truth. He wants to know not only his environment and its biological resources (this need exists also in animals), but also the meaning of life and reality (philosophy), the nature and functioning of the material universe (the sciences). This need is developed to a greater or lesser extent in different individuals, but it is always present to some extent. Nobody wants to be led into error by others, or takes pride in consciously being wrong, although quite a number of people occasionally find it useful to deceive themselves.

As a being who loves man wants to possess not only himself but also other creatures. This desire for the possession of other creatures may assume three fundamental forms.

1. Some people want to possess or to use other creatures merely as a means for their own self-realization, without any regard for the nature or the rights of these others. Such people consider themselves the center of the universe. They have excluded God from their thought and from their love, and everybody and every thing must serve them and help them reach their own happiness. This is the picture of the completely egotistic individual.

2. Some people want to possess and use other creatures with due respect for their nature and their rights. They use some creatures merely as means (minerals, plants), others as means but with certain restrictions, imposed by their higher ontological perfection (animals), others never merely as means, but as associates, models, companions, friends—in short, as fellow men. Here possession is of a higher kind, and takes the form of knowledge, reverence, admiration, sympathy and love. No explicit reference is made to the final end for which these creatures exist, to God. The absolute for which such people live is duty, or the progress of mankind, or social justice. Their ideal is a moral ideal.

3. Others want to possess and use other creatures with due consideration for their nature and rights and refer them explicitly to God. Theirs is a religious ideal, which includes and transcends the moral ideal described in 2.[3]

Here again we meet a source of conflict in human life. Very few individuals belong entirely to any one of the three groups outlined above. Every human being is strongly impelled towards egoism, and will at least occasionally yield to it. On the other hand, most persons are attracted, however faintly, by the moral or the religious ideal. Even those who have definitely opted for ruthless egoism

[3] Compare with the three stages of Kierkegaard in *Stages on Life's Way.*

will generally clothe their designs in the garb of morality, thus paying an involuntary tribute to the moral ideal.

Another higher tendency which man possesses because he is a spirit in matter is the striving towards beauty, both the enjoyment and the creation of beauty. Part of this striving derives from the sex drive and appears to some extent in animals. But above this biological drive towards beauty there is a spiritual craving for the enjoyment and the creation of esthetically satisfying objects. That this drive is deeply ingrained in man may be demonstrated by the fact that every human culture shows some artistic production, and that very few human beings are absolutely indifferent to every form of beauty. However, this drive is strongly influenced by the environment, and it remains very rudimentary in many individuals.

Summarizing, we may say:

Man wants happiness because he possesses a will. But his desire for happiness is vague and, on the conscious level, not specified. He himself must specify it, staking his all on himself or on some Absolute distinct from himself. This Absolute may be God consciously intended, or God unconsciously intended under the guise of duty, the progress of mankind, social justice. God, on the other hand, may be explicitly rejected as the Absolute, and the will may strive towards an egoistic form of happiness based on the possession of some creature. Man's craving for happiness includes a desire for knowledge and truth, a desire for loving possession of other beings and a desire for beauty.

Shall we say that there is a religious drive in man? We can admit the existence of such a drive if we take the word religious in a very wide and rather vague sense. The striving towards truth and happiness is objectively a striving towards God, and it is not surprising that in most cases it is subjectively, although vaguely, felt as such— that is, as a religious tendency. We must remember, however, that, like all other conscious drives, this one depends greatly on the influence of the environment, that it may remain at a very rudimentary stage of development, that it may be hampered or inhibited by other drives and even consciously counteracted by the will. The fact that all human races and cultures show some kind of religious consciousness is a strong argument for the existence of an inborn religious drive in man.

MAN'S INTERMEDIATE DRIVES

We call intermediate those drives in man which contain both intellectual and sensory components. Because they contain sensory components we find them in animals also; but because in man they are taken over and animated by the will they present in him a radically different aspect.

We have mentioned these drives on p. 156, as "propensities showing no clear organic rhythm," that is, as drives which are not physiological but strictly psychological. We should mention them here again and study the way in which they manifest themselves in man, when taken over and animated by the intellect and the will. But treating all these drives in that way would be beyond the scope of this book, and we shall therefore consider only one example, the social drive.

The social drive is present in many animals, especially in the higher vertebrates. It is manifested in animals by the fact that they seek the company of their fellows, they "assume by primitive sympathy the feelings of the group . . . evoke emotional responses from others"[4] and imitate them.

Man is the most social of all vertebrates. His social drive is implied in the need for the possession of others, mentioned above. It is not simply assumed by the will, as is the case with the hunger or the sex drive. In man the spiritual need for contact with others combines harmoniously with the sensory need for "belonging to the group" and produces together with it one of the deepest cravings of human nature.

Man needs the company, protection, help, example, admiration and love of his fellow men. During his long childhood and youth he needs continual care, protection and love. He cannot reach the full development of his capabilities without a protracted education. During the first years of his life, he remains for the most part at the receiving end of these social relations. But gradually another need matures which makes him desire to influence, to help and instruct others; to be accepted, esteemed, admired and honored by

[4] R. B. Cattell, *Personality,* p. 181.

them. He needs to communicate to them not only his emotions but also his ideas and his intentions. Complete self-realization is impossible without a loving donation of one's self to others. Solitary confinement is one of the most terrible punishments which can be meted out to a human being. The feeling of being rejected, of being useless and of no importance, produces acute mental suffering. Even the hermit living alone in his cave cannot, without doing violence to his own mental and spiritual development, entirely forget that he belongs to the human family. He has given up the bodily presence of his fellow men only in order to influence them spiritually.

All the other psychological propensities mentioned on p. 156 are, in the same way, "sublimated" through combination with man's spiritual tendencies. Thus animal curiosity blends with the need for truth and manifests itself in man's unending quest for knowledge.

Even the drives which have clearly physiological roots, such as the hunger and the sex drive, are considerably transformed through their assumption under the will. Man needs food, just like the animals. But he has learned to need certain kinds of food, prepared in a certain way, presented in a manner which suits his taste, enjoyed with a certain ritual in the company of others of his kind. His hunger drive, although it may occasionally show itself in grubbing or hunting, manifests itself more frequently in agriculture, industry, business and the huge economic system of modern society. Equally remarkable are the great differences existing between animal mating and the complexities of human courtship and marriage.

Note:

At the end of this empirical study of man's rational life we should like to point out that we have totally neglected one important sector of that life: man's higher feelings, his sentiments—for instance, the sentiment of anxiety, of duty, of beauty. The reason is simply the great difficulty of such a study. Neither experimental psychology nor philosophy can tell us much about man's higher affective functions. Needed here is the phenomenological method. Cfr. the works of Dietrich von Hildebrand, also S. Strasser, *Das Gemüt*. For a shorter study, P. Lersch, *Aufbau der Person,* 6th ed., pp. 180-260.

READINGS

J. Nuttin, *Psychoanalysis and Personality,* pp. 159-256.

Philosophical Study of
Man's Rational Life

15

The Human Intellect

THE POSITION and value of a philosophical system depend primarily on its conception of the human intellect. In order to gain a better understanding of our own conception, it is useful to compare it with some other systems. Such a comparison will help us to see where we stand in philosophy and will show that the Aristotelian-Thomistic system tends to take the middle road between the untenable positions at either extreme.[1]

THE POSITION OF OUR SYSTEM

From the point of view of knowledge, we can divide the systems into five main groups:

1. The first group rejects the value of knowledge in general. We know nothing, none of our faculties gives us certain knowledge of reality. This is SCEPTICISM, a system professed by the Greek sceptics of the fifth and the third centuries before Christ. This system cannot be either set forth or defended without internal contradiction, as Aristotle demonstrated. It has no adherents among modern philosophers.

2. The second group holds that only the senses give us certain knowledge. In fact, we have only sense knowledge; that which is called intelligence is only a higher sense, or the sum-total of the senses. This doctrine, variously called SENSISM, EMPIRICISM, POSITIVISM, leads to MATERIALISM. The system existed in Antiquity,

[1] This review of the systems must be very brief, and is therefore necessarily oversimplified. It cannot point out the many good features in these philosophies. The reader is referred to any good history of philosophy.

but it was presented in its purest form by the British Empiricists of the seventeenth and eighteenth centuries, especially David Hume. In some form or other it prevails in many American philosophical circles, and it constitutes the unconscious philosophy of many scientists.

3. At the opposite extreme is a third group of philosophers who maintain that only the intellect gives us knowledge of reality. They either overlook sense knowledge or fail to distinguish it from intellectual knowledge. This system is called IDEALISM, and it leads to Idealistic PANTHEISM. It was presented in its purest form by the great German Idealists of the eighteenth and the beginning of the nineteenth century, especially Fichte, Schelling and Hegel.

4. A fourth group admits the existence of both sense and intellectual knowledge, makes a distinction between the senses and the intellect and affirms that both participate in human knowledge. But it fails to make a satisfactory synthesis of both. This error seems to be very natural to the human mind, and it has been presented in many forms.

a. According to Plato (427-347 B.C.) our soul existed before we were born into this world. In its pre-natal dwelling place the Ideas subsisted in a pure form, not embedded in material things. In that heaven of Ideas, the soul contemplated not trees or horses or men but the Idea of Tree, Horse or Man. Now confined in the body as in a prison, the soul has lost this contemplation of pure Ideas. But when physical impressions from individual trees, or horses or men impinge on our senses, our soul "remembers" the ideas corresponding to them, which it contemplated in its former state. Therefore our sense knowledge is real; however, it is not a cause but only an occasion of our intellectual knowledge.

b. Although he did not admit the pre-existence of the soul, Descartes (1596-1650) professed a somewhat similar doctrine. One of the central tenets of his system is that soul and body are both complete substances. He rejected the traditional explanation of body and soul as complementary principles, of matter and form constituting together one complete substance. As a consequence he had great difficulty in explaining such elementary facts as that, when our senses are impressed by a physical object, we conceive the idea of that object in our minds, or that, when our will wants us to move a part of our body, the body executes that movement. At some point in his system he acknowledged the interaction between soul and body and asserted that it had its seat in the pineal gland; but then again, impressed by the impossibility of a material substance influencing a spiritual substance, he denied all interaction. This forced him into the position of denying that our ideas come from the senses and asserting that they are inborn in the mind. The unsolved problem of the interaction between body and soul has plagued Descartes' successors, who have presented the strangest theories in their attempts to solve it.

c. A first attempt was made by Malebranche who taught the system of Occasionalism. Like Descartes he considered body and soul to be two complete substances and rejected the possibility of any direct interaction between them. How then did he explain the obvious fact that, when our eye sees a tree, our mind conceives the idea of a tree? By saying that the sense perception of the tree was an *occasion* for God to put into our mind the corresponding idea—i.e., when our body is influenced by a material object, our mind is simultaneously endowed by God with the idea of that object.

d. Even to Malebranche's followers Occasionalism seemed artificial and improbable, and therefore another follower of Descartes, Leibniz, starting from the same principles (body and soul complete substances, no interaction possible between them), devised the doctrine of "pre-established harmony." God does not intervene every time I have a sensation. He has pre-established a perfect harmony between the series of my sensations and the series of my ideas, so that every time I have a sensation, the corresponding idea arises in my mind; thus the sensation has no influence on the formation of the idea. He used the comparison of two clocks which mark the same time, neither having any influence upon the other. They have been made in such a way as to mark time in perfect harmony. If we wanted a modern example, we could say that whenever Donald Duck opens his mouth we hear him speak, although the movements of his mouth have not the slightest influence on the sounds we hear. Between the film and the sound-track there is a pre-established harmony.

e. For Leibniz the two series of events, one physical, the other psychic, had been freely synchronized by God. For Spinoza they are necessary emanations of God. Spinoza's system is one of realistic pantheism. Everything which exists is a necessary attribute or mode of God. According to Spinoza, God may be compared with a gigantic tree with many branches which grow out of it of absolute necessity. We know only two of these branches, the branch consisting of the physical events and that which consists of the psychic events. They are perfectly parallel in their development, so that to each event in the physical branch corresponds an event in the psychic branch. Our sensations are physical events, our ideas are psychic events. Therefore, to every one of our sensations corresponds an idea, although the sensations have no influence upon the formation of the ideas.

All these philosophers reasoned logically from their premises. Yet their systems are untenable, especially the most logical and coherent of these systems, the doctrine of Spinoza. He was led to affirm that God possesses spatial extension because he deduced inexorably all the consequences deriving from his own and Descartes' starting point: body and soul are two complete substances; the senses and the intellect do not really co-operate. Since the consequences are false, the starting point must be false. The errors contained in the system of Spinoza are among the best arguments for our conception of the intimate collaboration of sense and intellect in the formation of our ideas, and therefore also of the substantial unity of man.

5. A fifth group of philosophers admits that the senses and the intellect collaborate in the formation of our ideas, and that without the co-operation of both we can have no intellectual knowledge.

a. Immanuel Kant (1724-1804) was one of the first modern non-Scholastic philosophers who rejected the fundamental assumptions of Cartesianism and Empiricism. At first he had been indirectly influenced by Descartes, but he soon discovered that Cartesianism could not be held. The influence of the British Empiricists made him lean for a while towards Empiricism, but it did not take him long to uncover its weaknesses. By dint of much labor he finally rediscovered the middle position which had been held by Aristotle and Aquinas, and he claimed that both sense and intellect are the necessary sources of all human knowledge. But he did not rediscover the traditional position completely and was thus led into some serious errors which have had a very great influence on the whole of modern philosophy.

Kant was right when he affirmed that the senses and the intellect co-operate in every human thought, but he was wrong when he maintained that intellectual knowledge does not reach beyond the domain of the senses. For him the function of the intellect is to arrange and unify the data of the senses by imprinting its own subjective categories on them. It follows that we can know only sensible, material beings, and that whatever is not material is beyond the range of our knowledge. Man cannot know such realities as God, the soul, liberty. Here lies Kant's fateful error. He did not understand that, although all our knowledge starts with the senses and is accompanied by sense knowledge, our intellect can reach further than the senses. He did not realize that we can "mean" more than we can "represent." Kant rediscovered an important part of the great Aristotelean-Thomistic synthesis and enriched it with many interesting developments which we gratefully accept. But he did not rediscover the whole synthesis; he underestimated the real power of the human intellect and rejected all metaphysical knowledge as illusory. He did not deny the existence of God or of the soul, but he claimed that our intellect as such, our theoretical intellect, could not reach them. Such a system is known as AGNOSTICISM.

b. Hence there are good reasons for maintaining the age-old synthesis, first discovered by Aristotle (384-322 B.C.), strengthened and sharpened by Aquinas (1225-1274). Body and soul are incomplete substances, constituting together not a union but a unity. Sense and intellect co-operate in all our knowledge. But the intellect does more than organize sense knowledge. It reaches far beyond the senses, it can know immaterial realities. In the following pages we shall study how this is possible.

IMMATERIALITY OF THE HUMAN INTELLECT

Our intellect is immaterial: this means, it is not intrinsically dependent upon matter. The brain is that portion of matter which has the closest relation to the operations of our intellect. We claim, therefore, that our intellect is not intrinsically dependent on our brain, that our brain is not a cause of the operations of our intellect, that it does not think.

Since we cannot study our intellect directly, we must turn to its operations and show that they are immaterial. For, as a being is, so it acts. If the operations of our intellect are immaterial, their cause, our intellect, must likewise be immaterial.

We shall consider three operations of the intellect: ideas, judgments and reflection.

Every philosopher admits that our intellect is not material in the way a stone is material; it cannot be seen or touched or photographed like a stone. It is not material in the strict sense; that needs no demonstration. But many philosophers claim that there is no difference between the immateriality of our intellect and that of our senses. We claim that our intellect is immaterial in a higher way; that, unlike the senses, it is intrinsically independent of matter.

Therefore we must compare the operations of our intellect with those of our senses, both external and internal, and show that there is a radical difference between them, which involves a radical difference in the nature of the faculties.

COMPARISON OF SENSATIONS OR IMAGES WITH IDEAS

Sensations are always of single objects or single groups of objects. I see *this* cat, I hear *this* plane, I touch *this* table, I see *this* crowd, I hear *this* squadron flying overhead.

Images likewise always refer to a single object or group of objects. I cannot imagine a tree which is at the same time a poplar and a birch, big and small, with leaves and without leaves. The clearer my image is, the better I realize that it applies only to one individual object or group of objects.

My ideas, on the other hand, are universal. They apply to each and every individual of a species. The idea which I have of a tree applies to all trees, poplars and birches, big and small, with or without leaves, present, past and future, real and possible. Not only are my ideas universal, I am also aware of their universality.

I even possess a few ideas which apply to absolutely every reality. Such are the ideas of "being," "something." They can be used for whatever exists or is possible, and I am aware of this fact.

Hence there is an essential difference between sensations and images, on one hand, and ideas, on the other hand. There must be a corresponding difference between the senses and the intellect. The root of that difference is in the materiality of my senses as opposed to the immateriality of my intellect. Wherever there is matter (prime matter or second matter), or intrinsic dependence on matter, there is quantity, therefore spatiality and temporality. An object which is in space and time is necessarily individual, singular, concrete. It follows that where there is generality, universality and abstractness, where there is no localization in space and time, there can be no intrinsic dependence on matter. Therefore my ideas are not intrinsically dependent on matter and my intellect, which produces them, is strictly immaterial.[2]

COMPARISON OF SENSATIONS AND IMAGES WITH JUDGMENTS

Sensations and images are always of contingent objects or actions. That means that the objects which I perceive or imagine do exist, but do not exist necessarily; they could also not exist. And the actions which I perceive or imagine happen, but do not happen necessarily.

On the other hand, in all judgments there is an element of neces-

[2] It should be noted that an idea, inasmuch as it is a real accident of my intellect, is a singular, individual being. Singularity and individuality do not always involve matter. But universality always excludes it. Now the meaning, the scope of my idea is universal, and therefore my idea excludes any materiality.

sity. Even a judgment referring to a contingent event contains a core of absolute necessity.

It is raining. That is a contingent, not a necessary fact. I may perceive it or imagine it; it remains perfectly contingent. When, however, I pronounce the judgment, "It is raining," this judgment, although referring to a contingent event, contains a core of necessity. If it is raining, it is raining, it cannot not be raining. It is absolutely impossible that at the same moment and at the same place it should be raining and not raining.[3] We have here a hypothetical necessity. Hypothetical: If it is raining. Necessity: It is necessarily raining. That necessity is absent from all my images and perceptions and present in every one of my judgments.

But the necessity in our judgments appears more clearly in certain kinds of judgments, especially in all mathematical and metaphysical judgments. Two plus two makes four. Every effect has a cause. Whatever is, is. A being cannot exist and not exist at the same time. These judgments are absolutely necessary, universally and eternally true. By means of such judgments we dictate, in a certain sense, our law to reality. I do not know what exists or happens on the other side of the moon. But I know that if there are two moon craters and two others besides, there are necessarily four craters, and it is absolutely certain that these craters have a cause.

Therefore we have discovered one more essential difference between the operations of the senses and imagination and some operation of the intellect, which implies a corresponding difference between these faculties. That difference is rooted in the materiality of sensation and imagination, as opposed to the immateriality of the judgment. Potency, and especially its lowest form, prime matter, is the radical principle of contingency and mutability. Wherever we find necessity in the sense of eternal, immutable existence,[4] we know that there can be no intrinsic dependence on matter. There-

[3] It will be noticed that these contingent judgments are necessary inasmuch as they embody the first principle.

[4] Necessity in the sense of eternal, immutable existence, is to be carefully distinguished from necessity in the sense of determinism. The former is a perfection of being, which is found in its highest form in God. The latter is an imperfection, found in material beings. We are speaking here of the first kind of necessity.

fore the judgments produced by my intellect are not intrinsically
dependent on matter, and my intellect itself is strictly immaterial.[5]

COMPARISON OF THE IMPERFECT REFLECTION
OF THE SENSES WITH THE PERFECT
REFLECTION OF THE INTELLECT

One of the most remarkable properties of my intellect is its
power of reflecting perfectly on its own activity. I think that I
think, I am aware of being aware, I am conscious of being conscious. The intellect not only performs an activity, but it knows
that activity while it is going on.

The senses possess no perfect self-reflection. My eye sees, but
it does not see that it sees. My imagination imagines, but it does
not imagine its own imagining.[6] The senses act, but they do not
reflect upon their own activity. It is true that the animal is aware
that it sees or hears. But we have already shown that this fact must
be explained through the central sense. No external sense is aware
of its own activity; the central sense is not aware of its own activity; but the central sense is aware of the activity of the external
senses. This is called imperfect self-reflection.

Since the intellect is capable of perfect self-reflection, whereas
none of the senses is, there is an essential difference between the
senses and the intellect. This difference is based upon the materiality of the senses, as opposed to the immateriality of the intellect. Perfect self-reflection means self-consciousness, a very high
kind of consciousness. But consciousness is opposed to matter,
and self-consciousness excludes any intrinsic dependence on matter. Self-consciousness makes a being capable of coinciding with
itself. Matter involves spatiality, and in a spatial being every part

---

[5] It should be noted again that our judgments, as real accidents of our
intellect, are contingent and mutable. They come and they go and they
change. But their content and scope extends to something which is hypothetically or absolutely necessary, eternally and immutably true. That excludes any intrinsic dependence on matter.

[6] When we say, "I imagine that I imagine," the first "I imagine" is taken
in the sense of "I suppose," which denotes an act not of the imagination,
but of the intellect.

is outside every other part, and cannot coincide with any other part without destroying itself.

We may again conclude that our intellect is intrinsically independent of matter, is strictly immaterial.

OBJECTIONS AGAINST THE FOREGOING PROOFS

Objection 1: The fact that our ideas are universal is not a proof of their immateriality. There are many universal relations and tendencies which are not immaterial. A cat has a universal tendency to kill mice. It is not just looking for this or that individual mouse, but just for mice, for any mouse. Our eye has a universal power of seeing colored objects, any colored object. A hammer is a universal tool for driving nails into boards, any nail into any board. All these are universal tendencies or relations without any immaterial element.

Answer: The universality of these tendencies, powers or relations is purely potential until it is actualized by and in some intellect. The cat has a universal tendency to kill mice, but is not aware of it and kills only this or that individual mouse. The same remark applies to the eye and to the hammer. The universality exists only in an actual or possible intellect. Therefore the objection confirms our position. But it suggests that we should say more precisely that "universals known as such" are a proof of immateriality.

Objection 2: There are universal images, concrete and individual representations having a universal meaning. For instance, the poster featuring the typical U.S. Marine, the picture of the typical Yankee farmer, the cartoon of the typical professor. These are material objects, standing for all the representatives of a class, and therefore truly universal.

Answer: In reality these pictures represent a whole class for us because we have an idea of that class. The picture evokes that idea in us, and it is only through that idea that it has this universal power of representation. If we had no idea of the U.S. Marine, the poster would represent only the individual who modeled for it.

Objection 3: "Whether others have this wonderful faculty of abstracting their ideas, they best can tell: for myself, I find indeed I have a faculty of imagining or representing to myself the ideas of those particular things I have perceived, and of variously compounding and dividing them . . . *whatever hand or eye* I imagine, it must have some particular shape and colour. Likewise the idea of *man* that I frame to myself, must be either of a white, or a black, or a tawny, a straight, or a crooked, a tall, or a low, or a middle-sized man."[7]

Answer: The answer to that objection is contained in the objection itself, in the words which have been italicized. "Whatever hand or eye" and "man" does not represent a hand or eye or man in particular, but just any hand, eye or man. Berkeley confuses "imagining" and "conceiving." He is quite right when he affirms that we must always imagine a definite individual; he is wrong when he denies that we can conceive or think a universal nature. The confusion may be explained by the fact that every one of our ideas is accompanied by an image.

Objection 4: "Abstract ideas are . . . individual, however they may become general in their representation. The image in the mind is only that of a particular object, tho' the application of it in our reasoning be the same, as if it were universal."[8]

Answer: This is another way of putting Berkeley's objection. It is true that the *image* in the mind is of a particular object. But the corresponding *idea* or *concept* is universal. Hume admits only that it is universal in its representation, that we apply it as if it were universal. He explains that fact as follows: To similar objects we apply the same name. When we recall that name, it evokes the idea of one of the individuals to which we have applied it and gives rise to a tendency to evoke many more individuals of that kind.

But how then can we use the general idea, as we often do, for the *totality* of the individuals, real or possible, to which it applies? Do we then have to evoke all these individuals?

Of course not, says Hume. "We abridge that work by a more partial consideration." We recall a certain number of individuals, just enough to make sure of the limits of applicability of the given

<hr>

[7] G. Berkeley, *Principles of Human Knowledge,* Introduction, #10. (Our italics.)

[8] D. Hume, *Treatise of Human Nature* (1888), p. 20.

name, and for the rest we trust the evocative tendency itself. "However this may be, it is certain *that* we form the idea of individuals, *that* we seldom or never exhaust these individuals; and *that* those which remain, are only represented by means of that habit, by which we recall them whenever any present occasion requires it."[9]

Thus Hume admits a "habit by which we recall them whenever any present occasion requires it." This habit, this awareness of being able to evoke any and all individuals of a certain class, is precisely what the universal idea is. Hence we may say that Hume, like Berkeley, admits that universal ideas exist, although he does not call them by that name.

Objection 5: Against the argument taken from necessary judgments, the following objection is raised by the Logical Positivists: The truths of metaphysics are either tautologies or they are meaningless. In neither case do they tell us anything about reality, nor can they be used as a demonstration of the immateriality of the intellect.

Since Logical Positivism is held by many philosophers in the English-speaking countries, we must devote some attention to it.[10]

The statements of what you call metaphysics, say the Logical Positivists, are either analytic or synthetic. If they are analytic, they are mere tautologies. Their validity depends on the definition of the terms; they tell us nothing about reality, but only about the meaning we attribute to certain words. Examples of such tautologies are the principle of identity (Whatever is, is) and the principle of contradiction (It is impossible for a being to exist and not to exist at the same time).[11]

If the principles are synthetic, such as the principle of causality (Whatever is not self-existent depends in its existence on the Self-Existent being), they are meaningless, containing words but conveying no sense.

Answer:

1. The objection claims that a principle such as "Whatever is,

[9] *Ibid.,* p. 22. Cfr. Maréchal, *PDM,* II, pp. 212 ff.

[10] For a good discussion of Logical Positivism, see F. Copleston, S.J., *Contemporary Philosophy.*

[11] ". . . the reason why these propositions cannot be confuted in experience is that they do not make any assertion about the empirical world, but simply record our determination to use symbols in a certain fashion." A. J. Ayer, *Language, Truth and Logic* (Dover Publication, 1946), p. 31.

is" tells us nothing about reality, that it refers only to our way of using words. When we say that a house is a house, this does not exclude the possibility that the house in reality, outside the mind, should not be a house. The house might be a tree. Only we are not supposed to talk that way, because to say that a house is not a house, that a house is a tree, would violate the rules of language.

Why does such a way of speaking violate the rules of language? Is it not because the rules of language are based on the rules of reality, of being? Are these rules purely arbitrary? Could they be changed by some universal convention? It is obvious that if, by some such convention, we gave up the principle of identity, both thought and speech would become impossible. Nobody would know what you meant when you spoke of a house, since that house could just as well be a tree, a cat or an umbrella. This is not a mere convention, it is the most fundamental law of all reality. It is true that when I say of a house that it is a house, I do not announce anything new or startling; yet I affirm of that house the thing which is of the greatest possible importance concerning it, namely the fact that it is a house. No statement about it can be more fundamental.[12]

The error of the Logical Positivists derives from their failure to realize that the principle of identity is not only analytic but is also synthetic. As a rule of language it is analytic. As a rule of thought it is synthetic. In its synthetic form it means: that which is real is intelligible. Or: being as it is in itself is identical with being as it is in the intellect.

Logical Positivists deny this interpretation of the principle. But such a denial involves a contradiction, because it implies the very thing that is denied. When the Logical Positivist asserts: it is not true that being as it is in itself is identical with being as it is in the intellect, he is claiming that this is true not just in his mind, but in reality. He is asserting that the non-identity, which he affirms between being as it is in itself and being as it is in the intellect, is an objective state of affairs. In other words, he is claiming that, in this instance, reality as it is in itself is identical with reality as it is in his intellect. He is therefore using the principle of identity as a

[12] See an interesting discussion on this topic in John Hospers, *An Introduction to Philosophical Analysis*, pp. 135-137.

synthetic principle in the very act by means of which he denies its synthetic nature.

2. If we ask the Logical Positivist why he asserts that a statement such as "Whatever is not self-existent depends on the Self-Existent Being" is meaningless, he answers that "a statement is meaningful if, and only if, it is either analytic or empirically verifiable." Since the principle of causality, as it is expressed above, is neither analytic nor empirically verifiable—i.e., verifiable directly or indirectly through sense experience—it follows, according to the Logical Positivist, that it is meaningless.

Hence the value of his objection depends on the truth of the assertion that "a statement is meaningful if, and only if, it is either analytic or empirically verifiable." Logical Positivism does not demonstrate this statement on which its whole position is based. And the fact is that it cannot be demonstrated, because it contains its own refutation. For the statement itself is obviously neither analytic nor empirically verifiable; hence, in terms of Logical Positivism, it is meaningless.

Of course, the statement could be postulated as an axiom (Let us agree that. . . .), or it could be affirmed with the necessary exception, "All statements which are neither analytic nor empirically verifiable are meaningless, except this present statement." But the dogmatism of such a position would be so obvious that we may be excused from giving our attention to it.

What we have been saying does not imply that the statements of metaphysics are not verifiable at all. It is true that they are not empirically verifiable if by empirically we mean through sense experience.

But they can be verified by transcendental experience—that is, by the experience of our own thinking. Our thinking is a fact, although it cannot be observed by sense experience. It is a fact of which we are absolutely certain, since we can only deny it by means of the thinking process itself. But it can be shown that the basic principles of metaphysics are implied in our every act of thought, that they are explicitly or implicitly affirmed in every one of our affirmations; so that whenever anybody denies them he contradicts himself.

We have shown that these principles apply to reality. Hence we are in possession of some absolutely certain, immutable knowledge about the whole of reality. Our point is that knowledge of this kind cannot be "caused" by a material brain, hence that our intellect is an immaterial faculty.

Objection 6: The so-called necessary principles are not a proof of the immateriality of the intellect. Their necessity is derived from frequent association: because in our experience we have always seen A followed by B, we affirm that B follows necessarily upon A (lightning-thunder: cause-effect). But the laws of association operate on the sense level, they do not imply an immaterial faculty. This is one more objection presented by Hume.

Answer: Hume's explanation of the necessity of laws could perhaps be defended with reference to physical laws, although even there it does not seem sufficient. But it does not apply to the laws and principles of geometry, mathematics and metaphysics. We shall not, however, insist here on the case for geometry and mathematics, although it is a very good one, since so many modern philosophers hold that the statements of these sciences are mere tautologies.

So let us give immediate consideration to the basic metaphysical affirmations. We call them metaphysical, although the Positivists consider them merely logical, principles. We have shown above that the principle of identity is a law of logic only because it is, more fundamentally, a law of metaphysics. The same thing applies to the other metaphysical principles.

Everybody admits the absolute certitude of these principles. But the basis of this certitude has been explained in many different ways. Briefly reviewing these explanations will allow us to strengthen the argument drawn from the necessary judgments of our intellect.

1. The first principles of metaphysics are actually inborn in our intellect. We do not accept this explanation; there are no actually inborn principles in our mind. We can have no knowledge without sense experience.

2. These principles derive from experience and induction, like the laws discovered by the Sciences. That answer is quite insufficient. Induction can never lead to absolute certitude. Moreover, a vast amount of strictly controlled observation is required before

physical laws are firmly established. Finally, these laws apply only for those conditions in which they have been ascertained. In a different kind of universe these laws might not apply. On the other hand, the metaphysical principles are absolutely certain, are immediately evident, apply to all reality, even to merely possible reality.

That last statement might be questioned. Would it be possible for God to create a universe in which none of the physical or scientific laws would apply? Without any doubt, Yes. Would it be possible for God to create a universe wherein the metaphysical principles would not apply? a universe in which, for instance, what is, is not?—that is, in which a being could exist and not exist simultaneously? No, it would be utterly impossible.

But how can we, finite and contingent beings, make such sweeping assertions? Are we not, to a certain extent, dictating our own law to reality? Are we not telling God that He can do this but cannot do that? True, and this shows that our mutable and contingent minds are bearers of immutable, necessary and eternal truths, that in some way, through the principles of metaphysics, the Eternal Truth itself is speaking in us. How, then, could our minds be material faculties?

Supposing that a hypercritical opponent or doubter were to say: "It is true that I cannot conceive of a universe wherein that which is, is not; but does this imply that in reality such a universe cannot exist? Might not I be wrong?" We would answer: "Your objection involves a contradiction, and it is thus self-refuting. You say that you cannot conceive of a universe in which that which is, is not; and then you immediately try to conceive of such a universe. You suppose that, even though you cannot conceive of it, a universe would be possible in which that which is, is not, in which a being could exist and not exist at the same time. But you take it for granted that this strange universe and whatever it contains is that which it is—namely, a universe in which that which is, is not. Your question has about the same value as the following questions: "I know that a circle cannot be square, but suppose it were square, how many angles would it have?" "Is it possible to think without thinking?"

3. Textbooks of Scholastic philosophy generally say that these

principles are immediately evident, because we notice that the predicate is contained in the definition of the subject, because we are at once aware of the necessary connection between these two terms. This is true, but it leaves one question unanswered: Why do we at once see this necessary connection? Is it on the basis of our former experience? Obviously not. Then it must be owing to the very power of our intellect, without direct dependence on sense experience, from within, a priori. This leads us to the real solution of the problem.

4. Our intellect possesses the habitual knowledge of the first principles (*habitus primorum principiorum*). In their light we judge of everything else, and therefore every one of our judgments has a core of necessity. We have received that habitual knowledge of the first principles from God Himself, not in the form of actually inborn knowledge, but in the form of potential or virtual dispositions, which are actualized as soon as they enter into contact with exterior reality reaching us through the senses. Therefore we see these principles *in* sense experience, although they do not come to us *from* sense experience.

The habitual knowledge of the first principles of metaphysics is our way of sharing the intuitive knowledge of the pure spirits (principle of proportionality). It follows that a faculty which contains such principles—albeit only virtually—must be a spiritual faculty.

Although the human intellect is not intrinsically dependent on the brain, it is extrinsically dependent on that material organ. The brain is a necessary condition for the operation of our intellect. Without a brain in good condition, our intellect, in ordinary circumstances, cannot produce its operations. In this way the human intellect differs from the angelic intellect, which is entirely independent of matter.

That the intellect is extrinsically dependent on matter can be demonstrated in the following ways:

1. We know that a serious impairment of the brain, either by a lesion or by intoxication, makes intellectual operations impossible or difficult.

2. Every one of our ideas is accompanied by an image. But this

image, being a product of the senses, is intrinsically dependent on matter. If there can be no thought without image, there can be no thinking without some co-operation of the brain.

3. Every human operation is the operation of a being composed of form and matter. Therefore no human operation is possible without some co-operation of matter. Since our thought is not intrinsically dependent on matter, as we have demonstrated above, we must admit an extrinsic dependence of our intellect on matter for its operations.

THE ORIGIN OF OUR IDEAS

How do our ideas originate? They are not inborn and the senses have a part in their formation. That much is evident from ordinary experience. From sense knowledge we pass to intellectual knowledge, from the phantasm[13] we derive the idea.

But the phantasm or image is material and the idea is immaterial. How then do we pass from a material image to an immaterial idea? Or, in terms of the underlying faculties, how can the material senses influence the immaterial intellect? To this question only three answers can be proposed, and each one has been defended by a group of philosophers.

1. The intellect receives the ideas from the imagination as the imagination receives its images from the senses, and as the senses receive their sensations from the outside world.

Such is the thesis of the empiricists and of the sensists. It leads necessarily towards materialism. According to this conception the intellect is nothing but a higher kind of sense, passively receiving its ideas from the imagination. Senses and imagination can passively receive their contents because they are material faculties. The intellect, being immaterial, cannot passively receive anything from a material object or faculty.

[13] "Phantasm" is the technical term used in Scholastic philosophy to designate the highest product of the combined senses. It is generally considered synonymous with image, but it may also stand for a perception. The highest product of the combined senses is a perception when the object is present, it is an image when the object is not present, to the senses. In the following pages we shall use the term "image" instead of the obsolete "phantasm."

2. The intellect receives its ideas directly from God. This solution has been defended by Malebranche and, in a slightly different way, by all philosophers who admit the existence of inborn ideas. It involves no contradiction; God could put our ideas directly into our mind. But that solution is utterly improbable since God generally uses secondary causes, and since all appearances point to some influence of our senses in the formation of our ideas. Moreover it implies inacceptable consequences. Malebranche's occasionalism finds its logical conclusion in Spinoza's pantheism.

3. If the ideas cannot come from the objects through the senses, and if they do not come directly from God, there remains only one other possible solution: the ideas are produced by the intellect itself. The intellect, in this hypothesis, is both active and passive. As active it imprints the ideas upon itself, as passive it receives them. The active function of the intellect is generally called the *agent intellect,* whereas the passive function is known as the *possible intellect.*

When a student is listening to his professor, it looks as if the professor were putting new ideas into the student's mind. In fact, he is doing nothing of the kind; he is only emitting certain sounds with the hope that these sounds will help the student to develop in his own mind ideas which correspond to the professor's ideas. Somewhat in the same way the agent intellect, taking the image as a model, imprints the corresponding idea on the possible intellect. Thus any question of passivity of the intellect under a material influence is avoided; the intellect is passive only in relation to itself.

In the traditional phraseology it is said that the agent intellect "abstracts" the idea from the image and puts it into the possible intellect. To abstract the idea means to leave out of consideration all the material, individual, concrete features of the image and to keep only the general and universal features. In the image of this individual tree the intellect ignores the fact that it is an oak or a maple, big or small, leafy or without leaves. It keeps only the "treeness"—that which is common to all trees.

But an obvious difficulty arises at once. In order to discriminate between what must be excluded and what must be retained in the image, the intellect should know it.

But the immaterial intellect cannot know the material image. To know it means to be influenced by it, and the immaterial intellect cannot be passively influenced by a material agent.

The solution of this difficulty must be sought in a consideration of the unity of man and the close co-operation of his powers. In man body and soul together constitute one being. Therefore the intellect and the senses are most intimately united, they cannot operate independently of each other. Neither the intellect nor the senses know, it is man who knows through them.

Technically speaking, the intellect is the final cause of the senses, and also, in some way, their formal and efficient cause.

1. The intellect is the *final cause* of the senses because in man sense knowledge is made to serve intellectual knowledge. Sense knowledge has undoubtedly a biological or survival value in man, as in animals. But it does not end there. It is potentially intelligible, which means not only that it can eventually be transformed into intellectual knowledge, but that, in some way, it desires this transformation, that it is penetrated with intellectual finality.

But this does not explain how we can pass from sense to intellectual knowledge, without any material passivity of the intellect. In order to solve that problem, we must consider the two other kinds of causality which we have mentioned above.

2. The intellect is, in a certain way, the *formal cause* of sense knowledge. We say: in a certain way. For, if we were to take this expression literally, we should make our ideas into material entities, since the union of a spiritual form with matter results in a material being.

Yet we may compare the relation of the intellect to sense with that of form to matter. As the spiritual soul does not hover over the body, but lives in it, penetrating and animating it throughout, so the intellect does not (as we are too prone to think) stand above the senses, but lives in them, animating, inspiring and guiding them. Hence, when the imagination produces its image, it does so not only *for* the intellect, but also *under its unconscious guidance and inspiration,* in somewhat the way in which all the cells of a living being work under the unconscious direction of the vital principle. The intellect, inasmuch as it unconsciously directs the construction of the image, is known as the agent intellect.[14] This vital but unconscious co-operation in the construction of the image makes the intellect "live," "exercise," unconsciously know the essential structure, the universal features of that image, provides it with the intelligible "impression" (*species impressa*). This unconscious intelligible impression is uttered, expressed, affirmed in and by the possible intellect, thus becoming the "intelligible expression" (*species expressa*), that is the mental word, an affirmed concept or idea.

A comparison may help. The best way of knowing the structure of your radio set is not to look at it or to read about it, but to take it apart and rebuild it. If you can reassemble the parts of your radio set, you know it very well. And you know not only this individual set, but all sets of the same make; you have acquired the idea of it. Suppose now that you should know it so well that you could rebuild your set unconsciously, in your sleep. You would then possess an unconscious knowledge of the general structure of this kind of radio set. Something similar is true of the intellect, as a result of its unconscious intervention in the formation of the image; and what it knows unconsciously in one of its aspects— the agent intellect—becomes luminous and conscious in its other aspect—the possible intellect.

3. The intellect is also, in a certain way, the *efficient* cause of the senses. This again should not be understood literally. Yet we may say that the intellect brings forth, begets, produces sense by some kind of emanation, as the only possible means for a spiritual faculty of getting into touch with material reality.[15] The image, on the other hand, may be called an *instrumental* cause, a tool, used by the intellect in the production of its ideas. Not, however, as if the agent intellect used the image as some kind of tool for writing the ideas upon the possible intellect. A material tool cannot exercise its function on an immaterial object. The image is a tool of the

---

[14] It is important to note that the *conscious* image (*in actu secundo*) is produced by the imagination in the imagination, and that the intellect has nothing to do with it. But the *preconscious* construction of the image (*in actu primo*) stands under the influence of the higher faculty.

[15] "Sense, moreover, is a certain imperfect participation of the intellect, and therefore, according to its natural origin, *it proceeds from the intellect*, as the imperfect from the perfect." *S. Theol.*, I, 77, 7, c. (Italics ours.)

intellect just by being an image, by being a specification of the imagination whose construction the intellect has unconsciously guided, acquiring in this very activity a living attitude to, a dynamic relation to that image, whose conscious reflection in the possible intellect is the mental word, the affirmed concept or idea.[16]

It is possible to shed further light on this mysterious connection between intellect and imagination by considering what is called a "scheme." A scheme is the law according to which we construct an image. Thus the scheme of a circle is: "Make a straight line revolve around one of its ends." A scheme has a sense component, because the figure which results from it is a singular, concrete figure, this imagined or perceived circle. It has an intellectual component, because it is a law. Combining both intellectual and sense components, the scheme bridges the gap between the intellect and the imagination.

Nobody will deny that we possess such schemes for the construction of geometric figures. Do we have anything similar for the ordinary images of everyday life, for a tree or a house or a dog? Undoubtedly, although these schemes do not have the uniformity and the clearness of geometric schemes. Everyone is capable of imagining, if not of drawing, a sketchy outline of these concrete objects. That outline or image is constructed according to a vaguely conscious law which is its scheme.

In the above examples we passed from the concept to the image by means of a scheme; the intellect consciously directed the imagination in the formation of the image. In the first acquisition of a new concept the process is reversed. A certain number of sense data deriving from the object are combined to form an image, a phantasm, of the object. This requires a unification of spatial elements, since knowledge is essentially unification. This unification is performed by the imagination under the unconscious guidance of the agent intellect, and from this active co-operation with the imagination, the agent intellect gains an "intellectual impression" of the object, which becomes an "intellectual expression" of that object in the possible intellect.

[16] K. Rahner, *Geist in Welt,* pp. 292-293.

16

Nature and Functioning of Our Intellectual Knowledge[1]

THE IMPRESSION AS A DYNAMIC RELATION

The impression is not some kind of intellectual image, it is not an ethereal copy of the image. It can never be known without reference to the image. It may be compared with the beam of light issuing from a movie projector. This beam alone will never produce a picture on the screen. There will be a picture only if the beam of light passes through the film. The image functions in somewhat the way the film does; the impression is comparable to the beam of light carrying an invisible picture. As the picture becomes visible only when the beam of light, having passed through the film, hits the screen, so the impression becomes conscious, is transformed into an idea, only when in actual contact with the image it is actively impressed upon the possible intellect. This explains why we can become aware of our ideas only by turning to the corresponding image.

The formation of our ideas is often conceived in a too mechanical way. It is believed that, once the image has been formed by the sense powers, the intellect extracts from it an idea which, in some mysterious way, was hidden in it. In this rather naive conception

---

[1] The following pages represent an attempt to introduce the student into the heart of the mystery of intellectual knowledge. They are rather difficult, and not as essential as the previous chapter. Therefore they may be omitted in an elementary course.

Throughout this chapter the word "image" is used instead of "phantasm," and the words "impression" and "expression" stand respectively for *species impressa* and *species expressa*.

267

the image is a *concrete* representation of the object; from it the intellect draws an *abstract* representation of the same object, which is known as the idea. Both the senses and the intellect have a representation of the object. This conception smacks of the Cartesian dualism of body and soul as two complete substances.

We do not have two representations of the same object, any more than we have within us two powers of knowing which operate independently. There is only one representation, the image produced by the senses. But as the soul animates the body, so the intellect animates the senses. Hence, when there is an image in the sense powers, our intellect in some way animates that representation, it maintains a dynamic relation to it. This relation is the impression. And the idea, the expression, is the active uttering, the conscious awareness of this relation.

Therefore the process of abstraction does not consist in an operation by which the intellect extracts the hidden intelligible content from the image. It is rather a living attitude, by which the unity of the intellect is referred to the multiplicity of the senses. We shall try to demonstrate later that this unity of our intellect is none other than the unity of Being.

THE UNDERSTANDING AND THE INTELLECT

The impression is the specification of the activity of my intelligence. When I consider my intelligence, carrying an impression, in its connection with the lower term of the relation, the multiplicity of the senses, I call it the Understanding. When I consider my intelligence, carrying the impression, in its connection with the higher term of the relation, the unity of Being, I call it the Intellect.[2]

[2] This problem is beset with serious terminological difficulties. St. Thomas called the lower aspect of our intelligence *ratio* (reason) and its higher aspect *intellectus*. The moderns use respectively "understanding" and "reason." Hence "reason" means the lower aspect for the Scholastics and the higher aspect for the moderns. Therefore we shall avoid the term "reason" altogether, and we shall call the lower aspect "Understanding" with the moderns, and the higher aspect "Intellect" with St. Thomas. In that specialized meaning we shall always write Intellect with a capital I. Intellect with a lower case *i* is used as a synonym of intelligence. Cfr. *S. Theol.,* I, 58, 3, c.; 79, 8, c.; *Ver.,* 15, 1, c.

Both Understanding and Intellect are aspects of the selfsame human intelligence. Intelligence is the cognitive faculty of the human soul. But the human soul is both the substantial form of a material body and a spirit in matter. When we consider our intelligence as the cognitive faculty of the substantial form of a material body, we speak of the Understanding. When we consider it as the cognitive faculty of a spirit in matter, we speak of the Intellect.[3]

The Understanding always works in intimate connection with the senses. It is a faculty which organizes sense experience, as Kant would have it. It resembles, although on a higher scale, the "intelligence" of animals; it can be measured by intelligence tests; it develops with age and education; it differs from one individual to another. Since it is so intimately connected with the image, the senses and the brain, we can expect an increase of knowledge about that faculty from the new Science of Cybernetics, which studies the functioning of calculating machines and of "electronic brains."

The material object of the Understanding is any material reality, anything which affects our senses. Its formal object is the quiddity, the "whatness" of these beings.

The Intellect, on the other hand, although it needs the collaboration of the senses, transcends the domain of the senses and can reach supra-sensory reality. It is capable of complete self-reflection. It resembles, although on a lower scale, the intellect of the angels. It cannot be studied experimentally; it does not grow with age; it is the same in all human beings. In it we find the habitual knowledge of the first principles. By means of our Intellect we know things as they are in themselves; for, as things appear to the Intellect, so they are in themselves. The point of view of the Intellect is not relative, but absolute, because it is the point of view of a spirit, of the spirit.[4] The object of metaphysics is "being as being." The meaning of that expression "being as being" becomes clear when we realize that it means "being as known by our Intellect."[5]

[3] We have mentioned a similar distinction in the empirical study of human intelligence. Cfr. p. 207. What we called there "human intelligence" as opposed to "animal intelligence" corresponds to the Understanding.

[4] ". . . notre esprit juge en tant qu'esprit du point de vue de l'esprit tout court."—A. Marc, S.J., *Psychologie Réflexive*, Vol. I, p. 195.

[5] What we have been saying makes it possible to state in a simple yet profound way the relation between Metaphysics, the Sciences and everyday knowledge. Man is composed of soul and body; so is, analogically speaking,

The material object of the Intellect is any being, whether material or immaterial. Hence that object is coextensive with the whole of reality. The formal object of the Intellect is truth or intelligibility. That means that the Intellect can know any being whatsoever inasmuch as it is true or intelligible.

We must always bear in mind that Understanding and Intellect are not two distinct faculties but two aspects of the same faculty, the intelligence. Taking the terms "material" and "formal" in a wide and analogical sense, we might say that the Understanding is the material, the Intellect the formal, aspect of our intelligence. That implies that our Understanding can never operate without the "inspiration" of the Intellect, and that the Intellect requires, in its every activity, some collaboration of the Understanding.

When speaking of the object of human intelligence, we may distinguish not only a material and a formal aspect, but also a proportionate and an adequate object. The proportionate object of human intelligence corresponds to the object of the Understanding. It is anything which affects our senses (material object), inasmuch as it possesses a quiddity or a nature (formal object). The adequate object of human intelligence corresponds to the object of the Intellect. It is any reality whatsoever (material object), inasmuch as it is true or intelligible (formal object).

UNIVERSAL IDEAS, THE CENTER OF
HUMAN KNOWLEDGE

Some people wonder why Scholastic philosophy insists so much upon the existence and the objective value of universal ideas. The reason may now become apparent. Universal ideas[6] are the center of human knowledge. The seat of universal ideas is the Understanding. Inasmuch as the Understanding collaborates intimately with the

---

human knowledge. The soul of human knowledge is Metaphysics; its body is constituted by everyday and scientific knowledge. As the body is nothing without the soul, so everyday or scientific knowledge is impossible without its metaphysical core. As the soul cannot act without the body, so metaphysics is impossible without the co-operation of everyday knowledge. Yet the soul is not intrinsically dependent on the body; neither is metaphysics on everyday or scientific knowledge. See P. Scheuer, S.J., "Notes on Metaphysics."

[6] More precisely: *affirmed* universal ideas.

senses, universal ideas put us into contact with outside reality, with the material world, and ultimately with prime matter. Inasmuch as the Understanding is "animated" or "informed" by the Intellect, universal ideas put us in contact with the unity of Being, with the Pure Act.[7] Whenever we have a universal idea we embrace, unconsciously but really, the whole extent of reality, from prime matter to Pure Act. In every one of our universal ideas the whole of metaphysics is implicitly contained. When studying metaphysics we do not, as in the study of the Sciences, discover new knowledge which we in no way had before. We make explicit and conscious a knowledge which was with us from the moment we got our first universal idea.

This is denied by all nominalists. For them we have first intellectual knowledge of single individual beings. When we have acquired sufficient knowledge of that kind, we set out upon the discovery of metaphysics. But this would be a perfectly hopeless undertaking. Kant has demonstrated that the knowledge of material and finite reality, as conceived by the nominalists, will never yield the knowledge of immaterial beings and of the Infinite Being.

We may show this in a slightly different way. Let us consider a certain number of universal ideas: house, man, dog, tree, bridge. If we try to discover what these concepts have in common, we discover that they all refer to *something* which affects *our senses*. That is precisely the material object of our Understanding. Notice how this object connects the multiplicity of the material world (which affects our senses) with the unity of being (something, a being). We might put it schematically as follows:

Something, a being	Object of the Intellect
which affects our senses	Object of the senses
Something which affects our senses	Object of the Understanding

KNOWLEDGE OF THE UNIVERSAL AND OF THE SINGULAR

In our everyday knowledge, what we know first is a singular, individual, concrete object. But such an object is known by the whole

[7] This will be demonstrated in the following paragraphs.

man, intelligence and senses combined. Intelligence alone knows only the intelligible features of the object, its substantial form. The substantial form is the same in all individuals of the same species. Therefore to know only the substantial form of an object is to know only that which the object has in common with all other individuals of the same species. That which distinguishes one individual from another is its relation to quantified matter. But an immaterial faculty such as human intelligence cannot directly know quantified matter. Therefore it does not know that which distinguishes one individual from another. However, in our ordinary knowledge we always use intelligence and senses together. Intelligence gives us the universal intelligible features of the object; the senses apply and restrict these features to a particular individual.

Does our intelligence, by means of its ideas, penetrate the essence of material objects? In a certain sense, yes. But not in the sense that it knows at once whatever can be known of that object. Such knowledge is acquired gradually, by everyday experience and scientific investigation. What our intelligence knows at once about the object is its quiddity. In knowing this quiddity our faculty proceeds from the most fundamental and general features to the more specialized ones. Thus with regard to a new object we find out first that it is "something" (a being, a substance); next we may discover that it is living, sentient.

With regard to most objects our quidditative knowledge remains very vague and must be supplemented by data from the senses, which are not properly intelligible. Thus the common starling may be defined as "a bird with black plumage, in parts iridescent and in parts spotted with buff." Of this lengthy definition only the word *bird* is "intelligible" without direct reference to the senses, inasmuch as it means "a living, sentient substance." The remainder of the definition refers directly to sense knowledge.

Universal ideas are not reached by a process of comparison and elimination. We might be inclined to believe that, in order to reach the universal idea, say, of "starling," we must first know a few birds of that species. We should then compare them with each other, eliminate their individual features and keep only the common ones, thus slowly arriving at the universal idea of starling.

That is the scientific procedure of the ornithologist; it is not the natural procedure of our intelligence. The first contact of our intelligence with any new object yields a universal idea. It may and will generally be a rather imperfect one, but it is a universal idea. Suppose I have never seen a starling. I notice one for the first time, dimly, in a fog, and I say, "something black." That is a universal idea. It is very imperfect, and it applies to many more things than starlings. Experience will help me refine it and complete it, but it was a universal idea from the very beginning.

ANALOGICAL KNOWLEDGE OF
IMMATERIAL REALITIES

We have referred several times to the connection of our intelligence with the supreme unity of Being. We said that the impression is a dynamic relation connecting the multiplicity of the senses with the supreme unity of Being; we have affirmed that our universal ideas put us implicitly in contact with the Pure Act. This requires further explanation.

It is evident at once that in our ideas the multiplicity of the senses is connected with the unity of being. Every universal idea refers to "something which affects our senses." That which affects our senses is thus connected with "something," that is with "a being."

But that being is always a quantitative being, and therefore the unity of being to which the multiplicity of our senses is referred seems to be unity of quantitative being. That is the position of Kant and of all Agnostics. They claim that the unity to which all our knowledge is referred is the unity of quantitative being and that our intelligence cannot reach above that unity, is therefore unable to reach immaterial realities, such as the soul or God. We admit that the highest unity of our Understanding, that is of our intelligence considered in its direct collaboration with the senses, is the unity of quantitative being.

But we maintain that the highest unity of our Intellect extends far above and beyond quantitative being, all the way to the supreme unity of Being, of God Himself. In other words, our human intelligence inasmuch as it is a spiritual faculty, refers every object it knows to God Himself.

In this connection Aquinas makes an important distinction between that which our concepts *represent* and that which they *mean,* between their element of *representation* and their element of *signification.*[8] Our concepts can represent only material beings, but they can mean immaterial objects.

To represent signifies: to picture by means of intelligible notes. *To mean* signifies: to intend, to point towards, to affirm. When we distinguish between "that which is represented" and "that which is meant" we claim that the object which we intend, which we want to affirm, is not necessarily the same as the object we picture before our mind.

It is especially in our concepts of immaterial objects that the difference between the element of representation and the element of signification is striking. Thus when we have the concept of soul, we observe in our consciousness a picture, an image of a material reality. That which is represented in our concept refers to this picture. It may be a vague picture of some subtle fluid permeating our whole body, of some ethereal double of our body, but it is the picture of a material reality. Yet, even while using it, we are aware that this material representation is not correct, that it does not exactly correspond to what the soul really is. We know that the soul is immaterial, even while we picture it before our mind by means of a material image. We mean, we intend something different from that which we represent, from that which we picture before our mind.

But if the representation is so inadequate, why do we use it at all? Because we are not pure spirits, because we need an image and a representation for every one of our thoughts, and because this picture of the soul is partially correct. We pictured the soul as something which subtly permeates our whole body. In fact our soul does permeate our whole body, it "informs," it "animates" the body. The picture is partially true. But the soul does not permeate the body in the manner of a fluid, however subtle. The picture is partially false.

That is the meaning of analogical knowledge. In the analogical knowledge of an immaterial reality, we use a material representation. Our representation is partially true and partially false, and what we

[8] Cfr. *S. Theol.,* I, 13, 2, c.

mean implies affirmation, negation and supereminence. We really mean that the soul permeates the whole body (affirmation), not, however, in the manner of a fluid (negation), but in a more perfect immaterial way (supereminence).

It is in the same way that we know God. God is known to us not directly but through His effects. Between God's effects and God Himself there is a relation. However, the concepts expressing these effects and God, their cause, cannot be univocal, they cannot apply to God and His creatures with the same meaning. These concepts are not equivocal either, their meaning is not entirely different. They are analogous, they apply to God and His creatures partly with the same meaning and partly with a different meaning.

Thus we can say of God that He is a being, that He is not a being, and that He is a super-being. In a certain sense these three statements are true, and they exemplify again the three steps in our knowledge of immaterial realities: affirmation, negation and supereminence. When we know God we have in our mind the representation of a being: God is a being. But that representation comes from an image; it is the representation of a material being, and therefore it does not really apply to God: God is not a being. Yet we must use a representation if we are to know God at all, but we must correct and transcend that representation: God is a super-being.

That which is represented in our concept of God is a material reality, that which is meant transcends all material reality. Our representation of God falls far short of the mark, but that which we mean is really the Infinite Being.

The proportionate object of our intelligence, the object of our Understanding, comprises that which we can represent and mean. The adequate object of our intelligence, the object of our Intellect, reaches farther and comprises also certain realities which we cannot represent but which we can mean.

OUR INTELLIGENCE A DYNAMIC FACULTY

We have seen that the analogical knowledge of God supposes in our mind a representation of God which we must correct. But how can we correct that representation unless we have some other representation of God which is the right one? Any correction which we make in the representation by means of which we know God seems to presuppose an exact knowledge of God.

This is a serious difficulty against the theory of analogy, and one which cannot be solved if our intelligence is conceived as a static faculty, a window opened upon the world of intelligible reality, a camera passively undergoing the imprint of that reality.

But our intelligence is a dynamic faculty—that is, a faculty which strives actively towards its object, towards knowledge, truth, intelligibility. We are aware of that striving in every one of our intellectual operations. That striving is not an elicited but a natural appetite; that is, an appetite which is not preceded by knowledge.[9] Every act of knowledge is a passage from potency to act, a real movement. But every real movement has an end. What is the end of the movement of our intelligence?

Not the knowledge of this or that particular being, or any collection of particular beings. Such knowledge satisfies the craving of our intelligence for awhile, but very soon that faculty resumes its quest. These objects are an intermediate end, not the ultimate end of our intelligence. The striving of our intelligence goes beyond them both extensively and intensively. Extensively because we want to know many more beings. Intensively because we want to know in a more perfect manner the beings which we do know. These beings do not explain themselves, they are not perfectly intelligible of themselves, and our intelligence wants to explain them, wants to make them perfectly intelligible. No finite object, no accumulation, be it ever so comprehensive, of finite objects, satiates the appetite of our intelligence. In the presence of any kind or collection of finite objects our intelligence continues to

---

[9] A strong objection may be raised against the dynamic or striving nature of our intelligence. Striving, so goes the objection, belongs to the appetite, not to knowledge. This is quite true for all elicited appetite. But all objects in nature possess a natural appetite, and this applies also to our intelligence. To be more exact we should say that it is not the intelligence, but man himself who strives towards knowledge, with elicited appetite by means of his will, with natural appetite by means of his intelligence. Inasmuch as man is a being endowed with an immaterial intelligence, he strives naturally, unconsciously, towards the possession of all truth. "The true is something good, inasmuch as the intellect is a given reality, and truth is its end" (*S. Theol.*, I, 82, 3, ad 1).

search, to inquire, to ask questions and seek explanations. It follows that all these objects are only intermediate ends of our intelligence, and that, even while knowing them, that faculty strives beyond them towards some ultimate satiating end.

What is that ultimate end of our intellectual quest? If we examine this appetite of our intelligence, we shall note that any limited object does not satisfy it, *precisely because it is limited.* It is *limitation as such* which keeps our intelligence from ever finding perfect rest in any of its objects. But if limitation as such keeps our intelligence striving always further, only the Unlimited can perfectly satisfy it. The very fact that our intelligence, although it can represent only limited realities, is always conscious of their limitation, demonstrates that it is impelled by an urge going beyond these limits. For a limit can be known as limit only by one who actually or potentially, in fact or in aspiration, goes beyond that limit.

It follows that the deepest appetite of our intelligence carries it beyond any limit of space and time, beyond any finiteness whatsoever, towards the Infinite Being. And this is precisely the way in which we know God. Not by means of an ordinary concept (although such a concept is a prerequisite), but as the end towards which, in every single act of knowledge, our intelligence keeps striving.

We inquired above how it is possible for us, in our analogical knowledge of God, to correct the representation which we have of Him, since such a correction seems to presuppose a correct knowledge of God.

Here we touch with the finger the most delicate point in analogical knowledge. We can, in a very real sense, compare God with the creatures without knowing God directly in Himself. For let us suppose that a definite relationship connects the creatures to God, and that this relation as such is known to us in its lower term; then, knowing the lower term *as relative,* we should have by this very fact and to the same extent, some notion of the higher term, somewhat as, when we see an arrow leaving the bow, we have an indication of the position of the target in the very direction which the arrow takes. And this is in fact what happens to us: we know creatures as *relative* to an absolute Principle, *as contingent,* and in that way—and only in that way—do we know God.[10]

How do we know creatures as relative, as contingent? Not by means of concepts—relativity and contingency do not belong to the intelligible notes of any creature, they are not a part of their definition—but through the very striving of our intelligence. We want to know these objects; therefore they are an end of our intellectual activity. But once we know them, we are not satisfied, we want to go beyond them. Therefore they are not the ultimate, but only an intermediate, end of our intellectual striving. Therefore the very activity by which we know these objects implies that they are intermediate ends, hence relative and contingent. Every time we know an object, we affirm implicitly that it is for us a means of reaching God. But every means is referred by him who uses it to the end which he intends. Therefore, in every act of knowledge we implicitly refer the object of that act to the Infinite Being, to God.[11]

Thus we have demonstrated the statements made a few pages earlier: that the impression is a dynamic relation connecting the multiplicity of the senses with the supreme unity of Being, that our universal ideas put us implicitly in contact with the Pure Act.

The demonstration of God's existence consists precisely in making explicit what we "exercise" implicitly in every act of knowledge; it expresses in concepts what we affirm through the very activity of our mind. The hinge of every such demonstration is the principle of metaphysical causality, which states that every being which is not self-existent depends on the Self-Existent Being; or the principle of sufficient reason, which affirms that whatever is not intelligible in itself is intelligible only because of its relation to that which is intelligible in itself. Both these principles are "exercised" in every one of our judgments; we affirm them implicitly every time we think.[12]

[10] Maréchal, *PDM,* V, p. 258.

[11] "All knowing beings know God implicitly in every object they know. For as nothing is desirable but through some resemblance with the first goodness, so nothing is knowable but through some resemblance with the first truth" (*Ver.,* 22, 2, ad 1).

[12] Does the fact that our intellect strives towards God imply that God really exists? Although this problem belongs properly to Natural Theology, we shall briefly put down the main lines of an answer. The striving of our

KNOWLEDGE OF METAPHYSICAL PRINCIPLES

We can demonstrate the same thing in the following way. Whenever we know an object, we affirm, implicitly or explicitly, that "This object *is*." Such an affirmation is absolutely true only of God. Strictly speaking, only God *is*. In all other judgments of that kind the predicate is too wide for the subject. Our affirmation is true only if we add implicitly to the subject a "complement of being," which consists precisely in its total dependence on God." Our statement really means: This object, inasmuch as it depends on God, is. Therefore in every affirmation we affirm implicitly not only the existence of God but also the principle of metaphysical causality and the dependence of the object of our affirmation on the Infinite Being.

Such is precisely the way in which the *habitus primorum principiorum,* the habitual knowledge of the first principles, operates in us. We can briefly indicate how the other first principles are exercised in the same way. It is immediately evident that the first principle in its positive form, "Whatever is, is," and in its negative form, as principle of contradiction, "A being cannot exist and not exist at the same time," is implicitly affirmed in every judgment.

Furthermore, when we know an object intellectually, we affirm implicitly that it is *true,* since our intelligence uses it as a means towards its end, which is truth. We affirm implicitly the *goodness* of that object, since we strive towards it as an object of our intellect and a possible object of our will. We affirm that it is *composed of act and potency,* because it is an end of our intelligence, but not a satiating end.

---

intellect is a natural striving, independent of our will. Such a striving cannot be one towards the impossible. A natural striving towards an impossible end would be absurd. Hence we may conclude that the Unlimited Being, the Pure Act, is possible. But the Pure Act is possible if, and only if, He exists. Hence the Pure Act exists. This sounds like the ontological argument, yet it is quite different from it. Here we do not demonstrate the possibility of God through an examination of concepts, but we show that the possibility of God is demanded or implied by a necessary fact, the fact of affirming. Cf. Maréchal, *PDM,* V, pp. 448 ff. See also A. Grégoire, S.J., *Immanence et Transcendance;* J. Defever, S.J., *La Preuve Réelle de Dieu.*

If the object of our knowledge is a material object, we affirm implicitly that it is *composed of a substantial form and prime matter,* that is, of an intelligible and an unintelligible element. The concept of such a being involves a necessary and intrinsic relation to an image, that is, to sense knowledge, to something which is, from its very nature, impervious to the intellect. This implies that the essence of that being, as expressed in its concept, contains an unintelligible element. This element is prime matter. Prime matter is that component of a material being's essence which is and always will remain impervious to a human intelligence.

Therefore when our intelligence knows an object, it "exercises" the whole of metaphysics in that knowledge, it invests that object with all the metaphysical attributes. This conception of metaphysics undermines the negative, agnostic part of Kant's *Critique.* Kant believed that we reached metaphysical principles and concepts only after first acquiring ordinary concepts of material beings. For him these ordinary concepts can be formed without any intervention of metaphysical principles. Once we have a certain number of such concepts, we use them as a starting point in our attempts to reach solid metaphysical knowledge. Kant has no trouble showing that such an attempt is futile, and that the knowledge of material beings as he conceives it can never yield any real knowledge of immaterial realities.

Metaphysical principles and concepts are "exercised" in every one of our judgments. There can be no object in the intellect except one invested with the whole of metaphysics. The affirmation of metaphysics is a condition of the very possibility of any object in our mind.

JUDGMENT AND AFFIRMATION

In the foregoing paragraphs we have constantly spoken of the impression, the concept and the idea; we have not mentioned the judgment. We must now recall the statement made earlier in this book (p. 177), that every concept presupposes a judgment, since it originates in a judgment. Often what would seem to be a mere concept is actually a simple judgment. For example, while you are walking with your bird-fancier friend he points to a bird and says, "A bobolink." Never before having heard the name of such a creature, you have now acquired a new concept, the concept of "bobolink," which has come to you in the implicit judgment you have made: "This is a bobolink."

Wherever, therefore, in the foregoing paragraphs we have spoken of a concept or an idea, we meant "a concept in a judgment" or "an affirmed idea." That the judgment is the central point of our intellectual life becomes evident as soon as we consider the dynamic nature of our intelligence. We have emphasized the dynamism, the movement, the activity, the striving of our intelligence. But a concept as such is a static representation. It is evident, then, that the concept cannot be the foundation of our intellectual life, that the foundation must consist in some activity. The judgment, the affirmation, is such an activity.

We should remember that there is no consciousness of the object in our intelligence until we have a *species expressa,* an "intellectual expression." When the agent intellect, having abstracted the impression from the image, imprints it on the possible intellect, all the conditions are set for the act of knowledge, but there is still no real knowledge. The possible intellect must now express this impression, utter it to itself, affirm its "adequation" to exterior reality. That is the "expression," the mental "word," and it is always a judgment involving an affirmation. Of the object known in the expression our intelligence always affirms that it is, or at least that it is possible. Every object of knowledge, it should be remembered, is referred to the Absolute End of our intelligence, and such a reference involves an affirmation of reality, of actual or possible existence.[13]

Man is a spirit, albeit in matter. A spirit knows through intuition; that is, through direct contact with the object, without the mediation of mental pictures or representations. This intuition is abso-

---

[13] St. Thomas sometimes speaks as if the intellect could produce simple concepts without a previous judgment. When he speaks technically, however, he affirms that even the knowledge of simple concepts can be called true or false, that is, involves some judgment . . . "Although the non-complex itself, or even a definition, is not in itself true or false, nevertheless the intellect that apprehends 'what a thing is' is said to be always true in itself—although it may be accidentally false" (*ScG.,* I, 59).

lutely perfect in God, the Infinite Spirit, who knows every reality by knowing Himself. It is less perfect in the angel, pure spirit but finite, who finds in his own intellect all that is needed for knowledge but must receive this infused knowledge from God.

In man, finite spirit in matter, intuition becomes so imperfect that it is no longer intuition in the strict sense of the term. Only the first principles of all knowledge are directly received by man from God. But of themselves they yield no knowledge, since they are only potentially conscious and need the intervention of an object derived through the senses in order to become conscious.

Yet there is in the human intellect an element which corresponds, in its own way, at its own degree, to the intuition of the pure spirits. It is intuition in the wider sense of the word, intuition not of the object of knowledge but of *the very activity by which man affirms the object of his knowledge*. When he affirms an object, he is aware of the fact that he affirms it. That awareness requires no concept or judgment whatsoever; it is direct and intuitive. And since the object of his knowledge is always the object of an affirmation, that object itself falls indirectly under this intuition. Therefore in man affirmation is the substitute for the intuition of pure spirits.[14]

We can show this in another way: "The human mind is a faculty in quest of its intuition; that is to say, of assimilation with Being."[15] The mind is in search of an object which will fill it to capacity. That capacity is infinite, and only the Infinite Being can fill it. The mind strives towards some reality which will entirely equate its formal object. Its formal object is truth or intelligibility as such, and only the perfect Truth will completely exhaust it. The mind is constantly impelled to seek an object which it can affirm without any restriction, about which it can say: "This being *is*." Only God can be affirmed in that way; concerning all other beings our intellect must say: "This being is *this* or *that*." Therefore our intelligence cannot reach the intuition which will fully satiate it during this life; it constantly strives towards this goal by means of countless partial affirmations.[16]

[14] Defever, *op. cit.*, pp. 20-25.

[15] Maréchal, *Studies in the Psychology of the Mystics*, p. 101.

[16] This does not imply that man has an appetite for the intuitive vision of God, but only that he is capable of being raised to the divine vision by

By way of conclusion we reprint a passage from Maréchal, which summarizes what we have been explaining:

The human intelligence is not merely a mirror passively reflecting the objects which pass within its field, but an activity directed in its deepest manifestations towards a well-defined term, the only term which can completely absorb it—Absolute Being, Absolute Truth and Goodness. The Absolute has set its mark on the basic tendency of our intelligence; moreover, this tendency constantly surpasses the particular acts of the intellect; the mind is driven by its internal dynamism from intellection to intellection, from object to object; but so long as it gravitates in the sphere of the finite, it attempts in vain to liken itself to its internal movement, to rest in the fullness of its act, to affirm being, by identity, purely and integrally. . . . The affirmation of reality . . . is nothing else than the expression of the fundamental tendency of the mind to unification in and with the Absolute; this affirmation would only have its full objective value by becoming a direct intuition of the Absolute; it keeps, however, a diminished and analogous value in its application to every object which sets the activity of the mind going and allows itself to be co-ordinated with the totality of objects already affirmed. . . .[17]

READINGS

St. Thomas Aquinas, *Summa Theologica*, I, Q. 79, a. 1,2,3,4; Q. 84, a. 1,2,3,6,7,8; Q. 85 a. 1,2,3,5; Q. 86, a. 1. Gilson, *The Philosophy of St. Thomas Aquinas*, pp. 233-259, and *The Spirit of Mediaeval Philosophy*, pp. 229-268. Marc, *Psychologie Réflexive*, Vol. I, pp. 165-375. Maréchal, *Le Point de Départ de la Métaphysique*, Cahier V, pp. 185-233, 248-259, 296-355. Rahner, *Geist in Welt*. Rousselot, *The Intellectualism of St. Thomas*. Wild, *Introduction to Realistic Philosophy*, pp. 441-467.

---

the grace of God. Cp. J. Maréchal, "De Naturali Perfectae Beatitudinis Desiderio," in *Mélanges Joseph Maréchal*, I, pp. 323-337.

[17] Maréchal, *Studies in the Psychology of the Mystics*, p. 100.

17

The Human Will

THAT MAN possesses some tendencies is denied by nobody. The existence of sense appetite, of the many drives by which man strives towards pleasure and away from pain, is strongly emphasized by modern psychologists. But quite a number of them deny that man has a rational appetite, a *will*, essentially different from and superior to the sense drives. Others admit the existence of the will but deny its *freedom*. Therefore, in this chapter, we must first demonstrate the existence of the will, next the freedom of the will. Although we shall treat these two problems separately, it should be noted that the existence of the will is really demonstrated only when we have established that man's highest tendency is free.

EXISTENCE AND NATURE OF THE WILL

The existence of the will can be demonstrated philosophically and confirmed by data derived from everyday experience.

The philosophical demonstration is rather simple. It rests on the supposition that we have demonstrated the existence in man of some knowledge which is essentially different from and superior to sense knowledge, of a cognitive faculty which is immaterial and only extrinsically dependent on matter.

Now it is generally admitted, and it follows from the very nature of appetite as previously explained, that the nature of the appetitive faculties corresponds to the nature of the cognitive faculties. Therefore, if man possesses an immaterial cognitive faculty, he must also possess an immaterial appetitive faculty.

The opponents of the concept of the will do not deny the general

285

principle; they reject the existence of the intellect as we conceive it. But since we have demonstrated the existence of an immaterial intellect, we are justified in concluding that there is in man an immaterial tendency, not intrinsically dependent on matter, which we call the will.

An empirical confirmation of this philosophical argument is derived from everyday experience. Every act of real self-control is an implicit manifestation of the will. In such an act we are conscious of the fact that some tendency in us is held in check by a higher tendency. That higher tendency is the will.

Against this argument the following objection may be raised. Animals also exercise self-control. Thus a hungry but well-trained dog will not take the meat he sees on the table.

This, however, is not real self-control. The sight of the meat has aroused in the dog two conflicting tendencies: hunger and fear. The fear is a product of his experience. On a previous occasion his grabbing the meat has been followed by some very disagreeable sensations. The memory of these painful sensations is now associated with the perception of "meat-on-the-table." If the fear is stronger than the hunger, the animal will not take the meat. If hunger exercises the stronger influence, he will take it, although the struggle between the two tendencies may be apparent in the furtive way in which he snatches his loot.

It must be granted that in some men apparent self-control can be explained in the same way. When a dishonest man keeps his hands off a well-filled wallet because he is afraid of the police, his behavior resembles that of the hungry dog. But there are plenty of cases in which man checks his lower tendencies for purely intellectual or moral reasons, not in order to avoid physical pain or to win some pleasure.

The Freudians have a deterministic explanation even for these cases. They say that man's Super-ego explains such instances of self-control. For them the Super-ego is a product of instinctive tendencies and social pressure and involves no will or real freedom of choice. We shall see that there are cases in which man's apparently moral conduct can be explained in terms of the Super-ego understood in that sense. But the morality which rests on the Super-ego is a pseudo-morality, an instinctive morality differing essentially from rational morality. The Freudian interpretation may explain some, it does not explain all, instances of self-control. We shall come back to this problem in a later chapter.

Another empirical confirmation of the existence of the will derives from the fact that we sometimes will an object which is repugnant to our body and our sense tendencies; for instance, when we swallow a bitter medicine, or submit to a painful operation or perform a disagreeable duty. In all these cases we are not attracted by a material, sensible good but by some good presented by our intelligence.

We can also use the phenomenon of voluntary attention as a confirmation of the existence of a rational appetite in us. Voluntary attention is distinct from spontaneous attention. Spontaneous attention is present in animals; it is the concentration of the senses and of the mind on some object which appeals to one of the lower drives. In voluntary attention we concentrate our senses and our mind on some object which does not spontaneously interest us. We concentrate because we want to concentrate, and we want to concentrate because our intelligence tells us that it is good for us to concentrate. Compare the attention you pay to an interesting moving-picture with that given to a dull but important textbook.

The object of the will is the same as that of the intellect, but considered from another point of view. This means that the material object of the will coincides with that of the intellect, but that their formal objects differ. The material object of the will is being, any being presented by the intellect. The formal object of the will is goodness in general, the good as such. Whatever the will wills is willed because it is good.

Should the will ever be confronted with an object which embodied its formal object completely, with the "good as such," it would necessarily embrace that object. God is the good as such, and if the will should ever meet Him as He is, it would necessarily adhere to Him. But on this earth we have no adequate idea of God, and therefore this hypothetical circumstance is never realized.

Yet in its deepest nature, if we consider its "natural" striving as contrasted with its elicited volitions, the will unconsciously and naturally strives towards the Infinite Good which is God. This general, unconscious, necessary striving towards God must be translated into specific, conscious, free volitions. These volitions may advance in the direction of God or they may deviate from that direction (sin). But even when deviating from the Supreme Good, they take their impetus from His attraction, while the specification of that impetus comes from a particular good presented by the intellect.

The possession by the will of the good as such constitutes happiness. Objectively, therefore, man's happiness consists in the possession of God, and he strives towards that possession in every one of his volitions. But man may freely decide that his happiness consists in the possession of some finite good, and in that case, there will be a cleavage between the natural and the elicited striving of his will, between his fundamental general willing and his superficial specified volitions, between his willing will and his willed will.

The will may strive towards a material or an immaterial good, a physical or a moral good, a real or apparent good. A physical good is an object which is good for man as a being in the material universe. A moral good is that which is good for man as a free being. When the will strives towards an apparent good, it strives towards something which is objectively evil but appears to be good. It is evil for man's spiritual nature, but it attracts one of his sensory drives and the will yields to that attraction. In such instances the will strives towards something which is evil, but not inasmuch as it is evil. Evil as such cannot be the object of the will because it is not a real being, but only the privation of some perfection which an object should possess.

The will strives towards some good which is presented by the intellect. The will itself does not know the good, it is not a cognitive faculty. Every one of its elicited acts must be preceded by an intellectual cognition. The relation of the will to the intellect is analogous to the relation between the engine and the steering wheel of a car. Movement in general comes from the engine, but the direction of the movement derives from the action of the wheel.

As the intellect knows not only itself but also all other faculties and their objects, so the will wills not only itself but also all other faculties and their objects. As the intellect knows that it knows, the rational appetite wills its own willing. It can move itself, it can command itself to will.

The will can also will that the other faculties perform their actions, it can command them to act. It commands the intellect to think, the memory to remember, the eye to see and the leg to move. The will can command the eye to see, but what the eye sees depends on the object presented to it. The *exercise* of vision depends on the will, but its *specification* comes from the object. Indirectly the will can also influence the specification of the other faculties.

We should always remember that it is not really the will which wills, but man, the person, who wills by means of his rational appetite.

FREEDOM OF THE WILL

In the paragraphs which follow we shall explain what we mean by the freedom of the will; consider the position of the determinists; demonstrate the freedom of the will; explain why the human will is free.

THE MEANING OF FREEDOM

Freedom in general means the absence of restraint. There are different kinds of restraint and of freedom. Physical freedom is the absence of physical restraint. When a prisoner is released from prison, he is physically free, since he is no longer restrained by the prison walls. Moral freedom is the absence of moral restraint, of an obligation, of a law. Thus in this country we are morally free to criticize the Government.

Psychological freedom is the absence of psychological restraint. Psychological restraint consists in drives which force a subject to perform certain actions or make it impossible for him to perform them. Thus a hungry, untrained animal is forced by its hunger to eat the food which is set before it, a scared rabbit cannot help running away. These animals are not forced into their actions by any external power or moral obligation; they are forced to act by the compelling influence of their own drives, they possess no psychological freedom. A hungry man, on the contrary, can refrain from taking food, and a soldier frightened by a heavy bombardment can stay at his post. Men possess psychological freedom.

Psychological freedom is also called freedom of choice, since it allows the free subject to choose between different courses of action. It has been defined as that attribute of the will whereby it can act or not act (freedom of exercise), can act in this way or in that way (freedom of specification).

THE MEANING AND KINDS OF DETERMINISM

Many modern philosophers and psychologists deny the freedom of the will. They are called "determinists" and their system is known as "determinism." They claim that in spite of some contrary appearances, man is forced or "determined" in all his actions.

All materialists and sensists are necessarily determinists. For them man is a purely material being. But matter is perfectly determined and possesses no freedom. When we know a material system perfectly, we can foresee and predict all its future activities. Thus an astronomer predicts with great accuracy all future eclipses. The materialists claim that if we knew the material system called "man" perfectly, and if we were aware of all the influences working on him, we should be able to predict all his future activities; we could write his biography on the day of his birth.

Determinism has taken different forms. Biological determinism maintains that physiological factors exert a compelling influence in man's life. We do what we do because of the kind of body we have inherited from our parents, because we are "born that way." The biological determinists emphasize especially the role of the endocrine glands and the genes in determining our conduct.

Psycho-social determinists emphasize a combination of psychological and social factors as explaining human conduct. On the psychological side they point to the different drives and tendencies which impel the individual; on the social side, to the continual pressure of the environment—words, customs, fashions, propaganda, but most of all education, in particular education during the first few years of life.

The psychological determinists insist upon the compulsive influence of the motives presented to our minds, asserting that when two motives are opposed to each other, the stronger necessarily prevails. In this view the will is like a balance, which necessarily tips toward the heavier weight. Thus our will necessarily chooses the greater good and follows the stronger motive.

Theological determinism holds that our life is irresistibly directed by God. We may be under the impression that we are free, but that impression is false, since our actions are determined by the Divine Will. This kind of determinism often takes the form of a vague fatalism—"It is so written." All pantheists are determinists, since they deny freedom in God Himself and claim that everything—in God, in the universe and in the individual—is but the blind necessary development of the one all-pervading divinity.

We shall see later that there is a grain of truth in some forms of determinism. But as they stand, these deterministic theories are false. We shall show this by demonstrating that the human will is free.

DEMONSTRATION OF THE FREEDOM OF THE WILL

We shall consider four arguments, which may be called: (1) the argument from common consent, (2) the psychological argument, (3) the ethical argument, (4) the philosophical argument.

The Argument from Common Consent. The great majority of men believe that their will is free. This conviction is of the utmost practical importance for the whole of human life. Therefore, if there is order in the world, the majority of mankind cannot be wrong in this belief. Hence the will is free.

The great majority of men believe that their will is free. The judgment of common sense is that there is freedom of the will. The man on the street is sure that he is free and that his neighbor is free. Only among the sophisticated does determinism find acceptance, and even among them only in theory, not in practice.

It must be admitted that the majority of mankind have in the past accepted certain things as facts which later investigation proved to be untrue. Thus for centuries it was universally believed that the sun revolved around the earth. But this kind of fact has no practical bearing on human life, and the universality of such a mistaken notion involved no disorder in human nature itself. However, the question whether or not we are free, masters of our own destiny and responsible for our actions, is of the greatest practical importance, and to suppose that the majority of mankind had for centuries erred in holding this belief would not be compatible with the concept of an ordered universe.

This argument has no value for those who deny order in the universe. For them there is nothing absurd in the idea that most people should be convinced of something false, even if that erroneous opinion had an essential bearing on the conduct of their lives. But for all who admit that the world makes sense, this argument is very strong.

It could be objected that in scientific and philosophical matters we should follow those who have studied the question, even if they constitute only a minority, rather than acquiesce blindly in the opinions of the ignorant majority. And the proponents of determinism are precisely those who have arrived at their deterministic conclusions after studying the question.

To this objection we give three answers:

1. If all those who studied the question theoretically arrived at deterministic conclusions, we should indeed have to follow them. But even among philosophers the majority uphold the freedom of the will. In continental Europe only the Dialectical Materialists or Marxists claim that man is subject to determinism; almost all other professional philosophers, whether existentialists, phenomenologists or Thomists, are firm upholders of the freedom of man's will. Some existentialists credit man with even more freedom than he actually possesses. In the English-speaking countries, it is true, many philosophers (although probably not the majority) profess a belief in determinism. This deterministic trend stems directly from the influence of Logical Positivism and indirectly, as we shall see, from the doctrine of Hume and Kant.

2. Whether one professes determinism or the freedom of the

will has a great practical influence on life. Why should a man try to control himself if he is convinced he cannot do it anyway?

. . . I am firmly convinced that the belief that nobody is ever morally responsible, in addition to being false, is quite certain to have a mischievous effect and to increase the amount of needless cruelty and suffering. For it justifies Smerdyakov's formula in *The Brothers Karamazov:* "All things are permissible." One of the commonest experiences is to meet someone whose belief that he can't help doing what he is doing (or failing to do) is often an excuse for not doing as well as he can or at least better than he is at present doing.[1]

A belief in determinism may have a far-reaching influence on one's life. On the other hand, the way a person lives may have a deep influence on his attitude toward the doctrine of free will, to the extent that opposition to this doctrine is sometimes based more on practical than on theoretical grounds.

This remark should not be misconstrued as implying that determinism is only a handy way out of the obligation of moral effort. Such an allegation would be unfair. There may be instances of that kind. More often, however, these influences of one's way of life on one's philosophical doctrine are unconscious, emanating, as they do, from the environment, the early education and the intellectual climate in which one has been reared.

3. Far from shunning moral effort, great numbers of determinists make a consistent effort to be decent and honest persons. It is difficult to see how there is no contradiction between the doctrine they profess and the kind of life they try to lead. And all determinists often conduct themselves as if they admitted the freedom of the will, of their own will and especially of the will of other people. But this leads us to our next argument.

The Psychological Argument. We have said that most people naturally hold that the will is free. Why do they cling to that conviction? Because they are directly and indirectly aware of the freedom of their own decisions. They are directly aware of their

---

[1] Sidney Hook, "Necessity, Indeterminism, and Sentimentalism," in Sidney Hook (ed.), *Determinism and Freedom in the Age of Modern Science*, p. 179. In future references this book will be quoted as *DF*.

freedom in the very act of making a free decision; they are indirectly aware of it because of the many instances of behavior
which can only be explained by admitting the freedom of the will.

1. *Direct* awareness of the freedom of our free decisions: In
this argument we claim that at the very moment in which we are
exercising our freedom we are aware of it. We do not claim, on
the other hand, that we are *directly* aware of being able to choose
freely *before* the choice is made or *after* it has been made.

It is true that before reaching a free decision we see several
courses of action lying before us and have the feeling that we can
freely choose any one of them. Tonight I may start working on
that term paper which is due next Monday, or I may visit my
friends or go to the movies. I feel very clearly that the decision
is up to me, that I can freely choose any one of these ways of
spending the evening.

True, if this means that from past experience, hence indirectly,
I know that in such situations the choice is entirely up to me. False,
if it is claimed that I am actually aware of some power in me
which I am not actually exercising, the power of freely choosing
between these different eventualities. How could I be conscious of
something which is merely potential? Only that which is actual can
be the object of an act of consciousness.

Are you capable of lifting a weight of fifty pounds? of running
a quarter of a mile in a minute? You can answer these questions
only if you have actually tried to do these things, or if you judge
from the experience of people whom you consider to be about your
equals in physical stamina. The power of doing these things is or
is not present in you, but your consciousness cannot tell you anything about it until you try to exercise it.

Suppose New York City were suddenly attacked by a fleet of
enemy bombers carrying thermonuclear weapons. In such an emergency some people would be heroically courageous; others would
behave in a cowardly way; most men would stand somewhere between these two extremes. Which way would I behave? Unless I
have been in extreme danger before, I do not know, and I would
find out only if the catastrophe occurred.

Would you have the courage to run into a burning building, liable to collapse at any moment, in order to save trapped children? You cannot tell until you actually have to make the decision.

Of course, you feel that you could do it in this sense—that you could perform the bodily movements required to run into that building. You could do it if you wanted to do it. The question is: could you want to do it? Man is free not because he can do what he wants to do (many animals have that power, and the determinists admit that we have it), but because he has it in his power either to want or not want to do it.

Our point in this discussion is, then, that we are not aware of our power of choosing freely except in the very act of exercising that power. We are aware of the possible courses of action, we may know from past experience that when no great difficulties lie in the way we are capable of choosing any of these courses. But we are not conscious of our power of free choice as such, except while we are actually exercising it.[2]

Once we have reached a decision, we continue to have the impression that, although we have chosen A, we could as well have selected B or C. Here again we have no present awareness of a power of choosing which we are no longer actually exercising. The awareness is indirect, based on memory, not upon an actual perception of the power of choice. If, in order to demonstrate that power, we change our mind and pick B instead of A, this is another decision, not a mere repetition of the previous one.

Therefore we do not claim that we have an awareness of our freedom of choice before exercising it or after having exercised it. But we possess that awareness while we are choosing, while we are deciding to take A rather than B. At that moment we are conscious that we are selecting A without coercion, without constraint; we feel that we are not being impelled by blind impulses, that we are not being manipulated like a puppet.

In order to demonstrate this to ourselves, we should not take the case of some trifling choice of everyday life which does not affect our deeper personality—v.g. choosing between a ham or cheese sandwich—nor the case of a decision which is taken

---

[2] Even then we are aware of our free *act* rather than of our *power* of performing such acts. The existence of such a power is inferred from the existence of the acts.

instantaneously, without apparent reflection. In the latter instance a decision may be free, but it is not easy to show it.

But take the following example: As a public official you have confidential information that a major road is going to be built across a piece of property which is available at a very low price. You could buy that land through some intermediary and sell it later at a handsome profit. This idea has come into your mind quite spontaneously, you are not free in the matter. You realize at once that such behavior, if not downright dishonest, would be at least unethical. You can at once, *freely,* banish that "temptation" from your mind. It may, and probably will, come back, even if you do not want it. But it is up to you to reject it. You may, on the other hand, *freely* decide to consider it for awhile, to begin a deliberation. After several days of hesitation, you finally "make up your mind"; you decide No or Yes. Now especially, you are clearly aware that putting an end to the deliberation and choosing either course of action are free decisions, of your own making, entirely up to you, for which you assume the responsibility, which make you a better or a worse man. In these free decisions you were *influenced* by many factors which are not of your own making (your heredity, early education, environment, by public opinion, etc.). But these factors cannot force you to decide one way or the other. The final decision comes from deep within you, from the core of your personality, from your own free will. When you thus make a decision, especially an important one, in the moral order, you are aware of it and of the fact that this decision is free, does not have to be taken, could be a different one.

True, the awareness of freedom is not overwhelming; it is not difficult to overlook it if for some reason you choose to do so. As Professor De Finance writes, "Clear does not always mean distinct, much less reflectively known. There is a perception of values which entails neither words nor images, and that is why it may seem to go unnoticed, *but in order not to notice it, you must already have refused it in your heart.*"[3] That may explain why some people assert that they are not aware of the freedom of their decisions. Although this does not necessarily involve bad faith, it

[3] *Existence et Liberté,* pp. 9-10. See also K. Rahner, S.J., *Schriften zur Theologie,* Vol. III, p. 130, note.

involves more than merely theoretical reasons. Our free decisions are so central in us that in a certain sense we *are* our free decisions. The process by which we become aware of what we are is quite different from scientific or everyday knowledge.

2. *Indirect* awareness of the freedom of our decisions:

Many facts of our daily life, of which we are clearly aware, can be explained only if we are free. We deliberate before taking a decision, we weigh the reasons for and against it, we regret some of our past choices; and this implies that we should, and by inference could, have acted differently. We admire, praise and reward virtuous and heroic actions and manifest through our attitude the implicit belief that the person who performed them was not forced to do so. If Doctor Albert Schweitzer cannot help staying with his patients in tropical Africa, there is no reason for admiring him. We react with spontaneous indignation in the presence of certain crimes, a reaction quite different from the shock we feel in face of some natural calamity. If Hitler was not acting freely when he decreed the wholesale extermination of the Jews, his action was just one more natural disaster, and there was no reason for any indignation about it.

In most countries the administration of justice is based on a belief in the freedom of at least some human actions. Most courts try to find out the degree of deliberation (that is, of freedom) with which a crime was committed. And the punishment is generally proportioned to the degree of freedom. If man is not free, there is no reason for punishing a "first degree" murder more severely than the killing of a pedestrian in an automobile accident.

This psychological conviction of freedom is so strong that even determinists act on it if they do not watch themselves. Determinists deliberate, they praise virtue and heroism, they regret some of their past decisions, they hold a moral view of the actions of others— they are morally indignant in the presence of heinous crimes, etc.

One teacher of psychology I know works his course up to a fine climax wherein he declares that freedom of the will is man's greatest delusion. (Note): Privately this same psychologist sees his dilemma, and laments that he finds it necessary to administer praise and blame to himself and to others, "as if" people were responsible for their acts.[4]

It is now widely recognized among moral philosophers that, no matter how irrefutable the logic of absolute psychological or naturalistic determinism may be, sane and rational human beings, in order to retain their sanity, their rationality, and their human purposefulness in living still stubbornly insist on deciding, choosing, and acting as though they were autonomous, dignified, and free individuals. This is the phenomenon, above all, that still needs to be explained.[5]

The [Communist] Party denied the free will of the individual—and at the same time it exacted his willing self-sacrifice. It denied his capacity to choose between two alternatives—and at the same time it demanded that he should constantly choose the right one. It denied his power to distinguish good and evil—and at the same time it spoke pathetically of guilt and treachery. The individual stood under the sign of economic fatality, a wheel in a clockwork which had been wound up for all eternity and could not be stopped or influenced—and the Party demanded that the wheel should revolt against the clockwork and change its course.[6]

However, if you point to these inconsistencies, the determinists try to explain them away. "We admire and praise a hero just as we admire and praise a heavyweight champion, or a winning race horse. Our admiration for the horse does not imply that the animal is free. Why should our admiration for the hero imply that belief?"

It is true that we admire and praise performances which involve no freedom—for instance, that of a race horse, of a champion, of a great singer. But that kind of admiration differs from the admiration which we pay to virtuous or heroic actions. Great performances in sport or art involve the overcoming of great physical difficulties. Great performances in the sphere of morality do not; from the physical point of view, anyone could accomplish them. It is *physically* no more difficult to run into a burning building in order to save trapped children than it would be to run into that building when there is no danger; the difficulties are not physical

---

[4] Allport, *College Reading and Religion*, p. 102.

[5] H. W. Hintz, "Some Further Reflections on Moral Responsibility," in *DF*, p. 166.

[6] A. Koestler, *Darkness at Noon* (New York, Macmillan).

but psychological, internal to the subject and freely overcome by him. Freedom consists precisely in overcoming such internal obstacles; hence admiration here implies a belief in freedom.

"We want a criminal to be punished, not because we believe that he could have refrained from committing his crime, but because the punishment will be a deterrent for other potential criminals." This may be true as far as the punishment is concerned, but it does not explain the spontaneous outburst of indignation with which even a confirmed determinist reacts to certain crimes, v.g. the extermination of millions of innocent people by Communists or Nazis.

"We have the impression of freedom because we are not aware of the motives which determine us. These motives are unconscious." This is the Freudian form of determinism. We shall take it up later in detail in our study of the Unconscious. The following remarks will suffice for our present purpose: Such a decision, which would force itself on the mind unaccompanied by any awareness of the motives prompting it, is in fact not a free choice but a compulsion. When a person cannot help doing something and does not know why he wants to do it (v.g. washing one's hands every few minutes) he is not free; he is suffering from a compulsion, he is abnormal. But our ordinary choices do not assume that pathological form.

"The very fact that, although I am determined and I know that I am, I often act as if I were not, is a proof of determinism. I cannot help it, I am not free."

If I were determined, I would know nothing about it. Animals are unfree, and totally unaware of it. In order to be aware of space, I must, in some way, stand outside space. I can know time only because something in me is above time. I can speak of determinism only because I am not totally in its grip.[7]

The Ethical Argument. If there is no freedom, there is no real responsibility, no virtue, no merit, no moral obligation, no duty, no morality. The necessary connection between freedom and these spiritual realities is quite obvious and is demonstrated in Ethics.

[7] See De Finance, *op. cit.,* p. 13.

This is a strong argument, because the sense of duty and the belief in morality and moral obligation come naturally to man, and even those who deny their existence in theory live in practice as if they admitted it.

Kant, who claimed that the existence of freedom was not demonstrable by theoretical reason, nevertheless was convinced that man is free, and he derived this conviction from the fact of duty, which he considered to be immediately evident to the practical reason.

Among the first principles which, as we have argued, are virtually inborn to the human intellect there is at least one that refers to the moral order: "The good must be done and evil must be avoided." This fundamental dictate of conscience, this moral "ought," is virtually inborn in every human mind. It is the basis of all moral obligation, and it implies freedom of the will, since obligation is nothing but the necessity of doing something freely.

The determinist who denies the existence of duty nevertheless, to a certain extent, implicitly affirms it. For in his discussion with an opponent he will take it for granted that both he himself and his opponent *ought* to be sincere and truthful, *ought* not to distort the adversary's statements and *ought* to abide by the rules of polite discussion.

He may assert, of course, that all these things have nothing to do with duty, that they are mere conventions, like the rules of etiquette or of a game. But when I move in polite society, why do I abide by the rules of etiquette? When I play games, why do I observe the rules? Is it an inborn necessity, such as my need for breathing? Is it a drilled-in performance, such as the tricks learned by a dog? There may have been some drilling; fundamentally, however, observing the rules of social intercourse or of the game is a duty, an obligation. But obligation supposes freedom, it is necessity as it applies to a free agent.

No social life is possible without obligations and duties. In our relations with other people we are aware of certain obligations we have in regard to them, and we are even more aware of their obligations towards us. Therefore we are continually taking it for granted that man is free.

Those who maintain that all obligations are mere conventions will have to admit, in accordance with their own logic, that no obligations are absolute, no duties are sacred, no rights are inalienable. Hence a majority might one day decide that the extermination of a minority was good and permissible.

The Philosophical Argument. This argument can be presented only in a philosophical context. It presupposes the two following philosophical statements, which we shall not demonstrate here:

1. Every kind of knowledge evokes a corresponding kind of striving. This follows from the fact that knowledge and striving, as we have tried to show earlier,[8] are the two fundamental functions or aspects of being;

2. Immaterial striving is free at least in this sense, that it is not determined from outside. Determinism derives from matter.

If these two principles are admitted, the argument for the freedom of the will is easy to set up:

There is in man an immaterial kind of knowledge, as we have demonstrated above. Hence there must also be in him an immaterial kind of striving. And since immaterial striving is free, there is in man a free kind of striving, which is called the will.

WHY THE HUMAN WILL IS FREE

The following explanation of the deeper reason why the human will is free is often presented as one more argument for the freedom of the will. It is indeed such an argument, because the explanation of why man's will is free implies the reasons for admitting this freedom.

Man's freedom does not consist merely in being able to do what he wants to do. Many animals can do what they want to do. But it is not within their power to decide what they want to do: their nature and their environment decide this for them. Man, on the other hand, is able not only to do what he wants to do but also to decide that he wants to do one thing or another. What he wants to do is up to him, it is not dictated to him by any exterior or interior influence.

We must show, therefore, the fact that, and the reason why,

[8] See p. 197.

the human person does not will the things he wills out of necessity; the fact that, and the reason why, he wills them freely. In order to make our explanation as clear as possible, we proceed in four stages:

1. Man wills a thing necessarily as soon as he has decided: "This is good."

The will is a faculty whose object is the good. When a faculty meets its object, it is not free, it must embrace it. Therefore the will must necessarily embrace the good.

But the will does not know its own object, it is not a cognitive faculty; it meets its object through the intellect. Hence as soon as the intellect judges: "This is good," the will is presented with its object and must necessarily embrace it.

Therefore we must find out in what circumstances the intellect, or rather man through his intellect, has to decide: "This is good." If this statement follows automatically on the presentation of certain goods, man possesses no freedom. If this statement is of the person's own making, he is free. Man is free if he can freely decide: "This is good." He possesses no freedom if he decides necessarily that something is good.

2. Man decides *necessarily* that a thing is good when it conforms to his standard of goodness.

The person judges the goodness of things not arbitrarily, but according to a certain norm or standard. When an object fulfills the requirements of that standard it is necessarily called good. If man's standard of goodness were pleasure, everything pleasurable would have to be judged good, and his will would necessarily embrace it. Should this standard be finite goodness, man would have to will every good object.

3. Man's standard of goodness is "goodness as such."

The will is guided by the intellect. The intellect knows being as such, desires truth as such. The object of the will has the same extension as that of the intellect which guides it: it is the good as such; and goodness as such is the standard according to which man judges the objects of his will. The good as such means the perfect good, without any restriction, imperfection or limitation.

4. No object on earth comes up to man's standard of goodness.

On earth we never meet the perfect good. Many things are

good, but they are not absolutely good, they all have their limitations, their defects. Even God as we know Him on earth does not necessarily appear to us to be the good as such, since if we want to adhere to Him, we must give up certain forbidden pleasures which satisfy some of our drives and, to that extent, seem good to us.

5. Hence there is not a single object on earth with regard to which man is forced to decide: "This is good." There is not a single object in relation to which we are not free.

In other words: We are free to will or not to will, because we can always say: "This is good but not perfectly good."

We can say: "This is good but not perfectly good," because we are capable of comparing every good presented to us with the perfect good.

We are capable of comparing every good presented to us with the perfect good because our intellect provides us with the idea of the perfect good.

Our intellect provides us with the idea of the perfect good because it is immaterial.

It follows that our freedom is ultimately based on the immateriality of our will and our intellect. We are free because we are spirits.

MECHANISM OF A FREE DECISION

In every free decision we may distinguish several steps. Although frequently the decision matures so quickly that we are hardly aware of these steps, they must be present if the decision is to be really free.

First Step. The first step consists in the attraction exercised by some good either on the will or on some other drive. Thus, while we are writing a term-paper, the idea comes up in our mind that it would be nice to see the picture at the neighborhood theater. We are immediately attracted by that pleasure.

Such an attraction is natural and unavoidable. Our sense appetite is necessarily attracted by any pleasure presented to it by the senses. Our will also is attracted, because, from the point of view of the senses, this pleasure is a real good. No freedom is involved in this step, and therefore no responsibility, no possible guilt. A temptation is precisely such an attraction exerted on the will by some moral evil presented as a pleasure.

Second Step. The second step consists in considering and examining the attractive good. Besides its desirable aspect it shows other features which are not so desirable. It is agreeable to go to the movies, but it is disagreeable to go to class tomorrow without that term-paper and to receive a poor grade for the course.

Because there are good sides to the object, we are attracted. Because there are bad sides to the same object, we are not forced, we remain free. As we concentrate on the good sides, we feel more and more attracted. As we emphasize the bad sides, we feel more and more free to resist that attraction. If our mind were so entirely occupied by the goodness of the object that there was no room for any other considerations, we should not be free. In that case the object would appear to be simply good, perfectly good. Before the perfect good, which is its necessitating object, the will is not free. It is only by comparison with other goods, and ultimately with our standard of goodness, that the deficiencies of the object become apparent. Therefore this second step is essential in any free decision.

Sometimes such a comparison becomes impossible. Thus in hypnosis, in psychosis, in severe neurosis, when the mind does not function normally, a person may be unable to see the dark sides of the object: he is "fascinated" by it; there is no room in his mind for anything but its allurements.

This may also occur in more normal circumstances; for instance, when the sense appetite or the emotions are so strongly aroused that the object occupies the whole mind and excludes any other content. In such cases of extreme emotional disturbance the mind sees only the good sides of the object, it is unable to advert to its deficiencies. This may happen in intoxication, drug addiction, great sexual excitement, extreme fear or anger. In such cases freedom may be strongly curtailed, with a corresponding decrease of responsibility and of eventual guilt, or it may be entirely abolished.

Since these states are connected with strong physiological disturbances, there is some truth in the doctrine of biological deter-

minism. Some bodily conditions interfere with the exercise of freedom. Some cases of unbalance of the endocrine glands, of pathological heredity, result in frequent physiological upheavals which,
if they do not entirely eliminate freedom, at least considerably decrease it. But these are pathological conditions. In the normal individual such extreme circumstances do not usually occur, and it
is one of his duties to see to it that they do not occur. He is obliged
to avoid the occasions which may put his body into such a state of
turmoil that he can no longer exercise real freedom.

Third Step. The third step consists in deliberation, in which the
reasons for and against a course of action are examined by the intellect. This step may take a long time or it may be instantaneous.

Movie or term paper? We weigh the pros and the cons. Our
mind when thus engaged is like scales; the weights are the advantages of either course of action. The side on which the heaviest
weights pile up will finally go down and stay down, and our will
necessarily follows it.

But how do these diverse considerations arise in the mind? If
they arise independently of the will, under the influence of circumstances, environment, the laws of association, without any
possibility on our part of influencing them, then we are merely
witnesses of the struggle between the motives, and whatever may
be the outcome of that struggle, we must join the winning side.
Such is the position of the psychological determinists, who claim
that the will always accepts the objectively strongest motive.

But that position is not supported by our inner experience. We
can influence that struggle which the motives wage in our mind; we
can strengthen the force of some motives by concentrating our attention on them; we can weaken others by turning our attention
away from them. Circumstances, environment, the laws of association, our present state of body and mind do influence the presentation of the motives. But we can always intervene and support one
side against the other. The side to which we lend our support will
finally prove the stronger and will determine the issue.

Here again, in the process of our deliberation, neurosis, strong
emotions, a violent passion may have a disturbing influence. They
render a cool, accurate appraisal very difficult, they make it hard

for us to concentrate our attention. All these influences may decrease, or even in extreme cases abolish, human freedom.

Psychological determinism holds that the will always follows the strongest motive. This position can be maintained only if we add that in normal circumstances that motive will be the strongest which *we make* the strongest. It is untenable if we interpret it as meaning that the strength of the motives is determined independently of our intervention.

Fourth Step. Sooner or later we decide, "This is good for me now." We overlook the bad features of the object, we concentrate our attention on its attractiveness. Once that decision has been reached, the will must follow it and embrace the object presented by the intellect.

This decision is not the result of a purely intellectual process nor of the objective state of affairs, nor of social pressure, nor of our past education. All these factors *influence* our decision, they do not *determine* it. It is the product of our own personal intervention, of a factor which comes from the very depths of our personality. It is a free decision.

Everything in this material universe is determined by and in its causes. The only exception to this rule is the freedom of the human will in its free decisions. In and through them we share, in an analogous and very lowly way, something of God's own creative power.

18

Further Elucidation of Man's Free Decisions

THE PRACTICAL SYLLOGISM OF THE WILL

The mechanism of a free decision can be explained in another way, which will allow us to shed more light on this essential feature of man's nature. When a person makes a free decision, he uses what has been called "the practical syllogism of the will." It can be presented as follows:

That which is good must be willed.

But this action or object is good for me now.

Therefore this action or object must be willed.

This syllogism is not explicitly used by the subject, but it can be read into his deliberation. It contains not the usual three, but four terms, since the middle term is not the same in the major and in the minor premise. In the major "that which is good" refers to the good as such, to that which is absolutely good, for only the good as such must be absolutely willed by the rational appetite. The minor, on the other hand, refers to "that which is good for me now." Therefore the syllogism is invalid, and it cannot force the assent of the intellect. It becomes valid only if "that which is good for me now" is in some way equated with "that which is good."

The intellect of itself cannot equate these two terms, but in a free choice the intellect under the influence of the will is capable of equating them. Voluntary attention, which is an activity of the intellect influenced by the will, overlooks the finite and defective aspects of the object, makes it appear to the intellect as good without restriction, or as a means for reaching the perfect good. By a

307

fiat of the will "that which is good for me now" has become just "that which is good." Now the practical syllogism is valid, the conclusion follows, the decision is reached.

Although man can freely decide that a finite object is perfectly good, or a means for the acquisition of the perfect good, he does not reach such a decision without good reason. Freedom does not mean arbitrariness. The reasons which make him reach such a decision are summarized in the words, *for me now,* which point to the dispositions of the subject.

As a person is, so things appear to him. The impression which objects make upon a subject depends not only on the objects but also on the state of mind, the dispositions of the subject. Some of these dispositions are stable or permanent (*for me*), others are of a more transitory nature (*now*).

The transitory dispositions are all those which temporarily affect the subject at the moment of his choice. Such are his state of health, his mood, the weather, the present environment. When these transitory dispositions have a greater impact on the choices than the more permanent factors, we have a fickle subject whose life lacks unity, the general direction of whose choices changes from day to day.

The more permanent dispositions which influence a man's decisions are indicated by the words, *for me.* What a person is because of his inherited dispositions and has become as a result of his education, his environment, his own personal experiences and efforts, the influence of God's grace upon him, makes some things appear good and others not good for him. Thus his whole past life has a share in his free decisions. A person who leads a moral life comes to decide with increasing ease and spontaneity that those objects or actions are good for him which happen also to be morally good in themselves, whereas an individual who yields again and again to his animal nature reaches a state in which he experiences a constantly increasing facility in considering as good for himself whatever suits his passions and his lower drives. This pressure of the past on a man's free decisions never amounts to compulsion, but it is very real and it increases as time goes on. "Man shapes his own being daily by the exercise of his freedom, but yesterday's freedom lies heavy on today's, and the latter already casts its shadow over tomorrow's."[1]

THE DOMINANT INCLINATION

This influence of the past on free decisions has been called a "dominant inclination."[2] It is an inclination because it inclines, or pushes, the will towards certain kinds of objects. It is not a determining inclination, because the will can always resist it,[3] but it is a dominant inclination, because its influence tends to prevail more and more in the process of man's decisions. It is a habit of the will which, depending on the direction it has taken, impels some men toward the moral good, making it easier for them to be faithful to their moral ideal, and other men towards moral evil, making it more difficult for them to lead a virtuous life. It becomes part of man's character, not, of course, as one of its inborn, spontaneous features, but as acquired and controlled by the action of the will.

The theory of the dominant inclination allows us to answer serious objections against the freedom of the will. Thus Professor John Hospers writes:

How can anyone be responsible for his actions, since they grow out of his character, which is shaped and molded and made what it is by influences—some hereditary, but most of them stemming from early parental environment—that were not of his own making or choosing?[4]

It is true that our actions grow out of our character, if character is understood as including our will and our dominant inclination. But it is only partly true to say that our character is molded and made what it is by influences which are not of our own making.

---

[1] Mouroux, *The Meaning of Man* (New York, Sheed & Ward, 1948), p. 157.

[2] *Ibid.*, p. 156.

[3] "The infinite amplitude of the will can never be ontologically suppressed and the possibility of recovery is always real, and even if a man bears all the marks of enslavement, the only determinism that holds him is one that has been *willed and constructed,* and is therefore capable of being *refused and destroyed.*" *Ibid.*, p. 157.

[4] "What Means This Freedom?" in *DF*, p. 119.

That indeed applies to the determined, unfree elements of our character (what we shall later call our spontaneous character). It does not apply to our will and to our dominant inclination, to our controlled character.[5]

In the neurotic person the determined elements of character have a tendency to prevail. That is why his freedom and responsibility are more or less restricted. But in a normal individual's character those elements which are of his own making (dominant inclination) or under his own control (free-will) are, or should be, predominant. A person's moral growth consists precisely in a gradual extension of this autonomous sphere of his personality.

In other words: although the early environment may have a bad influence on the development of our character, we can, to a great extent, overcome that influence by dint of voluntary effort.

But, continues Professor Hospers, "If we *can* overcome the effects of the early environment, the ability to do so is itself a product of the early environment. We did not give ourselves this ability and if we lack it we cannot be blamed for not having it."[6]

The ability to overcome the effects of the early environment is not a product of that environment. Neither our free-will nor our dominant inclination derives from our environment. We have slowly built the latter up through the use of the former. Our free-will was given to us with our very being: the First Cause, which gave us existence, gave us existence as free agents. As the Supreme Good this same First Cause continually invites and attracts us. We do not consciously experience this attraction as deriving from the Supreme Good. It reaches us on the conscious level under the guise of attractive finite goods. It is up to our free-will to accept or to reject the invitation of the Supreme Good, to yield to, or to resist, His attraction. We accept and yield when we freely choose only those finite goods which lead us to Him; we reject and resist when we freely prefer those finite goods which lead us away from Him. Our will is not something which we give ourselves; the attraction of the Supreme Good is not of our own making. What does lie in our power is the way we use our God-given will in the pres-

[5] See our study of spontaneous and controlled character in chapter 20, p. 364.
[6] *Op. cit.*, p. 126.

ence of the God-sent attraction. Our volitional life is not a monologue but a dialogue.[7]

Thus we see at what point Professor Paul Edwards errs in the course of the following remarks:

> It is true that A helped to form his own later character. But his starting point, his desire to change, his energy and courage, were already there. They may or may not have been the results of previous efforts on his own part. But there must have been a first effort, and the effort at that time was the result of factors that were not of his making.[8]

We reply that the first effort was the result of A's *freely using* factors which are not of his making. His first free act was a free welcoming or rejecting of the invitation of the Supreme Good. It may have assumed the following shape:

As a child, say, of seven, A discovered a few coins lying on a table. He felt like taking them to buy candy. Suppose that he was already past the mere Super-ego stage, that he was more or less vaguely aware that stealing was not wrong because it was forbidden, but forbidden because it was wrong.[9] If he chooses to steal the coins, he decides implicitly that for him the supreme good or happiness consists in following his own egoistic inclinations. If he resists the temptation, he decides that for him the supreme good or happiness consists in respecting the more or less vaguely perceived moral order. The first free act means a total orientation of life, either towards or away from the Infinite Good. That explains why St. Thomas attributed so much importance to it.[10] If the child A has chosen to steal, it will be easier for him to be dishonest again when the next occasion occurs; if he has overcome this first temptation, it will be easier for him to be honest next time. He

[7] To the attraction of the Infinite Good in the natural order, which can be known by reason, is added the supernatural attraction of God as Author of Grace, which is known only by faith.

[8] "Hard and Soft Determinism," in *DF*, p. 109.

[9] "Wrong because forbidden" is a Super-ego evaluation; "forbidden because wrong" is a conscience evaluation, implies real morality and freedom. We do not know at what age the transition from the former to the latter occurs. On the Super-ego, see chapter 21, pp. 388 ff.

[10] *S. Theol.*, Ia IIae, 89, 6. See the penetrating study of Maritain with regard to the first free act in *The Range of Reason*, pp. 66-85.

has made a start at developing a dominant inclination—or, as Professor Edwards puts it, at forming his own later character.[11]

Suppose now that A, having stolen the coins with a bad conscience, experiences no disagreeable consequences. The adults around him do not care; as a matter of fact, they act in the same way, only on a larger scale. Neither at home nor in the school is A's dawning sense of duty and of responsibility given support or encouragement. Everybody in his environment is out for a good time without any regard to the moral law. Why should A not follow their example? Almost unavoidably the child's conscience will be warped, and his will-power will remain undeveloped. No less than his intelligence, these powers need to be educated during childhood and adolescence. His conscience will be warped: he will not be clearly aware where his duties lie, what he must do and what he must avoid. His will-power will be undeveloped: even if he knows the moral law, he will not have the strength to live up to it, owing to insufficient motivation and a dominant inclination in the wrong direction. Accordingly, A's responsibility will be considerably less than that of a person of his age who has enjoyed a solid moral education. He is a victim of his environment. He may, in spite of advancing age and even intellectual development, remain morally infantile throughout his life.

Does that mean that he is not free at all? By no means. A certain amount of freedom is retained by all men who are not totally insane. Furthermore, there are some domains in which he clearly continues to see his "duty," and where it is up to him to listen to the "voice of his conscience." For example: he belongs to a gang, and he would consider any "squealing" on it as a hideous crime. Should he be induced to do it all the same, he would do it in full freedom, and well aware of this freedom and the ensuing responsibility.

In such a person freedom is undeveloped, owing to a deficient education. It is not totally absent, even within the field of objective morality, and within some restricted areas it may be as strong as it is in the average individual.

[11] This example shows again that the most important free decisions occur in the moral order.

From what we have said about the dominant inclination it would seem to follow that both the man who lives a moral life and becomes increasingly subject to a dominant inclination towards virtue, and the man who follows the lead of his lower drives and becomes increasingly subject to a dominant inclination towards sin, see their freedom gradually decline with the mounting pressure of the inclination which holds sway in their life. Only the man who wavers between good and evil, trying to lead a moral life but frequently straying from the right path through weakness, would keep the full unhampered use of his freedom.

This strange conclusion is true in a certain sense, if we take freedom to mean only the power of choosing indifferently between moral good and evil. But this very conclusion makes it clear that such cannot be the real meaning of human freedom. Experience confirms this view. The main, if not the only, field in which human freedom is exercised is that of moral endeavor. Now we observe that individuals who have been supremely successful in that endeavor become in practice more and more unable to choose evil, when a choice is to be made between good and evil.[12] In the Saints such choice is practically eliminated, yet the Saints are supremely free. Therefore real freedom cannot consist essentially in the power of choosing between good and evil.

FREE-WILL AND LIBERTY

Freedom presents two problems which might be called, in Augustinian terms, the problem of free-will and the problem of liberty. The first is a problem of mechanism, and it concerns the power of choosing, essential to every spiritual creature, making him master of his own acts, of his own objects, of his own judgments. The second is a problem of meaning or purpose, and it concerns the power of self-realization which characterizes the person, and enables him to respond to his vocation and to achieve his destiny. The two problems are implied in each other as a partial problem and a total, as a problem of structure and a problem of dynamism, as a problem of the means

[12] We do not say that they are completely (or physically) unable to choose. As long as man lives he is capable of falling away from the good.

and a problem of the end. For free-will is a means to liberty, and the power of choosing is there to serve a power of self-achievement.[13]

According to this conception free-will, or the power of choosing between opposite values, is not an end in itself, it is only a means. The end is the acquisition of perfect liberty. That liberty consists essentially in this: that the elicited, conscious acts of our will shall coincide more and more with the natural, unconscious striving of the same faculty. The natural, unconscious striving of our will is necessarily directed toward the Absolute Good, which is God. Whenever we use our free-will in the right way, freely choosing what is morally good and rejecting what is morally evil, our elicited, conscious activity coincides with that fundamental craving of our will.

As we repeat such actions, what is morally good tends to appear, more and more, as that which is "good for me now." Our dominant inclination is leading us to the real good; what we like to do is exactly what we must do. Our liberty is growing, whereas our power of choosing, our free-will, is becoming gradually a factor of less importance. All normal human beings are free, in the sense that they possess the power of choosing. All human beings must become free, in the sense that they should acquire perfect liberty. The main purpose of education, psychotherapy, ascetical effort—in fact, of all attempts at self-improvement—should be the acquisition of this perfect liberty by means of a prudent use of free-will.

In this connection we must mention the theory of the "final option," which is being accepted by an increasing number of philosophers and theologians. According to this theory, the series of free decisions which succeed each other in a man's life culminate, at the very moment of death (and this even when he dies in a coma, apparently deprived of any kind of consciousness), in a final, momentous decision or option by which he chooses either the objective good or his own subjective advantage; by which he either humbly and lovingly acquiesces in God's will or proudly and egoistically asserts himself as the center of everything. This choice is free, and fully conscious. As a matter of fact, it is more free

[13] Mouroux, *op. cit.*, p. 143.

and more fully conscious than any choice made by a man during his life. Through it he fixes his eternal attitude towards God and himself.

But this option stands very much under the influence of the dominant inclination. The person who has consistently tried to prefer God to his own egoistic pride will almost certainly (although freely, not necessarily) confirm these previous choices in his final choice. On the other hand, the individual who has regularly put his own pleasure and pride above a humble surrender to God runs a very great risk (although he is not forced, he remains free) of sealing his eternal destiny by a final decision of the same kind.

This final option is not made in the light of eternity. It remains really free. It is the final act of man's life, the very act of transition from time into eternity. It is, as it were, the irrevocable signature which a man, in full consciousness, puts down under the script of his life. It is the first and the last time he can commit himself forever.

As this last free choice will be decisive of man's attitude for eternity, it must have features which differentiate it from the free decisions of everyday life. Since man's first free decision is very important, his last free choice must be even more momentous. It seems inadmissible that a spiritual being should assume his eternal attitude in an unconscious way, slip unawares into the posture which will be his forever; hence there are good reasons for accepting that the final option must take place in a last intense burst of mortal consciousness and freedom.[14]

THE THREE KINDS OF FREE ACTS

A dominant inclination is not determinant. Powerful as its influence may be upon all of a person's actions, it can never force him to follow its lead. Furthermore, the inclination itself, having been freely willed and constructed, can at any time be freely resisted and destroyed.

[14] See E. Mersch, S.J., *Theology of the Mystical Body*, pp. 262 ff.; R. Troisfontaines, S.J., "Death: a Test for Love, a Condition of Freedom," *Cross Currents* 7 (1957), pp. 201-212, and also *"Je ne meurs pas. . . .,"* pp. 120-151; R. W. Gleason, S.J., *The World to Come*, pp. 69 ff. Catholic readers are referred to p. 467 in the Appendix.

Therefore we may distinguish three kinds of free acts. The first is exercised in the direction of the dominant inclination, it carries into detail the plan of life which a man has slowly come to accept. As the inclination grows, such actions become gradually easier, so as to seem instinctive and automatic. They remain free actions nevertheless, for the inclination itself has been freely constructed and is freely maintained.

The second kind of free actions go counter to the dominant inclination. People who ordinarily follow the lead of their animal drives or their egoism occasionally perform acts of charity, kindliness or generosity, while others whose effort is ordinarily directed towards the good sometimes deviate from their ideal. Such deviations from the main trend of one's life indicate that the personality has not yet been perfectly unified around a dominant ideal.

The third kind of free actions are the most important. More than merely deviating from the dominant inclination, they break with it, they cut the personality free from it and give a new orientation to an individual's whole life.

. . . these are acts that put the end itself in question, which touch the roots of liberty, the whole trend of a life, the spiritual being of the person. These are acts of conversion, whether involving a total break—on the plane of willing—with the past, or a decisive deepening, a radical purification or perversion, carried out in accordance with the habitual inclination but through an option that puts a whole destiny in question. Such acts are creative. They constitute the most splendid proof of the abiding liberty of man; and from that standpoint the apostate is as good an example as the convert. Such acts are always possible since the essential core of the will remains inviolate, and its infinite capacity will never be satisfied with the finite. They are difficult, because they demand a total resumption of the self. . . . They are rare, because no one can repeatedly make a clean sweep of the whole orientation and mechanism of his life, the equilibrium and play of his powers. . . . But such acts are the deepest expression of a personality, they are acts of the person as such, that is to say self-constructive. Whenever they appear, they initiate or resolve a crisis of growth or collapse in the history of the man, and mark him for time and eternity.[15]

[15] Mouroux, *op. cit.*, pp. 158-159. For a striking example of such a free action, see the gospel according to St. Mark, x, 17-22.

Although at times such a fundamental decision may seem to emerge rather suddenly into consciousness, it is nevertheless most often the outcome of a slow process of maturation. The clear, explicit decision may have been preceded by a period of subconscious groping, as the new orientation sought to express itself, to embody itself, in the many actions of daily life, preparatory to its emergence into the full light of awareness. Many complex factors are in interaction here. From the innermost depths of the human person such a basic decision slowly emerges in a perpetual dialogue between the divine invitation and attraction[16] and human assent or refusal. On the one hand the option, before it is fully explicit, is already influencing man's actions, giving them a general orientation in its own direction; on the other hand these actions are slowly endowing the option with concrete form—allowing it to take on a body, as it were—until finally it is able to emerge into the full light of consciousness. It is in this mysterious interaction of the Infinite and the finite spirit, in the exchange between the core of the person and its countless surface activities, that a human destiny slowly shapes its course.[17]

INTERACTION BETWEEN INTELLECT AND WILL

The mechanism of a free decision as explained above in the practical syllogism of the will raises a serious difficulty. The minor premise of that syllogism becomes acceptable to our intellect only under the influence of the will. An act of the will is required to make us admit that "this object or action is good." But we know that the will acts only under the guidance of the intellect. The will cannot force our intellect to admit the minor premise unless its movement is guided by some judgment such as, "It is good to force the intellect to accept the minor premise." But this judgment is not self-evident; hence the intellect can pronounce it only under some influence of the will. And so on, indefinitely. We are obviously in a vicious circle.

[16] This is true on the natural level, but much more so on the supernatural.

[17] See P. Fransen, S.J., "Towards a Psychology of Divine Grace," in *Lumen Vitae,* 12 (1957), pp. 203-232.

The way out of this difficulty is to remember that my intelligence does not know, nor does my will, will; but I know and will through these faculties. The difficulty arises from an exaggerated objectification of the faculties. Intellect and will are not substances but accidents. It is not really the intelligence that leads the will and the will that influences the intelligence, but I myself, as knowing, lead myself as willing; and I, as willing, influence myself as knowing. In an act of free choice it is the whole person, in his most intimate originality and spontaneity, who expresses himself. There is something deeply mysterious in every free decision. A finite spirit in matter is necessarily, in some respects, a mystery to itself.

There is another kind of influence of the will upon the intellect which has great practical consequences. Every intelligent student of spiritualistic philosophy has wondered at some time why its main truths are rejected by so many philosophers. These truths seem obvious, and they are supported by strong arguments. Yet many good minds are impervious to the arguments and reject the doctrines. They adhere to other philosophical systems which, to their minds, follow logically from self-evident principles. Thus philosophy presents the bewildering spectacle of many conflicting systems, each of which is defended as the only logical expression of the truth.

The ultimate reason for this state of affairs is the fact that in all matters which vitally involve man's major interests, his will, his tendencies, his habits and attitudes exert an unconscious influence on his intellect.

Consider a concrete situation. This thinker has been brought up in a materialistic environment and considers man to be a product of blind evolution, a complicated mechanical system differing from other material beings only in degree of complexity. His whole outlook on life—his way of regarding others, his habits and attitudes— is derived from this basic conception. If such a man were to be convinced of the truth of a spiritualistic system, he would have to revolutionize his whole way not only of thinking but also of living. Is it surprising, then, that arguments for that system meet greater resistance in his mind than would be met by a geometrical demonstration or a scientific theory?

Add to this the fact that philosophical truths are reached by a difficult process of reasoning. In philosophy the demonstrations proceed through a series of affirmations linked by reasoning. At every link difficulties may occur to the mind, and the affective resistance lurking in man will make the most of these difficulties in order to put him off the right path.

All this involves no bad faith. The factors making for bias have developed in the individual's mind without his knowledge or consent, under the impact of his education, environment, the spirit of the time.

In other cases, however, bad faith may be involved. The individual may use "rationalization"—that is, in a vaguely conscious way deceive himself as to the real foundation for his intellectual convictions. Consider a concrete example. A young man has been brought up as a Christian. He has a fair grasp of the Christian conception of man, finds it satisfactory and appreciates the strength of its arguments. After leaving college, however, he falls into serious moral disorder. His conscience bothers him, and he seeks a means of escaping its painful reproaches. Only two means are available: straighten out his conduct or stifle his conscience. If he does not have the courage to follow the former course, he will be tempted more and more to adopt the latter. He will not clearly announce to himself that he is going to smother his conscience, but he will begin to see all kinds of intellectual difficulties against the Christian conception of man. Arguments which once seemed strong begin to lose their hold on his mind, and objections which he used to brush aside take on ominous proportions. He may struggle for a while, but finally he arrives at a stage where he gives up his former ideas and embraces one of the current philosophies which reject the very notion of moral responsibility and hence of sin. On the surface this young man may believe that he has arrived at his deterministic convictions through a purely intellectual process of reflection. Yet deep within himself he knows that he has adopted his new philosophy because he wanted to adopt it, and that he wanted to adopt it because it would provide him with a valid excuse for the kind of life he is living. This young man is in bad faith, and he is aware of it and responsible for it.

All this goes to show that our conception of man and of life is based on some fundamental option which depends primarily on our will.

One is a theist or a pantheist, a materialist or a spiritualist, because the will has imposed its choice; and the will imposes its choice because the doctrine in question is in accord with the kind of love it has already chosen. The condition for arriving at the whole truth consists not so much in the natural excellence of the apprehensive faculties as in the rectitude of the will, *which decides to love according to that which is, and not to judge that which is according to a previously adopted love.*[18]

NOTE ON DETERMINISM

For a better understanding of determinism, it is useful to explain its derivation. It is apparent that many contemporary determinists have been strongly influenced by Kant's third Antinomy, and more particularly by its Antithesis.

Kant's Thesis was: "Causality according to the laws of nature is not the one causality from which all phenomena of the world can be deduced. In order to account for these phenomena, it is necessary also to admit another causality, that of freedom."

And his Antithesis was: "There is no freedom; everything in the world takes place entirely according to the laws of nature."[19]

Kant claimed that the Thesis could not be demonstrated by Theoretical Reason, but was postulated by Practical Reason. The Antithesis he considered absolutely certain for the domain of our experience. Many moderns, affected by Kant's agnosticism, continue to consider the Thesis indemonstrable, and they moreover deny that it is postulated by Practical Reason. With Kant they uphold the absolute certitude of the Antithesis.

This explains why a number of contemporary philosophers, especially in this country, consider "caused event" and "determined event" synonymous, why they equate "free" and "uncaused." For them the idea of a free cause seems like a contradiction in terms;

---

[18] P. Scheuer, S.J., "Deux Textes Inédits," in *Nouvelle Revue Théologique*, 79 (1957), pp. 822-823. This should not be construed as a profession of irrationalism. Human intelligence is naturally capable of discovering the truth. But in this investigation of the truth it may be helped by moral dispositions or hampered by moral obstacles. Cp. *S. Theol.*, IIa IIae, 45, 2. See also the Encyclical *Humani Generis*, #34; J. Maritain, *The Range of Reason*, pp. 22-29. Many excellent things about this important topic in J. Levie, S.J., *Sous les Yeux de l'Incroyant*, Part I.

[19] Kant, *Critique of Pure Reason*.

they can conceive of no causal connection other than that which exists between an antecedent and a consequent. As they understand it, the doctrine of free-will is therefore absurd, since it maintains that events occur which are uncaused.

Hence the following strange utterances, which it is instructive to ponder if we want to understand the determinists:

> To salvage moral responsibility one must resort to certain odd metaphysical notions that have long since been out of fashion and that are admittedly most difficult to comprehend clearly. What is needed, that is, is a view according to which (a) there is a reason for everything that happens, but (b) some such happenings—viz. some human acts—are contingent. . . . [This view] . . . involves the conception of a self or person . . . that is not merely a congeries or series of states or events. . . . it involves an extraordinary conception of causation, according to which something that is not an event can nevertheless bring about an event—a conception, that is, according to which a "cause" can be something other than a sufficient condition. . . . Now, both of these conceptions—that of an *agent* as distinct from the states or events of his history, and that of *performing* as distinct from being a sufficient condition—are certainly odd and hard to conceive of clearly. Indeed a philosopher could not be accused of stubbornness if he preferred to give up moral responsibility rather than embrace these two notions.[20]

Such conceptions seem to be diametrically opposed to our own; yet our position, properly understood, is not as far removed from that of the moderns as may at first appear.

We accept both Kant's Thesis and his Antithesis—though not, of course, from the same point of view. Kant's Thesis applies to the noumenal order, to the domain of things as they are in themselves, to the order of intelligible being. His Antithesis is admitted for the phenomenal order, for the domain of things as they appear in our everyday experience, for the domain of the natural sciences. This is the way Kant himself solved his famous Antinomy; but his agnosticism led him to affirm his Thesis only problematically, hypothetically, whereas we affirm it absolutely, as following from the very laws of being.

[20] Richard Taylor, "Determinism and the Theory of Agency," in *DF,* pp. 215-216.

In practice, this distinction means that our free decisions possess at the same time one cause and many antecedents. The cause, that which produces the decisions in the order of being, is our will—or, more precisely, our Ego operating through our will. The antecedents—the factors which are prior to the decisions in time—are the ideas, images, judgments, memories, doubts and fears, attitudes and tendencies, etc., which precede and accompany these decisions. A scientist as such can study only the antecedents. He must admit the hypothesis of universal determinism. To him it looks as if the decision D follows as necessarily on its antecedent C, as C followed on B and B on A.

Yet on a higher plane, animating the psychic phenomena somewhat as the soul animates the body, another causality is at work, the ontological causality of the person reaching a free decision. But like the soul itself, this kind of causality can be known only by the philosopher (or by any man acting as a philosopher). It escapes the most penetrating investigations of the scientist (or of the philosopher unable to transcend the scientific attitude), who discovers only a stream of consciousness in which phenomena follow each other with absolute necessity—where in reality a sovereign being is shaping his own essential attitudes.[21]

There is no doubt about it: the causality of a free agent freely reaching a decision is mysterious to us. Here is a cause which can equally well produce effect B or effect C without being predetermined to produce either. Where is the sufficient reason of either effect?

. . . The principle of sufficient reason is intangible, but not univocal; its application is different in the world of exterior objects from what it is in the world of spiritual interiority. A thing cannot produce a different effect if it is not itself modified in its being. And since every created spirit is to some small extent a thing, its free acts are always accompanied by real modifications. But in their pure essence as spiritual acts, they are exempt from the law of things. Their sufficient reason resides in the very spontaneity of the spirit.[22]

[21] See Maréchal, *PDM,* V, pp. 579-581.

[22] De Finance, *Existence et Liberté,* p. 207. The author adds in a note: "When we say that the subject is the sufficient reason of his acts, we do not claim, of course, that he determines himself without reason. The subject is the *sufficient reason of the effective sufficiency of his reasons.*"

We should recall here a remark made several times in this book. A higher cause may operate in and through a lower order of causality without producing any apparent disturbance in the latter, yet in some mysterious way informing it with purposes which wholly transcend those which are contained in the lower causes.

When determinists try to explain a free decision entirely as the necessary consequent of its psychic antecedents, it is as if a physiologist, asked to explain how Beethoven wrote the *Ninth Symphony*, should do it in terms of the cerebral motions, nerve impulses and muscular contractions involved in handling the quill and putting down the notes of the score on paper. In a certain sense our scientist would be right: physiologically, that is all there is to writing a symphony. Yet somehow, mysteriously, from within, and forever beyond the reach of the most astute physiologist, the master's genius or inspiration was at work in and through these muscular contractions, guiding the hand which wrote the immortal score. Likewise the human spirit is at work in and through the psychic phenomena which precede and accompany, and in a certain sense constitute, a free decision.

READINGS

S. Thomas Aquinas, *Summa Theologica*, I, Q. 82, a. 1,2,3; Q. 83, a. 1,2,3,4; Ia IIae, Q. 8, a. 2; Q. 9, a. 1,2,3,6; Q. 13, a. 1,3. De Finance, *Existence et Liberté*, pp. 5-96; Farrer, *The Freedom of the Will*. Gilson, *The Spirit of Mediaeval Philosophy*, pp. 304-323. Marc, *Psychologie Réflexive*, Vol. II, pp. 62-186. Maritain, *Scholasticism and Politics*, pp. 94-113. Mouroux, *The Meaning of Man*, pp. 143-195. Wild, *Introduction to Realistic Philosophy*, pp. 475-493.

19

Man's Soul and Body

EXISTENCE OF THE SOUL

In the four preceding chapters we have demonstrated that man possesses an immaterial intellect and a free will. The intellect is not man, nor is the will: both are powers through which man operates. Technically we call them faculties—that is, the immediate principles of mental operations. Since these faculties are not the person himself, they must exist *in* the person. But since they are immaterial, they cannot exist in the person's body, which is material.

Hence there must be in the human person, besides his body, some other component in which his spiritual faculties inhere. We call this component the soul.

Therefore our first provisional definition of the soul might be: that component of man in which the intellect and the will inhere; or, that component which manifests itself in man's thinking and willing.

You might here object: Why not simplify things and say that man is composed of a body plus an intellect and a will? What need is there for that extra component you call the soul?

Our reason for postulating the soul as the substratum for the intellect and the will is that these faculties, since they are not substances, must inhere in something; and since they are not material, they cannot inhere in the body.

You press your objection: But the soul itself is not man, hence it must be in man. It cannot inhere in his body, inasmuch as it is the substratum of spiritual activities. Hence it is either a substance

—and then, in the substance "man" we must admit another substance, "soul"—or it is an accident. But if it is an accident, it must
inhere in one more substratum. And so on, indefinitely.

It is true that the soul is not man, and that it does not inhere
in the body. How, then, can it be united to the body? The objection
forces us to mention briefly here certain points which can be
fully treated only later on.

Remember what we said about organisms in chapter 2. An
organism is composed of prime matter and a substantial form.
The substantial form is also called the vital principle, or soul. The
soul of an organism is its substantial form, makes it exist as a
material substance; it is also its vital principle and makes it exist
as a living body.

Man is an organism. Hence he possesses a soul which makes
him a material substance and a living body. It is the same soul
which we meet here as the substratum of man's intellectual and
volitional activities. Hence we must further define the soul as that
which makes man a material substance, a living body, a sentient
organism and a rational animal.

One of man's essential components is his soul. What is the
other? His body? Not quite—at least, not the body in the usual
meaning of the word. The other component is prime matter, a
principle of being that of itself is totally undetermined and unable
to exist; that exists only in union with the substantial form by
which it is determined and together with which it constitutes one
complete essence.

Hence the soul is not man, the soul is in man. Yet it does not
inhere in man's body. We cannot even say that it exists in man
besides his body. The soul is that essential component of man
which, united to prime matter, makes of man a rational, sentient,
living, material substance. We shall come back to this important
point in the second part of this chapter.

How do we know that the same soul performs all these functions? Could there not be several souls in man? say, three—a vegetative, a sentient and a rational soul? This theory was accepted by
a few of the ancients. But if we conceive of several souls in man

we deprive the concept of a soul of all its explicative value. This concept is profound and difficult to grasp.

The soul is a higher kind of substantial form. Now a substantial form is of itself an incomplete being; it is a principle of being, a formal cause which requires a complementary material cause to produce a being. The combination of these two causes does not result in a union of two distinct elements but in a real unity; it produces not a couple but an individual.

Hence a substantial form, or a soul, cannot be added to a complete being without ceasing to be a substantial form or a soul. That is where the theory of a plurality of souls in man breaks down. Suppose man were a living body by virtue of his vegetative soul. A living body is already a complete substance; many accidents or accidental forms may be added to it, but no other substantial form or soul can be superadded. Hence the sentient and rational souls of man posited by the theory of a plurality of souls could only be accidents, not real souls. Suppose even that we were willing to consider the sentient soul as an accident. Still we cannot see how the rational soul, the substratum of man's immaterial faculties of intellect and will, could be the mere accident of a material body.

Once we have admitted the existence of a rational soul in man, it may be asked why we should still hold to the concept of the faculties of intellect and will. Could we not say that the soul itself does the thinking and the willing, without the intermediation of faculties?

There are several reasons why we must admit the concept of faculties as really distinct from the soul. We shall mention only the most obvious and the easiest to grasp. The soul is to prime matter as act is to potency. The soul, since it is act, always actually produces the effects of which it is the immediate principle. For instance, the soul is the immediate principle of life; therefore that which possesses a soul is always actually alive. Thus if our soul were the immediate principle of our thinking and willing, we should always be actually thinking and willing. But we know from experience that this is not so. Hence our soul cannot be the immediate principle of our rational activities, and we must ad-

mit, as their immediate principles, faculties really distinct from
the soul.[1]

It is, of course, very important to realize that, although the
intellect and the will are faculties really distinct from the soul,
they are not independently acting entities but powers by means of
which the person acts. Although for the sake of conciseness we
often say that the intellect thinks and the will chooses, we should
always keep in mind that these expressions are misleading and
create false problems. In reality the person thinks and chooses
through his faculties.

Faculties are accidents, in the sense that they do not exist in
themselves, but in something else, namely in the soul. But they
are necessary accidents, emanating directly and necessarily from the
very essence of the soul. A human soul without intellect or will is
as inconceivable as a circle without roundness. Therefore we call
the faculties proper accidents, or properties.[2]

Having established that man possesses a soul, we must inquire
more closely into (1) the nature of the human soul; (2) its relation
to the body; (3) the relation of the human body to the rest of nature.

NATURE OF THE SOUL

THE HUMAN SOUL IS SPIRITUAL

Spiritual means intrinsically independent of matter. A being is
spiritual if it does not require matter as a co-cause of its operations
and of its existence.

But we have demonstrated that the intellect and the will, through
which the soul acts, are not intrinsically dependent on matter.

But as a being is, so it acts. Therefore the human soul is not
intrinsically dependent on matter, it is spiritual.

We have demonstrated also that the intellect and the will are
extrinsically dependent on matter—that is, that they need matter
as a condition of their operations. The same thing holds true for
the soul; it is extrinsically dependent on matter, at least during our
present life. That is why the human soul is not a pure spirit. The

---

[1] *S. Theol.*, I, 77, a. 1.
[2] *S. Theol.*, I, 77, Q. 1, ad 5.

pure spirits (God and the angels) are neither intrinsically nor extrinsically dependent on matter.

Objection: How can we say that the human soul is spiritual, in view of the fact that it is the radical principle not only of man's thinking and willing but also of all his sense activities, of his vegetative functions and his very corporeity? It has been shown earlier that the functions of growth, nutrition and reproduction, and all the sensory and instinctive activities, are to be explained by a co-operation of matter and the soul, acting as co-causes. Thus it is evident that the human soul is intrinsically dependent on matter for most of its operations, and hence that it is material.

Answer: It is true that man's soul is intrinsically dependent on matter for its vegetative and sentient activities. Yet it is not therefore a material soul, since for some of its operations it is not intrinsically dependent on matter. Such intrinsic independence of matter is utterly impossible in any material being. The level of a being's nature must be taken at the highest point of its operations. *Qui potest plus, potest minus.* A man who spends 10¢ for a cigar and $100,000 for a yacht is a wealthy man despite his dime cigar.

Man's soul is at once the substantial form of a material being and a spirit in matter. It is a spirit which, besides its own spiritual activities, performs also, in co-operation with matter, all the functions of a vegetative and of an animal soul.

What distinguishes it from all other substantial forms is its spiritual activities; that is why we call it *specifically rational.* But it possesses all the powers or virtualities of a corporeal form, of a vegetative and sentient soul; that is why we call it *virtually corporeal, vegetative and sentient.*

Man is the lowest of the spirits and the highest of the material beings. He, and he alone, belongs to both the realm of the spirit and the realm of matter. This meeting in him of spirit and matter explains his greatness but also the tragic nature of his destiny.

THE HUMAN SOUL IS SIMPLE

A being is simple when it has no really distinct parts. Parts may be either essential or integral parts. Therefore we distinguish essential and integral simplicity. The human soul possesses both kinds of simplicity.

Essential parts are the parts of the essence, substantial form and prime matter. When we say that the human soul is essentially simple, we mean that it is not composed of substantial form and prime matter. But that is obvious for two reasons: (1) the soul *is* a substantial form; and (2) beings composed of substantial form and prime matter are material beings. But we have demonstrated that the human soul is not material. Hence it is not composed of substantial form and prime matter, it possesses essential simplicity.

Integral parts are extended or quantitative parts, such as the legs, the trunk, the head of our body. Such parts exist only in material beings, since prime matter is the principle of quantity and extension. But we have demonstrated that the human soul is not material. Therefore it has no quantitative or integral parts, it possesses integral simplicity.

THE HUMAN SOUL IS IMMORTAL

Immortal means not subject to death or to destruction, destined to exist forever. We shall consider briefly two arguments, which have a certain value but are not cogent. Then we shall study more intensively an argument which strictly demonstrates our statement.

The first argument is taken from the common consent of mankind. Man by nature believes in immortality, as is evidenced by the spontaneous belief in immortality of all peoples, even the most primitive. But if there is order and purpose in the world, such a universal belief cannot be mistaken. (Cfr. what we have said about this kind of argument in the demonstration of the freedom of the will, p. 292.)

The second argument is taken from Ethics. It starts from the obvious fact that on this earth good people are often unhappy and harried by pain and adversity, whereas many wicked people are healthy, wealthy and prosperous. In other words, it is evident that in this life virtue does not always receive its reward nor vice its punishment. But if there is order and purpose in the universe, there should be a perfect sanction for the moral law. This is possible only if there is another life after death, where reward and punishment are meted out to those who deserve them.

This argument will not, of course, convince those who claim that the world and man are products of blind chance. Nor will it carry much weight with those who consider virtue to be its own reward. Finally, it demonstrates only survival after death, not immortality. It cannot prove that the reward and the punishment must last forever.

The third argument is strictly philosophical. It demonstrates not only that the soul survives death, but that it survives forever, that it is immortal. Its method is to consider all the ways in which a being can cease to exist and to exclude the possibility of any of these ways affecting the human soul.

A being ceases to exist either for intrinsic or for extrinsic reasons. The intrinsic reasons affect its essence, the extrinsic reasons its existence.

A being's essence can be destroyed directly by decomposition, indirectly by loss of essential support. A being's existence is destroyed by annihilation.

The human soul cannot be destroyed by decomposition or by loss of essential support, and it will not be destroyed by annihilation.

The human soul cannot be destroyed by *decomposition.* Decomposition means the resolving of a composite being into its constituent elements. Thus water is destroyed when it is decomposed into oxygen and hydrogen; a table is destroyed when it is burnt and reduced to ashes and gases.

Only composite, or material, beings can be decomposed. Since the soul is simple and immaterial, it cannot be destroyed by decomposition.

The human soul cannot be destroyed by *loss of essential support.* There is loss of essential support when a being which is intrinsically dependent on matter for its operations and for its existence loses the support of that matter. For example, the soul of an animal is intrinsically dependent on matter, on its body. Therefore, although the soul of an animal cannot be decomposed, it can be destroyed when the body of the animal is considerably modified by a wound or a disease. Likewise a flame ceases to exist not by decomposition but because the fuel which feeds it is exhausted or modified.

But we have demonstrated that our soul is not intrinsically dependent on matter for its specific operations. Therefore it cannot be destroyed by loss of essential support.

The third way in which a being can be destroyed is by *annihilation*. Annihilation is the reduction of a being from existence to non-existence. It is the opposite of creation and, like creation, it can be performed only by God. God could, strictly speaking, reduce our soul to the state of non-existence by withdrawing His creative influence which holds it in being. But God will never annihilate the human soul.

We have demonstrated that the soul cannot be destroyed by decomposition or by loss of essential support. By its very nature the soul has no potency to non-being.[3] God creates it as a being destined to exist forever. But God's will is immutable. Therefore He does not annihilate a being which he creates as a being destined to exist forever.

In other words, in the divine simplicity creation and conservation are absolutely the same act. As God creates a being, so He keeps it in existence. If He creates a nature which is destined to exist forever, He conserves it as such. To say that God might perhaps annihilate it would mean that we have surreptitiously introduced a time element into the creative action.

Therefore, although the possibility of annihilation cannot be excluded with reference to a finite being as finite, the immortal soul, inasmuch as it is created as such, is not subject to annihilation.

We can also present man's craving for perfect happiness as a proof that God will not annihilate the human soul.

That craving is natural, inevitable, deeply rooted in man's very nature, implanted therefore by the Maker of that nature. But if this craving comes from God, its realization must be possible. We say possible; it will not necessarily be realized, for God has made

---

[3] To human souls "the necessity of existing belongs according to their very nature, and the possibility of not existing is removed from their nature" (*De Pot.*, Q. 5, a. 3, c).

man free, the master of his own destiny. It would be contrary to God's wisdom and goodness to put into man a craving whose realization would be impossible.

But man cannot be perfectly happy unless he is immortal. Man has an intellect which conceives the idea of an existence without end. Therefore, if man, whatever his state of felicity, knew that this felicity was to end, he could not be perfectly happy. Hence man's soul is immortal and God will not annihilate it.

Answer to Objections. Against this demonstration quite a number of objections may be raised. They refer not to that section of the proof which shows that the human soul cannot be decomposed, or disappear indirectly through the disappearance of the being of which it is a part, but to the third section of our demonstration, in which we try to show that God will not annihilate the human soul, or to its conclusion, which is claimed to be untenable. Let us consider a few of these objections.

1. The demonstration assumes the truth of that which must be proved. It states: "God does not annihilate a being which He creates as a being destined to exist forever." But that is precisely the point at issue: that the soul is destined to exist forever is still to be demonstrated.

Answer: That point has been demonstrated. The first two steps of the proof demonstrate that the human soul is destined to exist forever. *Of its nature* it cannot stop existing, it will exist forever. The meaning is this: suppose that God maintains the soul's nature unchanged; then the soul will exist forever.

This statement may be further clarified by a consideration, for the sake of contrast, of the material creation. *Of its nature* this world and all the material things in it—this city, this house, my body—is destined to fall apart, to cease to exist. Even while God preserves the nature of these beings unchanged, they will disappear, because it is of their nature to change and slowly to disintegrate. That is the way God has made them.

It is of the nature of the human soul, on the contrary, never to disintegrate. It cannot break down into its parts because, being immaterial, it has no parts to break down into. Thus God has made it. The disappearance of the human soul can be the result only of a modification of the divine plan as we know it from a study of the nature of the soul. But God's immutability excludes such a modification.

2. If your demonstration holds for the human soul, it applies also to the material universe. For, although every individual material being will eventually disintegrate, its components, that into which it distintegrates, will continue to exist. Only an act of annihilation might put an end to them, and your demonstration excludes the possibility of such an act. Hence, under ever-changing forms, the matter of the universe will exist forever.

Answer: It is true that this conclusion follows from our argument. We see no difficulty against it. As a matter of fact, if the human soul is to exist forever, matter too must always be. For, as we shall point out, even after death the human soul retains a relation to matter.

3. If the human soul is destined to exist forever, it should also have existed from eternity. Otherwise there would have been a modification of the divine plan when, through creation, the soul passed from non-existence to existence.

Answer: The soul's transition from non-existence to existence does not imply a modification of the divine plan. From all eternity God decided that, when certain conditions should be fulfilled, this soul would be created.

4. Why, then, could God not have decided from all eternity that when certain conditions should be fulfilled this soul would stop existing?

Answer: God could have thus decided. But He shows us that He did not so decide by the very fact of His creating a soul which of its nature will exist forever. Our argument is based on the fact that in the nature of the human soul, as we know it from our philosophical study, we discover the divine intention with regard to man. We discover no such intention prior to man's existence from which we should have to infer a change in the divine plan.

5. You have not mentioned all the ways in which a being can cease to exist. There is a further one: absorption into a more comprehensive whole. Thus oxygen and hydrogen cease to exist when they combine in order to form water. In like manner the human soul might cease to exist by being absorbed into a more

comprehensive soul, v.g. a world soul, or by being absorbed into the infinite Spirit.

Answer: The example given in the objection provides a first answer. Oxygen and hydrogen are not really destroyed, since electrolysis can recover them.

We cannot, at least not from reason alone, demonstrate that an absorption into a more comprehensive whole which would not destroy the soul is impossible. But an absorption which would eliminate the soul as a self-conscious substance would destroy the nature of the soul, would amount to a real annihilation, and against this possibility our previous arguments hold.

6. You have not only demonstrated that God will not annihilate the human soul, you have demonstrated that He *can* not do so. If it is true that the annihilation of the human soul conflicts with divine immutability, God cannot annihilate the soul. But a being which cannot be annihilated is a necessary being. Hence, according to your demonstration, the human soul is not a contingent but a necessary being.

Answer: It is true that God cannot annihilate the human soul; however, it is not because the soul is necessary, but because God cannot change. It is not true that it follows from this that the human soul is not contingent. A being is contingent not because it begins or ceases to exist, but because it is not of its essence to exist. That it is not of the essence of the human soul to exist is evident from the fact that it has not always existed, and from the further fact that, at every moment, it receives its existence from God. The human soul will exist forever as a creature—that is, as a contingent being.

7. The argument derived from the desire for happiness supposes that every human being desires to exist forever. But that is not true. Some people wish not to exist, they desire their own annihilation.

Answer: It does not seem possible really to desire non-existence. For non-existence is nothing, and it is impossible to desire nothingness, just as it is impossible to have a real idea of it. These people may desire the end of their present unhappiness, of their present existence, with the vague feeling that they would *be* better off if they did not exist. Thus, under that desire for extinction lies a desire for existence.

8. There are many natural cravings of man which are never realized. Most people desire affection, success, good health, a long life, etc., and quite a number never obtain what they crave.

Answer: These things which so many people desire are possible, their unfulfilled wishes might have been realized. We do not assert that a natural desire can never be frustrated, but only that it cannot have the impossible as its object. A natural desire for the impossible is an evident contradiction. Hence perfect happiness must be possible to man. But it is impossible unless the human soul is immortal. Hence the human soul is immortal.

9. How can the soul continue to exist after its separation from the body, since it requires the co-operation of the body for all its activities? It has been shown earlier that all the vegetative and sentient activities of the soul require matter as a co-cause, and that the intellectual and volitional activities need matter as a necessary condition. Hence the soul after death would continue to exist but would be unable to act. A being unable to engage in any kind of activity seems like a contradiction in terms, an impossibility.

Answer: Before trying to reply to this objection, we might as well admit that for the answers to this question we are to a considerable extent groping in the dark. We know that the human soul survives after death because we cannot see any way in which it could cease to exist. But how it exists and how it operates in that state of separation from the body is not easy to comprehend.

It is obvious at once that vegetative and sense activities of any kind are impossible in the state of separation, since matter is a co-cause of such activities.

It is not so certain that intellectual and volitional activities are impossible, since for them matter is only a necessary condition. Such a condition might be supplied by some other agent, by God or by a pure spirit.

Furthermore, although all our ordinary ideas and judgments require images for their production, there is one kind of knowledge which does not directly require such an image: the knowledge which the soul has of itself. In this case the knower and the known are identical, knowledge is intuitive and requires no intermediary.

However, as long as the soul is united to the body, such knowledge is possible only with regard to the soul's action, not with regard to the soul's essence. For example, as concerns the soul's action: I have a direct, intuitive knowledge of myself thinking and of myself freely deciding. Hence this kind of knowledge too seems impossible after death, since it presupposes an act of ordinary knowledge, and that is impossible without an image deriving from the body.

However, the fact that the human soul does not possess during this life an immediate intuition of its own essence seems to be due to the union of that soul to the body. Therefore, when that union is interrupted the soul should enjoy intuitive self-knowledge. Now such knowledge of itself by the soul surpasses any kind of knowledge which man possesses on earth. Intuitively knowing its own essence, the soul would also know in and through that essence the divine causality which keeps it in existence, and the countless relations which unite it to all other human souls and to the world of pure spirits. The soul's intuitive self-knowledge implies, therefore, a very perfect kind of natural knowledge of God and of all other spirits. And that knowledge is accompanied by a corresponding activity of the will. Hence we have good reasons for admitting that, after its separation from the body, the human soul continues to perform real activities of cognition and volition.

Furthermore many authors claim that the separated soul can reactivate the intelligible "impressions" (*species impressae*) which it has acquired during its mortal life, and thus know again the objects corresponding to them. This doctrine, however, introduces a serious difficulty, as we have seen that the "impressions" can be known only in the images,[4] that they should not be considered as reproductions of objects, but as relations uniting the intellect to the images supplied by the senses.[5] How these two positions may be reconciled would be too difficult to explain here.[6]

10. Should the human soul survive its separation from the body, it would become a pure spirit. But of pure spirits there can be only one in each species. Hence, either the human soul does not survive,

---

[4] *S. Theol.*, I, 84, 7, c. and ad 1.
[5] P. 268.
[6] The interested student is referred to K. Rahner, S. J., *Geist in Welt,* 2d ed., pp. 316 ff.

or else all separated souls, having survived death, become united into one being, which is as much as to say that the human soul does not survive.

Answer: The human soul does not become a pure spirit after death. It remains a spirit destined to inform prime matter. It retains a transcendental relation to matter. A transcendental relation is one which is not superadded to a fully constituted being, but which is constitutive of the essence of that being.

How this transcendental relation to matter, which the soul keeps even after death, looks and works in reality, we do not know. Only speculations are possible in this field. Since this is a fascinating topic, we might be excused if we briefly mention one of these speculations, especially as it is presented by one of Europe's foremost thinkers.

Karl Rahner wonders whether our thinking about the soul, the body and death has not been too much influenced by Neoplatonism. We have a tendency to think of death as meaning a total separation of the soul from matter, since we regard matter, neoplatonically, as an obstacle to the soul's union with God. On the other hand, we are forced to maintain a relation between the soul and matter.

But might not death be considered as an opening up to matter rather than as a separation from it? Could we not say that at the moment of death the soul becomes not acosmic but pancosmic? During this life the soul is united to prime matter. But prime matter is one, pervading the whole material universe, and thus through its union with prime matter the soul is connected with the totality of the universe. As long as we live, this pancosmic connection is obscured by our more intimate connection with one segment of the cosmos, our own body. But when the body is gone, the pancosmic connection is the only one which remains for the soul. This does not mean, of course, that the whole material universe becomes the body of the separated soul, or that the soul becomes omnipresent to the whole universe. But it might mean that

the soul which has thus, in death, by giving up its limited bodily shape, opened up to the whole, does in some way influence the totality of the world, not only of the material world, but of the world considered as the foundation of the personal life of the rest of men, as beings composed of body and spirit.[7]

These speculations raise a host of questions which cannot be answered. One thing is certain, however: the state of separation is not natural for the human soul, and although reason cannot give proof of the resurrection of the body, by its very nature it is wide open to such a possibility.

THE HUMAN SOUL IS DIRECTLY CREATED BY GOD

Creation is the production of something out of nothing. We demonstrate that the soul is created by God by excluding all other possibilities.

The soul is either produced from some pre-existing substance or is not produced from any pre-existing substance, and therefore created. But the soul is not produced from some pre-existing substance.

That pre-existing substance would have to be either a material or an immaterial substance. It cannot be a material substance, since the soul is immaterial, and it is obviously impossible to make something immaterial out of a material substance.

Nor can it be an immaterial substance, such as the soul of the parents. An immaterial substance cannot be divided, because it is simple. It is impossible to take a part of it and make that part into a new soul.

Therefore the soul is not made out of some pre-existing substance. It is made out of nothing, it is created. But God alone can create. Therefore the human soul is directly created by God.

Although the parents do not produce the soul of their child, they produce more than just the body. They can really be said

[7] K. Rahner, S. J., "Zur Theologie des Todes," *Zeitschrift für Katholische Theologie*, 79 (1957), p. 10. As the title of the article shows, Fr. Rahner studies this problem mainly as a theologian and tries to confirm his above-mentioned ideas with arguments taken from Revelation. Engish translation of the article in A. R. Caponigri (ed.), *Modern Catholic Thinkers* (New York, Harper, 1958), pp. 138-176. See also R. Troisfontaines, S. J., "*Je ne meurs pas. . . .*", p. 116.

to beget the human being, since they produce a body which demands the infusion of a spiritual soul. Therefore the parents are not only the cause of the body, but also indirectly of the union of body and soul—that is, of the whole human being.

When is the soul created?

We cannot answer that question with certitude. From the very nature of the soul it follows that it cannot be created before the body. For it is essential to the soul to have a transcendental relation to matter. We can understand that this relation may subsist after the soul's separation from the body, but we do not see how it could exist before the soul's union with the body. Therefore the soul is created when it is infused into the body.

When is the soul infused into the body? St. Thomas, after Aristotle, defined the soul as the first (or substantial) act of a physical, *organized* body which has the *potency* of life. Therefore he held that the human embryo must possess a certain degree of organization before it can become the seat of a rational soul. It should have at least the beginning of a human shape, and the essential organs must be present. St. Thomas admitted, however, that the embryo is alive from the very moment of conception. But this first life is vegetative life, and the first soul is a plant soul. When a certain degree of organization is reached, the vegetative soul is replaced by a sensitive or animal soul. These two souls are not created but generated, called forth from the potency of matter. Finally, when the organization has progressed sufficiently, God creates and infuses a rational soul. St. Thomas's theory is known as the mediate animation theory.

Most present-day Scholastics reject this theory and hold that the rational soul is infused at the moment of conception. This "immediate animation theory" sprang up in the seventeenth century. The authors who first introduced it did not deny St. Thomas's contention that the embryo must have a certain degree of organization before it can become the seat of a rational soul; but on the basis of defective scientific observations they held that this organization was present from the very beginning of embryonic life. This "preformation" theory, according to which the later organism is already present on a microscopic scale in the earliest embryonic stages, was held for a long time by many scientists. Nowadays it is universally rejected.

Although the scientific reasons which prompted many Scholastics of the seventeenth and eighteenth centuries to reject the mediate animation theory of St. Thomas have lost their value, the great majority of present-day Scholastics continue to hold the immediate animation theory. They see no difficulty in admitting that a rational soul may inform an unorganized embryo, even when it consists of only a few cells.

A few recent Scholastic authors would like to return to the conceptions of St. Thomas. Prominent among them are Cardinal Mercier, one of the founders of Neo-Scholasticism, and Canon de Dorlodot.[8] At the present stage of our knowledge, it seems impossible to decide which theory is true.

RELATION BETWEEN BODY AND SOUL

The question of the relation between body and soul has given rise to quite a number of conflicting theories. The main opinions are briefly reviewed:

1. Body and soul are complete substances which act upon each other (Interactionism);

2. Body and soul are complete substances which do not act upon each other (Psychophysical Parallelism);

3. Body and soul are but two aspects of one fundamental reality (Panpsychism);

4. Only the body is a substance; what is called "soul" is only a collection of psychic phenomena (Actualism, Phenomenism);

5. The soul may be a substance, but we cannot demonstrate it by theoretical reason (Agnosticism);

6. The soul and only the soul is a substance; the body is a body only because of the soul (Hylomorphism).

Of these various theories we prefer the last one. We shall show the reasons for this preference first negatively, by pointing out

[8] See his spirited defense of mediate animation in E. C. Messenger, *Theology and Evolution*, pp. 259 ff.

the serious objections which may be made against the five other
opinions; next positively, by developing the theory of hylomorphism.

Interactionism. Body and soul are complete substances which
act upon each other. This position has been held by such great
philosophers as Plato and Descartes. It is also the implicit position
of common sense.

Common sense observes that the soul can act on the body: I
want to move my arm, and at once the arm moves. I am afraid,
and my heart beats faster. I am ashamed, and my face turns red.
Protracted worry and tension may produce gastric ulcers. On the
other hand, the body acts on the soul. When I am tired, my mind
becomes dull; when I am intoxicated, my thinking becomes hazy.
A concussion is followed by unconsciousness; lack of iodine in the
thyroid gland may produce cretinism. These are facts, and no
theory of the relation between body and soul can be accepted
which does not account for them.

We dissent from this theory not because it admits an interaction
between body and soul, but because it claims that this interaction
is between two *complete* substances, between two *efficient* causes.

If man is composed of two complete substances, he is not one
person. He is not a unity but a union; not an individual but a
couple. He should never speak as I, but only as we. Or else, when
he thinks, he should say: My soul thinks; and when he falls, he
should say: My body falls.

Furthermore it is very difficult to see how the body can act
on the soul as an efficient cause acts on its object. The body is a
material substance, extended in space. The soul is an immaterial
substance, not extended in space. Now, a material substance can
only produce material effects, which can be received only by
another material substance which is extended in space. It follows
that the body cannot influence the soul in the way demanded by
interactionism.

Psychophysical Parallelism. Body and soul are complete substances which do not act upon each other. This theory too holds
that man is composed of two complete substances, but it takes into
account the impossibility of any efficient causality being exercised
by one of them upon the other.

How, then, does it explain the instances we have mentioned as the observations of common sense? By stating that between the series of events in the soul (psychic events) and the series of events in the body (physical events) there is a perfect parallelism; so that whenever something occurs in the soul, there is a corresponding occurrence in the body, and vice versa. As for explaining this perfect parallelism in the absence of any interaction, see what we have said on p. 247 about the occasionalism of Malebranche and the pre-established harmony of Leibniz.

A first objection against this system is, again, that it denies a real unity to the human person.

Furthermore, its way of accounting for the perfect parallelism between the psychic and the physical series is so artificial that it leads almost naturally to the next position. It is not without reason that both Malebranche and Leibniz were so much opposed to Spinoza: they were vaguely aware that the logic of their own system pushed them towards his doctrine.

Panpsychism. Body and soul are but two aspects of one fundamental reality. The basic stuff of reality possesses two sides which always occur together: a psychic side and a physical side. What is true of all reality is also true of man; in him the psychic side is the soul and the physical side is the body. Now the perfect correspondence existing between mental and bodily events is easy to understand: they are fundamentally the same thing, looked at from different angles.

This theory leads to impossible conclusions. If all reality possesses a physical and a psychic side, the Supreme Reality will not constitute an exception to this rule. Hence God has a body and He is extended in space. Spinoza, the greatest proponent of panpsychism, was led by the logic of his system to call space a divine attribute. A system which leads to such a conclusion is false.

Actualism, Phenomenism. Only the body is a substance; what is called "soul" is but a collection of psychic phenomena. The philosophers who hold this view try to do away altogether with the notion of substance. As a matter of fact, we might say that it is precisely because they reject the idea of substance that they are forced into such a system. They claim that although the body really exists, the soul is only a figment of the mind. Yet they are not necessarily materialists; not all of them claim that the body thinks, judges or decides.

What, then, in me does perform these mental activities? Their answer is: Nothing, they just happen. They succeed each other in us like the links of a chain, like the days of the week, without any permanent underlying reality.

Hume's statements on this subject are famous. Man, he says, is "nothing but a collection of different perceptions, which succeed each other with an inconceivable rapidity, and are in perpetual flux and movement. . . . The mind is a kind of theatre where several perceptions successively make their appearance. . . . The comparison of the theatre must not mislead us. They are the successive perceptions only, that constitute the mind."[9] William James held similar views.

It is very difficult to understand how such a theory can be defended without contradiction. How, in terms of his own theory, could Hume at the end of his treatise remember what he had written in the first chapters? How could he ever make promises and keep them? How could he explain that when he saw a tree or enjoyed music (mental contents), he was at the same time aware of seeing that tree and enjoying that music (something underlying these contents)? How could he ever refer to himself as I? It seems evident that an intelligent man can be led into such a position only because he has decided that there can be no substances.

Nor does it help to assert, with William James, that the thing which remembers, collates, judges, is the present Thought, the present link in the series of mental events, which has in some way appropriated all the previous mental events.

For that Thought either exists in itself, or it exists in something else. If it exists in itself, it is a substance. If it exists in something else, the same alternatives occur for that "something else," until we finally arrive at a substance.

In fact, James himself admitted as much when he attributed all thinking to some underlying "world soul"; his difficulty seems to have derived from a mistake often made by the pioneers of

[9] D. Hume, *A Treatise of Human Nature,* part iv, section vi.

Empirical Psychology: they tried to explain scientifically what can be explained only philosophically, and thus they introduced philosophical explanations which they attempted to pass off as scientific explanations. The experimental psychologist as such does not know of any substantial soul and does not need it in his system. He is allowed to explain the present thought by means of its antecedents. But he is abandoning the scientific attitude and entering the sphere of philosophy when he claims that this present thought has no substantial cause.

Agnosticism. The soul may be a substance, but we cannot demonstrate this by theoretical reason.

This is Kant's objection. He admitted that the human mind, following its natural bent, inevitably reaches the conclusion that the human soul exists as a substance. Yet the conclusion is false, and the reasoning which leads to it is a "paralogism of Pure Reason."

How does man naturally reach that conclusion? In every categorical proposition, a predicate P is attributed to a subject S: S is P, a mammal is a vertebrate. But the subject of that proposition may, in its turn, become the predicate of a less general proposition: Man is a mammal. This can go on until we arrive at a subject which can only be a subject, never a predicate. An American is a man, I am an American. I, the subject of the last proposition, can never be predicated of anything else. And this subject, which is the ultimate substratum of all the properties predicated of it, and which does not itself inhere in any deeper-lying substratum— this absolute subject—is evidently a substance.

Hence Kant expresses the first paralogism of Pure Reason in the following syllogism:

"That which cannot be thought otherwise than as subject does not exist otherwise than as subject, and is therefore substance.

"A thinking being,[10] considered merely as such, cannot be thought otherwise than as subject.

"Therefore it exists also only as subject, that is, as substance."[11]

[10] In the first edition of the *Critique of Pure Reason* Kant explicitly equated this thinking being with the soul.

[11] I. Kant, *Critique of Pure Reason*, trans. by N. Kemp Smith (1933), p. 371.

Why does Kant reject this syllogism? Because he claims that it is affected by the fallacy of four terms. He says that the "subject" mentioned in the major premise is an ontological subject, while the "subject" mentioned in the minor premise is only a transcendental subject.[12] In other words, Kant admits that the major premise applies to the subject as it exists in reality: the subject which it affirms is thought as a real object, as real and as objective as the predicates attributed to it. The minor premise, on the other hand, refers only to the domain of knowledge, to things as we know them subjectively, as they appear to us. We do not know and we cannot know whether the minor is true objectively, in the domain of reality. The minor means only this: objects become conscious, become objects of thought, only because they are referred to my consciousness, because I can say of them, "I think." But that consciousness, that center of unity which says "I think," cannot itself become an object of thought. How could it, since knowledge is possible only when that center is the *subject* of thought?

Therefore, according to Kant, the subject mentioned in the minor premise is only a thinking subject as such, not an objective substratum of properties, like the subject mentioned in the major. It is but a function of knowledge, a group of formal a priori conditions of knowledge, a transcendental subject.[13]

Kant acknowledges our impulsion to say that this transcendental subject is also a real subject, endowed with substantial unity. But we have no way of justifying this belief. Therefore we must say: it may be that there is an ontological subject; it may be that there is no such subject (agnosticism).

Why does Kant claim that we cannot rationally justify our spontaneous belief that, underlying the transcendental subject, there is a real ontological subject, a substantial soul? Because we lack any kind of intuition about that subject or soul.

---

[12] What Kant means by "transcendental subject" may be simply explained as follows. We say that when a subject knows an object, that subject is a substance performing a function of knowledge. Suppose now that in this last sentence you drop the words "a substance performing" and you keep only the words "a function of knowledge." Then you have Kant's transcendental subject.

[13] Maréchal, *PDM,* III, pp. 229-230.

Kant, it should be remembered, claims that the categories of substance, of causality, etc., can be rightfully used only if they are accompanied by an intuition. But, in his view, man has no intuition of his substantial soul or I. He has a certain knowledge of his empirical I, his body as the center of his physical activities. He knows his transcendental I, the Ego as the necessary a priori condition of all knowledge. But he has no knowledge of his ontological I, and he cannot have such knowledge.

For only that can be known which can become the object of thought. But the thinking I is subject and can never become object, not even the object of thought, without ceasing to be a thinking I. Hence it can never be known.

Kant's mistake consisted in demanding a perfect intuition of the I. For him there was no middle ground between a perfect intuition, in which the knower coincides perfectly with the known, and no intuition at all. It is true that we have no perfect intuition of our soul or of our ontological I; our dependence, intrinsic or at least extrinsic, on matter, makes such an intuition impossible in this life. But we have an imperfect intuition of our soul in action —of our intellect in the act of thinking, of our will in the act of freely choosing. I know that man, and I am aware of knowing him. I freely make this decision, and I am conscious of making it. I am not a mere function of unification; while I am unifying the data of experience, I am aware that I am unifying them, I have an intuition of myself in the act of unifying them, I am a real unifier.

These are real intuitions, instances of knowledge without any intermediary. True, they are imperfect intuitions, because through them I do not directly reach the essence of my soul, but only its operations. Even so, these intuitions are sufficient to allow us to use the category of substance, to affirm that the I which emerges in every act of knowledge and of choice is not a mere unifying function or transcendental subject, but a real ontological subject, a substance.

Hylomorphism. The soul, and only the soul, is a substance; the body is a body only because of the soul.

In this position, the one we adopt, man is composed of two

complementary principles, a formal cause and a material cause. In this respect he resembles all other material beings, which are likewise composed of substantial form and prime matter. There are, however, some important differences between man and all material beings below him. In the latter, form and matter are both incomplete principles; neither is able to exist by itself; neither is able to perform any activity except in complementary union with the other. In man, on the contrary, only matter is an incomplete principle, totally dependent on its partner. Man's soul is more than an ordinary substantial form. It is that, but it is more than that; it is also a spirit. It is a spirit which performs all the activities of a substantial form, and in these activities it is intrinsically dependent on matter. But as a spirit it possesses, above and beyond these material powers, other virtualities of intellect and will, which do not require matter as a co-cause, but only as a necessary condition.

Furthermore, in the other material beings existence is received not by the substantial form, but by the essence, composed of substantial form and prime matter. In man existence is received directly by the soul, which passes it on to the matter which it informs.

But what happens to the body in this system? It is not identical with prime matter, but it is the first result of the union of the soul with prime matter. Man is a body, a living body, a sentient body and a rational body through the union of the one same soul with prime matter.

The reason we prefer this system is that it resolves such a variety of philosophical problems:

1. It explains man's unity without denying his duality. Man is matter and mind; yet he is not a union of these two elements but a real unity. Soul and matter are not united like the pilot and his plane, like the rider and his horse. When the pilot steps out of his plane, both he and the plane keep their individuality; when the soul leaves the body what remains is no longer a human body, but a "corpse"—that is, technically speaking, a collection of chemicals. Soul and matter are more intimately one than a statue and its shape, a sentence and its meaning, a symphony and the inspiration of the composer. Without the shape there is not a shapeless statue, there is no statue at all, but only a block of marble;

without the meaning, there is no meaningless sentence, but just a collection of words; without the inspiration, there would be a jumble of sounds, but no symphony. Without denying man's duality, hylomorphism clarifies and forcefully stresses his unity.

2. Hylomorphism can explain the interaction between what we call body and soul without endangering the concept of man's unity and without admitting the possibility that a material object can act upon an immaterial reality. Between the soul and matter there is indeed interaction; not, however, as between an efficient cause and the object on which it operates, but as between a determining and a determined component; as between a formal cause and its complementary material cause. It is the kind of interaction which exists between the marble and the shape, between the words and the meaning, between the sounds and the inspiration.

Every activity or event in man is always an activity or an event of the soul, and in every activity or event of man matter has a share. When I decide to move my arm, it moves. We tend to attribute the decision to the soul and the movement to the body. The fact is that the body has a share in the decision, and the soul in the movement. Extreme muscular fatigue makes the mind dull. We should not interpret this as if the fatigue were only in the body and the dullness only in the mind. The soul itself feels fatigued in the tired muscles, and matter has its share in the dulling of the mind.

3. Hylomorphism gives us the only consistent explanation of the origin of our ideas, as was shown in chapter 15, pages 262ff. We are now better prepared to understand that explanation.

It is very difficult to rid our minds entirely of the dualism of Plato and Descartes. Even while we reject it, we continue to think of the body as contributing to our mental life independently of the soul. The senses are conceived as powers of that body, acting independently of the intellect, doing their work first, and then passing on their information to the intellect. A nice example of interactionism! Just as the human soul is not to be conceived as existing somewhere outside and above the body, the intellect should not be conceived as standing outside and above the senses. As the soul dwells in the body, animating it throughout, so the intellect dwells in the senses, permeating them. Every activity of the senses is also an activity of the intellect, in the same way in which every movement of the body is also a movement of the soul. Hence there is no real passage from sense knowledge to intellectual knowledge but a steady "information" of sense knowledge by intellectual knowledge, corresponding to the steady animation of the body by the soul. As a being is, so it acts. We are composed of body and soul; our ideas likewise are, analogously, composed of a body and a soul: the body is the contribution of the senses, the soul is the contribution of the intellect. And just as our soul is the substantial form of a material being and is also a spirit, so that, far from being materialized by its function of informing matter, it always emerges above matter, as intellect and as will; so our intellect always transcends every sense image which it "informs," and remains forever open to the knowledge of supra-material realities.

If this explanation of the origin of our ideas is rejected, there seems no way of avoiding either materialism (the senses influence the intellect, which entails the supposition that the latter is material) or the theory of inborn ideas. This is a strong argument in favor of hylomorphism.

Objections: 1. According to hylomorphism, prime matter has only a passive and receptive causality in the constitution of man. All activity and determination comes from the soul. But this supposes that not only man's intellect and his senses, but also his drives, his instincts, his temperament, the sex to which he belongs, his weight and his height—in fact, all the positive features of his personality—derive from the soul. This contradicts what we know about prime matter as the individuating component of material beings.

Answer: It is quite true that not only the substantial reality, but also all the accidents in man, derive from the soul. Yet these qualitative differences are not present in the soul as such; otherwise two human souls would differ specifically from each other. The differences are actively produced by the soul and received in matter, but the soul produces them in matter according to the dispositions of matter, and owing indirectly to the influences of the environment, heredity, and so on. The differences in the dispositions of matter explain why specifically similar souls can produce such widely different accidents.[14]

---

[14] *Ver.,* 26, 2, ad 2. Cfr. Rahner, *Geist in Welt,* pp. 325 ff.

2. If the soul is a complete substance, prime matter can only be an accident. This not only is in contradiction with hylomorphism, it also seems to make of man a pure spirit, who puts on a garb of corporeity, as angels are reported to do occasionally.

Answer: The soul is a complete substance, but not a complete nature. A substance is complete as a substance and as a nature when it is not destined to enter into composition with another substantial principle, when it is capable of carrying out all its connatural operations. Thus a dog and a man are substances which are complete as substances and as natures. A substance is complete as a substance, but not as a nature, when it really exists in itself and not in something else, yet is destined to enter into composition with some other substantial principle in order to constitute a complete nature or species, in order to be able to carry out all its connatural operations. Hence prime matter is not a mere accident, it is really a substantial constituent of man, required to make of him not a spiritual substance but a human being, a man.

RELATION OF THE HUMAN BODY TO THE REST OF NATURE

SUMMARY OF THE SCIENTIFIC DATA

In a previous chapter we saw that there are good reasons for admitting evolution within the animal world: very slowly, through natural descent, new groups of animals originated from the previously existing species.

The most remarkable of these groups, the latest to appear on the scene, is that of the *Primates,* to which belong the monkeys and the apes. The primates are characterized by a great development of the brain, stereoscopic vision, lack of specialization in their limbs, and the prolongation of infancy in their young. The highest primates have developed opposable thumbs—that is, the hand is so constituted that the tip of the thumb can touch the tips of all the other fingers. This innovation has made of the hand a remarkable tool, useful for the performance of a variety of tasks, once it was no longer needed for walking or standing— as soon, in fact, as the animal adopted an upright posture.

Such upright posture is typical of man; the other primates use it only intermittently and imperfectly or not at all. However, about thirty-five years ago the paleontologists unearthed in South Africa the fossil remains of some kind of prehistoric ape which obviously had adopted an upright posture. These animals, known as the *Australopithecinae,* displayed other remarkable features which bring them anatomically nearer to the human body than any of the primates which have survived until our times. Thus their dental structure looks more like that of a human being than that of any present-day ape; and although they were smaller than the latter, they had brains whose average size (600 cubic centimeters or cc.) is comparable to that of the bigger modern apes. Most paleontologists agree that in spite of these advanced features, the Australopithecinae were apes, not human beings. They seem to have lived between half a million and a million years ago.

It is not claimed that these creatures belong to the direct ancestry of man. But their discovery has demonstrated that if man's bodily descent is traceable to some animal form, this form was not that of our modern apes, which have become too specialized in the simian direction, but that of some more generalized simian ancestor, possibly rather like the Australopithecinae.

More than sixty years ago the Dutch anthropologist Dubois discovered in Java a few fossil remnants of what he called "apeman," *Pithecanthropus.* Heated controversies followed upon Dubois' discoveries and conclusions. Now that the dust has almost settled and further discoveries have confirmed some of Dubois' first claims, the following conclusions seem to meet with general agreement among the experts: Pithecanthropus was a real man, although with his protruding eyebrow ridges, his lack of a real forehead, his brain size of about 900 cc.—halfway between that of the modern apes (500) and that of modern man (1350)—he appears to stand, anatomically, much nearer to the apes than does modern man.

These conclusions were confirmed by similar discoveries made more than thirty years later in China, near Peking, where a considerable number of fossil remnants belonging to what has been called *Sinanthropus,* or Pithecanthropus Pekinensis, were unearthed. As the latter name indicates, this man has strong points of resemblance with the Java fossils. The brain size, however, is slightly larger, averaging somewhat above 1000 cc. Pithecanthropus and Sinanthropus may have lived about half a million years ago.

We come nearer to present-day humanity with our next group of fossils, *Neanderthal man.* The first remnants of this type were discovered one hundred years ago near Düsseldorf in Germany. Since then many similar discoveries have been made in Europe, Africa and Asia. Although the size of the Neanderthal brain is on the average comparable to that of the average modern brain, its owner must have had a brutish appearance, with his retreating forehead, thick brow-ridges, protruding cheek-bones, and heavy limbs.

Paleontologists are increasingly doubtful of Neanderthal's right to a place in the direct ancestry of modern man. He seems to have stood in a collateral line, and he shows manifest signs of retrogression in this sense: that the older Neanderthal fossils, the ones which are more remote from us in time, look more modern than those which are nearer to us in time. Neanderthal man may have lived between two hundred thousand and one hundred thousand years ago; the group seems to have become extinct about 25,000 years ago.

The next fossil type in our present brief summary is *the man of Cro-Magnon,* found in Southern France, who lived about 20,000 B.C. He is in most respects indistinguishable from Homo Sapiens of today.

This extremely condensed, oversimplified account of human paleontology is presented here only to introduce our philosophical discussion of the origin of the human body. Many more types of fossils could have been mentioned. Those which have been considered seem to be the most important. What has been said about them is, in some instances, still controversial. Paleontology is a science characterized by great activity; it is continually discovering new facts, re-examining its data, devising and testing new hypotheses, revising its opinions—and occasionally even discovering a hoax! Only a specialist can keep abreast of its development. However, it does seem certain that its broad lines are firmly established, and the few preceding pages may give us an idea of what these broad lines are.

They suffice to show us that a certain number of anatomically intermediate stages have been discovered between animals and modern man.

Granted that these fossil forms have been correctly described and interpreted by paleontology, it does not follow that modern man is descended from them. It is quite possible that all of these forms, and it is most probable that some of them, represent offshoots of man's genealogical tree and are only collaterally related to him. But even so, they indicate that there has been a gradual transformation of the human organism, and that there is a wide collection of intermediary stages between the body of the apes and the human body.

It is not contradictory to claim that these forms have no connection whatsoever with man, that the human body was created by God as well as the human soul. But such an explanation is a philosophical or theological explanation, it is not a scientific explanation. A scientist as such does not know the meaning of creation and should never include God in his scientific system. Science looks only for secondary causes or antecedents; God is the first cause, not an antecedent.

For the scientist there remains only one explanation for the origin of the human body: it accounts for all the facts he knows; it is regularly confirmed by the new facts he discovers; there are no decisive facts against it, although plenty of gaps remain, and many difficulties and doubts. That explanation is evolution—the gradual transition, through genetic descent, of these different forms from one to the other, slowly leading up to the human body as we know it today.

This is, of course, only a theory. From the very nature of the case it will never be possible to demonstrate it strictly as a fact, since most of the evidence has been lost forever. But we must add that *scientifically speaking* it is the only tenable theory today.

Philosophically and theologically speaking, another explanation of the origin of the human body might be given: the human body was directly created by God. If we had solid philosophical or theological reasons for adopting it, we would give up the scientific hypothesis. If, however, such philosophical or theological reasons do not exist, there is no reason for not adopting the hypothesis of evolution to explain the origin of the human body.

In behalf of the Catholic reader,[15] the Appendix will try to show how the evolutionary origin of the human body can be reconciled with the data of Theology.

PHILOSOPHICAL EVALUATION

1. We have shown in a previous chapter that evolution in general has been explained mechanically, as resulting solely from the forces of matter and of chance, and that it could be explained finalistically, as resulting from these same forces acting under the guidance of an idea, a design, and therefore ultimately of a mind, which can only be the Creative Mind.

We have also shown why, although scientists as such can only accept the first kind of explanation, such an explanation remains essentially incomplete unless it is supplemented by the other one.

Similar considerations apply to evolution as it concerns the origin of the human body. The scientist as such is perfectly entitled, he is even obliged, to try to explain that evolution in a purely mechanical way, endeavoring to show how the forces of living matter could lead up to the different pre-human and human forms which paleontologists have unearthed (mechanism as a method).

Yet such an explanation remains essentially incomplete and must be supplemented, on the philosophical plane, by a resort to some guiding design, and therefore to some directing mind as the ultimate explanation of the whole process. Mechanism as a doctrine is false.[16]

Hence the evolution which we accept as a possible explanation of the origin of the human body may be attributed on the scientific or phenomenal level to the interaction of natural energies, of living matter and its environment. A deeper interpretation however, such as is expected of the philosopher, forces us to acknowledge the Creator as the first and fundamental cause of the process of evolution. God creates through evolution.

2. We have demonstrated earlier in this chapter that the human soul is directly created by God. It follows that evolution is abso-

---

[15] And also, to a certain extent, in behalf of all readers who consider the Bible the inspired word of God.

[16] See pp. 37, 57.

lutely excluded as an explanation of the origin of the human soul. A spiritual substance cannot derive from material causes. Evolution may explain the origin of plant and animal souls, because these souls are material, educed from the potency of matter. It may, to a certain extent, explain the origin of the human body. But it cannot be used in any sense to explain the origin of the human soul. Therefore man cannot be a product of evolution, since man is man only because he possesses a spiritual soul.

3. Strictly speaking, neither can the human body be a product of evolution. This follows from our doctrine of hylomorphism, which holds that the human body is a human body only because it is informed by the human soul. Thus, since the human soul cannot be a product of evolution, neither can the body of man. God creates the soul and makes the body of man. This does not imply a rejection of the theory of evolution. It means only that what the evolutionary process can produce is not a human body but an organism which may become a human body as soon as a human soul is infused into it.

4. Until a hundred years ago it was traditionally held that the matter into which God for the first time infused a human soul was inorganic matter (the dust of the earth). We have now very good scientific reasons for admitting that this matter was, in reality, organic matter—that is, the body of some apelike animal.

Aquinas held that some time during the course of pregnancy God infuses a human soul into the embryo which, until then, has been a simple animal organism, albeit endowed with human finality. The theory of evolution extends to phylogeny what Aquinas held for ontogeny.

Hence there is no philosophical difficulty against the hypothesis which asserts that the first human soul was infused by God into the body of an animal possessing an organization which was very similar to that of man. That animal was endowed with human finality in this sense: that, in our hypothesis, God Himself through the laws of nature, had prepared this organism and made it capable of receiving a human soul.

5. Some Scholastic philosophers claim that no animal body could receive a human soul until it had first been prepared for such an infusion by a special intervention of God.

Others hold that this transformation was effected by the infusion of the rational soul, which made the receiving body not only accidentally but essentially different from an animal body. In other words, the final preparation for the new form was effected by the very infusion of that form. We prefer this second opinion.

6. If the hypothesis of evolution is accepted for the human body, it follows that God infused the human soul into a body which had animal parents, or into an embryo carried by an animal mother. Although in either case some biological and psychological influences of the animal progenitors of that organism on the future man cannot be denied, it is evident that the first man had *no animal parents in any sense of this word,* since he received neither his human soul nor his human body from animals. The hypothetical prehistoric apes used by God for the formation of the organism into which He infused the first human soul are no more the father or the mother of the first man than the dust of the earth mentioned in the Bible is the progenitor of Adam.

End ecurse

READINGS

On the Human Soul:

St. Thomas Aquinas, *Summa Theologica,* I, Q. 75, a. 1, 2, 4, 6; Q. 76, a. 1-4; Q. 77, a. 1, 2, 3, 5. Gilson, *The Spirit of Mediaeval Philosophy,* pp. 168-188, *The Philosophy of St. Thomas Aquinas,* pp. 204-220, and *Elements of Christian Philosophy,* pp. 203-219. Marc, *Psychologie Réflexive,* Vol. II, pp. 290-376. Maritain, *The Range of Reason,* pp. 51-65. Messenger, *Theology and Evolution,* pp. 243-332. J. P. Ruane, S.J., "Self-Knowledge and the Spirituality of the Soul in St. Thomas," in *The New Scholasticism,* 32 (1958), pp. 425-442. Sertillanges, *Foundations of Thomistic Philosophy,* pp. 199-232. Siwek, *The Enigma of the Hereafter.* Troisfontaines, *"Je ne meurs pas. . . ."*

On Anthropological Evolution:

Broderick, *Early Man.* Coon, *The Story of Man.* J. F. Ewing, S.J., "Human Evolution, 1956," in *Anthropological Quarterly,* 29 (1956), pp. 123-139. Hooton, *Up from the Ape.* Howells, *Mankind in the Making.* Le Gros Clark, *History of the Primates.* Senet, *Man in Search of His Ancestors.* Teilhard de Chardin, *The Phenomenon of Man.*

PART FIVE

MAN AS A PERSON

In Section I of this Part human personality will be considered empirically and studied with scientific methods. Section II contains a philosophical study of human personality.

SECTION I

Empirical Study of Man's Personality

20

Personality and Its Components

DEFINITION AND COMPONENTS OF PERSONALITY

Personality has been defined in countless ways. For empirical purposes we shall use the definition presented by G. W. Allport, "Personality is the dynamic organization, within the individual, of those psycho-physical systems which determine his unique adjustment to his environment."[1]

It is an *organization* of *systems,* not just a sum-total of traits. The many traits which we can distinguish in a personality are organized in systems, and these systems themselves present a definite organization. That organization is *dynamic,* it changes, it acts upon the environment and is influenced by it. The systems are *psychophysical,* they have a bodily and a mental aspect. This dynamic organization of systems *determines the adjustment* of the individual to his environment. To survive and prosper everyone must adapt himself to his environment. The way in which he adjusts himself is determined or explained[2] by his personality. Every individual adjusts himself in his own typical way, which differs from the adjustment of all other individuals. The subject's personality explains the unique features of this adjustment.

The psycho-physical systems whose dynamic organization constitutes personality are: physique, intelligence, temperament and character. Physique refers to the body, all its organs and functions, its state of health or sickness, its beauty or deformity. All these features have a great influence upon the way in which an individual adjusts himself to his environment. Intelligence is taken here in the

[1] *Personality,* p. 48.
[2] Those who object to the word "determine" in Allport's definition may replace it by "explain." Allport *is* not a determinist.

wide sense of modern psychology, as the power of adapting oneself to new circumstances. It includes all the cognitive functions, not only intelligence proper, but also memory, imagination, the external senses. Temperament refers to the individual's "susceptibility to emotional stimulation, his customary strength and speed of response, the quality of his prevailing mood and the fluctuations and intensity of his moods."[3] It includes the kinetic and affective aspects of human personality.

Character can be taken in an ethical or in a psychological sense. Ethically considered, character may be defined as the power of self-control, or the capacity of regulating one's life according to principles. In that sense we speak of character education, we say that some person has a strong or a weak character. The power of self-control or of inhibition belongs properly to the will; character in the ethical sense is synonymous with will-power, as explained in a previous chapter.

In this section we shall consider character only in its psychological meaning.[4] Psychologically considered, character may be defined as the organized totality of the tendencies of an individual. Man possesses many tendencies, which are differently developed and integrated in different individuals. In some people, for instance, the aggressive tendency is so powerful that all other drives are organized around it; these people have an aggressive character. In others two tendencies may compete for leadership; still other individuals show no predominant drive. The total pattern of all tendencies differs from person to person, and explains the character differences between these persons.

Man's most important tendency is the will. Is the will one of the components of character? It may be considered as such, or it may be excluded. Therefore it is useful to make one more important distinction with reference to character, the distinction between man's spontaneous character and his controlled character.

Spontaneous character does not include the will; it is the organized totality of man's lower drives. It refers to the way in which

[3] Allport, *op. cit.*, p. 54.
[4] Allport does not distinguish these two meanings of character. He understands character exclusively in the ethical sense. This explains why he does not mention character as one of the constituent systems of personality.

the drives would react and the person would behave if he did not check the drives and control himself. When a person is intoxicated, very tired, stirred by a powerful emotion, he may behave very differently from his usual ways,[5] thus showing that his spontaneous character is quite different from his controlled character.

Controlled character is the organized totality of all man's tendencies, including the will; it explains the way in which the person behaves when he has normal self-control.

In weak-willed people who lack self-control the difference between these two aspects of character is negligible. On the other hand, in people who have learned to control themselves there may be a considerable difference between what they would do if they "let themselves go" and what they will actually do. Perfect self-mastery makes it almost impossible to discern a person's spontaneous character. In most individuals there are occasions when self-control falters, and the natural pattern of the spontaneous tendencies has a chance to show itself as it is.

THE THREE FACTORS WHICH MOLD PERSONALITY

Most textbooks of psychology state that our personality is determined by two factors, heredity and environment—nature and nurture, what we receive at birth and what education and social influences do to us. But even when applied only to empirical personality that statement is false, because it is incomplete.[6] Heredity and environment have a very great share in molding personality, but there is at least one more factor which is equally, if not more, important.[7] The way a person uses his inborn capabilities and

[5] William Sheldon writes that "in temperament study an ounce of alcohol is sometimes worth hours of the shrewdest inquiry."—*The Varieties of Temperament* (New York, Harper, 1942), p. 66. The same thing applies to spontaneous character. The reason, says the wit, is that "the will is soluble in alcohol." "You are right," says the philosopher, "if you mean that the will is extrinsically dependent on matter."

[6] Here again, however, the scientist as such is allowed to ignore the will, since it is a cause which, as scientist, he cannot know. That is why experimental psychology is essentially incomplete.

[7] From Revelation we know that one more factor must be included: divine grace, which acts continually upon man's intellect, will and other functions.

adapts himself to his environment depends to a great extent on his own free volition. He may consciously and voluntarily inhibit certain drives; he may, to a certain extent, hold in check his emotions, or at least their expression; he may even, albeit within narrow limits, act upon his physique, for instance by exercise or dieting. Finally, he is capable of influencing his environment, either by modifying it or at least by moving out of it.

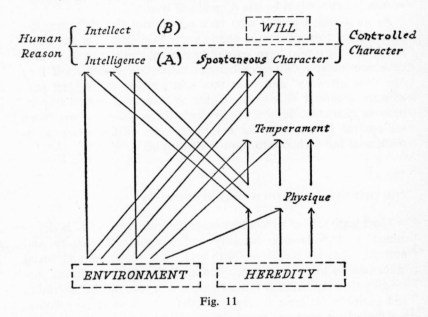

Fig. 11

The relation existing between the four constituent systems of human personality and the three molding factors of human personality is graphically represented in Figure 11.

This diagram requires a certain amount of explanation. The lower part (below the horizontal line) represents the sensory functions; the upper part represents the spiritual functions. The intimate connection existing between these two levels is manifested essentially in human reason and in controlled character. Human reason combines the intelligence which we share with animals with the Intellect which we share with angels. Controlled character is produced by the interaction of our free will with our spontaneous character, the organized totality of our lower drives.

As a matter of fact these two components should not be shown as simply standing one above the other, as in the diagram. The Intellect should be represented, if possible, as permeating intelligence, and the will as animating spontaneous character. The relation between the two components is not that which exists between the first and the second floor of a building; it is similar to that which exists between a statue and its shape, a sentence and its meaning, prime matter and the soul. This explains why, in spite of the essential distinction between the two levels, any trouble affecting the lower functions has its repercussions on the higher functions. The lower level has a certain autonomy in relation to the higher one: a morally wrong decision does not necessarily affect one's health. Nevertheless even in that direction there is a considerable amount of interaction.

Experimental psychologists as such are interested only in the lower part of the diagram. That is a scientifically correct attitude. Some of them deny the existence of the spiritual functions. That is no longer a scientific attitude, but the expression of a philosophical bias. For these crypto-philosophers man is only a superior kind of animal. The four constituent elements mentioned in the lower part of the diagram are present in animals, at least in the higher animals. Two dogs may differ from each other not only in physique and in intelligence but also in temperament (one is excitable, the other not) and in character (one is aggressive, the other is shy). In the case of animals such differences are due *entirely* to the influences of heredity and environment, and the animals themselves cannot modify their physical or mental constitution.

In the diagram the constituent systems of personality are printed in small type, the factors which mold personality are printed in capitals and boxed. The influence of each system upon the others and of each factor upon the systems within the sensory level is indicated (very roughly) by the direction and the number of the connecting arrows. One arrow means a slight influence, two arrows a considerable influence, three arrows a very strong influence. Thus we see that physique depends primarily on heredity, although the environment too has some influence on it. A child born of healthy stock will not become physically strong unless he is provided with adequate food. Intelligence depends mainly upon physique and heredity, but here again the environment is important: a talented child will not reach a high intellectual development without adequate schooling.

The influence of the environment is greater upon temperament and spontaneous character than upon physique. By environment is meant here especially the influence of the parents, as they mold the very receptive mind of the child during the first few years of life. Freud and his followers have rightly emphasized the importance of that influence.

A and B in the diagram show an open place for two functions which we shall mention only later: the Super-ego and Conscience. Conscience (B) is the Intellect inasmuch as it guides the will and judges its actions. It is a spiritual function. The Super-ego, according to Freud, is an outgrowth of the Ego, which helps the person adapt himself to his social environment. We shall consider it more thoroughly later. It is a sensory function, and it exists in some animals—v.g., a housebroken dog. The two functions generally are present in everybody; they co-operate and their relation is analogous to that which exists between the Intellect and intelligence or between the will and spontaneous character.

Other names could be used for some of the systems mentioned in the diagram. Thus it might help on occasion to replace the terms "temperament" and "spontaneous character" respectively by "the affective foundations of personality" and "the instinctive foundations of personality."

In the following pages we shall study the various psycho-physical systems which constitute man's empirical personality, with the exclusion of intelligence, which has been considered in a previous chapter.

SHELDON'S CLASSIFICATION OF PHYSIQUES

Human physique has been studied by a certain number of investigators, such as Kretschmer in Germany, Pende in Italy, MacAuliffe and Sigaud in France. But nobody seems to have been more successful in this investigation than the American William H. Sheldon, whose system we shall briefly set forth in the following paragraphs.

Sheldon based his study of human physiques on 4,000 photographs of young men of college age. These photographs were all taken from the same distance and the same angles: front, back and profile.

In this large collection of pictures Sheldon looked first for the extreme variants, for those types of body which depart most widely from the average male form. He found only three of them. Their departure from the average is very striking, "they seem to be made of different stuff." For Sheldon these extreme variants represent, in almost pure form, the three COMPONENTS which enter, in different proportions, into the making of every human body. These components are ENDOMORPHY, MESOMORPHY and ECTOMORPHY.

Endomorphy means relative predominance of soft roundness throughout the various regions of the body. When endomorphy is predominant, the digestive viscera are massive and tend relatively to dominate the bodily economy. The digestive viscera are derived principally from the *endodermal* embryonic layer.[8]

In more detail this component is described as follows:

. . . Central concentration of mass. Predominance of abdominal and thoracic volume over the extremities. Predominance of abdomen over thorax. Predominance of proximal segments of limbs over the distal segments[9] . . . High square shoulders with soft contours. Short neck. Head large and . . . almost spherical. Face wide. . . . No muscle relief throughout. . . . Short, tapering limbs . . . comparatively small hands and feet. . . . The skin is soft, smooth, and velvety, resembling the skin of an apple. . . . Massive chest hair is rare in endomorphy. A premature tendency toward baldness is often seen, even in youth. This is a round, even baldness, beginning at the top of the broadly domed

[8] W. H. Sheldon, *The Varieties of Human Physique* (New York, Harper, 1940), p. 5.
[9] The proximal and distal segments of the limbs are respectively those which are nearer or farther away from the trunk.

head and spreading peripherally in an almost perfect circle, leaving a highly polished surface.[10]

Mesomorphy means relative predominance of muscle, bone and connective tissue. The mesomorphic physique is normally heavy, hard, and rectangular in outline. Bone and muscle are prominent and the skin is made thick by a heavy underlying connective tissue. The entire bodily economy is dominated, relatively, by tissues derived from the *mesodermal* embryonic layer.[11]

In more detail:

. . . Rugged, prominent, massive muscling. Large, prominent bones. . . . The most conspicuous characteristic of arms and legs is the relative prominence and massiveness of the distal segments. . . . The wrist is heavy and massive, as are the hand and fingers. . . . Thoracic volume predominates over abdominal volume. . . . The shoulders are broad, . . . the pelvis is sturdy and powerful, with broad hips. . . . The head shows heavy supraorbital ridges, prominent and massive cheek bones, heavy, square jaw. . . . The head strongly suggests the cubical shape. The neck is usually fairly long. . . . The skin is thick and coarse with large conspicuous pores. . . . Because of its thickness and large pores, we have sometimes likened this skin to the skin of an orange. . . . The hair is generally coarse and may be either luxuriant or sparse. . . . Baldness is variable: when it appears, it usually appears first on the front of the head.[12]

Ectomorphy means relative predominance of linearity and fragility. In proportion to his mass, the ectomorph has the greatest surface area and hence relatively the greatest sensory exposure to the outside world. Relative to his mass he also has the largest brain and central nervous system. In a sense, therefore, his bodily economy is relatively dominated by tissues derived from the *ectodermal* embryonic layer.[13]

In more detail:

Slight, "thready" muscles . . . The general suggestion of decentralization of structure is strong. . . . The thorax is relatively long as compared with the abdomen . . . The shoulders are narrow. . . . Both

[10] *Ibid.*, pp. 37-38.
[11] *Ibid.*, p. 5.
[12] *Ibid.*, pp. 39-41.
[13] *Ibid.*, pp. 5-6.

the arms and the legs tend to be relatively long in the distal segments. Extremely weak thighs and upper arms are constant features of ectomorphy. . . . The neck is long and extremely slender. . . . The head as a whole is slight. The most constant feature of the head is the relatively small facial mass as compared with the cranial mass. The features of the face are uniformly small, sharp, and fragile. . . . The face presents a sharply triangular appearance. . . . Marked occipital projection is common and the result is often an exceptionally long head. . . . The skin is thin and dry. . . . We sometimes speak of ectomorphic skin as resembling the outer skin of an onion. The skin color is typically poor, that is to say, pale and ashy. . . . The hair is usually fine, often extremely fine, and it grows rapidly. . . . Baldness is rare.[14]

When the three fundamental components had been well established through a study of the extreme variants, Sheldon went over the 4,000 photographs again and arranged them in the order of increasing endomorphy. Physiques with the lowest endomorphy came first, next physiques with slight, with average, with great, with extreme endomorphy. Seven steps were used, 1 meaning the lowest observed amount of endomorphy, 4 average endomorphy, 7 extreme endomorphy. Each photograph received a mark designating its degree of endomorphy. The same procedure was used for mesomorphy and ectomorphy.

Each subject is now designated by three figures, one for his position on the scale of endomorphy, one for mesomorphy and one for ectomorphy. Thus an extreme endomorph received the three marks 7 1 1,[15] an extreme mesomorph 1 7 1 and an extreme ectomorph 1 1 7. Other individuals would receive marks such as 5 3 2, 1 6 2, 4 4 4, etc. The patterning of the three components as expressed by these figures is called the *somatotype* of the individual. Theoretically 343 somatotypes are possible, in fact only 76 were discovered. The sum of the components is never lower than 9 (for instance 171) or higher than 12 (for instance 444).

The somatotype seems to remain constant throughout life. Nutritional conditions and general health may produce changes in the body, but generally they do not affect its fundamental structure. A

[14] *Ibid.*, pp. 42-45.
[15] Read: seven-one-one.

631 who puts on 40 pounds does not become a 731 but changes from a lean 631 to a fat 631.

Sheldon also studied some second-order variables of human physique. "*Dysplasia* is the aspect of disharmony between the different regions of the same physique."[16] He distinguished five regions in the body. An individual who has a somatotype of 442 for the head region, 452 for the thoracic trunk, 542 for the arms, 443 for the abdominal trunk and 342 for the legs, shows a considerable amount of dysplasia.

"*Gynandromorphy* refers to the bisexuality of a physique. Members of each sex exhibit more or less the secondary characteristics of the opposite sex,"[17] such as widening of the hips, development of the breast, distribution of the hair. A measurement of these secondary sex characteristics gives an index of gynandromorphy.

Texture refers to the fineness or coarseness of the body structure. It is a more qualitative feature, and cannot be directly measured. *Hirsutism* refers to the hairiness of the body.

Sheldon's initial work is based on photographs and measurements of the male physique. Some preliminary work on the female physique, later confirmed by independent investigators, made him conclude that the same 76 somatotypes occur among women. Their distribution is slightly different. Endomorphy and combinations of endomorphy with ectomorphy are more common among women, whereas among men we find more mesomorphy and combinations of mesomorphy with endomorphy.

SHELDON'S CLASSIFICATION OF TEMPERAMENTS

Temperament, as shown in our diagram, is molded by two sets of influences, by physique and environment. That means that an individual will be more or less emotional, quick or slow in his motor reactions, usually cheerful or depressed, etc., because he inherited this particular kind of body from his parents and underwent a definite set of influences in his environment, especially during the first years of life.

[16] *The Varieties of Human Physique*, p. 7.
[17] *Ibid.*, p. 7.

The relation between physique and temperament has been studied in Sheldon's second volume. An extensive study of the temperament of 33 male graduate students, whose physiques were known, and another study of 100 male college students or graduates enabled him to establish the existence of three main components of temperament. These components occur in their purity only in a few extreme cases; generally they are blended in definite proportions. Here again numerals from 1 to 7 are used to indicate the intensity and the pattern of the three components in an individual temperament.

The three temperament components are: VISCEROTONIA, SOMATO-TONIA and CEREBROTONIA.

Viscerotonia, the first component, in its extreme manifestation is characterized by general relaxation, love of comfort, sociability, conviviality, gluttony for food, for people, and for affection. . . . The personality seems to center around the viscera. The digestive tract is king, and its welfare appears to define the primary purpose of life.

Somatotonia, the second component, is roughly a predominance of muscular activity and of vigorous bodily assertiveness. The motivational organization seems dominated by the soma. These people have vigor and push. The executive department of their internal economy is strongly vested in their somatic muscular system. Action and power define life's primary purpose.

Cerebrotonia, the third component, is roughly a predominance of the element of restraint, inhibition, and of the desire for concealment. Cerebrotonic people shrink away from sociability as from too strong a light. They "repress" somatic and visceral expression, are hyper-attentional, and sedulously avoid attracting attention to themselves. Their behavior seems dominated by the inhibitory and attentional functions of the cerebrum, and their motivational hierarchy appears to define an antithesis to both of the other extremes.[18]

Sheldon discovered 20 traits characterizing each of the three components. We give here the 10 most important traits of each component.

VISCEROTONIA: Relaxation in posture and movement, love of physical comfort, slow reaction, love of polite ceremony, sociophilia, evenness of emotional flow, tolerance, complacency, the untem-

---

[18] *The Varieties of Temperament*, pp. 10-11.

pered characteristic, smooth and easy communication of feeling, extraversion of viscerotonia.

SOMATOTONIA: Assertiveness of posture and movement, love of physical adventure, the energetic characteristic, need and enjoyment of exercise, love of risk and chance, bold directness of manner, physical courage for combat, competitive aggressiveness, the unrestrained voice, overmaturity of appearance.

CEREBROTONIA: Restraint in posture and movement, over-fast reactions, love of privacy, mental over-intensity and apprehensiveness, secretiveness of feeling and emotional restraint, self-conscious motility of the eyes and face, inhibited social address, vocal restraint and general restraint of noise, youthful intentness of manner and appearance.[19]

Within each of these three clusters the traits are positively correlated, that is, they have a tendency to increase and decrease together. Traits belonging to different clusters are negatively correlated.

Each of the clusters is positively correlated with one of the three physical components. According to Sheldon the correlation between endomorphy and viscerotonia is .79, between mesomorphy and somatotonia .82 and between ectomorphy and cerebrotonia .83.

More independent research is required before these correlations can be accepted as firmly established.[20] Temperamental components cannot be exactly measured like bodily dimensions. Therefore a subjective factor may enter into their appraisal. Sheldon may unconsciously have overestimated facts which favored his system. His researches have established the influence of physique, and directly of heredity, upon human temperament, even if that influence is not as strong as the above-mentioned correlations would suggest.

Temperament depends not only on the individual's physique but also on his life history, especially on his affective experiences during the very first years of his life. This important fact has been especially emphasized by Freud and his followers. Therefore, before proceeding with our study of empirical personality, we must know some-

[19] *Ibid.,* p. 26.
[20] See for instance in J. P. Guilford, *Personality* (p. 122), the correlations discovered by other investigators; they are positive but considerably lower.

thing about Psychoanalysis and the main systems derived from it. There are other reasons for studying these systems. The psychoanalytic conception of man is increasingly adopted by many people who reject the Christian conception of man. Furthermore although these systems contain serious errors, they also offer some important new findings about human nature which we cannot afford to ignore.

READINGS

Allers, *The Psychology of Character*, pp. 4-61. Allport, *Personality, A Psychological Interpretation*, pp. 3-54, 213-231. Harmon, *Understanding Personality*, pp. 3-36, 113-140. Roback, *The Psychology of Character*, pp. 155-162; 447-566. Sheldon, *The Varieties of Human Physique* and *The Varieties of Temperament*. VanderVeldt and Odenwald, *Psychiatry and Catholicism*, pp. 1-14.

21

Psychoanalysis and Systems Derived From It

THE FIRST part of this chapter will be devoted to a study of some aspects of Freud's psychoanalysis, which is and will remain the foundation of all modern systems of depth-psychology.[1] In the second part we shall briefly consider the systems of Alfred Adler and C. G. Jung.

PSYCHOANALYSIS AND THE DOCTRINE OF FREUD

Freud writes, "The theory of repression is the pillar upon which the edifice of psychoanalysis rests. It is really the most essential part of it."[2] By repression he means the unconscious and automatic inhibition of a psychic content.

The most important cases of inhibition are those in which one drive is stopped by another drive. A hungry dog seeing a piece of meat on the table does not grab it. His fear inhibits his hunger. At a party we fall in with a bore, and we should like to tell him that his jokes are stale; but politeness or charity prevents us from giving in to that impulse. In this case there is voluntary and conscious inhibition, or "suppression." There are other cases, says Freud, where the inhibition happens unconsciously and automatically, and then we have a "repression."

[1] These systems are called depth-psychology because they probe the depths of the Unconscious.
[2] S. Freud, "History of the Psychoanalytic Movement," in *The Basic Writings of Freud* (New York, Modern Library, 1938), p. 939.

What happens to the inhibited tendency? It does not just disappear, it continues to strive towards its goal, but now in an unconscious and roundabout way. It will eventually reappear in consciousness. If the repression does not succeed, the tendency may reappear as a slip of the tongue, as a case of misunderstanding, mislaying, forgetting, etc. Or it may come back in the shape of a dream image. Sometimes it comes back as a neurotic or a psychotic symptom. When repression is successful, the inhibited tendency is "sublimated" and may lead to valuable achievement.

PSYCHOPATHOLOGY OF EVERYDAY LIFE

This is the title of one of Freud's works, devoted to the study of lapses, slips of the tongue, small mistakes, cases of forgetting, etc., which have been lumped together under the name of "parapraxias." Freud was the first author to claim that these mistakes, which seem to result from pure chance, have a meaning, that they are both the effect and the sign of hidden tendencies. He applies the principle of "psychic determinism," according to which psychic phenomena, as well as the physical phenomena of nature, have causes, are determined by these causes, follow necessarily from them and can lead us back to them. Why does this man write that his fiancée is an "angle" instead of an "angel"? Why does he dream of a black cat? Why does this patient claim that she is the daughter of the Emperor of Japan? Before Freud, only general answers could be given to these questions. The slip of the pen was attributed to fatigue, the dream image to the fact that the man was sleeping, the delusion to the circumstance that this patient was schizophrenic. Freud claimed that these general factors may explain why there was a mistake, a dream image or a delusion. But they do not explain why we have *this* particular mistake, *this* dream image, *this* delusion, instead of some other. Freud claims that all these psychic phenomena are determined by definite causes, and that the discovery of these causes may throw much light on important factors in mental life.

The principle of psychic determinism applies to all psychic phenomena with the exception of our free decisions. (Freud, being a determinist, does not mention this exception.) Free decisions are not determined, they are spontaneous manifestations of our deepest personality. But all other phenomena—our moods, emotions, attitudes, associations, judgments, ideas, images, etc.—inasmuch as they are not under the direct influence of the will, are determined by certain causes. These causes cannot always be discovered, they are not necessarily deeply significant, but there must be causes, and from them these phenomena follow with absolute necessity. With the important exception mentioned above the principle of psychic determinism is perfectly acceptable.

In some cases of parapraxia one drive clashes with another drive and can be only partially discharged. You ask your friend, "Where is your brother? I have not seen him for quite a while." He replies, "Don't you know? He entered the cemetery . . . the seminary last fall." This is a typical slip of the tongue, which must have some cause. That cause may be superficial and without deeper meaning —the similarity of two words and the flagging of the speaker's attention through fatigue. But the cause may lie deeper and consist in the clash of two drives. Your friend has always been opposed to his brother's priestly vocation. "Why bury himself in that place?" Before strangers he suppresses his opposition. When he hears your question he wants to answer it. Here we have two drives: the desire to answer your question and the desire to criticize his brother's decision. The latter drive is suppressed, but it uses the similarity of two words (cemetery, seminary) to slip past your friend's attention and reveal his deepest feelings.

In other cases of parapraxia a drive may be completely inhibited by another drive; that is repression. Both the repressed and the repressing drive may be unconscious. Nothing seems to happen in the mind, although a lot is happening unconsciously. This is especially true in cases of forgetting. Freud claims that there are two kinds of forgetting. The usual instances of forgetting may be explained by the fact that the memory traces have been weakened by the lapse of time. Other instances of forgetting involve the clash of two drives: a forgotten element tries to emerge into consciousness; an unconscious force keeps it below the level of consciousness. The American psychoanalyst Frink[3] explains how, having forgotten the name of a drugstore, he tried to find out whether this

[3] M. F. Frink, *Morbid Fears and Compulsions* (New York, Moffat, Yard, 1918), pp. 51-53.

forgetting involved any deep-lying factors. The name of the drugstore owner was Pond. Now when Frink was a youngster he had,
through some imprudence, caused the death of his own dog *at a
pond* where they were playing together. This tragic event had upset
him awfully; he had been inconsolable for many days. The accidental killing of his pet produced a "psychic trauma," that is, a
deeply disturbing emotional shock. After some time, owing to a
natural tendency to forget painful and humiliating experiences,
everything connected with this trauma had been banished from
his memory, had been repressed. It is quite possible that this is
the reason he could not remember the word "pond" even in an
entirely different setting.

This example may not be convincing for anyone not familiar
with psychoanalytic interpretations. Yet it is a good illustration of
how two tendencies unconsciously clashing in our mind may explain what seems to be a simple case of forgetting.

We have insisted upon these examples because they are typical
of psychoanalysis and illustrate one of its main features: psychoanalysis emphasizes man's drives and the clashes occurring between
them. That is the reason why this kind of psychology is often
called "dynamic" psychology.

THE DREAM THEORY

Freud claims that the interpretation of dreams is the royal road
to a knowledge of the unconscious elements in our psychic life.
Dreams had been studied long before Freud, but no complete
theory had ever been presented. Freud used the data of his predecessors, enlarged them considerably, and was able to integrate
them in one coherent system because he had discovered a method
for interpreting dreams. This method is "free association."

Free association can be simply defined as "daydreaming aloud."
When we daydream we allow our minds to wander, without any
logical connections. The subject is supposed to do precisely that,
and to tell the psychoanalyst everything which comes to his mind.
A psychoanalyst who listens to these associations is sometimes able

to discover in them the meaning of the dream image from which the associations have started.

From the use of this method Freud derived two important conclusions.

1. The dream has a meaning. This is true only if a distinction is made between the manifest and the latent content of the dream. The manifest content is that which we remember of the dream, the latent content consists of the hidden causes which produce the dream images. The latent content, says Freud, has a meaning. The manifest content is not an expression but a symptom of that meaning.

2. The dream is a wish-fulfillment. This is very clear in many children's dreams, and sometimes in the dreams of adults. But how can this be said of the many meaningless dreams which we remember? Freud explains this by means of his hypothesis of the "censor." Many wishes which crave fulfillment during the dream are of a low, anti-social—we should say immoral—nature. But even during sleep the higher moral tendencies continue to oppose the fulfillment of these wishes. Freud calls the "censor" the sum of the drives which prevail in the consciousness of an individual and prevent the lower drives from becoming conscious in the dream. The forbidden wishes try to circumvent the censor by taking on a disguise; they appear in consciousness in a distorted, unrecognizable form. This explains why most dreams are so difficult to interpret. For Freud most dreams are the disguised fulfillment of a repressed wish.

The wish is the efficient cause of the dream; its material cause consists of sensations experienced during sleep and past memories. Many authors have noticed that dreams weave some of these sensations, which we may experience vaguely during sleep, into their own framework. Thus we may dream that we are drinking a long draught of ice-cold water, and a little later wake up with a strong sensation of thirst.[4] Some of the peculiarities of dream memory also had been observed before Freud. The dream often reproduces events of the previous day; it selects preferably unimportant events;

---

[4] This simple example illustrates several peculiarities of the dream; how it uses vaguely conscious thirst sensations; how it fulfills a wish; how it protects the sleep by satisfying a wish which tends to wake us up.

it often revives memories and impressions going back to the first years of life.

Freud has thoroughly studied what he calls the dream mechanisms, that is, the ways in which the dream arranges and elaborates the materials on which it is constructed. These mechanisms are one more reason why dreams are often so difficult to interpret. The most important mechanisms are:

Condensation. The manifest content of the dream is often an abbreviation of the latent content. In other words, the images of the manifest content are often overdetermined, they have more than one cause in the latent content. This is sometimes very clear in "collective persons" as they may appear in our dreams. We may dream of a person we do not recognize, who combines the features of several individuals and stands for all these individuals.

Displacement. The affective charge of the dream is often detached from its proper object and attached to an accessory object. For instance a woman who hates her sister-in-law dreams that she strangles a small white dog. Analysis shows that the hatred is directed against the sister-in-law, although in the dream it is directed against the dog. The hatred has been displaced from its real object onto an object which is accidentally associated with it.

Dramatization. The content of the dream is not expressed by means of ideas or judgments, but by means of images, generally visual images. The dream is acted out, not expressed in words. The dream regresses from the abstract to the concrete, from ideas to images.

Symbolization. One concrete object in the dream may stand for another concrete object of which it is the symbol.

Much of what Freud says about the dream is true. Unfortunately, as is usual with Freud, he generalizes too easily; when he claims, for instance, that *all* dreams have a meaning, that *all* dreams are wish-fulfillments (except the few cases which might be attributed to repetition compulsion). Furthermore he attaches too much importance to the sexual element in dreams, although he admits explicitly that not all dreams have a sexual meaning.

Dalbiez summarizes the main idea of Freud's interpretation of dreams very well when he states that the dream is a kind of *psychic* expression, and that it is a *natural and individual psychic language.*

The dream is a kind of psychic expression. That means that the dream is a sign, not a physical or organic sign but a psychic sign. The signs which we use in our knowledge of men may be divided into four groups: (1) The sign and the thing signified are both organic. Such signs are used especially in medicine. Fever, for instance, is an organic sign of some organic disorder. (2) The sign is organic and the thing signified is psychic; for instance, blushing, grinding one's teeth. (3) The sign is psychic, the thing signified is organic, v.g., a toothache. (4) Both the sign and the thing signified are psychic. This kind of sign was almost entirely neglected before Freud. The dream is such a sign; it could be called a psychic symptom of a psychic disturbance. It is a psychic symptom because it is expressed in images which should not be taken at their face value but interpreted according to certain rules. It is the symptom of a psychic disturbance, namely of some thwarted tendency or drive.

The dream is a natural and individual language. It is a language because it expresses something; a psychic language because it consists not of words but of images; an individual language because it means something different for every individual; a natural language because it is neither intended nor even understood by the individual who uses it.[5]

AFFECTIVE DEVELOPMENT

If we were to cling to a strictly Freudian terminology, we should have to entitle this chapter, "Freud's Conception of Psycho-sexual Development." For him every affection or love is based upon the sex drive, and the development of that drive measures the affective development of the person.

We shall not follow Freud into that extreme position, but by transposing some of the things he said and correcting them in the light of a more comprehensive view of man we can gather important and generally accepted conclusions about affective development, about the development of temperament under the influence of the environment.

Under the influence of Freud a great transformation has taken

[5] R. Dalbiez, *Psychoanalytical Method and the Doctrine of Freud* (New York, Longmans, 1941), Vol. I, pp. 122-125.

place in our conception of the needs of the human baby. A few decades ago pediatricians insisted above all upon hygiene for the baby. Nowadays an equal emphasis is placed on the baby's need for love and affection. As one psychologist says tersely, "Babies who are not loved die." It has been shown that, even if they do not die, such babies, although they may be reared according to the rules of the strictest hygiene, do not develop as well as other babies surrounded by less hygiene and more affection.[6]

Even if the physical health is perfect, it will be evident later that something is lacking in their psychic makeup. Their capacity for loving others, for easy, trustful, friendly relations with their fellow men remains stunted. Later they may be able to love others with their mind and will but not with their emotions, and this cerebral kind of love will leave an aching void in their life.

It is, of course, especially from the mother that the baby first expects a warm and continual love. If the mother herself is stunted in her affective life, she will be unable to satisfy the baby's need for affection, and she may unwillingly be the cause of a serious deficiency in her child's development.[7]

It is one of Freud's most valuable contributions that he emphasized—although in terms we cannot accept—the supreme importance of the very first months and years of the child's life for the building of what we shall call a harmonious affective basis for all future development. In the light of this doctrine some apparently unimportant activities of the mother in relation to her child have assumed great psychological importance.

First the activities by which the mother feeds her child. No feeding equals breast feeding, because none comes up to it as a manifestation of real maternal love or offers so great an opportunity for manifesting such love. The way in which the mother feeds her baby is very important, not only for his physical, but also for his psychic development. If she performs that duty patiently, willingly, cheerfully, her happy dispositions will, in a sense, be imbibed with her milk by the infant. Tenseness, nervousness, impatience, dislike for

[6] The common sense of mothers has always felt that babies needed to be loved and fondled. Science spurned this intuition for awhile in favor of more hygiene, but it has now discovered that the mothers were right.

[7] More specifically in the development of the affective and instinctive foundations of personality—temperament and spontaneous character.

this task of love are felt by the baby and affect his psychic development in an unfavorable manner. Even some of the physical features of the nursing process may have important psychic repercussions. If the mother's milk flows freely and abundantly, so that the baby gets its food without effort, he will slowly develop a disposition of confidence and trustfulness and lay the foundation for a cheerful and optimistic temperament. If the baby has to make undue effort to get his food, or if the milk does not flow in sufficient abundance, he may feel frustrated, and the chances are that he will acquire traits of distrust and greediness, or at least a disposition to develop such traits later in life.

The way in which the child is weaned has also assumed great psychological importance. Gradual, patient, cheerful weaning will have no harmful repercussions. Abrupt, impatient weaning may leave the child with far-reaching psychic scars.

The mother gives her child his first social training; she teaches him to make his first personal sacrifices in behalf of those with whom he lives. Because this represents the first step of the child in the field of social relationships, it has a great impact upon his sensitive mind. This first social training is a very simple one; it consists in training the child for cleanliness. Great stress is now laid on the way in which the mother performs this homely duty. Here again impatience, abruptness and nervousness may evoke in the child an incipient rebellion and foster traits of stubbornness or stinginess which will be woven into the very fabric of his budding personality. If, on the other hand, the mother is patient and kind and succeeds in coaxing the child to do what he is supposed to do out of love for her, a great step has been taken in the right direction and a basis has been laid for the development of a generous and charitable character.

As the child becomes more and more aware of the other members of the family—father, brothers and sisters—social relations assume an increasing importance. If these relations are easy and smooth, the child is well on his way towards easy and harmonious relations with other people in his later life. If, on the other hand, there are strains and stresses in the family, if the parents do not get along with each other or quarrel frequently, even if they try to hide their mutual dislike from the children, there is something in the family atmosphere which will affect the child unfavorably and make his own later social life more difficult. If his father is too stern and authoritarian, the child will always fear him, and he may develop a basic strain of timidity which will make him feel ill-at-ease before people in authority. If the behavior of his mother is unpredictable, so that he never knows whether to expect affection or rebuke from her, he may become unable to love anybody trustfully and it may be difficult for him later in life to enter into a happy marriage.

Freud attaches great importance to the Oedipus complex, which makes its appearance around the age of three. The intense love which the little boy has for his mother leads him to crave her undivided attention and love. He notices that the mother is also very much interested in the father and resents it; he becomes jealous of his father, wishes him to go and stay away, to die, to be dead. These feelings of hatred towards the father may be combined with sincere love for him. Unconscious affective life is not ruled by logic.[8]

The Oedipus complex is slightly different in the little girl. She also starts life with a great attachment to the mother. But later on she transfers this attachment to her father and develops jealousy, hatred and unconscious death-wishes in relation to her mother.

Freud claims that the attachment of the child for the parent of the opposite sex is a sexual attachment. In a few pathological cases this may be true. In most cases there is no reason for calling this attachment sexual. It is an affective attachment without spiritual elements, based on instinct, and may therefore be called "sensual." But usually there are no sexual elements in it, if the word sexual is taken in its ordinary meaning.

With these restrictions we have no difficulty in admitting that the Oedipus complex occurs frequently in children. It consists then in a tendency for the little boy to prefer his mother and for the little girl to prefer her father. The relation with the other parent, in either case, is a mixture of affection and jealous or rebellious aversion. This complex must not be attributed to incestuous leanings; it may often be explained by the fact that a parent has a tendency

---

[8] Such a mixture of contradictory feelings for the same person or objects is called "ambivalence."

to favor a child of the opposite sex; also, the training and disciplining of a child is generally the task of the parent of the same sex, and this relation may give rise to a certain parent-child tension.

According to Freud the Oedipus complex disappears around the age of five or six. Or rather, it is repressed; it becomes unconscious and may continue to exert some effects out of the depths of the unconscious. On the conscious level it is normally replaced by an identification of the child with the parent of the same sex. The boy takes his father as a model and an ideal, and the girl tries to shape her behavior after that of her mother.

For Freud the age of five marks the beginning of the latency period. According to him the sex drive has been very active during the first five years of the child's life. Around the age of five to six, the inhibitory tendencies, such as shame, modesty and sympathy, make their first appearance. Under their influence, helped by pressures in the environment, the sex drive is repressed and goes underground.

Transposing this in terms of a more comprehensive view of the human person, we shall say: Around the age of five to six, the rational faculties of the child enter into action. During the first few years the child was predominantly a creature of instincts,[9] led by his senses, egoistically looking for pleasure and avoiding pain, capable of receiving a certain amount of training, of very much the kind that an animal can be given. With the emergence of the rational faculties, real moral training can start.

Yet even before that time, the child has undergone a welter of influences which will leave indelible imprints on the affective and instinctive foundations of his personality, on what we call his temperament and his spontaneous character.

It is not necessary to admit with the psychoanalysts that these infantile experiences will *determine* the whole future development of the personality. But there is no reason for denying that they will greatly *influence* it. A child who has lived in a favorable environment has laid foundations on which a harmonious and well-adapted personality can easily be built up. A child who has undergone noxious, and especially traumatic, experiences may be handi-

---

[9] There is no sufficient evidence on which to accept Freud's theory that most of these instincts are of a sexual nature.

capped in his later development; he may have to struggle against serious internal difficulties throughout his life. Yet, by dint of personal effort and with the help of prayer, the latter may succeed, despite his handicaps, in developing a strong moral personality, whereas the former may go seriously astray if his happy beginnings are not taken up and reinforced by conscious voluntary effort.

FREUD'S CONCEPTION OF THE HUMAN PERSONALITY

According to Freud the human person comprises three levels, which he calls the Id, the Ego and the Super-ego. The Id is the sum-total of the sensory drives; it is unconscious, it strives only after pleasure and takes no account of reality. The Id corresponds to what we call "sense appetite."

The Ego is derived from the Id. It comprises the perceptual functions by means of which we enter into contact with reality and the executive functions which help us influence the outside world. Freud's Ego does not correspond to what we call the Ego or the Conscious Personality. He considers the Ego as passive and determined by three sets of influences: the Id, the Super-ego and the outside world. In this view, we do not direct our life, but whatever we do is a resultant of the interaction of these three groups of forces. In other words, Freud is a determinist who denies human freedom. Although we readily admit that our Ego is *influenced* by sense appetite and the outside world, we deny that it is *determined* by these influences.

The Super-ego derives from the Ego. When the child becomes aware of his environment, he notices that, in order to receive approval and affection from his parents and to escape rebuke and punishment, he is supposed to do certain things and to omit others. The child "behaves" at first for these extrinsic reasons. He does what he is told to do and abstains from that which is forbidden by his parents. Gradually, however, the need for direct parental orders or prohibitions becomes smaller; he begins to "tell himself" what to do and what to avoid. There is now in his own mind a substitute for the parents which directs his conduct in their name. The child has "introjected" the parents, he has "identified" himself with them. This substitute for the parents is Freud's Super-ego. Its influence is strongly supported by the inhibitory tendencies which we have mentioned above and which, in Freud's conception, are but transformations and sublimations of the sex drive.

From all this it is evident that Freud's Super-ego does not coincide with what we call "conscience," despite the contrary claims of many psychologists. The Super-ego is passively received from without, whereas conscience develops actively within. The Super-ego is a social and instinctive agency, conscience is a moral and rational power. The Super-ego "would produce a personality completely caked with custom and shackled by tribal mores,"[10] it produces conventionality and a pseudo-morality such as was found in the Pharisees and in many Puritans of the Victorian age. Conscience is man's intelligence inasmuch as it judges his actions in the light of reason and, for the Christian, the light of Revelation; it is the basis of the mature moral personality.[11]

When Johnny, aged five, says his prayers before going to bed, he does so because he has been bidden by his mother, he is led by his Super-ego. If John continues at the age of twenty-five to say his prayers *only* for that reason, he has not reached real morality, he is still guided by his Super-ego. It is more probable, however, that he says his prayers because he realizes that he needs prayer or that he owes worship to his Creator. In that case he is led by his conscience. The same action which was initiated under direct pressure from the environment and carried on for awhile under the influence of the Super-ego has now been freely assumed by his moral conscience.

The Super-ego is not conscience. But it exists and operates in most individuals.[12] In young children, before the age of reason, the action of the Super-ego is obvious. They "behave" just because they have been told to by their parents. Gradually, as the higher

[10] G. W. Allport, *Personality*, p. 218.

[11] For a profound study of the differences between real morality and the pseudo-morality inspired by the Super-ego, cfr. the remarkable book of Dr. Ch. Odier, *Les deux Sources, Consciente et Inconsciente, de la Vie Morale* (Neuchâtel, La Baconnière, 1947).

[12] And in intimate union with conscience, as explained by Fr. Gustave Weigel, S.J., in his excellent remarks in *The Proceedings of the Institute for the Clergy on Problems of Pastoral Psychology* (1955), pp. 25-26.

functions develop, conscience takes over the function of the Super-ego. But rare are the individuals, even among adults, in whom this substitution is ever complete. In most people there is a fringe of Super-ego around the core of conscience. In some that fringe is very wide, because a great part of their actions is a mere routine carrying on of customs and habits acquired during childhood, without any personal assimilation of the motives for such conduct. Such people remain morally infantile in most of their actions, their morality is mainly convention. However, in all normal individuals, there is at least a core of real conscience. They admit at least that "good should be done and evil avoided," not just because of what they have been told by their parents but because their intelligence grasps the truth of this statement.

Moral development consists precisely in widening the domain of conscience at the expense of the Super-ego, and in morally developed persons only unimportant actions may continue to stand under the guidance of the Super-ego.

Furthermore, even in those who have developed their moral personality, there may be remnants of Super-ego influence in the manner in which they conceive or execute their duties. Such traits as moral rigidity or formalism may be explained in this way.

It is especially in the pathology of moral life that the Super-ego is a useful concept. Morbid scrupulosity is a neurosis which must be attributed to the action of the Super-ego. The individual, in spite of his own better judgment, is unable to rid himself of the impression that some unimportant or innocuous action constitutes a serious sin. Freud claims that the Super-ego is often irrational, tyrannical, compulsive. A morbidly scrupulous person suffers from the insidious action of such a Super-ego.

SOME OTHER IMPORTANT FREUDIAN CONCEPTS

The concepts which we shall consider here are those of the Unconscious, repression and sublimation.

The Unconscious. Freud makes a distinction between conscious, preconscious and unconscious phenomena. Preconscious phenomena are those of which we are not actually aware, but of which we can easily become aware. All our habitual stock of knowledge consists of such preconscious contents.

A phenomenon is unconscious when we are not aware of it and cannot become aware of it by the ordinary methods. It takes hypnosis or free association to bring such contents back to the level of consciousness. The psychoanalysts claim that there are such unconscious contents in our mind, because without them it is impossible to explain certain facts. In post-hypnotic suggestion, the subject executes during the waking state an order which he received during hypnotic sleep and of which he is totally unaware. There are many mental phenomena, such as sudden likes and dislikes, hunches, prejudices, attitudes, feelings, strange dreams, the vast domain of neurotic and psychotic symptoms, for which we can find no cause in our conscious mind and which nonetheless must have a psychic cause.

It is now generally admitted by psychologists that there are unconscious psychic processes, especially that there are unconscious factors which explain the presence in us of certain states of consciousness. This is especially observable in the domain of feelings, emotions, attitudes, prejudices, etc. Thus at my first meeting with a person, I may at once experience an intense dislike for him. There must be a cause for that feeling, yet I am not aware of it and cannot account for my reaction, try as I may. Later on I may realize that this person resembles an uncle whom I feared and disliked when I was a child. The unconsciously perceived resemblance explains my dislike.

In this case, the feeling of dislike is conscious, its cause is unconscious. In other cases all the symptoms of a certain trait, of a habit, may be clearly conscious; taken all together they give a precise indication of their common root. The subject nevertheless is unaware that he possesses such a trait because he has never connected all its single manifestations (of which he is aware) with any common cause. If these manifestations were put down on paper for him to read and ponder, he would at once recognize the common root from which they spring. Yet it may take him years before he realizes the presence in himself of a deep-lying trait which he would have no trouble recognizing at once in another person. This character trait is unconscious for the person who possesses it, although his relatives and friends are clearly aware of it.

Some psychoanalysts place much emphasis on unconscious motivation. They try to eliminate human freedom by attributing all man's choices to the influence of unconscious motives.

Consider the case of hypnosis: a subject who has been hypnotized is told to carry out a certain order, and without the slightest hesitation he obeys. He feels that he is performing his task freely, although we know that his behavior is determined.

Still more striking are the cases of post-hypnotic suggestion. Here is a normal person who, at 10 A.M., while under hypnotism, has received the order to come back to the hypnotist's office with his umbrella at 3 P.M. Having emerged from the hypnotic sleep, he returns home without remembering, without even being able to remember, the suggestion he has received. Yet, lo and behold, around 3 P.M. he feels strongly impelled to take his umbrella and walk back to the hypnotist's office. Asked why he does so, he may hesitate a moment, then come up with a more or less plausible reason—which, however, is not the real reason. He does not know the real reason; he invents one, he "rationalizes." Throughout, of course, he feels that he is acting with unhampered freedom. Here is an action, performed in the waking state, by a normal person, with a full sense of freedom; yet, says the psychoanalyst, it is in fact determined by an unconscious motive, there is no shred of freedom in it.

Why, then, should not all instances in which man feels free be instances of his not knowing what forces him to do, with a sense of entire freedom, whatever he may do?

We are willing to admit that during the hypnotic sleep there is no freedom. Even if the subject feels no compulsion, we know that he is obeying the hypnotist blindly. Yet even here freedom is not always completely eliminated. There are a number of cases on record where a subject, having received from the hypnotist an order diametrically opposed to his deepest moral convictions, yielded only after a real struggle, or yielded only partially, or did not obey at all. We would not say that this is the general rule, as contrary instances are reported. But this balking on the part of man's deepest will does occur occasionally even during the hypnotic trance, where we are willing to admit the absence of real freedom.

The situation is different in post-hypnotic suggestion. Supposing that the subject is normal, we do not see any reason for admitting that the feeling of freedom he has while carrying out the hypnotist's suggestion does not correspond to the real state of affairs. He is fully aware of his desire to return to the hypnotist's office, although he does not know the origin of that desire. He can examine this suggestion which comes up in his mind, and he can freely decide that there is no serious reason why he should not do what he feels like doing.

Such things happen to us frequently in everyday life. We may all of a sudden develop a very strong craving, say, for a steak with onions. We have no idea why we suddenly feel that way, but it is a fact, right now nothing looks more desirable than that steak. Does that mean that we are not free to accept or to reject that impulsion? Suppose it is Friday and I am a good Catholic. I shall simply reject that craving. It may persist, come back time and again during the day. I am not free to feel it or not to feel it. Its origin is unknown to me. But I can freely yield to it or resist it.

The mother blames her daughter for choosing the wrong men as candidates for husbands; but though the daughter thinks she is choosing freely and spends a considerable amount of time "deciding" among them, the identification with her sick father, resulting from Oedipal fantasies in early childhood, prevents her from caring for any but sick men, twenty or thirty years older than herself. Blaming her is beside the point; she cannot help it, and she cannot change it.[13]

True, she cannot help it, she cannot change it. But she can resist this inclination, and if the complaining mother has taught her daughter not to yield to her every impulse, but to use her head and act reasonably, she will do so. The fact that this morbid attraction for sick elderly men has an unconscious root does not take away the daughter's freedom.

These two everyday situations resemble the case of the post-hypnotic suggestion in all respects but one. In each case there is a strong desire to do something, there is unconsciousness of the

[13] J. Hospers, "What Means This Freedom?" in *DF*, p. 114.

origin of that desire, there is the possibility either of freely accepting or of rejecting it. The only difference—which is immaterial for our purposes—is the origin of the desire. The desire to walk back to the hypnotist's office derives from the suggestion received during previous hypnosis; the desire for the steak has probably some physiological source; the attraction for sick and elderly men derives from the daughter's Oedipus complex.

Coming back to post-hypnotic suggestion, let us suppose that a normal subject was given the following order, to be executed a few hours after the end of the hypnotic trance: At 6 P.M. you will take the big carving knife and cut the throats of your two children. What would happen at 6 P.M.? Around that time the subject would probably be bothered by some very wild and crazy ideas and impulses. Although he would not remember having received any suggestions of that kind during hypnosis, he would suspect that something must have happened then which would explain the emergence of these weird fancies in his mind. And although he may continue to be plagued by them for a while longer, there is no danger (supposing him to be normal and not addicted to hypnotism) that he will yield to the awful suggestion. The fact that these ideas come up in his mind is determined, beyond his control; their origin is unconscious; but the ideas themselves are fully conscious and his reaction to them remains fully free.[14]

By way of conclusion we may say this: It frequently happens that while we consider a certain course of action we are influenced by factors of whose origin we are not aware, by motives which, although conscious, possess unconscious roots. As long as we are aware of the motives themselves, our freedom is not essentially impaired.

But unconscious motivation is sometimes understood in a different way. We are unconsciously motivated when we make a decision for reasons which we do not know. In such a case not only would the origin of the motive be unknown, the motive itself

---

[14] Cf. J. Nuttin, *Psychoanalysis and Personality*, pp. 123-131. Subliminal suggestion, the latest procedure of advertising gone wild, does not endanger the freedom of normal people. The most it can achieve is to suggest certain ideas or to arouse certain impulses. But it can never force the customer to act on these ideas or to yield to these impulses. Its success depends upon the gullibility, and especially upon the lack of self-control, of most people.

would remain unconscious. We believe that we make a decision for this or that conscious reason; in fact we are determined by the pressure of unconscious motives. The conscious reasons are only a "blind," an instance of "rationalization."

This kind of unconscious motivation does not occur in normal people, at least not when important decisions are involved. A decision made under such motivation would not be felt as a free choice, but as a pathological compulsion. "I have to do this, I cannot do anything else, and I do not know why I do it." Such cases do happen, they exclude freedom, they are abnormal.

Let us take a concrete example again. A young man, having completed his studies, deliberates about the choice of a career. He hesitates between becoming a sailor or a salesman. He has the motives for and against each job clearly in his mind. Finally he decides in favor of a sailor's life; he can tell you all the motives which have prompted his choice. This is a conscious and free deliberation, leading to a conscious and free decision.

Not at all, says a psychoanalyst. The conscious motives are only rationalizations. The decision is determined by an unconscious motive, the young man's unconscious hatred for his father, which prompts him to get away from home.

What does the analyst really mean when he offers that interpretation? He may mean several things:

1. The young man may be aware of his strong aversion for his father, but he does not know why he dislikes him so much. There is conscious hatred with unconscious roots. That is what psychoanalysts generally mean when they speak of unconscious hatred, unconscious guilt, etc. But then we are back in the previously discussed case. This conscious aversion, whose origin is unconscious, will be taken into consideration by our young man when he freely makes up his mind. Whether or not its roots are conscious, as long as the motive itself is present in consciousness, it does not interfere with freedom.

2. The young man chooses the sea apparently for the motives which he alleges, in fact because of his aversion for his father. He is dimly aware of this, but he does not want to admit it to himself. He is trying to deceive himself, he lacks sincerity with himself. Such cases are rather frequent; they do not involve un-

conscious motivation, they do not exclude freedom. Professor Nuttin considers them as instances of what he calls "psychic intimacy":

It is a fact that in our culture, at least, one can divide the psychic contents into several layers, belonging either to the "intimate" or to the "public" part of personality. As lived at the most intimate level of personal consciousness, personality is not absolutely identical with the personality which lives and unfolds in the realm of public and social life.[15]

These intimate contents are "those psychic contents which do not fit in with the explicit constructive image which the person is tending to realize within himself."[16] Not only does the person not want to show these intimate layers to others, he is disinclined to look at them himself, he turns his inner eye away from them, he tries to act as if they did not exist. Yet these contents are not unconscious, and the subject remains always vaguely aware of them. He is obscurely conscious also that they remain vague because he looks away from them and that he has an obligation to check their influence upon his life.[17]

3. The young man is certain that he chooses the life of a sailor because of the motives which are consciously before his mind. In fact, his choice is *determined* by his unconscious hatred for his father. In such a case freedom would indeed be excluded. But we repeat that such cases do not occur in normal people, when an important decision is at stake. If the psychoanalyst asserts the reality of such cases, he will have to demonstrate it. He cannot do so by asking the subject, since the motives are supposed to be totally unconscious. His only possible method consists in dream interpretation and analysis. Such procedure is admittedly very

---

[15] Nuttin, *op. cit.*, p. 192.

[16] *Ibid.*, p. 196.

[17] Dostoevsky wrote, "Every man has reminiscences which he would not tell to every one, but only to his friends. He has other matters on his mind which he would not reveal even to his friends, but only to himself, and that in secret. But there are other things which a man is afraid to tell even to himself, and every decent man has a number of such things stored away in his mind." ("Notes from the Underground," quoted by W. Kaufman, *Existentialism from Dostoevsky to Sartre* [Meridian Books, 1956], pp. 81-82.)

subjective, its conclusions cannot be checked, and we shall need more reliable arguments before giving up the well-founded reality of free-will in man.

We can transpose this whole discussion into other terms. Most of our choices are influenced at once by drives and by motives. Drives have a physiological basis, they push us blindly towards some pleasure or away from some pain. Motives, on the other hand, are based on higher values; they are consciously and freely accepted by the Ego. In the example we have been discussing the drive would be the hatred for the father, the motives are the various conscious reasons which impel our young man to choose a career as a sailor.

Sometimes the drive and the motive push in the same direction; for instance, in real love, the sex drive and the spiritual love for another person. Sometimes there is a conflict between drive and motive; for instance, when the sex instinct pushes us towards a forbidden act, there is a conflict between that drive and the motives which come naturally to a Christian mind (chastity, keeping God's love, etc.).

It may be that a person yields to the drive and is unwilling to admit it. He tries to convince himself that he acts for a motive. Thus a student of English reads a pornographic novel, allegedly for its style, in fact because of its salacious content. He is rationalizing; or, in terms of Christian asceticism, his intention is not pure.

The main question we are debating can now be put in the following terms: Is it possible that in an important decision our choice is determined by an unconscious drive, while we are convinced that we make it freely for some conscious motive? We answer that in normal people this does not occur. Such a decision would not be felt as a free choice, but as a blind compulsion. In such a case the individual cannot really say: "I can take it or leave it." He must take it.

There can be no doubt, however, that in many of our decisions, drives which may be more or less conscious have some influence. We may try to convince ourselves that we adopt a certain course of action only for this or that conscious motive. It may be true that if this motive were not present in our mind, we should not make that decision. Nevertheless we are dimly aware that we are also prompted by a drive, and we consent to be prompted by it. Our decision is free, but it is not explained entirely by the motive by which we would like to explain it. There is a certain amount of self-deception, a lack of perfect sincerity. It is not easy to be perfectly sincere with one's self.

Where a decision is made apparently for a motive but in reality with great help from a drive, there may be difficulties ahead. The force of the drive may wane or the drive may reverse itself, and unless by then the motive has taken deeper root it may be insufficient to sustain our resolve. That is the reason why marriages based predominantly on sex attraction are often doomed to failure, why a religious vocation embraced in great part out of a desire for security will not stand the test of the unavoidable difficulties.

It is important to notice, however, that some courses of action may begin under the predominant influence of a drive and be continued under the influence of motives. A student may have started the study of chemistry out of fear of failing in his major subject, but he gradually becomes so much interested in this field that he enters it as a career. Or take the example of a marriage entered predominantly under the influence of sex attraction, when the partners later discover in each other moral and spiritual qualities which will constitute a strong bond when the sex attraction has waned.

In conclusion to our extended study of the unconscious, we may say that we admit its existence and its importance in human life. We insist, however, that the essential human functions of judgment and free decision, although they may be and often are influenced and affected by the unconscious, emerge sufficiently above it to allow the normal person to steer his own life according to the light of his reason and the dictates of his conscience.

Some authors have advocated the use of the term "superconscious" for some very important elements of our mental life which escape the direct reach of our consciousness and yet do not belong to the affective or instinctive foundations of our personality. Such are in particular the "superconscious" striving of our intellect towards the Infinite Truth and of our will towards the Infinite Goodness.

Repression and Suppression. Freud says that repression is the most important concept in psychoanalysis. Repression is the unconscious and automatic inhibition of a drive; it differs from suppression, in which the inhibition is both conscious and voluntary.

Suppression is a very old idea. The concept of repression is new and was first introduced by Freud. Let us show, by means of an example, how Freud explains the origin of a repression. A little boy three years of age acquires a baby brother. He notices that the attention of his parents, which had been concentrated upon him, is now to a great extent diverted to the newcomer. As a result he starts to dislike, then proceeds to hate his baby brother. When he expresses these feelings his parents are shocked and tell him that he must love and protect the baby. The child tries to get rid of his forbidden feelings. At first he does it consciously, after awhile it is done unconsciously. Suppression has been followed by repression. The hatred for his brother seems no longer to exist. In fact, says Freud, that hatred persists unconsciously in the boy's mind. It may flare up again in certain circumstances, or it may reappear in parapraxias, in the dream, or under the form of neurotic symptoms.

There are indeed repressions of that kind in most normal people. But they are not always totally unconscious. The individual may be dimly aware of some tendencies of which he does not approve; he may try to keep them as much as possible out of the focus of consciousness. They belong to his "psychic intimacy," they hover on the fringe of consciousness.

Freudians seem to postulate that every drive which ever stirred in an individual continues to exist in him in a repressed state when it is no longer consciously felt. That is an exaggeration. After a good dinner, my hunger drive is not repressed, it is satisfied and quiet for awhile. The same is true for other drives.

In individuals who live chaste lives the sex drive, although never receiving any satisfaction, may be inactive, quiescent, without any real repression. It may be stirred up occasionally either by some organic condition or some stimulus coming from outside. In that case it will be suppressed, without any harm, for the sake of a higher good. People who live chaste lives do not repress their sex drive, they suppress the occasions which would stir up that drive, and if it is aroused, they suppress the drive itself.

Some people entertain the false notion that suppression or repression is always dangerous for mental health and must be avoided. Even Freud does not accept this. He knows that man must suppress or repress some of his drives if he does not want to wreck his own life.

Suppression is not dangerous, especially if we avoid two mistakes: (1) We should not multiply needlessly the occasions of suppression. It is not wise to allow a lower drive to be continually aroused and be continually obliged to suppress it. Translated into Christian language this means: Avoid the occasions of sin. (2) Suppression should not be conceived as something purely negative. When we deny a lower drive its forbidden object, we should not concentrate on that negative aspect. We deny that object *in order* to obtain something higher. The negative attitude is not the ultimate end but a means for something positive. It is healthier to concentrate on that positive aspect of suppression.

Sublimation. Freud's concept of sublimation represents a clever attempt at explaining away all higher functions in man. By sublimation Freud means the redirecting of the sex drive from its ordinary goal (sexual activity) to some higher goal (artistic, scientific, moral or religious activity). For him the writing of a symphony, the pursuit of scientific discovery and the heroic virtues of a Saint are all alike to be explained in terms of a redirected, canalized sex drive.

Understood in that sense the notion of sublimation corresponds to nothing real. Man's spiritual activities cannot be explained as derivations of his sex drive, they must be attributed to his spiritual faculties, whose existence Freud denied.

But sublimation is sometimes understood in other senses which may be acceptable.

1. It is possible to overcome a lower drive (sex, anger) by directing one's attention to some other object, by distracting the drive. In this case there is no real sublimation but rather a substitution.

2. When a lower drive is stirred up, it generally induces a state of restlessness. This restlessness may sometimes be overcome by keeping busy, by fatiguing the body. A certain amount of athletic activity helps some individuals to control their sex drive. Here again there is no real sublimation of that drive.

3. A person may inhibit his sex drive for the sake of a higher purpose. He prefers the satisfaction of a higher drive to that of his sex drive. As Professor G. W. Allport puts it: "An individual may without serious conflict forego some specific gratification, provided that he finds other sources of equal satisfaction. . . . In such instances, the individual simply disregards his unfulfilled desires, letting them atrophy, or repressing them without disaster, in the interest of an alternative plan of life that satisfies not these desires, but satisfies *him* as a whole man.[18]

Thus a young woman who has been jilted by her fiancé may presently enter a convent and consecrate her life to God. Freud would consider this an example of sublimation, and so could we. But we should use the same term with an utterly different meaning. For Freud it is the selfsame sex drive that first urged this girl towards marriage which now presses her to enter the religious life. We say that she foregoes the satisfaction of her sex drive, that she suppresses that drive, and that she can do it without harm because she finds happiness in satisfying a higher drive, her love for God.[19]

4. In the human person the biological sex drive is usually accompanied by complex feelings and sentiments. These may be diverted from the sex drive and attached to a higher tendency. Thus, to come back to our example: in the convent the young woman may direct towards God some of the feelings and sentiments which, in wedlock, she might have experienced for her husband. Her biological sex drive is not sublimated, it is suppressed. Her spiritual love is directed towards God. This spiritual love may now, and should be, clothed in feelings and sentiments which, in other circumstances, might have accompanied her love for her husband. In this case the affective processes have been sublimated, not the sex drive itself.

5. We have already pointed out that the will should not be conceived as standing above the drives any more than the soul hovers over the body. If there is to be moral growth, the will must orientate the drives in the direction of its own higher ends, use their energies for its own purposes, try to penetrate them more and more with spiritual finality. This cannot be done directly with all

[18] *Personality*, p. 185.
[19] Such a vocation should, however, be tested rather strictly. It may be prompted, in part, in an unconscious or vaguely conscious way, not by the sex drive, but by discouragement or resentment.

drives. Those which are essentially somatic can be put at the service of the will; they cannot be really spiritualized or sublimated. It is impossible to sublimate hunger, thirst and the biological sex drive. Other drives which are not somatic can really be spiritualized. Take, for instance, ambition. The drive to excel, to be strong and outstanding, is inborn in most human beings; it needs a favorable environment to reach its full development. When it has thus reached full strength, this "instinct" can be assumed by the will, animated and spiritualized by it, sublimated in the real sense of that word. We might even say that outstanding achievements will rarely occur except when a naturally ambitious "character" is thus animated by some higher purpose, whether that purpose be egoistic, as with Napoleon, or altruistic and idealistic, as with St. Paul or St. Ignatius Loyola. The same real sublimation may occur with other non-somatic drives, such as curiosity and gregariousness.

GENERAL EVALUATION OF FREUD'S SYSTEM

We have two major objections to Freud's system, one philosophical, the other scientific.

Philosophically we reject Freud's materialism, which makes him reduce all the higher functions of man to the level of the animal. He admits no basic distinction between animal and man; man is only a more highly evolved animal. The things which distinguish him from animals—his scientific, artistic, moral and religious ideas and achievements—are only transformations or derivations of the sex drive. Great parts of Freud's system have been vitiated by this materialistic prejudice, which Freud seems to have unconsciously imbibed from his materialistic environment.

Scientifically speaking, Freud's great weakness is that he is prone to unwarranted generalizations. He had a very keen psychological insight, which enabled him to unravel problems the solutions of which had eluded all former investigators. But he also had the unfortunate tendency to generalize from one or a few cases. He discovered some peculiarities in the neurotic patients whom he studied and concluded at once that the complexes and aberrations which he found in them were present in every individual. Such unwarranted generalizations are alien to a really scientific mind. The great emphasis which modern science puts on statistical methods has among its main purposes that of helping the scientist avoid unwarranted generalizations.

Freud's materialism and his tendency to rash generalizations are most apparent in his pansexualism. The fact that he explains almost everything in man as a derivation from the sex drive is a result of his inability to see the spiritual aspects of man and his tendency to ascribe to all individuals the abnormalities which he had discovered in some of his neurotic patients.[20]

It is rather difficult to separate the valuable elements in Freud's system from those which are worthless, or vitiated by his materialism. After that badly needed sifting there remain a great number of very valuable elements, which no student of human nature can afford to ignore. We have tried to point out some of them and to show how they can be integrated in a spiritualistic conception of man.

SYSTEMS DERIVED FROM PSYCHOANALYSIS

Adler and Jung were at first faithful disciples of Freud and borrowed many elements of their systems from Freud's pioneering work. Both of them gave up "orthodox" psychoanalysis because they came to realize that Freud exaggerated the importance of the sex drive.

THE SYSTEM OF ALFRED ADLER

The main differences between Freud and Adler can be summarized as follows: (1) For Freud the main drive in man is sex, for Adler it is the will to power, the drive towards superiority and self-assertion. Sex is only a manifestation of that fundamental

---

[20] A remarkably illogical procedure seems to be responsible for overemphasis on sex by psychoanalysts (by Freudians especially). Whatever form of behavior or thought is *ever* found in *any* life, to be associated with sex, they seem to assume to be *always* connected with sex in *every* life" (G. W. Allport, *Personality*, p. 188).

drive. (2) Adler gives much greater weight than Freud to the social factors influencing man's life. (3) Adler's approach is finalistic, Freud's approach is genetic. Adler tries to explain such psychic phenomena as dreams, neurotic symptoms, etc., by discovering their unconscious purpose, whereas Freud explains them by discovering their origin or genesis.

According to Adler man's life gravitates between two poles: the drive for power and the social drive. The purpose of education and therapy is to harmonize these two fundamental tendencies. They can be seen at work very early in the life of the child. They determine what Adler calls the "plan of life." Under the influence of the environment and of his own make-up, the child unconsciously builds up a conception of life, of society, of his own purpose in life and society, of what he expects from them, etc., which will unconsciously direct all his later activities. A fundamental unconscious law of behavior from which all the conscious principles directing his life will derive is thus written in his mind.[21] For instance a child with a weak physical constitution, living in a "soft" environment, with parents who spoil him, will quite naturally expect that, because of his weakness and helplessness, everybody will always be at his service. He develops what has been called the "Clinging Vine" plan of life.

In order to understand an individual it is indispensable to discover his plan of life. Adler claims that it is manifested in every single action of the individual. There are, however, some typical experiences which reveal that plan of life more clearly than any others. They are especially the earliest memories, the favorite story or hero of one's childhood, the dreams.

The plan of life is built mainly under the influence of organic factors and of the environment.

Organic Factors Affecting the Plan of Life. Adler insists especially on the importance of the factor of organic inferiority, whether general or specific. General organic inferiority has existed at some time in every individual. Every child feels small, weak and ignorant as compared with the big, strong and omniscient adults. This pro-

---

[21] Because this plan of life is characteristic for each individual, Adler has called his system "Individual Psychology."

duces normally a strong feeling of inferiority, which evokes, by reaction, a powerful striving towards superiority.

The effects of specific organic inferiority are more important. Such inferiority may consist in a real bodily defect, especially when it is visible to others (lame arm, hunchback, squint, harelip), or in some non-pathological peculiarity which attracts unfavorable comments (big nose, long ears, being too short or too tall). These defects or peculiarities attract scorn, mockery, pity, compassion, so that the individual develops not only a normal feeling of inferiority but frequently a pathological *inferiority complex*.[22] The complex itself automatically arouses a strong reaction in the form of an urgent drive towards superiority. This reaction may take one of several forms.

It may take the form of *compensation:* the individual works so hard to overcome his inferiority that he becomes as able as those who do not suffer such a handicap. Sometimes there is *overcompensation:* the effort to overcome the handicap has been so strong that the individual surpasses those who have no inferiority. Compensation and overcompensation may exert their effects in the very field where the inferiority is experienced (Demosthenes, the stutterer, becoming a great orator), or in a different field (Napoleon, a short man, becoming a great leader).

When, owing to lack of talent or energy, compensation is not possible, there will generally be what Adler calls *compromise* or *arrangement,* mechanisms whose purpose is again to overcome the unbearable feeling of inferiority. Compromise happens in several ways. It may be a purely negative attitude by which the individual withdraws, as it were, from life and society, becoming a mere spectator, a critic, a scoffer, who rejoices in the failures of others, belittles their efforts, professes a cynical and blasé attitude towards everything. It may be a positively anti-social attitude, when the person who has been unable to assert himself through positive achievement attracts attention by means of anti-social or criminal conduct.

Finally, it may be escape into illness, into dullness or neurosis. Certain forms of illness, called "functional illness," are very much under the influence of psychic factors. They are sometimes used

[22] A complex is a deeply buried, partly unconscious feeling or group of feelings, which affects the psychic life in a morbid way.

unconsciously as ways of getting out of a situation where the person feels hopelessly inadequate. A businessman facing bankruptcy comes down with an acute case of hypertension which requires immediate medical attention. He may now with a good conscience give up the hopeless battle for financial survival. His failure does not affect his feeling of self-importance, because he can convince himself that it is due not to mismanagement but to illness, to something which is quite independent of his own volition. Other people may find an escape into neurosis, and among young children the same mechanism may even assume the form of a flight into dullness.

Environmental Factors Affecting the Plan of Life. Social or environmental factors may produce a feeling or a complex of inferiority, with all the effects mentioned above—for instance, belonging to a linguistic, religious or racial minority. The more that minority is discriminated against, especially when its members are intellectually developed, the more the effects of the inferiority complex will show themselves. Many traits of Jewish psychology can be explained in that way. As the American Negroes develop culturally, the same reactions will become more frequent among them.

The fact of being a woman may be the cause of a feeling or complex of inferiority. That applies especially to milieus in which women have a lower social position than men—for instance, in China and Japan before the recent emancipation.

Adler lays great stress on the "family constellation" or the position of each child in the series of his siblings. It makes quite a difference whether a child is the oldest, or the youngest, or a middle child; whether he is an only child or one among many. As the most exposed positions, psychologically speaking, he mentions that of the only child, of the oldest and of the youngest child.

The only child is most likely to be spoiled and pampered. He is therefore not well prepared for social life and will often keep a fundamental egoism in his later social relations.

The oldest child has been an only child for some time. When a younger brother or sister arrives, the transition from the center of the family to a more secondary role may produce a psychological crisis. When more brothers and sisters arrive, the oldest child may be given a certain amount of authority over them, which makes him side with the parents, aligns the others against him, renders him old before his age. Or the parents expect him to be a model for the other children, which may produce discouragement and a feeling of inadequacy.

When there are only two children in the family, they are sometimes very different in spite of their similar heredity and environment. In fact neither heredity nor environment is quite the same for both of these children. Brothers and sisters, except for identical twins, have different genes. When there are only two children, the elder child will always be bigger, stronger, more experienced. The younger one feels that it is hopeless to compete with his brother in the fields where the latter is proficient. He will naturally turn his efforts towards other domains. That explains why, when the elder brother is a good student, often the younger one will not succeed so well in the classroom, but will become outstanding on the ballfield or in social relations.

The youngest child feels his inferiority more than any of the others. He may be spoiled, because the others take care of him. He may feel inferior, because the others are so much ahead of him. If he has an energetic nature, he may strike out in a new direction, not tried by anybody else in the family, and show great inventiveness and enterprise.

Adler's system is more optimistic than Freud's. All the deviations mentioned above may be avoided if the parents are aware of the factors which lead to them. His system contains many useful notations, especially for child and adolescent psychology. Like Freud, however, he overlooks the higher aspects of man and he stresses one drive too exclusively. Furthermore, his exaggerated emphasis on society, which he considers the ultimate end of man, is opposed to the Christian conception of man as an end in himself, although subordinate to God.

THE SYSTEM OF CARL GUSTAV JUNG

Jung's system, which is called Analytical Psychology or Complex Psychology, is difficult to explain clearly in a few pages, because it is rich and sprawling, in a state of continual flux and growth, and because it has never been summarized by its author in one comprehensive work. It is too important, however, to be passed over in silence. Therefore we shall attempt to point out, in the following paragraphs, a few important aspects of it.

1. Jung admits, besides the personal Unconscious mentioned by Freud, a collective Unconscious, which is shared by all the members of the human race, and which "consists of the inheritance of the psychic experiences of mankind. . . . Jung was obliged to postulate this 'collective Unconscious,' in addition to the 'personal Unconscious,' owing to the fact that certain symbols—or, more precisely, dispositions to form certain symbols—are found uniformly all over the world, and that similar symbols emerge in dreams, in daydreams, in the phenomena of 'second sight,' in religious and magical figures and emblems, in myths and fairy stories, in gnostic visions, in alchemy, and in automatic and 'inspired' designs and utterances."[23]

2. Transcending the unilateral conceptions of Freud and Adler, who attributed the whole of mental development to the influence of one specific drive, whether the sexual instinct or the will to power, he considers the "libido" to be the driving force which explains man's mental life. This libido is not the sex drive or a derivation of it. It is the name Jung gives to the totality of undifferentiated psychic energy, not only feeding the sex drive and the drive towards self-assertion, but also giving rise to higher tendencies, such as the religious drive.

3. For Jung the psyche is a self-regulating system, that is a system which tends unconsciously to counteract any one-sided development which circumstances may have forced upon the individual. Thus a scientist may easily develop his brain at the expense of his emotions. His Unconscious compensates automatically and develops in the direction of great emotionality. Sooner or later this man will be faced with a sudden eruption of this unconscious, and therefore infantile, archaic emotionality; he will go through a psychic crisis which, if skillfully handled, may give him the opportunity of consciously assimilating the long-neglected affective sphere of his per-

[23] G. Frei quoted in V. White, O. P., *God and the Unconscious* (Chicago, Regnery, 1953), p. 238.

sonality and building his psychic life again on a wider base. Jung calls the unconscious, undeveloped sides of our personality the "Shadow" and opposes them to the "Persona" which consists of those traits which we have consciously developed and which we show to our environment.

4. It is evident from (3) that Jung looks on a psychic crisis—a complex, a neurosis—not merely as a breakdown of the mind, but also as an opportunity for mental growth and development if it is well treated. It is not only the outcome of some previous mistake, it should also be the starting point of new mental gains. Likewise for him the dream is not entirely explained by the past experiences of the dreamer. It possesses also a "prospective" aspect, through which the person may become aware of aspirations and possibilities which have been neglected or repressed and which crave satisfaction. Among these aspirations Jung emphasizes the need for contact with the Absolute, the religious tendency of man. Very famous are the following words of Jung written in 1932, "During the past thirty years people from all the civilized countries of the earth have consulted me. . . . Among all my patients in the second half of life— that is to say, over thirty-five—there has not been one whose problem in the last resort was not that of finding a religious outlook on life. It is safe to say that every one of them fell ill because he had lost that which the living religions of every age have given to their followers, and none of them has been really healed who did not regain this religious outlook."[24]

5. Jung discovers these yearnings of man especially in what he calls the "archetypes," a product of the collective Unconscious which emerges often in dreams. Archetypes are inherited collective ways of conceiving, or rather of imagining reality, "in situations of general human character, e.g. such situations as those of fear, danger, struggle against superior force, the relations of the sexes, of children to parents, . . . of reaction to hate and love, to birth and death. . . ."[25] Men have met such situations over countless generations and they have reacted to them in their own typical way. The innumerable repetitions of these reactions have left an imprint in

[24] C. G. Jung, *Modern Man in Search of a Soul* (New York, Harcourt, 1936), p. 264.

[25] J. Jacobi, *The Psychology of C. G. Jung* (New Haven, Yale University Press, 1951), p. 12.

the mind of the human race, which explains why, even before the individual meets these situations, he possesses the ability to symbolize them and his reactions to them. Jung has studied these archetypes and their symbols in a great number of cultures, both ancient and modern. Many of these symbols refer to religious realities, and by studying them Jung has been able to demonstrate the existence in the collective Unconscious of many vague aspirations which correspond to some of the dogmas of revealed religion.

This mixture of psychology and theology in Jung's works has given rise to many misunderstandings. Quite a number of authors accuse Jung of being an atheist, or a pantheist, or a modernist who reduces supernatural realities to mere psychological symbols. Although his way of speaking may sometimes justify these accusations, Jung does not seem to deserve them. He has made it increasingly clear, especially during later years, that his intention is not to evaluate the reality of supernatural facts (that is the work of the theologian), but only to show as a psychologist that, deep in his Unconscious, every human being shows a yearning towards them and a readiness to accept them.

SYSTEMS DERIVING INDIRECTLY FROM FREUD

Depth-psychology has come a long way from Freud's rejection of religion as an illusion, a collective hallucination, to Jung's statement that the absence of a religious outlook on life is the cause of many psychological troubles. Jung's ideas on this topic have been developed by a school of psychotherapy flourishing in Vienna. They refer to their system as "logotherapy," "a psychotherapy which not only recognizes man's spirit, but actually starts from it."[26] The followers of this school claim that the religious need is one of the strongest needs of man, that it is present in every individual but often repressed. Such a repression may be harmful to psychic health, and psychotherapy must counteract it. An atheist is a person who represses his religious drive, and he may suffer ill effects from that repression even on the natural level. "Nobody

[26] V. E. Frankl, *The Doctor and the Soul: An Introduction to Logotherapy* (New York, Knopf, 1955), p. xi.

will convince us that man is a sublimated animal—since we can demonstrate that he carries within himself a repressed Angel."[27]

Thus our previously demonstrated assertion that man's intellect and will alike strive continuously towards the Absolute finds an unexpected confirmation in one of the most recent systems of psychotherapy. It seems undeniable that some individuals work themselves gradually into neurosis or psychosis because they repress this, one of their most basic cravings, the craving for the Absolute. It would be an exaggeration, however, to attribute all or even most cases of mental disturbance to this cause and to ignore the possible influence of other thwarted drives.

The Logotherapists are not the only ones who show a tendency to come back to the traditional conception of man. Under the influence of Otto Rank, Karen Horney and Carl Rogers, many psychotherapists are again stressing the spontaneity, the initiative, the "will" of their patients and the moral values which are so essential for maintaining mental health. They no longer consider the patient as a helpless victim of disordered drives, but as an individual who must be helped to help himself recover the direction of his life. The "will" of Rank may not be the will of our philosophy; it is nevertheless a factor which brings the conception of man in some of the most recent trends in psychotherapy considerably nearer to our position.

Philosophy, which Freud ignored (or tried to ignore) completely, has regained a prominent influence in the psychiatric writings of the Existential Analysts. They try to combine the insights and the methods of Freud, and his successors, with some of the central teachings of the great modern phenomenologists and existentialists. They are not looking for new techniques, but for a deeper insight into the nature of man, or, as they prefer to put it, into the "basic structures of the human condition."[28]

[27] V. E. Frankl, *Der Unbewusste Gott* (Wien, Amandus-Edition, 1948), p. 88. See also I. A. Caruso, *Bios, Psyche, Person* (Munich, Albers, 1957).
[28] See Rollo May et al., *Existence.*

CONCLUSION: INFLUENCE OF THE ENVIRONMENT
UPON TEMPERAMENT

Temperament is molded both by physique and by the influence of the environment, especially the early environment. The system of Sheldon has shown us the relations existing between physique and temperament. The data collected in this chapter give us an idea of the influence of the environment upon human temperament.

It seems probable that if the environment, especially the early environment, were absolutely the same for all individuals, each would develop a temperament corresponding perfectly to his physique. But the environment is far from identical for all men, and temperament does not correspond perfectly to physique.

Concerning this influence of the early environment on human temperament, and indirectly on human personality, we can learn much from Freud and the other depth-psychologists. They have demonstrated the great importance of the first childhood impressions upon the affective foundations of personality. Factors which would hardly affect an adult may have a deep influence on the receptive mind of the child. They may establish ways of feeling and reacting which will affect all his later development.

Above and beyond biological needs, the young child has psychological needs, especially the need for affection, for feeling important and for security.

Freud has emphasized the sexual needs of the child. If we drop the manifest exaggerations of some of his statements, we see that what he often means is the need for affection. The way in which this need is satisfied, first by the mother, later by the other members of the family, has a far-reaching influence upon the temperament of the child.

Adler has insisted on the need of a feeling of strength and importance, which the child develops as soon as he becomes aware of himself and his environment. If that need is not satisfied, he may develop a feeling or a complex of inferiority which may mark him for life. When parents know the factors which may produce these unhealthy reactions they can easily avoid or counteract them.

Horney, another disciple of Freud, has emphasized the need for security which is very strong in young children. That need may be considered as a combination of the two previously mentioned needs: being loved and feeling strong produces a feeling of security.

It should be noted that harm may be done to the child not only when these needs are not satisfied, but also when they are too well satisfied. Too much affection or security, allowing the child to feel too strong or too important, may interfere with right development as seriously as neglecting his psychological needs. Such treatment may pamper and spoil the child and make him overdependent, overconfident, conceited and anti-social.

READINGS

About Freud:

Allers, *The Successful Error*. Dalbiez, *Psychoanalytical Method and the Doctrine of Freud*, Vol. I, pp. 1-125, 369-409; Vol. II, pp. 1-87, 280-327. J. Donceel, S.J., "Second Thoughts on Freud," in *Thought*, 24 (1949), pp. 466-484. Ford, *Depth-Psychology, Morality and Alcoholism*, pp. 3-43. Harmon, *Understanding Personality*, pp. 81-90, 102-109. Maritain, *Scholasticism and Politics*, pp. 114-134. Moore, *The Driving Forces of Human Nature*, pp. 60-95, 231-320. Nuttin, *Psychoanalysis and Personality*, pp. 1-155. Stern, *The Third Revolution*. VanderVeldt and Odenwald, *Psychiatry and Catholicism*, pp. 110-124, 141-159.

About Adler:

Allers, *The Psychology of Character*. Allers and Barclay, *Practical Psychology*. Ansbacher, *The Individual Psychology of Alfred Adler*. Nuttin, *Psychoanalysis and Personality*, pp. 259-275. Shoobs and Goldberg, *Corrective Treatment for Unadjusted Children*.

About Jung and Others:

Clark, *Six Talks on Jung's Psychology*. Curran, *Counseling in Catholic Life and Education*. Fordham, *An Introduction to Jung's Psychology*. Hostie, *Religion and the Psychology of Jung*. Jacobi, *The Psychology of C. G. Jung*. Karpf, *The Psychology and Psychotherapy of Otto Rank*. Rogers, *Counseling and Psychotherapy*.

About All Above Systems:

Munroe, *Schools of Psychoanalytic Thought*.

Some Practical Applications:

Hagmaier and Gleason, *Counselling the Catholic*. Oraison, *Love or Constraint? Some Psychological Aspects of Religious Education*. Oraison, *Union in Marital Love: Its Physical and Spiritual Foundations*.

22

Characterology and Experimental Study of Character

WE HAVE made a distinction between temperament, spontaneous character and controlled character. Temperament refers to the totality of the affective functions, spontaneous character to the totality of the uninhibited drives, and controlled character to the totality of the drives as directed and controlled by the will. In fact, this distinction is difficult to maintain in practice. The relation between emotions and drives is so intimate that it is difficult to distinguish between temperament and spontaneous character. The diagram on p. 366 shows that, like temperament, spontaneous character is a product of heredity and environment. Even a differentiation between spontaneous and controlled character, although real and founded on the distinction between the will and the drives, is difficult to maintain in practice because of the subtle interaction between the lower tendencies and the human will.

Sheldon's work has provided us with a valuable classification of physiques and temperaments. Do we have anything comparable in the domain of character?

EUROPEAN SYSTEMS OF CHARACTEROLOGY

Many classifications of character have been presented since the earliest attempts of Theophrastes and Galen. All these classifications suffer from the same defect: they are not based upon a solid foundation of scientific facts. Their authors rely on their own experience and on second-hand information and build their systems on this rather flimsy foundation. Even where some experimental data are available, they are not sufficient to bear the ambitious systems based upon them. These constructions frequently demonstrate great psychological insight and a solid knowledge of human nature; but such ingredients are not sufficient for scientific work.

Despite these weaknesses the empirical study of character has been carried on with great vigor by many European psychologists and has given rise to a special science known as "characterology." While American and British psychologists have given up these attempts and concentrated on a more experimental approach, some Continental authors have developed classifications which have become famous enough to deserve brief notice.

One of the most famous of these systems is that of E. Kretschmer.[1] We shall not set it forth here, because the valuable elements of his work have been taken over by W. Sheldon in the classifications we studied in a previous chapter.

Eduard Spranger classifies individuals according to the values which are foremost in their life. He distinguishes six major domains of values: the theoretical, aesthetic, economic, religious, political and social values, and an equal number of types. In the pure types of his system one of these values commands the entire life of the individual. Consequently we have the following six types: (1) the theoretical type, who is in contact with reality and with other people only through his intelligence; the influence of his affective and volitional life is reduced to a minimum and disinterested knowledge is his main pursuit; (2) the economic type, who looks at everything from the point of view of its usefulness; (3) the aesthetic type, who is always looking for artistic beauty and expression; (4) the social type, who puts the stress on understanding and helping his fellow men; (5) the political type, who strives towards the full development of his personality by subordinating all other people to his own ends; and (6) the religious type, who refers whatever he knows or does to the totality of being and of reality.

Spranger emphasizes that his types are ideal types, seldom occurring in reality. In most people two or more values compete for the direction of life.[2]

---

[1] *Körperbau und Charakter,* 22d ed. (Berlin, Springer, 1955).
[2] E. Spranger, *Types of men,* trans. by P. J. W. Pigors (Halle, Niemeyer, 1928).

C. G. Jung classifies all people in two categories, the introverts and the extraverts (or extroverts). The extravert is interested in objective reality and in practical affairs; he is a realist, who pays little attention to his own mental life. He is tough-minded and pragmatic. The introvert is more interested in the interior world of his own feelings, attitudes and dreams; he has a rich affective life and he is impractical in daily life.

Both extraverts and introverts are further subdivided according to the mental function which is predominant in their lives. Jung distinguishes four functions: thought, feeling, sensation and intuition. Thought approaches reality by means of concepts and deductions; feeling evaluates it according to its pleasantness or unpleasantness; sensation observes it in a conscious and systematic way; intuition takes it in by noticing and interpreting in a vaguely conscious or unconscious way the many small cues which lead to a deeper understanding.

According to Jung most individuals possess one "superior" and one "auxiliary" function. One of the four functions is clearly predominant in an individual's life, while another function, although not as well developed as the superior function, plays a certain part in his conduct. The two other functions are undeveloped and unconscious. Thus an extravert whose superior function is thought and whose auxiliary function is intuition can be classified as an intuitively speculative extravert.

We must remember here what we have said previously about Jung's conception of the psyche as a self-regulating system. He claims that the Unconscious of an individual always develops the attitudes and functions which that individual neglects in his conscious life. Thus the Unconscious of the intuitively speculative extravert will be introverted; its superior function will be feeling (as opposed to thought) and its auxiliary function will be sensation (as opposed to intuition).[3]

[3] C. G. Jung, *Psychological Types,* trans. by H. G. Baynes (New York, Harcourt, 1926).

HEYMANS' CLASSIFICATION OF CHARACTERS

The system of characterology which, in our opinion, works best for *practical* purposes is that of Gerard Heymans. That system has recently been presented again with great skill by a famous French philosopher, René Le Senne.[4] Le Senne did not obviate the scientific weaknesses which modern psychologists attribute to Heymans' system. Notwithstanding his deep psychological intuitions, the classification remains pre-scientific.

Heymans' classification is based on a considerable number of facts, collected by means of a questionnaire and a biographical survey. The questionnaire consisted of 90 questions, referring to a great number of character traits. Heymans (in collaboration with Wiersma) sent this questionnaire to all the physicians of the Netherlands, asking them to answer it with regard to a few persons with whom they were well acquainted. Answers were received from 458 doctors, containing detailed accounts of the characters of 2,523 individuals. The biographical survey consisted in a thorough study of 110 biographies, giving plentiful information about the character of a certain number of artists, scientists, statesmen, generals, etc.

Among the many traits thus collected Heymans discovered three traits whose influence is predominant in the individual's character. He called these three traits the fundamental traits. They are emotionality, activity and secondary function.

An individual is classified as emotional or not-emotional according to the frequency and the intensity of his emotional reactions as compared with their causes. He is considered active or not-active according to the frequency and the intensity of his activity as compared with its motives.

The notion of secondary function requires more explanation. We shall make use of another term, retentivity, and we shall speak of retentive and not-retentive individuals. Every person's behavior is, at each moment, influenced partly by the present situation, partly by his past experience. There are great individual differences in the

---

[4] G. Heymans, *Einführung in die Spezielle Psychologie* (Leipzig, Barth, 1932). R. Le Senne, *Traité de Caractérologie* (Paris, Presses Universitaires de France, 1946).

relative strength of these two influences. Retentive individuals are those who are more influenced by their past experiences than by the present situation. Even when they are no longer aware of these past experiences, they continue to be guided or directed by them. On the other hand, not-retentive individuals are more influenced by what they see, hear, feel or experience here and now. When a psychic content has slipped out of their consciousness, it loses most of its influence upon their conduct.

Take two boys, Paul and John, who have both lost their mothers a few days ago. After the funeral they come back to school. Paul is not changed, he is the same cheerful, lively boy as before. When he thinks of his mother, he feels a surge of sadness in his heart; when he does not think of her, his loss does not seem to affect him. Paul is not-retentive. John, on the other hand, has changed. He has become more serious and more withdrawn. Even when he does not think of the death of his mother, that sad experience continues to weigh upon him and to affect his whole conduct. John is retentive.

This is an important distinction. It is immediately evident that retentive individuals have more unity and consistency in their lives, since the continual changes in their environment do not influence them too much. But they have some trouble in adapting themselves easily to new circumstances. Not-retentive individuals, on the other hand, show little unity in their lives, precisely because they adapt themselves so readily to every new situation. Retentivity is to character what a fly-wheel is to an engine; it makes movement smooth and even but renders sudden changes in speed difficult.

Theoretically these three fundamental traits can occur in eight different combinations. In fact, Heymans claims that the data of his questionnaire and survey show that these eight combinations really occur. He has given each of these combinations a name taken from everyday language, as shown in the following table:

not-emotional	not-active	not-retentive	AMORPHOUS
		retentive	APATHETIC
	active	not-retentive	SANGUINE
		retentive	PHLEGMATIC
emotional	not-active	not-retentive	NERVOUS
		retentive	SENTIMENTAL
	active	not-retentive	CHOLERIC
		retentive	PASSIONATE

The three fundamental traits and their eight combinations can be represented by a cube (Fig. 12). Every dimension of the cube represents a fundamental trait, and each corner stands for a character.

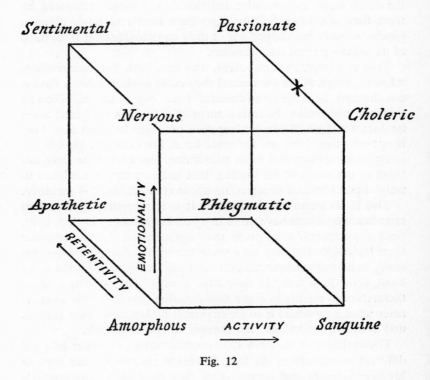

Fig. 12

This diagram makes it clear that the pure types are exceptional, that most real characters are, in various degrees, combinations of these pure types. Every point in the cube represents a possible character. Thus X represents a character which combines emotionality and activity but which is intermediate in retentivity. It is a blend of the choleric and the passionate types.

Heymans tried to show that these eight types are not mere "armchair constructions," but occur in reality. He considers a certain number of traits and finds, from his questionnaire and survey, how often such a trait occurred, say, in the nervous type, as compared with the average for the seven others. He claims that he can demonstrate in that way that there are real differences between his eight characters.

The main objection of present-day psychologists to Heymans' system is its statistical weakness. The statistical procedures with which he worked during these early years of experimental psychology are rather crude, and they did not enable him to demonstrate that the differences between his eight types are scientifically reliable. In other words: if Heymans had sent out the same questionnaire once more and obtained the same number of replies, what are the chances that the results would have been approximately the same? Because of the primitive nature of his statistical methods, he would have been unable to answer that crucial question.

Yet a sufficient number of these differences seem to be reliable, and for lack of any better system of characterology, we might use this classification, as many scientists used empirical classifications of plants and animals before their scientific classification had been established by Linnaeus.

1. The Emotional Inactive Types

The nervous and the sentimental have two striking features in common: a subjective outlook on life and irregular bursts of activity. Subjective outlook on life: Both types are emotional, so that feelings, emotions and sentiments are uppermost in their life. Furthermore, they are inactive, so that they cannot "unload" these emotions into activity, they cannot work them off. Hence, they are continually brooding over them, they "feel" their way through life, they rarely take an objective stand towards reality.

Irregular outbursts of activity: these individuals are active only under the influence of a strong emotion. Then they may show a feverish activity which they carry on for quite a time. But when the emotion fades away, the activity disappears with it. Real activity feeds on ordinary stimuli and is always present.

(1) The Nervous Type (emotional, not-active, not-retentive):

In his biographical survey Heymans discovered the following outstanding representatives of the nervous type: Lord Byron, Dostoevsky, de Musset, Edgar Allan Poe, Lawrence Sterne and Richard Steele.

Moral effort is not easy for them, theirs is a difficult character. Because they are emotional, they are carried away by every strong stimulus. The lack of activity leaves them open to many temptations. The lack of retentivity deprives them of the steadying influence of the past. Sometimes the nervous individual seems to be retentive, because he may brood for a long time over some emotion; he feeds it, he keeps it alive in his mind. But when it finally disappears it exerts no further influence on his life.

Nervous people often show strong contrasts or even contradictions in their lives. Their conduct may be entirely different from one day to the next, so that different people will make different judgments about them.

Nervous individuals are often distracted. They are rarely profound, often shrewd and keen of mind. Their judgment is absolute, but changes quickly. They are very sensitive to all bodily stimulations or stimulants, to cold and to heat, to a small quantity of coffee or alcohol. They easily worry about their health. They prefer to work during the evening or at night, rather than in the morning.

The great resources of the nervous type lie in the domain of social talents and artistic endowment. Nervous people are generally witty, they easily discover the funny aspects of a situation, they are good narrators and good actors. They can be most brilliant in society, but they will display their talents only when they are in "good form," when they are stimulated by the right environment. Otherwise they can be very dull. In his biographical survey, among the twenty individuals whom he considered as nervous, Heymans discovered thirteen artists, not a single philosopher or scientist. Nervous people lack the qualities which are required for philosophical and scientific work: exactness, power of observation, perseverance.

(2) The Sentimental Type (emotional, not-active, retentive):

Biographical survey: Charlotte Brontë, Amiel, Kierkegaard, Maine de Biran, Malebranche, Thackeray.

A sentimental individual can be singled out early in life. Sentimental children do not like to play with others, they prefer to dream, to read books, to listen to adult conversation. They come up with strange questions about profound problems.

The sentimental differs from the nervous only by the presence of a strong retentivity. That is enough, however, to hold in check the inferior tendencies, to correct the inconstancy and fickleness of the nervous type.

The judgment of the sentimental person is often biased by his emotions. He frequently shows great aptitudes for mathematics and languages. Theoretical speculation appeals to him only when it can help him feed his sentiments. Heymans found in this group several philosophers with strong religious tendencies, v.g. Kierkegaard and Malebranche.

Like the nervous, the sentimental is impulsive and irritable. More often than any other type he is gloomy, downhearted, shy and bashful. His affective life is deep, he is very serious. Moral and religious ideas have a great influence in his life; he is often fond of bold theories; he likes extreme positions, conservative or radical, strongly religious or cynical. He has a strong tendency to analyze and criticize himself. He generally prefers a simple life in the country to the busy social life of the city.

He is not used to tackling his work and carrying it out without delay. He is not clever in practical life. He has trouble making up his mind; when he has succeeded, execution remains difficult. He is honest, trustworthy, thrifty, disinterested, compassionate and ready to help others.

II. The Not-Emotional, Not-Active Types

The two negative features of these individuals have a tendency to strengthen each other. Because they are not-emotional, they do not even have the passing fits of activity which we have observed in the two previous types; because they are not-active, the few emotions they have are but weakly expressed.

Their attention, both voluntary and spontaneous, is weak and rigid; their associations are slow; they have a poorly developed intellectual life. But they adapt themselves easily to their environment, especially the amorphous type, for the simple reason that their lack of psychological backbone makes them fit every framework.

No individuals belonging to these types were discovered in the biographical survey. Le Senne claims that Louis XV was amorphous and Louis XVI apathetic.

(3) The Amorphous Type (not-emotional, not-active, not-retentive):

All their fundamental dispositions are negative; they are passive and impersonal. They go where they are pushed, they are driven and directed by the circumstances or by the people with whom they live. They borrow their ideas from their last conversation, from the last book they have read, or from the newspapers. One could almost say that they have no character.

Their interior life is poor and empty, which explains why they suffer from chronic boredom. To rid themselves of that oppressive feeling, they are liable to reach for every available pleasure.

Very few things interest them. They are not ambitious, nor concerned with political or moral questions. They do not like social intercourse, and when they have to join it, they are dull-witted and reserved. Even in danger or an emergency they stay undisturbed, and in such cases they may be more helpful than more brilliant types. Their affective life is quiet, even, often cheerful. They are tolerant and unable to get angry.

Amorphous people are often good actors. Heymans explains this as follows: having no character of their own, amorphous individuals have no trouble donning the character of somebody else.[5]

(4) The Apathetic Type (not-emotional, not-active, retentive):

Owing to their retentivity they are not as impersonal as the amorphous, and they oppose some resistance to exterior influences. But the lack of emotionality and of activity explains why their retentivity manifests itself above all in the formation of habits and routines. They are, to a great extent, the slaves of their own past. They think, feel and speak as they have always thought, felt and spoken. They may produce the impression of having a strong character, but that strength is purely negative and consists in psychic inertia.

They have few personal ideas, but they cling to these with great energy. They lack imagination, and their minds are slow-working. They are often distracted and narrow-minded; they are neither clever nor witty. Their mood is often sad and depressed. They rarely laugh. But they are quiet, not impulsive nor irritable.

They have trouble making up their minds; they hold grudges; they are taciturn, and inclined to grumbling and to miserliness.

With old age many people develop the traits of the apathetic character.

III. The Not-Emotional Active Types

Feeling and emotions do not dominate their whole lives, as with the nervous and the sentimental types. Hence they possess a more balanced character. Everything which favors activity is stressed in their thought. Their activity is not the feverish one of the nervous type in his moments of exaltation, it is steady and adaptable.

(5) The Sanguine Type (not-emotional, active, not-retentive):

[5] It does not follow, of course, that all good actors are amorphous!

Biographical survey; Francis Bacon, Lessing, Montesquieu, and Mme de Sévigné.

It may seem strange that the sanguine type is tagged as unemotional. We are accustomed to think of sanguine people as people who react strongly upon every impression and who display their emotions without much restraint. It is true that the sanguine type expresses his emotions very freely, but it does not follow that he experiences many and strong emotions. In him expression often exceeds impression.

The activity of the sanguine differs from that of the phlegmatic type because it is less steady and systematic. His lack of retentivity does not favor perseverance, and he will easily be discouraged in meeting obstacles. Not for a long time, however; soon his activity will prompt him to resume his efforts, to try other ways of reaching his end. The phlegmatic type may wear down the obstacle, the sanguine type takes a roundabout way.

The sanguine has a happy and genial character. There is something in him which reminds one of the cheerfulness and spontaneity of a child. His lack of retentivity makes him very adaptable and capable of getting along with all kinds of people. He takes life as it comes and enjoys the small pleasures it brings. No type is fonder than the sanguine of all kinds of athletic activities.

His mind is quick and alert but rather superficial. He is the man who always remembers a good joke or a fitting quotation, who is ready to make a speech or to tell a story. Owing to his activity, his practical judgment is often sound.

All these elements taken together: balanced character, easy social contacts, adaptability to new circumstances, a certain perseverance, quick and right judgment, explain why the sanguine is often a good leader, especially in circumstances where many quick decisions must be made. For long-range planning and leading the phlegmatic type is superior.

(6) The Phlegmatic Type (not-emotional, active, retentive):

Biographical survey: Buffon, Benjamin Franklin, Gibbon, Hume, Locke, John Stuart Mill, St. Thomas More.

Their most striking feature is, as their designation implies, their phlegm, their coldness. This is the result of their lack of emotionality combined with retentivity. But their activity too is quite remarkable. It is a calm, steady, regular activity. They rarely become discouraged, even before the strongest obstacles, and they cling to their purpose with unshakable tenacity. With low intellectual development this steady activity may turn into a simple routine and a worshipping of "red tape." With higher intellectual development one finds phlegmatics who devote their whole life to the pursuit of some goal—politicians, generals, businessmen who foresee to the last detail every move they will make and follow persistently the course they have mapped out.

As a rule the phlegmatic is intelligent, broadminded, personal in his judgment. He is rarely distracted; he reads much and remembers well what he has read. He is not brilliant or witty. But he is systematic, methodical, patient. He is generally better endowed for scientific than for artistic work. Among the twenty-four phlegmatics whom Heymans studied in his biographical survey, he found only four artists as against fourteen men of science.

The phlegmatic character differs from the nervous character through all its fundamental traits. Moral self-control is very difficult for the nervous, it is rather easy for the phlegmatic. However, his altruistic tendencies are poorly developed.

IV. The Emotional-Active Types

Their emotionality differs much from that of the nervous and the sentimental type. Owing to their activity, they do not brood over their emotions but convert them into activity. Their life is not dominated by their feelings but by practical considerations. Passive emotions, such as fear and sorrow, are replaced by active emotions, such as anger and love.

The activity of this group differs from that of the preceding group because it is fuller, richer, enlisting the whole personality. This is an effect of their emotionality.

(7) *The Choleric Type* (emotional, active, not-retentive):

Biographical survey: Danton, Dickens, Goethe, Mirabeau, Walter Scott.

Despite their lack of retentivity the cholerics do not lack perseverance. But their perseverance resembles that of the sanguine more than that of the phlegmatic type. They cling to their purpose because they like activity. This is especially true when they meet obstacles. The choleric enjoys a struggle and even a fight. Every occupation which opposes some kind of resistance stirs up his activity, because he considers it a challenge.

His emotionality has an active aspect. As a rule his emotions result from his activity and lead back to it. He does not pity those who are unhappy, he helps them, and if he cannot help them, he forgets them.

The cholerics' minds are easily biased by emotions, and they are better at executing orders than at issuing them.

They dislike pure science, being more interested in its practical applications. In the religious domain their faith is active, in politics they are opportunists.

They do not like to weigh the pros and the cons, but they trust their intuitive judgment, which is often right, at least in practical matters. Their tendencies show something rough and primitive. Above all they like liberty and loathe any kind of compulsion, so much so that even the social conventions may be felt as a burden. Yet frequently they do not grant to others the liberty which they claim for themselves. They like to meddle in everything and to dominate everybody. Despite its roughness this is generally a lovable type, in whom one finds many traits of a rough but unspoiled boy.

(8) The Passionate Type (emotional, active, retentive):

Biographical survey: Carlyle, Flaubert, Luther, Marat, Michelangelo, Napoleon, Pascal, Swift.

They differ from the cholerics by more unity in their lives, owing to their retentivity, and from the phlegmatics through more warmth and intensity, owing to their emotionality. Their name derives from the fact that their life is often dominated by a passion, that is by an intense and lasting tendency which commands all their activities.

Their emotionality does not show as much as that of the nervous or of the choleric, because their retentivity puts brakes on any kind of expression. Sometimes, however, they are carried away by a sudden and violent outburst of bad temper, especially when they are thwarted in their activity or when they meet petty opposition.

Their emotionality, abetted by a strong retentivity, has often an unfavorable influence upon their mind. Passionate individuals are often biased in their judgment; they have settled ideas about everything, they are clever in defending their ideas, but they seem blind to every point of view which is opposed to their own.

In the passionate type all the fundamental dispositions are positive, which explains the richness of their character. Cleverly used, this psychic wealth can produce great results. But it also frequently becomes a cause of friction between the individual and his environment. The passionate individual has trouble adjusting himself to others, and he readily clashes with his superiors or his equals, especially when he meets other strong personalities. With his subordinates and with people who oppose no resistance he is often kind and gentle. In general, however, he is admired and feared more than he is loved.

The passionate has a strong tendency to self-analysis and intro-spection. His mood is often gloomy; he is aloof, impatient, inclined to criticize more than to idealize. More often than any other type, he is ambitious.

Passionate individuals work regularly and easily become absorbed in their work. They are persevering, not easily discouraged by men or circumstances. The passions which dominate their life are more often egoistic or idealistic (ambition, religious proselytism, science) than altruistic passions. They do not care much for sport, pleasure, com-fort, social life. They sometimes feel a vague longing to get away from civilization into a more simple kind of life.

EXPERIMENTAL STUDY OF CHARACTER

When we said that no scientific classification of character is yet available, we did not mean to imply that experimental psychology has made no progress in this line. During the last quarter century psychologists have made great strides in the study of human char-acter and personality.[6] The following pages present a non-technical summary of this promising group of investigations.

METHODS

Experimental psychology uses four main methods in the study of personality.

1. The Clinical Method. This method is used in psychiatry, ab-normal psychology and clinical psychology. It starts with the study of abnormal behavior. When an individual is mentally abnormal, whether mildly (neurotics) or severely (psychotics), he presents a certain number of symptoms. Each mental illness has its own rather well-defined pattern of symptoms, which is called a syndrome. Examples of such syndromes are: mania, paranoia, hysteria. Many

---

[6] In this country the word personality is often used to designate what we have defined as "character." Therefore the title of this chapter could also be "Experimental Study of Personality."

psychiatrists and psychologists hold the view that these syndromes are but exaggerations of normal trait patterns. This view is confirmed by the fact that it is possible to line up individuals who present such a pattern in various degrees of intensity, from a clearly normal to an evidently abnormal stage. Thus a transition can be shown between the manic patient and the normal "cyclothyme," over various forms of hypomanic or cycloid personalities. All these individuals possess the following common features: liveliness in movement and expression, need of social contact, euphoria and cheerfulness, with occasional let-downs into depression. In the normal person these traits do not assume extreme forms. In the psychotic they are clearly abnormal, whereas the intermediate stages show a gradual deterioration from normal to borderline to abnormal. Psychology cannot use the microscope, which is so useful an instrument in most other sciences. But nature itself has provided cases where the workings of the mind are enlarged and available for closer study. These cases are the various neuroses and psychoses. True, many authors have serious objections to this view, which seems to regard the normal as a weaker form of the abnormal. We cannot enter into a discussion of this point here. It is enough to say that many psychologists hold that conception and that, whatever may be its theoretical value, it has in practice shed much light on some types of personality.

2. Behavior Ratings. This method is continually used in everyday life. From the words and actions of an individual we conclude that he possesses certain traits of character. Simple as this method seems to be, it is exposed to many errors. Therefore the psychologists have tried to refine it and to find the conditions required in order to make it as reliable as possible. Professor Allport mentions, among others, the following conditions: (1) The traits on which the subject is to be rated must be clearly defined. (2) The judges, those who rate the subject, must be trained in rating. (3) The judges should be invited to tell how certain they are that their rating is correct (as their certainty increases, the reliability of the ratings becomes greater). (4) The judges should be, as much as possible, of the same sex, the same nationality, the same social group, etc., as those who are to be rated (in general, the more the judges have in common with the subjects, the better they under-

stand them). (5) Care should be taken to avoid the "halo effect," which results from a tendency to rate the subject on a certain trait, not according to his real standing in this trait, but according to the general impression he makes, an impression which frequently derives from a single outstanding feature of the subject.[7]

3. Self-inventories. This method generally takes the form of a written character or personality test, in which the subject is supposed to answer a considerable number of questions referring to personality traits or to behavior connected with such traits. This method is rather easy and has been used extensively. Yet it has serious weaknesses. The subjects may not know themselves well enough to give reliable information about their own characters. They have no sufficient basis of comparison with others because of their insufficient knowledge of these others. A person cannot tell whether he worries more than the average person unless he first knows how much the average person does worry. The subject may easily cheat in such tests and try to make a good impression on the experimenter. If information is requested not about traits, but about activities which are supposed to demonstrate the existence of traits, there remains the danger that the same activity may be caused by different traits. Thus, as Allport remarks, a person may always seek a front seat at public meetings either because he is aggressive or because he is hard of hearing.

Several methods are used to eliminate these shortcomings. Purely subjective, introspective questions are avoided. Special questions are introduced which may trip a subject who tries to fake his answers. In this way the self-inventory method, if carefully used, may yield valuable information, especially in the domain of general behavior (including neurotic behavior), interests and attitudes.

4. Objective Test Measurements. In this method the subject is examined in situations which resemble those of real life (miniature life situations). His behavior is observed, and if possible measured, by others, and conclusions are drawn about the traits underlying his reactions. The most famous of these experiments are those of Hartshorne and May, in which thousands of children were examined on honesty, persistence, co-operativeness, etc. Example: in an examination the children were given an opportunity to improve

[7] *Personality*, pp. 436-447.

their marks by cheating, apparently without risk of detection, but actually with full knowledge of the experimenter.[8]

In this group we must also mention the projective techniques, as exemplified in the ink blot test of Rorschach, the Thematic Apperception Test of Murray, and many others. Used by expert investigators they may yield valuable information.

RESULTS

There are two ways in which the character of an individual may be described: we may classify him under a certain *type,* or we may enumerate the *traits* which we have discovered in him.

A type is an ideal model abstracted from a large group of individuals or personified in one single individual. Most types are continuous, that is, they possess two poles between which all the individuals of a group can be classified. Jung's famous dichotomy of Introverts-Extroverts defines a type. Some people belong clearly to one pole, they are introverts; others are extroverts (extraverts) and they belong to the other pole. Quite a number of people belong to neither extreme but occupy positions which are intermediate between the two poles.

A few types are discontinuous, they have no clearly defined opposite. They are often exemplified in a single individual. Only a few people can be subsumed under them. When we say that somebody is an "eager beaver" or a "Beau Brummell," we put him under a discontinuous type.

Traits are characteristic dispositions of an individual which make him behave in a more or less predictable way in a given situation.[9] When we know that a person is stingy, we can more or less foresee how he will react when money is involved.

Traits may be individual or common. They are individual when we consider them in the total context of a person's personality, as they are affected by all his other traits. Since each personality is unique, every trait, considered in that way, is strictly individual.

[8] H. Hartshorne and M. A. May, *Studies in Deceit* (New York, Macmillan, 1930).

[9] For the distinction between trait, habit, attitude, etc., cfr. G. W. Allport, *Personality,* pp. 290 ff.

They are common when we abstract them from their personal framework and compare them with similar traits discovered in other people.

Traits may be considered genotypically or phenotypically. A trait is considered genotypically when it is considered in relation to its origin, to its underlying causes in the person's life experience. A trait is considered phenotypically when it is considered only in its external manifestations. The first way yields individual traits, the latter common traits. Two individuals may be equally aggressive. The first one is aggressive because he is unconsciously compensating for a feeling of inferiority; the other one because he has a strong somatotonic component. The aggressivity is phenotypically the same in each case but genotypically quite different.

For scientific purposes the most important distinction is that which exists between surface traits and source traits. A clear comprehension of these terms would require considerable knowledge of statistics. We shall try to explain them without introducing statistical terms. A surface trait involves a group of traits which tend to appear together and to vary together in the behavior of many individuals. It corresponds, in the normal personality, to what a syndrome is in an abnormal personality. An example of such a surface trait, as given by Professor R. B. Cattell, is Integrity-Altruism, which contains the following trait-elements: honesty, self-control, self-denial, loyalty, fairmindedness and reliability.[10]

A source trait is the underlying factor which explains the presence of such a surface trait and the degree to which it is realized in an individual. We say "factor" rather than "cause," because experimental psychologists are not ready as yet to affirm that the source trait is a real cause. They have statistically demonstrated that source trait and surface trait vary together, but more evidence is required before a real causality can be affirmed.

One surface trait generally derives from several source traits. On the other hand, the same source trait makes its influence felt upon more than one surface trait. The number of surface traits is considerably greater than that of the source traits, and seems capable of indefinite extension. The psychologists hope to be able, sooner or later, to explain the presence and the intensity of these

[10] *Personality*, p. 37.

countless surface traits by means of a relatively small number of source traits and their mutual interaction. The following example, taken from Professor Cattell, illustrates the relation between surface traits and source traits.

Consider, for example, one of the surface traits or types[11] already mentioned—that revealed by the three positive correlations that exist among the three measures: (a) size of vocabulary, (b) arithmetical ability, (c) tactfulness in social situations. If we ask how this surface trait might have come into existence, attention turns first to the influence of innate mental capacity. Other things being equal the individual of greater general mental capacity will achieve a greater size of vocabulary, will handle arithmetical problems more capably, and will also be more clever and tactful in social situations. Some of the observed positive correlations among the three variables in the surface trait will therefore have their *source* in the fact that the performances all spring in part from a single root, namely, general mental capacity. But it also happens that these three performances are about equally the objects of educational attention, so that the individual who has longer or better schooling will tend to do better at all three of them. Consequently another part (perhaps the remaining part) of the positive intercorrelation seen in the surface trait goes back to this second source—length of education. *General mental capacity* and *amount of education experienced* may therefore be considered two source traits accounting for the observed *surface trait*.[12]

The same author explains that two individuals may have vocabularies of the same size, the same arithmetical ability and the same amount of social tactfulness—in brief, the same surface trait—although the influence of the two source traits is quite different in them. The first individual has a great mental capacity but received little formal education; the other has a lower mental capacity but had the advantage of long years of education.

Elsewhere Professor Cattell enumerates and describes the "twelve primary source traits manifested in all data."[13] These data

[11] Notice how the author equates trait and type, although he maintains the theoretical distinction between the two terms. In practice, especially when we speak of common traits or surface traits, the difference seems to be mainly one of point of view.

[12] *Personality*, p. 22.

[13] R. B. Cattell, *Description and Measurement of Personality*, pp. 475–497.

are the results obtained by applying the four methods mentioned above. This enumeration is only tentative; much more work is required before a complete and final list of the source traits can be presented.

READINGS

The books mentioned in the footnotes. Further:
Allport, *Personality,* pp. 3-23, 55-97, 286-560. Cattell, *An Introduction to Personality Study.* Harmon, *Understanding Personality,* pp. 37-77. Roback, *The Psychology of Character,* pp. 3-446.

For further reading in the field of Personality, the following books are suggested. (The books marked with an asterisk are of a more specialized and/or technical nature.) *

Arnold and Gasson, *The Human Person,* * Eysenck, *The Scientific Study of Personality.* Guilford, *Personality.* Harsh and Schrickel, *Personality: Development and Assessment.* McClelland, *Personality.* * Mowrer, *Learning Theory and Personality Dynamics.* * Murphy, *Personality: A Bio-Social Approach to Origins and Structure.* * Stern, Stein and Bloom, *Methods in Personality Assessment.*

For readings in the field of Social Psychology:
Bonner, *Social Psychology.* Britt, *Social Psychology of Modern Life.* Curtis, *Social Psychology.* Dennis and Wayne, *Current Trends in Social Psychology.* Hartley and Hartley, *Fundamentals of Social Psychology.* Herr, *How We Influence One Another.* Newcomb, *Social Psychology.* Sargent and Williamson, *Social Psychology.* Swanson, Newcomb and Hartley, *Readings in Social Psychology.* Walsh, *Facing Your Social Situation.* Young, *Social Psychology.*

For readings in the field of Abnormal Psychology:
Cavanagh and McGoldrick, *Fundamental Psychiatry.* * Cobb, *Foundations of Neuropsychiatry.* Dennis and Wayne, *Current Trends in the Relation of Psychology to Medicine.* Dorcus and Shaffer, *Textbook of Abnormal Psychology.* Landis and Bolles, *Textbook of Abnormal Psychology.* * Rose, *Mental Health and Mental Disorder.* VanderVeldt and Odenwald, *Psychiatry and Catholicism.* White, *The Abnormal Personality.*

* This bibliography was compiled with the competent help of Father J. G. Keegan, S.J., to whom we express our sincere gratitude.

Philosophical Study of Man as a Person

SECTION II

Philosophical Study of
Man as a Person

23

Man as a Person

To UNDERSTAND man as a person is no easy task. It means penetrating into the central mystery of our own being. We shall try to do it by using several approaches.

First we shall examine what traditional philosophy has to say about man as a person. Next we shall borrow from modern philosophy a few interesting data about some aspects of the human person which have been rather neglected in traditional philosophy. Finally we shall say a few words about the paradoxes of the human person.

TRADITIONAL PHILOSOPHY OF MAN AS A PERSON

Traditionally, a person is defined as an individual possessing a spiritual nature. This definition contains a genus (individual) and a specific difference (possessing a spiritual nature). We shall briefly consider both elements.

MAN AS AN INDIVIDUAL

A person is an individual being. An individual being is a being which is one in itself and distinct from all other beings. All real beings are individuals; general entities exist only in the mind. But all real beings are not individualized in the same way. In general we may say that purely spiritual beings are individualized through their form, and purely material beings through the relation of their form to quantified matter.

God is one in Himself and distinct from all other beings through the very fullness and infinity of His being. Pure spirits, or angels, are individualized through their essence, or form, which represents in each one of them a unique, intensive degree of being. The difference between two angels is not like that between two men, not even like that between two different sorts of animals, but rather like the difference between an animal and a man. It is an intelligible difference; that is, a difference which, if known at all by the human intellect, would be known without direct recourse to the senses.

Purely material beings, on the other hand, are individualized, are distinct from all other representatives of their species, not through their form (which is the same in each one of them), but through the relation of that form to quantified matter. Two oaks possess the same form, but they differ in size, shape, and color, and ultimately in that they cannot occupy the same part of space at the same moment of time. Such a difference is not intelligible to the human mind; it can be known only through a direct recourse to the senses.

Since man is both a material and a spiritual being, he must share, to a certain extent, the two modes of individualization. Inasmuch as he is a material being, he differs from all other men through the relation of his form to quantified matter. But there must also be formal individualizing features in man. It would be hard to conceive that I, as a unique, incommunicable person, should differ from other persons only through the relation of my soul to matter; that my soul, considered in itself, should be interchangeable with any other human soul.

In fact, only those beings whose form is totally immersed in matter differ from each other only through the relation of their form to matter. As soon as the form emerges from matter and becomes capable of immanent operations, as soon as we find in a being

an internal and autonomous law of assimilation, from then on arises *even in a material being, an individual feature of the formal order,* intelligible by right, even if not in fact . . . constituting an object of science—even if that object, as individual, remains always for *our* science an inaccessible limit. As one rises in the hierarchy of living beings, from plant to man, the importance of this formal element in individuation, always combined, of course, with the material element, increases, and the "intimate history," written in each living being by its accumulated immanent actions, will become more completely original.[1]

Let us consider here only the case of man. We suppose that the only difference between individual men when they begin their existence is the relation of their form to matter. But as these men go through life they accumulate all kinds of experiences (perceptions, emotions, and especially judgments and free decisions) which leave something behind in the individual. In a conscious being, and especially in a self-conscious being like man, the past is not just something which has happened and is gone forever. Something of it remains with him, grows with him, modifies him, makes him different from all other men. Not substantially, of course, but in some of his accidents. And some of these accidents are not, like those deriving from the relation to matter, perceptible by the senses; they are really intelligible, although not always for our human intelligence. Therefore we may conclude that man is individualized basically through the relation of his soul to quantified matter, secondarily through his own personal history, as written in him by his immanent actions, especially by his free decisions.

MAN AS POSSESSING A SPIRITUAL NATURE

A person is an individual possessing a spiritual nature. What do we mean by a spiritual nature? As we have explained earlier, spiritual means immaterial, whether completely immaterial, without even extrinsic dependence on matter, or incompletely, with some extrinsic dependence on matter. In the first case we have a pure spirit, in the second a spirit in matter.

A spirit exists not only in itself (it is a substance), and for itself (it is self-conscious), but also, with due dependence on God in finite spirits, by itself (it posits itself).[2] Spirit is essentially self-knowledge, self-volition, self-consciousness, self-position. It is Ego, or I.

[1] Maréchal, *PDM,* V, pp. 245-246.
[2] See J. de Finance, *Existence et Liberté,* p. 107, Note 19.

Of its nature spirit is destined to exist forever, since it possesses no potency to non-being. Hence the only way in which a spirit can cease to exist is through annihilation. But such an action would involve a change in the divine intention, introduce a time element into God's eternity. Hence it is impossible, and we must conclude that every spirit is created forever, is naturally immortal.

Spirit is open to the whole of reality. It opens up into the infinite. Its capacity is unlimited. It is in a certain way "everything." *Quodammodo omnia,* as Aquinas says again and again throughout his writings. No being is alien to the spirit, nothing lies absolutely beyond its reach. This is evident whether we consider the human intellect or the human will.

The human intellect is capable of knowing all reality. It strives continually towards the knowledge of the Infinite Reality. As soon as it knows any being, it knows it as limited, as not self-explaining, as demanding a complement of intelligibility. As soon as it finds temporary rest in the possession of any finite reality, it immediately resumes its quest for more and ever more being. Limitation, as such, offends the spirit and keeps it on the move. Only the Infinite Being can really satisfy it.

The human will too strives towards the Unlimited, the Boundless, the Perfect Good. Because of this striving, which leads it beyond any finite reality, it can never be so fascinated by a finite good that it cannot resist its allurement. The human will is free because it strives towards the All.

This is one of the most significant characteristics of the human spirit. It is made to know and love *finite* objects during its union with matter, but the dynamism which animates this knowledge and this love carries both of them irresistibly, albeit unconsciously, beyond any finite object, thus exhibiting the spirit's *infinite* capacity and yearning for truth and goodness. This power of transcending while possessing, of possessing only while transcending, of affirming the infinite in every finite affirmation, of loving the infinite in any finite love, is an essential feature of the human spirit.

In its knowledge the human spirit shares the point of view of *the* Spirit. Its point of view is absolute. As things appear to the human spirit, so they are in themselves.

This seems at first sight impossible. How can we ever know anything as it is in itself, since an object can be known only as it is known—that is, as it appears to the knower? And if an object can be known only as it appears to the knower, any change either in the object *or in the knower* will modify the knowledge.

This is quite true for our sense knowledge, and also for our everyday human knowledge, inasmuch as it involves sense knowledge. But it is not true for our purely intellectual knowledge, considered in itself. It does not apply to our knowing as spirits. A modification of our spiritual nature would only result in a greater or lesser penetration or extension of our knowledge; it would leave its absolute value unimpaired.

Nobody can really deny this. One who tries to deny it affirms it in his very denial. If you deny that the point of view of the spirit is absolute, you imply that this, your affirmation, which is an expression of your point of view as a spirit, is not absolute. It is a relative, contingent statement, which may or may not correspond to reality. Hence you are not really denying; you may be casting some doubt upon our initial statement, but you cannot really deny it. A real denial would invalidate itself.

In its free decisions the human spirit shares some of God's own creative power, whereby it assumes autonomously, without any compelling necessity from the environment, without any complete dependence on antecedents, without any co-action from God Himself, although under the steady attraction of His goodness, its attitude towards God and the world, towards others and itself, slowly shaping its own moral being during the time of its union with matter until, in its final momentous option, it freely embraces its eternal attitude towards Reality.

Spirit is essentially self-consciousness. Consciousness is the core of being. Every being is conscious, each one according to its degree (principle of proportionality). Consciousness means active self-identity.

In God, who is ESSE, self-identity is absolute; it decreases in the lower degrees, as act is combined with its opposite. Where identity is not absolute, it is combined with its opposite, that is with distinction. Every being which is not God is, in a certain sense, distinct from itself. . . . Thus the angel, as existence, is distinct from himself as essence. The corporeal being, as form, is distinct from itself as matter. These diversities will be manifested by corresponding diversities in the mode of consciousness.

In man the self-identity is not absolute, it is nothing but the unity of matter and form. Hence human consciousness will be the actuation or the exercise of that unity. It will, therefore, contain two terms: it will be composed like its object: it is a composite being which will know its composition in a composite way.

Hence in human consciousness two terms face each other; we shall call them the I-subject and the I-object. This double I is one single and the same reality, self-present and duplicated in its own eyes. The I-*subject* is the form as such. In this duality $(I = I)$, it is present to itself, but opposed to the other term, with which it constitutes one being and which is its material element. And that element is the I-*object*. —Hence the I-*subject* expresses the presence and the activity of the *form*, it is the active principle of consciousness. The I-*object* expresses the presence of the material element, it is the *term* of the activity of consciousness.[3]

Spirit is essentially active self-identity. In man this takes the form of active self-affirmation. I am I. This is the most fundamental affirmation, to which all other affirmations owe their certitude. Throughout this book we have insisted that the first principles, the fundamental affirmations of metaphysics, are virtually inborn in us. We exercise them, we live them, before we become aware of them, before we can put them into words. This is especially true for the most fundamental of these principles, the principle of identity, the first principle. It is the *concrete* first principle (I am I) which gives the *abstract* first principle (Whatever is, is) its solid existential foundation. The abstract first principle is hypothetical. It means, "If something is, it is." The concrete first principle is absolute, implied in its very denial. Nobody has shown this more clearly than Pierre Scheuer in the following passage:

In the I *the real and the ideal meet.* Being in itself is the real; being as it must be according to the exigencies of thought, being as intelligible, is the ideal. Therefore, taken in both senses, being is identical with itself. That is the import of the principle of identity whose two terms are the real and the intelligible. But the I is precisely the active

[3] Scheuer, "Deux Textes Inédits," in *Nouvelle Revue Théologique,* 79 (1957), pp. 816-817.

identity: it is the point where the real and the ideal meet; it is the real thinking itself; it is a fact or an entity which is an idea; it is being present to itself; it is the intelligible.

Every certitude is but a sharing of the first certitude by which an I is certain of being I. No identification of the real and the intelligible, hence no thinking, could take place, if the first concrete identity were not posited. . . . Hence we can offer no other demonstration for our fundamental principle than to say that there exists a fact which thinks itself; that this fact is I; that, when I use the word "being," I do nothing but transpose this apprehension to other things; finally, that, if being is not conceived through homology with the presence of the I to the I, it has no more content, no meaning; it is just a collection of letters. . . .

Therefore human knowledge is not a system of abstract truths which unfold before the mind, which are only an object before the subject and exterior to the subject; it is a totality to which the subject itself belongs. Our existence is a part of the totality of things; inasmuch as this totality takes the form of the conscious subject, we say that it is known. . . .

Metaphysics cannot be a system of truths which are absolutely independent of the existence of the subject which possesses them. Such a metaphysics would be pure Idealism. . . . The truth lies neither in Idealism alone, nor in Realism, but in a conciliation of the two: the knowledge of the empirical fact must be identical with that of the necessary order; and on the other hand, a concrete case must likewise be an idea; this conciliation exists only in the I and is possible only if the I is made the concrete principle of all knowledge. Thus human knowledge resembles divine knowledge. God's knowledge is empirical in the most radical meaning of this word; it is entirely contained in the apprehension of the fact of the divine existence. It is absolutely idealistic, because it is the intuition of the first idea and of the supreme necessity. God is the fact which is identical with the idea; and no knowledge, at any degree, is possible except in so far as this synthesis is reproduced.[4]

MODERN PHILOSOPHY OF MAN AS A PERSON

The text of Fr. Scheuer, with its emphasis on the subject, will serve as a point of transition between what traditional philosophy

[4] *Ibid.*, pp. 818-819.

tells us about man and what we can learn about the human person from modern philosophy. Traditional philosophy treated man primarily as an object,[5] the highest of all material objects, the peak of material creation, but an object all the same. It emphasized human *nature* more than the human person. Many modern philosophers, on the other hand, including those who follow the Scholastic tradition, assert that man, although he is an object *also,* is primarily a subject. They place greater stress on the *person* than on the nature.

We shall understand the human person better by considering briefly what these philosophers tell us about (1) man as a subject; (2) man as an embodied subject; (3) man as a subject among subjects.

MAN AS A SUBJECT

When we speak of man as an object, we do not simply mean man as an object of knowledge or of study. That he is such an object is self-evident; otherwise nothing whatsoever could be said concerning him. By man as an object is meant, more precisely, man considered from the outside, as an individual belonging to a certain species; in a way in which he can be known by everybody; considered only with respect to that which is common to all representatives of his species. Man as an object has a definition which contains a genus (animal) and a specific difference (rational). Likewise the person as an object can be defined: it is an individual possessing a spiritual nature. We know man and the person objectively by means of universal concepts. When we consider them in that way, we disregard the fact that man speaks of himself as I. Man or the person considered as an object is never I, but only He (the person) or It (the human nature).

Man as a subject is not He or It, but I. Here man is no longer considered as a thing or as an object, but as a Self. "I" is not a universal concept, it cannot be defined. "I" is a singular; yet, al-

[5] It is an error to claim that Scholastic philosophy never considers man as a subject. In the study of man's higher functions, especially his freedom and his conscience, the subjective aspect of man's nature is not overlooked. In general, however, the approach remains objective.

though it involves a material component, it is, unlike the other material singulars, an intelligible singular. The purely material singulars of our everyday experience can be known only through sense perception, they can only be denoted, pointed to, "this oak here, that cow there." I know myself in a much more intimate way, not merely by a sense perception, by a concept or a judgment, but as the subject of all my perceptions, my concepts and my judgments, as the source of all my conscious activities. The fact that I know myself as the subject or the source of all my conscious activities explains why, although I know myself very intimately, this knowledge can never be exhaustive.

Attainable precisely as source, the subject transcends by its very abundance any revelation of itself in a particular activity and therefore is never equalled by the knowledge had of it. Attainable, on the other hand, only as a source, inseparable from the concrete activity which issues from it and of which it is experienced as the unique responsible origin, the subject as such is grasped only indirectly (*in actu exercito*) and remains in itself ineffable. . . . Even as I reflect upon myself, I am aware of the distinction between the "myself" about whom I am thinking and the "myself" who thinks; aware too of the inadequacy of the former as a conceptual expression of the latter.[6]

MAN AS AN EMBODIED SUBJECT

This important aspect of the human person has been studied especially by the phenomenologists. The phenomenological method is deceptively simple, and because of its simplicity, rather difficult to employ. The phenomenologist tries to describe reality as it appears to our naive, spontaneous, untutored gaze, without any attempt at interpretation, explanation or demonstration. He endeavors to describe what is given, simply as it is given. No effort is made to find out what underlies the appearances, what accounts for the present data. We are so much in the habit of seeing and understanding whatever we examine in function of previously ac-

[6] R. O. Johann, S. J., "Subjectivity," in *The Review of Metaphysics,* 12 (1958), pp. 206-7.

quired knowledge, and looking for the underlying causes of phenomena, that such a spontaneous, unbiased, naive outlook is
difficult to maintain. Yet that is the kind of approach to reality
which phenomenology demands.[7] It is immediately obvious why
phenomenology as a philosophy cannot lead us far, since it excludes God, the soul—in fact, all realities which we know only
through reasoning from their effects. But as a method phenomenology may be very useful, and we shall employ it here only as
such, not binding ourselves to refrain from eventual comments
which extend beyond its proper sphere.

I refer to myself in a variety of contexts.[8] I say, for instance:
"I wash myself, I weigh myself, I examine myself in the mirror, I
try to improve myself, I know myself." In each of these expressions the subject is the same. The object also seems to remain the
same throughout; however, when our references become more
specific, we note that the objects are different. "I wash my face,
I weigh my body, I examine my appearance, I try to improve my
character, I know myself." Nevertheless, although the subject uses
different organs or faculties in performing these actions, we do
not say, "My hands wash my face, my eyes examine my appearance," though we might say, "I wash my face with my hands, I
examine my appearance with my eyes." From this Professor Strasser concludes: "I am a unity insofar as I perform an act, and I am
a plurality insofar as these acts are exercised upon myself."[9]

Yet, although all these objects of my actions are different, they
all belong to me; they all *are,* to a certain extent, I. I refer to *my*
face, *my* body, *my* appearance. All these actions originate in me
and terminate in me. Yet they are not entirely in me; they involve
something which is not strictly I. This is evident from the fact
that they meet with some resistance—I tire of moving my arm—

[7] For more information about phenomenology, see Quentin Lauer, S. J.,
The Triumph of Subjectivity.
[8] The following data about man's animated corporeity are taken from
S. Strasser, *The Soul in Metaphysical and Empirical Psychology* (Pittsburgh,
Duquesne University Press, 1957), henceforward designated as *The Soul.*
Many useful data about the same topic are to be found in the works of
Gabriel Marcel.
[9] *The Soul,* p. 84.

and also from the fact that they do not succeed as completely as I want them to—I cannot examine myself entirely; self-improvement and self-knowledge are difficult and always incomplete.

I perform these actions upon myself; yet the performing I and the I on which these actions are performed are not quite the same reality; otherwise there would be no resistance and no difficulty. There is in me, besides the performing, originating I, besides the I as subject, something which is not entirely I, some not-I. But every material not-I belongs to the world, is part of the world. Hence part of me is both I and the world. That is my body. Through my body I am part of the material world, and the material world is part of me.

We can express this in another way. That in me on which the actions are performed (my face, my appearance, my character) is not I as subject. They are I as object: they are objects in me. Yet those objects differ completely from objects such as money, houses and the like in that they are objects for something in me, not objects for me in my totality. If known by others, they are seen as parts of me, not as objects for me. Professor Strasser calls them "quasi-objects."

Quasi-objects are things which we both have and are, to use the distinction of Gabriel Marcel. There are certain things which I am, others which I have, others still which in a certain sense I am, and in another sense I have. I am a person, I have a dog. But what about my body? Shall I say, "I have my body" or "I am my body"? I must say both, I must correct one statement by means of the other.

At first glance it seems as if I could say, "I have a body." But, as Gabriel Marcel explains, if we are to be exact, we should say, "I have whatever I have because of my body."[10] Having a body is the prerequisite, the indispensable condition, of all real having. When I have something, I try to establish between that thing and me the same kind of intimacy which exists between my body and me. Since my body itself is for me a condition of all "having," I cannot truthfully say that I have my body.

Why, then, should I not say that I am my body? This formula

[10] *Etre et Avoir* (1935), p. 119.

is incorrect if the intention is to identify my whole being with my body. It is correct if it is taken as meaning that I am also my body.

I appear to myself as a concentration at several distinct levels; there is the world all around me, with its beings and its things which constitute my situation and the aim of my intentions; there is my body, which makes it possible for me to exist in that world, to be influenced by it and to act upon it; there is my consciousness, which focusses everything and from which radiates my will. At different levels I am all these things. Furthermore, these different spheres, material, biological, spiritual, are not placed next to each other, they are unified and ever more concentrated. I am my body, to be sure, *but I am not only my body*.[11]

There is a gradual transition between what I merely have and what I merely am. Some of my quasi-objects lie on the surface of my being; I have them more than I am they—for instance, my hair, my fingernails. Others are very near the core of my being; I am they more than I have them—for instance, my feelings, my imagination and my memory. Between these extremes lie such quasi-objects as my heart, my eyes, my face, etc.

My body is the reality which I have and am. Better, it is the totality of all realities which I do not have in the absolute sense, because I am they, and those which I am not absolutely because I have them.[12]

My body is the extension of my "originating" ego in the direction of the "world." It is the bridge which connects the ego with "worldly" things and beings. It is the continuation of my subjectivity in the realm of the objectivisable.[13]

All this implies, of course, that there is in me something absolutely central, which I do not have, which I only am. It is that which has all the rest and is not itself had; which knows everything in me and is not itself known (at least not as an object or quasi-object). For if it were had, by what would it be had? If known, by what would it be known? It is that in me for which the

[11] Troisfontaines, "*Je ne meurs pas. . . .*", p. 63.
[12] *The Soul*, p. 100.
[13] *Ibid.*, p. 101.

quasi-objects are quasi-objects. It is my Ego, my soul with its intellect and will, my spiritual self, my consciousness, my originating I.

It is difficult to apprehend this without falling into Cartesian dualism. Almost unavoidably, we imagine the spiritual I dwelling in the innermost recesses of our material body or subtly permeating all its parts. We must keep reminding ourselves that without the soul the body is nothing. The body is continually held in being by the soul. On the other hand, if we try to think of the spiritual I as separate from the living body, we are imagining something which does not exist. I am continuously embodying myself. Embodiment, or incarnation, is not something which happened to me once, when the soul slipped into the body;[14] it is coextensive in time with my existence in the world. The way I exist is: embodying myself. I am a spirit continuously secreting a shell of corporeity; but it is a living shell, in which and through which this spirit inserts itself into the world of matter, undergoes its influences and acts upon it. From a certain point of view my soul is nothing but this living shell of corporeity, exhausts itself entirely in its production (i.e., my soul as substantial form); and in that sense I may say that I am my body. From another point of view my soul transcends the body, without which it cannot exist in the world. The comparison with the shell must not be carried too far. A shell is something solid and subsistent, which continues to exist after the animal has died. Better, then, to compare the body to the glow of a lighted bulb. That glow is not the same thing as the bulb; yet the lighted bulb cannot exist without it, and it cannot exist without the bulb, by which it is continually kept in existence. So our soul continually surrounds itself with the glow of corporeity; only thus can it exist and act in this world.

We have said that the originating I knows everything and is not itself known. At least not as an object or quasi-object. How then do we know it? It seems impossible for us ever to know it, since to be known means to be an object, and the most characteristic feature of the originating I is that it is never an object, always a subject. If it is known, by what is it known? By another, deeper I?

[14] *Ibid.*, p. 148.

And how, then, do we know about this fundamental I? On the other hand, it seems evident that we must have some knowledge of the originating I, since we speak of it. Even Kant, who claimed that it is unknowable, purely problematical, must have known it to the extent of being able to define it as unknowable, problematical.

We have met that problem before, and we answer it as we did then. The originating I knows itself not directly but indirectly; neither as an object nor as a subject, but as an activity. It knows itself knowing or willing. When it knows material objects, it is aware that it knows these objects; when it chooses something, it is conscious of choosing. If there were no objects to be known or chosen, it would never know or choose; it would never know itself. It is evident, therefore, that the I knows itself only in and through the body, since every instance of direct knowledge or volition involves the body. The body reveals the soul to itself, but this revelation is imperfect, as much remains hidden as is revealed. A pure spirit is entirely transparent to itself, possesses an intuitive knowledge of its own nature. A spirit in matter does not. The body makes it impossible for the human soul ever to gaze directly upon its own essence, at least as long as soul and body are united. The soul can become aware only of its own activities, but it is aware of them *as its own*. Thus the body is for the soul both a means of expression and a veil.[15]

MAN AS A SUBJECT AMONG SUBJECTS

The human person lives with other persons. From the very first moment of his life, the child is as much a part of a human as of a material world. Without the material aid provided by his human environment, the child would not be able to survive physically; without the intellectual stimulation continually emanating from that environment, his spiritual powers would remain undeveloped. Biological evolution may be continuing in the world of plants and animals. In the world of men it has been replaced by cultural evolution, which proceeds at a much faster pace, advancing more

[15] Mouroux, *The Meaning of Man,* chs. 3 and 4.

in a century than biological evolution did in a million years. Imagine what man would be—materially, intellectually and morally—if there were no education, if every individual had to start anew and discover for himself all the knowledge and the skills he would need. Cultural evolution and education are essentially inter-subjective.

We must admit that this aspect of the human person has been neglected in Scholastic psychology. Much attention is paid to it in ethics, but in psychology it is hardly ever mentioned. One of the reasons for this shortcoming seems to be—strange as this may sound—that it is not easy, in the traditional framework, strictly to demonstrate that other human beings exist. We see their bodies and their movements, we hear their words. But how do we know that, underlying all this, there is a consciousness, an intellect and a will, an Ego like our own? The usual answer to this question is: we know it through analogy. We are aware of our own consciousness and of the fact that it expresses itself in certain movements and sounds. Hence, when we see or hear similar movements or sounds elsewhere in space, we implicitly conclude, through analogy, that there must be other conscious centers, other Egos, other human persons.

But this explanation not only sounds very artificial, it is also obviously insufficient to explain some well-known facts. One has only to watch a baby smiling back at his mother to realize that the baby is aware of his mother as a human being long before any reasoning by analogy is possible.

The explanation which we reject smacks of Cartesian dualism. It supposes that human consciousness is hidden in the human body like a man in a tent; that it lies behind the muscular contractions which express it to the outside world. We should remember that man is one being, that his soul permeates everything in him and can thus be said to be visible in the smile of his face and audible in the sound of his voice.

We can perceive the others as mere objects in nature, v.g. when they obstruct our view or when we bump into them. But we can also discover the other as a person, as an autonomous center of consciousness, as another I, as a Thou.

The other, as a person, is known only indirectly, when I speak to him, or listen to him, or smile at him, or use any other kind of sign to get into touch with him. Hence the way of knowing the other person as such always assumes the form of a "dialogue," supposes that he is a "you" for me.

To seek to know the "you" apart from the activity of dialogue is immediately to change him into a "he," to make him an object at least to this extent, that he becomes for us a mere individual instance of certain abstract determinations with his very selfhood reduced to a characteristic common to all men.[16]

There can be no doubt that the intersubjective relations are of the utmost importance in the life of the human person. I cannot develop without the many "you's" all around me; I am stunted in my development unless I turn consciously to the infinite Thou towards whom my intellect and my will keep striving preconsciously. It is to be expected that this intersubjective aspect of human life will receive an increasing share of attention as philosophy advances in the knowledge of human nature in its concrete condition.

THE PARADOXES OF THE HUMAN PERSON

Man is a spirit in matter, he is spirit and body. This strange combination produces tensions in man and explains what Mouroux calls the paradoxes of the human person.

1. As a body man is subject to all the laws of matter, he is in space and time, he is divided from all other beings, and although he is a unified totality, his unity is not perfect but comprises many elements which are often at war with each other. As a spirit man is above space and time, perfectly present to himself, capable of assimilating the rest of the universe and making it one with himself.

And yet this spirit and this body are one being. That is the first paradox of the human person: he is the unity of this spirit and this body. . . . And therefore, with and in the body, [the spirit] enters into space and time, it becomes subject to all the variations of the

[16] Johann, *op. cit.*, p. 207.

appetitive feelings, it acquires a whole biological, psychological and social individuality—things which for a pure spirit would have no meaning. But it becomes the act of a body in the only way in which a spirit can do so—that is to say while still remaining spirit, and so knowing, surpassing, and infinitely transcending its body. At his pure point the person surpasses and escapes all definite proportion with the body, so dominating it as to remain in himself immaterial, intemporal, breathing his own native air, and, so to speak, infinite with respect to it. The person is thus a spirit at once immersed and emergent, immanent in the body and yet transcendent.[17]

2. The human person is at once subsistent and open. Subsistent, that is, existing in himself and for himself, closed upon himself, being himself and nothing but himself, unable to become anything else. The person is a little self-contained island in the universality of being, an autonomous realm ruling itself, into which no created being can ever penetrate. Every human being is an inviolable mystery, for his essential core, his self-consciousness, can never be shared by anybody.

Yet the same human person is open in two directions, vertically and horizontally. Vertically he is open to God, from whom he has received his being, from whom he continues to receive it at every moment, for the person is forever the term of a creative activity of the First Cause. He is open horizontally to other men, because he is an individual in a species, sharing the same human nature with all the others in his species. When God creates a material species, what He intends is the species, not the individuals. The individuals are there for the species, they are means subordinated to the end, which is the species. Inasmuch as man is a material being, an animal, the same applies to him. He is there for the human species, a link in it, a moment of it, an aspect of its indefinite variety.

But man is not a purely material being, he is a spirit. And as a spirit he cannot be a means but only an end, he cannot be a link but only a totality, a center on which everything converges.

This brings us to the essential paradox of the person considered in relation to humanity at large. In so far as he is a spirit informing a body, he is drawn towards the conditions of material substance; he is

[17] Mouroux, *op. cit.*, pp. 116-117.

a member of the species and exists for the sake of the species. In so far as he is a spirit, transcending the body, he shares the condition of the spiritual creature; he is marked by direct relation to God, and surpasses a species made for his sake. He is defined on the one side by his multiple ties with, and integration in, the species; and on the other, by his simplicity and capacity for interiorization. He is at once a member and a whole, an eccentric point and a centre. He is a living tension between himself and the whole, and neither can come to fulfilment save *in* the other and *by* the other.[18]

3. The person is existent and yet to be achieved. The person is existent, he is a substance existing in and for and by himself, a permanent principle of bodily, sensory and rational activities. But the person is not existent as something immutable, something which is complete from the very beginning.

We do not speak here of the bodily and psychological growth of the person. These are not specifically characteristic of the person, since we find them also in animals. And since that kind of development is not free, we can say that it is given from the beginning, at least virtually, in the environment and the circumstances in which the individual develops. We mean the free moral development, by means of which the person decides for himself and by himself what he shall be, how he shall act, in what direction he shall develop. We mean the free decisions and free actions which nobody can force upon the person and whose sovereign independence God Himself respects. God calls the person, He draws his intellect and his will to Him, but He does not force anybody to accept the call and to yield to the attraction. Yet the way in which the person responds to this attraction decides the meaning of his life, his real value, his eternal destiny.

In that sense the person, although existent, must achieve himself. He has no more important task on this earth than this free activity by which, in a certain sense, he makes himself.

Thus man is always a call and a response intermingled, or better, the embrace of call and response. He cannot choose but respond, but he chooses his response. Sometimes he welcomes the call, cleaves to it with all his might, and so closely that he seems to make it one with

[18] *Ibid.*, pp. 129-130.

himself: a pure and joyous response coinciding with an ever more and more potent and triumphant call. Sometimes he rejects the call, shuts his ears to it deliberately, and this refusal invests the call itself with a destructive power, a force of negation that obstructs his deepest impulse, divides, disaggregates, and prepares to torture. Sometimes a man offers himself and turns away, gives and takes back. . . . The inexorable embrace of this call and this response constitutes the whole drama of human vocation, and indeed of the person himself: an unending drama which has always a meaning—however mysterious—at any given moment, but is always ready to take on another. It is indeed a terrible choice whereby a man is to invest himself with his own meaning, his own validity, and if not exactly his own being pure and simple, at least, with his moral and spiritual being, his destiny to election or damnation. A terrible wrestle between divine love and human liberty, in which God Himself is not assured of victory.[19]

CONCLUSION

Real democracy is based on the inalienable rights of man. These rights are not conferred upon man by the State, and they cannot be withdrawn by the State. They are not based upon some covenant by which men would pledge themselves to respect each other's rights. They are not even bestowed by God upon man above and beyond man's nature. They are given by God to man in and with his nature, they are inseparable from this nature.

Man has inalienable rights, because he is a sovereign being, an end in himself, never merely a means; because he is a spirit, albeit in matter, because the core of his being is self-consciousness, self-possession and self-position.

True, man is subordinated to God, but not merely as a means. God's purpose in creating man is fully achieved when man perfectly fulfills his own destiny and obtains perfect happiness. God's design concerning man coincides with man's own real end. God's glory, which is the end of His creative activity, is perfectly realized when the person reaches his own supreme destiny which, in the present supernaturalized order of creation, consists in the beatifying intuition of the Divine Essence.

[19] *Ibid.*, pp. 131-132.

READINGS

St. Thomas Aquinas, *Summa contra Gentiles*, III, 37-40, 47, 48, 51-54, 61. Gilson, *The Spirit of Mediaeval Philosophy*, pp. 189-208. Marc, *Psychologie Réflexive*, Vol. II, pp. 269-290, 377-401. Maritain, *Scholasticism and Politics*, pp. 45-70. Mersch, *The Theology of the Mystical Body*, pp. 96-128. Mouroux, *The Meaning of Man*, pp. 115-142, 267-279. Sheed, *Theology and Sanity*, pp. 121-139, 320-329. Sheed, *Society and Sanity*, pp. 19-78. Strasser, *The Soul in Metaphysical and Empirical Psychology*.

APPENDIX

APPENDIX
Theology and Psychology

IN BEHALF of the Catholic student we shall discuss in this Appendix some of the theological problems raised by the philosophical doctrines presented in this book. The first and most important of these problems refers to evolution, especially as applied to the body of man.

THEOLOGY AND EVOLUTION

For Catholics (and for many believers in the inspired word of God) the theory of evolution, especially as extended to man's body, gives rise to a certain number of problems, because some of the statements of that theory seem to be in conflict with the data of Revelation, or with the teachings of the Church. In the following pages we shall try (1) to show that there is no real conflict between the certain facts of Science (as opposed to some of its speculations) and the certain teachings of Revelation and of Theology; (2) to point out that nevertheless some doubts and obscurities are involved which will make the Catholic scientist and philosopher prudent in this matter; (3) to give the latest authoritative directions of the Church about the Catholic position on evolution, as gathered from the encyclical *Humani Generis*.

In order to achieve our purpose, we shall briefly confront the hypothesis of evolution with the three sources of Catholic doctrine: Scripture, Tradition and the teaching of the Church.[1]

[1] The student will find an excellent, up-to-date treatment of this whole problem in C. Vollert, "Evolution and the Bible," in *Symposium on Evolution* (Pittsburgh, Duquesne University, 1959), pp. 83-119.

EVOLUTION AND SCRIPTURE

The origin of all things is explained by the Bible in the two first chapters of the book of Genesis. It is explained twice, in two parallel texts which, according to most Bible scholars, had been transmitted independently of each other before being put together by the inspired author of the Bible. The second chapter of Genesis is an older form, written in a popular vein and containing a certain number of anthropomorphisms. The first chapter seems to be more recent and to correspond to a higher stage of intellectual development. It contains no anthropomorphisms.

Are all the statements of these two first chapters to be accepted literally? Who is to answer that question? For a Catholic there can be no doubt about this: the Church herself, who has been appointed by God the official interpreter of the inspired writings.

The Church exercises her guidance in several ways. One of them is through the Biblical Commission. More than fifty years ago that Commission had already declared that it is not necessary to take all the words and phrases which occur in the aforesaid chapters always in their proper meaning, that we must not look for scientific exactitude of language in these chapters.

On the other hand, the Commission insisted that the literal historical sense cannot be called in doubt regarding certain facts, narrated in the same chapters, which touch the foundations of the Christian religion—such, for instance, as the creation of all things by God in the beginning of time; the peculiar creation of man; the formation of the first woman from the first man; the unity of the human race; the original happiness of our first parents in the state of justice, integrity and immortality.

There is no doubt that certain difficulties may occur when we try to reconcile these statements of the Biblical Commission and some aspects of the hypothesis of evolution. But these difficulties do not seem to be insuperable,[2] as appears from the following considerations:

[2] Especially when we are told that "these decrees do not close the door to further study, as was pointed out by J. M. Vosté, secretary of the Biblical Commission, in a letter to Cardinal Suhard of Paris in 1948." Vollert, *op. cit.*, p. 102.

1. The Commission insists upon "the peculiar creation of man." Some authors hold that it is enough to admit the peculiar creation of the human soul. Others claim that the human body too is included in the statement.

We have explained previously that the soul of man is certainly created by God, and that since the human body becomes human only through the infusion of a human soul, the body also comes from the divine hands. Hence this point presents no difficulties.

2. The formation of the first woman out of the first man. If we had to understand this as referring to a material or instrumental causality of Adam's body upon Eve's, it would be a serious difficulty in the path of the Catholic evolutionist. However, it seems to be sufficient to admit an exemplary causality of the former's body upon the latter's, in which case the difficulty disappears. The encyclical *Humani Generis* does not mention this point.

3. The unity of the human race. Some non-Catholic evolutionists hold that the human race is descended from many original human couples, each one of which would have evolved from animal stock. This hypothesis is known as the hypothesis of polygenism. Against it the Biblical Commission instructs us to hold the view that all men are descended from only one original couple (monogenism). This point is of great importance for Catholic doctrine, which teaches that all men have inherited original sin from the first parents. It has again been explicitly affirmed by the encyclical *Humani Generis*.

The Catholic evolutionist sees no great difficulty here. He holds that the transition from animal to man demands a special divine intervention, the creation and the infusion of a human soul into an animal organism. There is no difficulty in admitting that God infused a human soul into only *one* original human couple.

4. The original happiness of our first parents in a state of justice, integrity and immortality. The Catholic Church teaches that our first parents had been raised to the supernatural order, that they possessed sanctifying grace, that they were immune from concupiscence and endowed with immortality, not only for their souls but also for their bodies. From these truths about which there cannot be the slightest doubt, some conclusions have been drawn which are not so certain: that our first parents possessed the in-

fused science of all things in nature, that they lived a life of very great happiness, that they were perfect specimens not only of supernatural and moral but also of physical beauty.

The picture which has resulted from all this in Catholic consciousness is in sharp contrast with the picture drawn by paleontology, which shows the first human beings as hardly distinguishable from the animals from which they are supposed to have evolved.

How can these divergent views ever be reconciled? Several ways have been suggested. We mention only two of them:

1. Without modifying any of the dogmas or of the truths which belong to the deposit of faith, the conception of the primitive state of man should be slightly revised. The supernatural state in which man lived is not incompatible with a low degree of physical or of mental development. A very high knowledge of God and of morality, a perfect self-control, may go together with a low cultural development. As Father Mersch puts it, "These gifts did not in any way transport mankind to a region of fairy tales. Humanity thus described was real and concrete, and was not necessarily at variance with the human origins which paleontology and prehistory are able dimly to discern."[3]

2. The infusion of the spiritual soul, of sanctifying grace and of the preternatural gifts had their repercussion upon the physical features and the mental developmenet of our first parents, who may have been the ideal types which Christian tradition has always pictured. The loss of sanctifying grace and of the preternatural gifts has been accompanied by a physical and mental degeneration, without, however, impairing the essential nature of man. The fossils which paleontology has discovered are either fossils of pre-human beings or of human beings who may have degenerated after the Fall.[4] The curve of evolution would have shown a sudden

[3] Mersch, *The Theology of the Mystical Body*, p. 143. See also C. S. Lewis, *The Problem of Pain*, pp. 60 ff.

[4] Or, as some hold, of pre-Adamites—that is, of real human beings who existed before Adam and were totally extinct when Adam was created. This hypothesis is not excluded by *Humani Generis*, which tells us: "No Catholic can hold that *after Adam* there existed on this earth true men who did not take their origin through natural generation from him as from the first parent of all." (Our italics.)

tremendous upsurge at the moment of the infusion of the human soul, of sanctifying grace and of the preternatural gifts, and would have shown a sudden or a gradual drop after the Fall. That drop, however, would not have brought the curve as low as it was before the creation of the soul, since the soul remained human and real humanity had started.

EVOLUTION AND TRADITION

It is impossible in this work to study in detail the writings of the Fathers of the Church on the origin of humanity. The interested student is referred to the book of Fr. Messenger mentioned in the Readings and to the article of Msgr. Amann, cited below. We shall simply translate the conclusion of the article of Msgr. Amann:

The upshot is at least that all the Fathers have not felt themselves obliged to interpret literally the texts of Genesis which refer either to the creation of animal or plant species or to the apparition of man. The most philosophically minded among them have not hesitated to bend, with more or less violence, the sacred narration to their philosophico-scientific conceptions. It would be a manifest abuse to try to find in the explanations of the boldest among them a proof in favor of evolutionism; the least we can say is that they give us an example of the great freedom which has always been the rule in the interpretation of the Bible outside of the questions of a religious or moral nature. At any rate, we do not find in the Patristic tradition this unanimity of interpretation which alone would lend an absolute and traditional value to the teachings of the doctors of the past.[5]

EVOLUTION AND THE TEACHING OF THE THEOLOGIANS

We have mentioned the official teaching of the Church on this problem in connection with Scripture. But there is another kind of teaching in the Church which deserves our attention, the teaching of her theologians.

[5] E. Amman, "Transformisme," *Dictionnaire de Théologie Catholique,* Fasc. CXLI, Col. 1388 (Paris, Letouzey et Ané, 1946). (Translated.)

When the hypothesis of evolution was first presented, the theologians, almost unanimously, rejected it. This wholesale rejection can easily be explained by historical reasons. Most of the early evolutionists were materialists, for whom the theory of evolution meant the definite vindication of their conception, the proof that matter and chance alone could explain the universe and that there was no need of a Creator.

Is it surprising then that the official defenders of religious truth wholeheartedly opposed a theory which proffered such claims, and that in their zeal to defend that truth, they went even farther than necessary or than advisable? This hostile attitude was shared by most non-Catholic theologians.

Slowly, however, a great number of evolutionists discovered that matter and chance alone could not explain everything and that the great problems of man's nature and origin remained as mysterious as ever. They toned down their anti-religious claims. On the other hand, the Catholic theologians started to make a few necessary distinctions and some of them at least took a more favorable attitude towards the hypothesis of evolution.

In fact most theologians had long ago given up a too literal interpretation of the two first chapters of Genesis. They had noticed the serious difficulties arising from such an interpretation. Thus God is said to have created light on the first day and the sun on the fourth day. He is shown creating the firmament, that is the solid vault of heaven which, according to the ancient Hebrews, extended above the earth. Here was obviously one of these instances where, as the Biblical Commission would teach, reason forbids the adoption of the strict sense and where the sacred author uses a notion conformable to the ordinary language of those times.

The theologians had also noticed long ago that the Bible often omits to mention the secondary causes where they are most certainly at work:

If it rains, it is God who rains from the height of heaven. It is God who sends the wind, who causes the snow to fall like tufts of wool, who scatters hoar frost like ashes, who, when it hails, casts forth ice in tiny fragments, and it is likewise God who sends the intolerable cold of winter. Then, at His command and as a result of His breath, ice and snow melt, and the waters begin again to flow. It is God who forms the child in the womb of his mother from its very first beginning to the complete organization of its body, and it is God again who draws it forth from its mother's womb and brings it to the light of day. . . .[6]

All this is, of course, perfectly true. Since God is the first and universal cause, it is really He who performs all these actions. But nobody denies that He uses secondary causes in performing them.

While the theologians were pondering these facts, the data of paleontology kept accumulating, new fossils were discovered, the old conception of the earth as about 6,000 years old had to be given up. Under the influence of these developments some theologians were induced to swing from one extreme to another. They claimed that not only was moderate evolution not opposed to the teaching of the Bible, it was actually taught by the Bible. The six days of Genesis were interpreted as the geological ages of paleontology, and efforts were made to show that the archeozoic, the paleozoic and the other eras of paleontology corresponded to the "days" of the Bible.

Furthermore it was pointed out that the sacred author does not say that God created the plants and the animals, but that He ordered the earth or the sea to bring them forth. (Genesis I, 11, 12, 20.) Here is an explicit mention of the action of the secondary causes in the production of living beings. Moreover, a comparison of verses 20 and 21 shows that, even where the Bible speaks of creation, the secondary causes are not necessarily excluded.

This attempt to find scientific data about the origin of life in the Bible is known as Concordism. Concordism is no longer held nowadays by the best Catholic theologians. They insist upon the fact, emphasized by the Biblical Commission, that it was not the intention of the sacred writer to teach the complete order of creation in a scientific manner, but rather to give to his countrymen a popular notion, according to the ordinary language of these times and adapted to their opinions and intelligence.

Therefore quite a number of outstanding theologians hold today

[6] H. de Dorlodot, *Darwinism and Catholic Thought* (New York, Benziger, 1922), pp. 43-44.

that the Bible is not opposed to the hypothesis of evolution, but that it does not teach that hypothesis either. The Bible is not a textbook of paleontology. The first chapters of Genesis are really historical; they tell us of events which are real matters of fact—the creation of all things by God in the beginning of time and the special creation of the first human couple. But they explain these facts in a popular way, according to the ordinary language of their times and adapted to their opinions and intelligence.

CONCLUSION

Although there is no evident conflict between Revelation and the hypothesis of evolution, there are some difficulties in any attempt to reconcile a few traditional Catholic conceptions with some aspects of the theory of evolution.

Therefore Pope Pius XII warns us, in his encyclical *Humani Generis,* that this difficult problem should not be discussed "as if there were nothing in the sources of Divine Revelation which demands the greatest moderation and caution in this question."[7]

From the same encyclical, which is the latest official pronouncement of the Church on the problem of evolution, we quote, by way of conclusion, the following passages:

For these reasons, the teaching authority of the Church does not forbid that in conformity with the present state of human sciences and sacred theology research and discussions on the part of men experienced in both fields take place with regard to the doctrine of evolution in as far as it inquires into the origin of the human body as coming from pre-existent and living matter—for Catholic Faith obliges us to hold that souls are immediately created by God. However, this must be done in such a way that reasons for both opinions, that is those favorable and unfavorable to evolution, be weighed and judged with the necessary seriousness, moderation and measure and provided that all are prepared to submit to the judgment of the Church to whom Christ has given the mission of interpreting authentically the Sacred Scripture and of defending dogmas of faith.[8]

[7] *Humani Generis* (New York, Paulist Press, 1950), #63.
[8] *Ibid.,* #62.

When, however, there is a question of another conjectural opinion, namely polygenism, children of the Church by no means enjoy such liberty. For the faithful cannot embrace that opinion which maintains either that after Adam there existed on this earth true men who did not take their origin through natural generation from him as from the first parent of all, or that Adam represents a certain number of first parents. Now it is in no way apparent how such an opinion can be reconciled with that which the sources of revealed truth and the documents of teaching authority of the Church propose with regard to original sin, which proceeds from sin actually committed by an individual Adam and which through generation is passed on to all and is in everyone as his own.[9]

THE FINAL OPTION
(p. 314)

From the theory of the final option, as it is explained in the text, one may be inclined to conclude that all men will be saved. If, at the last moment, everyone is given a choice between eternal happiness in heaven and eternal damnation in hell, who would hesitate between these two possibilities?

The theory of the final option leads to no such conclusion. The final choice which confronts man is not a theoretical choice between everlasting happiness and eternal punishment, but one more final practical choice between humble, loving self-surrender to God and proud, egoistic self-assertion. This decisive choice is heavily mortgaged by all the previous choices made between these two attitudes. It does not take place in the light of eternity. It is an act of this mortal life. It is the last act of this mortal life.

If any doubt remains about this, one might try to imagine what some people would do if they were told that they were to die within a week. Some of them would prepare themselves for the momentous passage, others would have "a last fling." The theory of the final option is at once consoling and inexorable in its implications. We are allowed to infer that if we try steadily to lead good lives, a sudden weakness or accident would hardly have fatal consequences for our salvation. But it also contains the warning

---

[9] *Ibid.,* #64.

that putting off moral effort until the end is in sight is egregiously dangerous and foolhardy.

THE CONCRETE CONDITION OF HUMAN FREEDOM
(p. 319)

The freedom we have studied in this book is the freedom of man considered theoretically, in the hypothetical state of "pure nature." But man does not live in the state of pure nature. He is fallen and redeemed. Philosophy as such cannot establish the historical reality of this fact, but philosophers can and do observe that there is a fundamental disorder in man's nature.

The will, guided by the intellect, should lead all other drives, and this subordination of sense to reason should be easy and natural. But experience teaches us that the sense drives do not readily respond to the command of the will. They strive towards their satisfaction without regard for due order; they continue their importunities even after the will has exercised its choice; they press their solicitations on the rational appetite and frequently subvert it to their own ends.

Therefore experience and philosophy teach us that there is some disorder in man. Theology explains this disorder as a result of Original Sin. Before the Fall each of man's drives strove towards satisfaction, but it would obey will and reason without the necessity of a struggle. Before the Fall man possessed perfect liberty. The Fall has diminished this liberty, and man must now develop it by dint of personal effort.

It is a dogma of the Catholic Faith that it is impossible for any man to avoid serious moral disorder (mortal sin) for a considerable time without special assistance from God (grace).[10] Translated into psychological terms this means that man cannot control his lower or egoistic drives for any considerable length of time without special help from God. Man is free, and in every single temptation he is capable of rejecting or accepting the allurements offered

---

[10] "If anyone says that without God's special help it is possible for a justified man to persevere in the justice he has received . . . let him be anathema" (Council of Trent, Denz. 832). Cfr. the saying of Christ, "separated from me, you have no power to do anything" (John xv, 5, Knox translation).

by his drives. But in practice he will yield sooner or later to their importunities, unless he receives a special assistance from God. This special assistance is usually granted only in response to prayer. Hence, practically, in order to be really free, man must pray. He cannot develop fully even on the natural level without supernatural assistance. There is no perfect liberty without prayer. Man owes it to himself to acquire that perfect liberty; therefore he owes it to himself to pray.

IMMEDIATE ANIMATION
(p. 340)

The legislation of the Catholic Church seems to favor the immediate animation theory. Canon 747 of the Church Law enjoins that all living embryos, of whatever age, must be baptized unconditionally. And Catholic moralists consider abortion, at whatever stage of pregnancy it may occur, as the murder of an innocent human being. However, it does not seem to have been the intention of the ecclesiastical legislator to decide which of the two theories, immediate or mediate animation, is true, and voluntary abortion remains sinful, although for different reasons, whether the embryo is already a human person or not.

READINGS

On Theology and Evolution:
Dorlodot, *Darwinism and Catholic Thought.* J. F. Ewing, S.J., "Human Evolution, 1956," in *Anthropological Quarterly,* 29 (1956), pp. 123-139.* Hauret, *Beginnings: Genesis and Modern Science.* Johnson, *The Bible and Early Man.* Messenger, *Evolution and Theology* and *Theology and Evolution.* Vollert, "Evolution and the Bible," in *Symposium on Evolution,* pp. 83-119. Vawter, *A Path through Genesis.*
On the Final Option:
Troisfontaines, *"Je ne meurs pas . . .",* pp. 120-151.
On Mediate Animation:
Messenger, *Theology and Evolution,* pp. 239-332.

* Reprints of this excellent treatment of the whole problem of human evolution are available from *Anthropological Quarterly,* 620 Michigan Avenue N.E., Washington 17, D.C.

GENERAL BIBLIOGRAPHY

General Bibliography

Allers, R., and Barclay, V., *Practical Psychology*. New York, Sheed & Ward, 1934.

Allers, R., *The Psychology of Character*, trans. by E. B. Strauss. London and New York, Sheed & Ward, 1931.

————, *The Successful Error*. New York, Sheed & Ward, 1940.

Allport, G. W., *Personality, A Psychological Interpretation*. New York, Holt, 1937.

Ansbacher, Heinz and Rowena, *The Individual Psychology of Alfred Adler*. New York, Basic Books, Inc., 1956.

Arnold, M. B., Gasson, J. A., S.J., et al., *The Human Person*. New York, Ronald Press, 1954.

Aveling, F., *Personality and Will*. New York, Appleton-Century-Crofts, Inc., 1931.

Barclay, V., and Allers, R., *Practical Psychology*. New York, Sheed & Ward, 1934.

Barrett, E. J. B., *Strength of Will*. New York, Kenedy, 1915.

Bertalanffy, L. von, *Modern Theories of Development*, trans. by J. H. Woodger. London, Oxford University Press, 1933.

————, *Problems of Life: An Evaluation of Modern Biological Thought*. London, Watts, 1952.

Bierens de Haan, J. A., *Animal Psychology*. London, Hutchinson, n.d.

Bloom, B. S., Stern, G. G., and Stein, M. I., *Methods in Personality Assessment*. Glencoe (Ill.), The Free Press, 1956.

Bolles, M. M., and Landis, C., *Textbook of Abnormal Psychology*, 2d ed. New York, Macmillan, 1950.

Bonner, H., *Social Psychology*. New York, American Book Co., 1953.

Britt, S. H., *Social Psychology of Modern Life*, rev. ed. New York, Rinehart, 1949.

Broderick, A. H., *Early Man*. London, Hutchinson, 1948.

Bugelski, B. R., *A First Course in Experimental Psychology*. New York, Holt, 1951.

Carles, J., *Unité et Vie: Esquisse d'une Biophilosophie.* Paris, Beauchesne, 1946.

――――, *Vers la Conquête de la Vie.* Paris, Hachette, 1958.

Cattell, R. B., *An Introduction to Personality Study.* London, Hutchinson, 1950.

――――, *Personality.* New York, McGraw-Hill, 1950.

Cavanagh, J. R., and McGoldrick, J. B., S.J., *Fundamental Psychiatry.* Milwaukee, Bruce, 1953.

Clark, R. A., *Six Talks on Jung's Psychology.* Pittsburgh, Boxwood Press, 1953.

Cobb, S., *Foundations of Neuropsychiatry.* Baltimore, Williams and Wilkins, 1958.

College Reading and Religion. New Haven, Yale University Press, 1948.

Coon, C. S., *The Story of Man.* New York, Knopf, 1954.

Copleston, F., S.J., *Contemporary Philosophy.* London, Burns and Oates, 1956.

Crutchfield, R. S., and Krech, D., *Elements of Psychology.* New York, Knopf, 1958.

Curran, C. A., Rev., *Counseling in Catholic Life and Education.* New York, Macmillan, 1952.

Curtis, J. H., *Social Psychology.* New York, McGraw-Hill, 1960.

Dalbiez, R., *Psychoanalytical Method and the Doctrine of Freud,* trans. by T. F. Lindsay. New York, Longmans, 1941.

De Finance, J., S.J., *Existence et Liberté.* Paris, Vitte, 1955.

Dennis, Wayne, et al., *Current Trends in Social Psychology.* Pittsburgh, University of Pittsburgh Press, 1951.

――――, *Current Trends in the Relation of Psychology to Medicine.* Pittsburgh, University of Pittsburgh Press, 1950.

Dewey, J., *How We Think.* Boston, Heath, 1910.

Dimnet, E., *The Art of Thinking.* New York, Simon & Schuster, 1929.

Dodson, E. O., *A Textbook of Evolution.* Philadelphia, Saunders, 1952.

Dorcus, R. M. and Shaffer, G. W., *Textbook of Abnormal Psychology,* 4th ed. Baltimore, Williams and Wilkins, 1950.

Dorlodot, H. de, *Darwinism and Catholic Thought.* New York, Benziger, 1922.

Editors of *The Scientific American, The Physics and Chemistry of Life.* New York, Simon & Schuster, 1955.

Ellis, W. D., *A Source Book of Gestalt Psychology.* London, K. Paul, Trench, Trubner and Co., 1938.

Eymieu, A., *Le Gouvernement de Soi-Même.* Paris, Perrin, 1935.

Eysenck, H. J., *The Scientific Study of Personality*. New York, Macmillan, 1952.

Farrer, A., *The Freedom of the Will*. New York, Scribner, 1958.

Ford, J. C., S.J., *Depth-Psychology, Morality and Alcoholism*. Weston, Mass., Weston College, 1951.

Fordham, F., *An Introduction to Jung's Psychology*. London, Penguin Books, 1953.

Gaffney, M., S.J., *The Psychology of the Internal Sense*. St. Louis, Herder, 1942.

Gannon, T. J., *Psychology: The Unity of Human Behavior*. Boston, Ginn, 1954.

Ganz, J., *The Psychology of Alfred Adler and the Development of the Child*, trans. by P. Mairet. New York, Humanities Press, Inc., 1953.

Gasson, J. A., S.J., Arnold, M. B., et al., *The Human Person*. New York, Ronald Press, 1954.

Gilson, E., *The Philosophy of St. Thomas Aquinas*, trans. by E. Bullough, 2d ed. St. Louis, Herder, 1929.

———, *The Spirit of Mediaeval Philosophy*, trans. by A. H. C. Downes. New York, Scribner, 1940.

———, *Elements of Christian Philosophy*. New York, Doubleday, 1960.

Gleason, R. W., S.J., *The World to Come*. New York, Sheed & Ward, 1958.

———, and Hagmaier, G., C.S.P., *Counselling the Catholic*. New York, Sheed & Ward, 1959.

Goldberg, G., and Shoobs, N. E., *Corrective Treatment for Unadjusted Children*. New York, Harper, 1946.

Guilford, J. P., *Personality*. New York, McGraw-Hill, 1959.

Hagmaier, G., C.S.P., and Gleason, R. W., S.J., *Counselling the Catholic*. New York, Sheed & Ward, 1959.

Harmon, F. L., *Principles of Psychology*. Milwaukee, Bruce, 1953.

———, *Understanding Personality*. Milwaukee, Bruce, 1948.

Harsh, C., and Schrickel, H. G., *Personality: Development and Assessment*. New York, Ronald Press, 1950.

Hartley, E. and Hartley, R., *Fundamentals of Social Psychology*. New York, Knopf, 1953.

Hartmann, G. W., *Gestalt Psychology*. New York, Ronald Press, 1935.

Hauret, C., *Beginnings: Genesis and Modern Science*. Dubuque, Priory Press, 1955.

Herr, V. V., S.J., *How We Influence One Another*. Milwaukee, Bruce, 1945.

Heymans, G., *Einführung in die Spezielle Psychologie*. Leipzig, Barth, 1932.

Hilgard, E. R., *Introduction to Psychology*. New York, Harcourt, 1953.

Hook, S., ed., *Determinism and Freedom in the Age of Modern Science*. New York, New York University Press, 1958.

Hooton, E. A., *Up from the Ape*, 2d ed. New York, Macmillan, 1946.

Hostie, R., S.J., *Religion and the Psychology of Jung*. New York, Sheed & Ward, 1957.

Howells, W., *Mankind in the Making*. New York, Doubleday, 1959.

Jacobi, J., *The Psychology of C. G. Jung*, trans. by K. W. Bash, rev. ed. New Haven, Yale University Press, 1951.

Johnson, H. J. T., *The Bible and Early Man*. New York, McMullen, 1948.

Karpf, F. B., *The Psychology and Psychotherapy of Otto Rank*. New York, Philosophical Library, 1953.

Katz, D., *Animals and Men*. New York, Longmans, 1937.

Klubertanz, G. P., S.J., *The Discursive Power*. St. Louis, The Modern Schoolman, 1952.

Koffka, K., *Principles of Gestalt Psychology*. New York, Harcourt, 1935.

Köhler, W., *Gestalt Psychology*. New York, Liveright, 1929.

————, *The Mentality of Apes*, trans. by E. Winter. New York, Harcourt, 1926.

Krech, D., and Crutchfield, R. S., *Elements of Psychology*. New York, Knopf, 1958.

Landis, C., and Bolles, M. M., *Textbook of Abnormal Psychology*, 2d ed. New York, Macmillan, 1950.

Le Gros Clark, W. E., *History of the Primates*. Phoenix Book, University of Chicago Press, 1957.

Lersch, P., *Aufbau der Person*, 6th ed. München, Barth, 1954.

Levie, J., S.J., *Sous les Yeux de l'Incroyant*, 2d ed. Paris, Desclée de Brouwer, 1946.

Lillie, R. S., *General Biology and Philosophy of Organism*. Chicago, University of Chicago Press, 1945.

Lindworsky, J., S.J., *Psychology of Asceticism*, trans. by E. A. Heiring. London, Edwards, 1936.

————, *Training the Will*, trans. by A. Steiner and E. A. Fitzpatrick. Milwaukee, Bruce, 1929.

Lonergan, B., S.J., *Insight, A Study of Human Understanding*. New York, Philosophical Library, 1957.

Marc, A., S.J., *Psychologie Réflexive.* Brussels, L'Edition Universelle, 1949.

Maréchal, J., S.J., *Le Point de Départ de la Métaphysique,* Cahier V, 2d ed. Brussels, L'Edition Universelle, 1949.

————, *Studies in the Psychology of the Mystics,* trans. by A. Thorold. New York, Benziger, 1927.

Maritain, J., *The Degrees of Knowledge,* trans. by B. Wall and M. R. Adamson. New York, Scribner, 1938.

————, *The Range of Reason.* New York, Scribner, 1952.

————, *Scholasticism and Politics,* 2d ed. London, Bles, 1945.

Marquis, D. G., and Woodworth, R. S., *Psychology,* 5th ed. New York, Holt, 1947.

Martin, W. O., *The Order and Integration of Knowledge.* Ann Arbor, The University of Michigan Press, 1957.

Mason, F., ed., *The Great Design.* New York, Macmillan, 1934.

May, R., et al., *Existence, A New Dimension in Psychiatry and Psychology.* New York, Basic Books, Inc., 1958.

McClelland, D., *Personality.* New York, Sloane, 1951.

McGoldrick, J. B., S.J., and Cavanagh, J. R., *Fundamental Psychiatry.* Milwaukee, Bruce, 1953.

Mersch, E., S.J., *The Theology of the Mystical Body,* trans. by C. Vollert, S.J. St. Louis, Herder, 1950.

Messenger, E. C., *Evolution and Theology.* New York, Macmillan, 1932.

————, ed., *Theology and Evolution.* Westminster, Newman, 1949.

Meyer, D. R., and Wickens, D. D., *Psychology.* New York, Dryden, 1955.

Misiak, H., and Staudt, V. M., *Catholics in Psychology.* New York, McGraw-Hill, 1954.

Montpellier, G. de, *Conduites Intelligentes et Psychisme chez l'Animal et chez l'Homme,* 2d ed. Louvain, Institut Supérieur de Philosophie, 1949.

Moore, T. V., O.S.B., *Cognitive Psychology.* Philadelphia, Lippincott, 1939.

————, *The Driving Forces of Human Nature.* New York, Grune and Stratton, 1948.

Morgan, C. T., *Introduction to Psychology.* New York, McGraw-Hill, 1956.

Mouroux, J., *The Meaning of Man,* trans. by A. H. C. Downes. New York, Sheed & Ward, 1948.

Mowrer, O. H., *Learning Theory and Personality Dynamics.* New York, Ronald Press, 1950.

Muckermann, H., S.J., *Humanizing the Brute*. St. Louis, Herder, 1906.

Munn, N. L., *Psychology*, 2d ed. Boston, Houghton, 1951.

Munroe, R. L., *Schools of Psychoanalytic Thought*. New York, Dryden, 1955.

Murphy, G., *Personality: A Bio-Social Approach to Origins and Structure*. New York, Macmillan, 1947.

Newcomb, T. M., *Social Psychology*. New York, Dryden, 1950.

Nuttin, J., *Psychoanalysis and Personality*, trans. by George Lamb. New York, Sheed & Ward, 1953.

Odenwald, R. P., and VanderVeldt, J. H., O.F.M. *Psychiatry and Catholicism*. New York, McGraw-Hill, 1952.

O'Hara, Sister Kevin, and Walters, Sister Annette, *Persons and Personality*. New York, Appleton-Century-Crofts, Inc., 1953.

Oraison, M., *Love or Constraint? Some Psychological Aspects of Religious Education*. New York, Kenedy, 1959.

———, *Union in Marital Love: Its Physical and Spiritual Foundations*. New York, Macmillan, 1958.

L'Origine de la Vie sur Terre, Cahiers d'Etudes Biologiques, Facultés Catholiques de Lyon #3. Paris, Lethielleux, 1958.

Otis, L. E., *La Doctrine de l'Evolution*, 2 vols. Montreal, Fides, 1950.

Payot, J., *The Education of the Will*, trans. by S. E. Jeliffe from 30th ed. New York, Funk, 1909.

Pegis, A. C., ed., *Introduction to St. Thomas Aquinas*. New York, The Modern Library, 1948.

Pradines, M., *Traité de Psychologie Générale*, 3d ed., 3 vols. Paris, Presses Universitaires de France, 1948.

Pratt, J. G., and Rhine, J. B., *Parapsychology, Frontier Science of the Mind*. Springfield (Ill.), C. C. Thomas, 1957.

Rahner, K., *Geist in Welt*, 2d ed. München, Kösel, 1957.

Rhine, J. B., and Pratt, J. G., *Parapsychology, Frontier Science of the Mind*. Springfield (Ill.), C. C. Thomas, 1957.

Roback, A. A., *The Psychology of Character*. New York, Harcourt, 1927.

Rogers, C. R., *Counseling and Psychotherapy*. Boston, Houghton, 1942.

Rose, A. M., ed., *Mental Health and Mental Disorder*. New York, Norton, 1955.

Rousselot, P., S.J., *The Intellectualism of St. Thomas*, trans. by J. E. O'Mahoney, O.F.M. Cap. New York, Sheed & Ward, 1935.

Ruch, F. L., *Psychology and Life*, 3d ed. Chicago, Scott, 1948.

Ruyer, R., *Eléments de Psycho-Biologie*. Paris, Presses Universitaires de France, 1946.

Sargent, S. S., and Williamson, R. C., *Social Psychology*, 2d ed. New York, Ronald Press, 1958.

Schneiders, A. A., *Introductory Psychology*. New York, Rinehart, 1951.

Schrickel, H. G., and Harsh, C., *Personality: Development and Assessment*. New York, Ronald Press, 1950.

Schrödinger, E., *What is Life?* Doubleday, Anchor Books, 1956.

Senet, A., *Man in Search of His Ancestors*. New York, McGraw-Hill, 1956.

Sertillanges, A. D., O.P., *Foundations of Thomistic Philosophy*, trans. by G. Anstruther, O.P. London, Sands, 1931.

————, *La Philosophie de St. Thomas Aquin*, rev. ed. Paris, Aubier, 1940.

Shaffer, G. W., and Dorcus, R. M., *Textbook of Abnormal Psychology*, 4th ed. Baltimore, Williams and Wilkins, 1950.

Sheed, F. J., *Society and Sanity*. New York, Sheed & Ward, 1953.

————, *Theology and Sanity*. New York, Sheed & Ward, 1946.

Sheldon, W. H., *The Varieties of Human Physique*. New York, Harper, 1940.

————, *The Varieties of Temperament*. New York, Harper, 1942.

Shoobs, N. E., and Goldberg, G., *Corrective Treatment for Unadjusted Children*. New York, Harper, 1946.

Sinnott, E. W., *Cell and Psyche: The Biology of Purpose*. University of North Carolina Press, 1950.

Siwek, P., S.J., *The Enigma of the Hereafter*. New York, Philosophical Library, 1953.

Spearman, C., *The Abilities of Man*. London, Macmillan, 1927.

————, *The Nature of "Intelligence" and the Principles of Cognition*, 2d ed. London, Macmillan, 1927.

Staudt, V. M., and Misiak, H., *Catholics in Psychology*. New York, McGraw-Hill, 1954.

Stern, G. G., Stein, M. I., and Bloom, B. S., *Methods in Personality Assessment*. Glencoe (Ill.), The Free Press, 1956.

Stern, K., *The Third Revolution*. New York, Harcourt, 1954.

Stoddard, G. D., *The Meaning of Intelligence*. New York, Macmillan, 1943.

Stone, C. P., ed., *Comparative Psychology*, 3d ed. New York, Prentice-Hall, 1951.

Strasser, S., *The Soul in Metaphysical and Empirical Psychology*. Pittsburgh, Duquesne University Press, 1957.

Swanson, G. E., Newcomb, T. M., and Hartley, E. L., eds., *Readings in Social Psychology*, 2d ed. New York, Holt, 1952.

480 General Bibliography

Symposium on Evolution. Pittsburgh, Duquesne University, 1959.

Teale, E. W., *The Insect World of J. Henri Fabre.* New York, Dodd, 1949.

Teilhard de Chardin, P., *The Phenomenon of Man.* New York, Harper, 1959.

Tinbergen, N., *The Study of Instinct.* Oxford, Clarendon, 1951.

Troisfontaines, R., S.J., *De l'Existence à l'Etre,* 2 vols. Paris, Vrin, 1953.

————, *"Je ne meurs pas. . . ."* Paris, Editions Universitaires, 1960.

VanderVeldt, J. H., O.F.M., and Odenwald, R. P., *Psychiatry and Catholicism.* New York, McGraw-Hill, 1952.

Vawter, B., C.M., *A Path through Genesis.* New York, Sheed & Ward, 1956.

von Frisch, K., *The Dancing Bees.* New York, Harcourt, 1955.

Walters, Sister Annette, and O'Hara, Sister Kevin, *Persons and Personality.* New York, Appleton-Century-Crofts, Inc., 1953.

Werner, H. *Comparative Psychology,* rev. ed. Chicago, Follett, 1948.

White, R., *The Abnormal Personality.* New York, Ronald Press, 1948.

White, V., O.P., *God and the Unconscious.* Chicago, Regnery, 1953.

Wickens, D. D., and Meyer, D. R., *Psychology.* New York, Dryden, 1955.

Wild, J., *Introduction to Realistic Philosophy.* New York, Harper, 1948.

Williamson, R. C., and Sargent, S. S., *Social Psychology,* 2d ed. New York, Ronald Press, 1958.

Windle, B. C. A., *Vitalism and Scholasticism.* St. Louis, Herder, n.d.

Woodworth, R. S., and Marquis, D. G., *Psychology,* 5th ed. New York, Holt, 1947.

Young, K., *Social Psychology,* 3d ed. New York, Appleton-Century-Crofts, Inc., 1956.

INDEX

Index